Odette Boivin
The First Dynasty of the Sealand in Mesopotamia

Studies in Ancient Near Eastern Records

General Editor:
Gonzalo Rubio

Editors:
Nicole Brisch, Petra Goedegebuure, Markus Hilgert, Amélie Kuhrt, Peter Machinist, Piotr Michalowski, Cécile Michel, Beate Pongratz-Leisten, D. T. Potts, Kim Ryholt

Volume 20

Odette Boivin

The First Dynasty of the Sealand in Mesopotamia

DE GRUYTER

ISBN 978-1-5015-1943-7
e-ISBN (PDF) 978-1-5015-0782-3
e-ISBN (EPUB) 978-1-5015-0786-1
ISSN 2161-4415

Library of Congress Cataloging-in-Publication Data
A CIP catalog record for this book has been applied for at the Library of Congress.

Bibliographic information published by the Deutsche Nationalbibliothek
The Deutsche Nationalbibliothek lists this publication in the Deutsche Nationalbibliografie; detailed bibliographic data are available in the Internet at http://dnb.dnb.de.

This volume is text- and page-identical with the hardback published in 2018.
Printing: CPI books GmbH, Leck
♾ Printed on acid-free paper
Printed in Germany

www.degruyter.com

Preface

This book is a revised version of the dissertation I defended at the University of Toronto in 2016 for the obtention of the degree of Doctor of Philosophy. It could not have been written without the constant support of my supervisor Paul-Alain Beaulieu whom I warmly thank for his interest, time, trust, numerous and useful comments, and unsinkable good humour. I would like to acknowledge the financial support received from the Canadian Social Science and Humanities Research Council, the Government of Ontario, and the Faculty of Arts and Science of the University of Toronto during my doctoral studies. During the academic year 2016–2017 I revised the initial manuscript of this book while I held an appointment as Postdoctoral Fellow in the department of Near and Middle Eastern Civilizations at the University of Toronto.

Besides my doctoral supervisor Paul-Alain Beaulieu, several other scholars shared generously their time, thoughts, knowledge, and sometimes manuscripts ahead of publication with me. I am very much in their debt and would like to extend my thanks to them. Piotr Steinkeller, who was on my dissertation defense committee, formulated many very useful suggestions and throughts on various aspects of my research; Karel Van Lerberghe shared with me ideas, notes, and his edition of many texts from Dūr-Abī-ešuḫ ahead of their publication; Andrew George sent me material ahead of its publication and brought to my attention the discovery of additional Sealand I texts; Heather D. Baker, who was on my dissertation defense committee, shared many useful comments on the text; Elyze Zomer sent me her transliteration of the Epic of Gulkišar and brought to my attention another text mentioning this king; Daniel Calderbank shared with me a chapter of his dissertation on the Tell Khaiber pottery and answered my questions in a manner comprehensible to a non-ceramicist and non-archaeologist; Uri Gabbay commented on a portion of my manuscript and made interesting suggestions; Clemens Reichel, also on my dissertation defense committee, formulated useful suggestions; Mary Frazer brought to my attention an Assyrian list of names including some Sealand I rulers; Douglas Frayne shared several ideas and references; also, two anonymous reviewers of this book manuscript formulated several very helpful comments and suggestions. I thank all of them for their help.

I am also very much endebted to Stephanie Dalley, the editor of the palatial archive published in CUSAS 9, for producing an excellent edition of these texts, whose ductus is not easy and for which there were no direct comparanda. Her work made it possible for me to analyze this archive on a solid, and well-struc-

https://doi.org/10.1515/9781501507823-001

tured basis, including very accurate hand copies. I extend my thanks to her as well.

Last but not least, I thank my son Philippe for gracefully living with the consequences of my decision to embark on this project.

Contents

Tables and Figures

List of Tables

List of Figures

Conventions and Abbreviations

Dates are given in the following format: **day.month.year**

month: in Roman numerals;

year: RN n (where RN = abbreviated royal name and n = regnal year)

Ilī = Ilī-ma-ilu
It = Itti-ili-nībī
Di = Dam(i)q-ilišu
Gu = Gulkišar
Pe = Pešgaldarameš
Aa = Ayadaragalama
Eg = Ea-gāmil

Royal names of the Babylon I dynasty are abbreviated following Horsnell's (1999) conventions, with the exception of Aṣ for Az.

For the year formulae of the CUSAS 9 archive, for which the exact regnal year is not always clear, the capital letter attributed by Dalley (e.g., year N) is often used alone (see Appendix 2 and Dalley 2009: 11f.).

Most personal names are given in normalized orthography with diacritics. One notable exception is Hammurapi, whose name has entered usage so much as to justify this adapted orthography, instead of Ḫammu-rāpi.

Abbreviations follow those defined in the *Reallexikon der Assyriologie und Vorderasiatischen Archäologie*.

Other abbreviations:

ABC: *Assyrian and Babylonian Chronicles* (Grayson 1975)
BC: Belgian Collection (texts cited in Dalley 2009: *passim*)
BKL A: Babylonian King List A (BM 33332)
BKL A: Babylonian King List B (BM 38122)
DN : Divine name
Dūr-Abī-ešuḫ$^{\text{(canal)}}$: fortress located at the outflow of the Hammurapi-nuḫuš-nišī canal
Dūr-Abī-ešuḫ$^{\text{(Tigris)}}$: fortress located on the Tigris (see Section 4.3.1 for a full explanation)
DynKL: Dynastic King List (= ABC 18 = MC 3)
GN: Geographical name
MC: *Mesopotamian Chronicles* (Glassner 2004)
PN: Personal name
SynKL: Synchronistic King List (A.117)
TK: Tell Khaiber tablets (oracc.museum.upenn.edu/urap/corpus)
VR: Rawlinson, H.C. and Pinches, T.G. 1884. *A Selection from the Miscellaneous Inscriptions of Assyria and Babylonia*. The Cuneiform Inscriptions of Western Asia, vol. V. London: Jankowsky.

1 Introduction

Our knowledge of second millennium Babylonia is one in stark contrasts. A wealth of archival documents—epistolary, legal, and administrative—in the first few centuries (the Old Babylonian period) illuminates several aspects of private affairs and state administration in minute detail. Due to a substantial number of tablets, we also have for the same period a fairly good grasp of other scribal activity, for instance in mathematics, divination, and literature. In addition, we learn through the royal Mari archives of many an episode in the intricacies of supra-regional politics that marked the complex relations between the small, ever competing Amorite states; for the Middle Babylonian (Kassite) period in the second half of the millennium, some more limited information comes from the Amarna correspondence. But these relatively solid areas of knowledge coexist with several gray zones. For instance, the absolute chronology of the greater part of the millennium remains an extremely contentious issue. Also, the entire transition from the Old to the Middle Babylonian period is fraught with uncertainties and, it seems, more questions than answers because of the general ebbing of written and material sources. The situation is perhaps best captured in the words of Charpin describing the late Old Babylonian period, and of Brinkman discussing the early Kassite period: the former concludes that "il est impossible d'[en] écrire une histoire politique un tant soit peu continue" (Charpin 2004: 367), while the latter observes that "no amount of theorizing can compensate for the lack of clear and trustworthy evidence" (Brinkman 1976: 13).

It is indeed not only a political *Zwischenzeit* between periods of unified rule in Babylonia—Amorite, then Kassite –, it is an altogether dark age for which we are at a loss to describe and understand with anything approaching confidence most aspects of the demographic, economic, environmental, cultural, and political processes and events. This phase of high uncertainty in our understanding of Babylonian history sets in earlier for southern Babylonia. Indeed, if we trust the available material and written evidence—or rather the lack thereof –, the region appears to turn more or less into a wasteland after the rebellion against Samsuiluna, and to remain so until Kassite (re-)settlement. To fill this hiatus historians had until very recently barely more to go on than a handful of references to the enigmatic dynasty of Eurukug, also called Sealand, scattered in later king lists and chronicles and early on associated with southern Mesopotamia. The term commonly translated as Sealand is associated in Mesopotamian historiographic

https://doi.org/10.1515/9781501507823-002

sources with three distinct dynasties;[1] it is the first one, coeval with the late Old Babylonian and the early Kassite periods, which is investigated here. In the last years, primary sources from their kingdom have finally surfaced and allowed for a thorough re-examination of the question. The present work presents the results of this undertaking.

It is nonetheless worthwhile to take a step back and trace the major steps in our understanding of Sealand history, more particularly of its first dynasty and kingdom, as some questions raised in early discussions are still valid. I will therefore review the main contributions in order to follow the evolution of the idea of Sealand in Assyriology from the 1880s to the present.

1.1 Review of previous scholarship

The sole historical study entirely dedicated to the Sealand dates as far back as 1932 (Dougherty 1932). This is not very surprising since until recently little new evidence had become available to encourage any serious attempt to revisit this part of Mesopotamian history. Accordingly, the history of southernmost Mesopotamia in the middle of the second millennium usually remains confined to a few paragraphs in chapters about the Old Babylonian or the Kassite dynasty. The dire lack of sources has also resulted in conflicting, sometimes irreconcilable views and speculations on the Sealand. To cite but two on intellectual history, at opposite ends of the spectrum: Hallo (1975: 199; 201) suggested, before any directly relevant literary texts had surfaced, that scholars of Sumerian who fled to the Sealand after the fall of the Amorite dynasty were responsible for "a final flowering of Sumerian literature, or rather of bilingual texts;" a few years later, with the same evidence at hand, Civil et al. (1979: 8) considered that the "occupation of Nippur by the Sealand tribes was quite different from previous conquests by the more 'civilized' Larsa and Babylonian kings, and seems to have put an end to all scribal activities."

1.1.1 First discussions on the Sealand

As early as 1886, Tiele (1886: *passim*) discussed the "Dynastie Šisku (Uruku?)" and the "Dynastie Seelands" mentioned in the Babylonian King List A published

1 See Section 2.3. The term is also associated in various sources with an area in southern Babylonia; this is discussed in Section 2.1.2.

some years earlier. Without concluding, he proposed that the "Seeland" was a land along the Persian shore or around an inner sea. The association between the Sealand and the Persian Gulf was embraced by other scholars and in 1904 Hommel (1904: *passim*) assumed that the "Meerland" extended along the Persian coast from Bīt Jakīn in southern Babylonia down to where Bahrein lies. He also posited that Karduniaš might be synonym of "Meerland." Along similar lines, Hüsing (1906: 663–65) suggested that Karduniaš might be the Elamite word for "Meerland."

Other scholars, however, did not associate Karduniaš and the Sealand, and the idea of a separate political entity co-existing with the first dynasty of Babylon emerged. Johns (1913: 83) discussed the conflicts between Abī-ešuḫ and "Iluma-ilu, king of the Sealand" of the "Uru-azagga" dynasty. He considered the Sealand to have been located in "inaccessible swamps."

A first attempt to write a history of the Sealand was made by King (1915: 197 ff.), who in 1915 dedicated a full chapter to "The Close of the First Dynasty of Babylon and the Kings from the Country of the Sea" as part of his reconstruction of Babylonian political history. He drew from the chronicles he had published a few years earlier to write, from a Babylonian point of view, the history of the "Sea-Country." King situated the Sea-Country mainly in the marshy area in the south-east of Babylonia, a region offering a natural barrier against invaders, also a region which had constituted a sanctuary to Sumerian refugees displaced by the Amorite invasion. King considered that the southern rebellion during Samsu-iluna's reign was led by Rīm-Sîn (I) of Larsa, by then very old, who had bided his time since Hammurapi's conquest but seized the opportunity to strike Babylon when it was beginning to struggle with Kassite invasions. Following Samsu-iluna's brief success in crushing the rebellion, the revolt of "all the lands" had in King's opinion been caused by Sea-Country leader "Iluma-ilum." Basing himself on the fairly recent publication of legal and business documents from Nippur that used date formulae of the latter, King concluded that central Babylonia had passed into Sea-Country hands in Samsu-iluna's twenty-ninth year, a view that is still valid. He discussed Abī-ešuḫ's unsuccessful efforts to regain control of the south and the construction of shrines at Babylon, reproducing cult places which had passed under Sea-Country control—a phenomenon also observed by contemporary assyriologists. King believed that, before his fall at the hands of the Kassites, the last Sea-Country king had unsuccessfully attempted to invade Elam. He also discussed the reasons motivating the inclusion of the Sea-Country rulers in the Babylonian King List, positing that, following the Hittite raid, it was probably the sole stable power in the region; reflecting on the same problem, Thureau-Dangin (1927: 184) surmised that the dynasty was included in the list because at least one of its rulers reigned at Babylon (he considers that in fact two kings may have reigned there).

1.1.2 Dougherty's "The Sealand of Ancient Arabia"

A turning point in scholarship about the Sealand was Dougherty's publication of *The Sealand of Ancient Arabia* in 1932. In his book, Dougherty (1932: *passim*; in particular 4–10) created the idea of the Sealand as a long-lived polity, in fact even as a nation. Basing himself on written sources, including works of literature, he placed the formation of the Sealand in the third millennium, around 2500, on the basis of three main elements: his reading of a partly reconstructed passage of a chronicle of early kings (*ABC* 20 A); a Neo-Assyrian omen collection possibly referring to a *ma-a-ti* A.AB.BA, which Sargon would have crossed to bring back booty from the Levant; and a firm belief that the second millennium Sealand, being a separate nation with its own cultural identity and some military power,[2] had to be the result of a long process of formation. Dougherty considered that the Sealand stretched along the northern and western (down to Dilmun) shores of the Persian Gulf,[3] but also situated a large portion of it in the Arabian peninsula, which he saw as the logical route for Sargon after his western conquests. He (*ibid:* 24) also considered that Sealand kings had to control a very large territory since they represented at times a strong military power and were granted a place in king lists; the Sealand could hence not have been confined only to southernmost Mesopotamia.

After an episode of Kassite domination and the short-lived second Sealand dynasty, Dougherty (*ibid.: passim*; in particular 102–05) depicted a ninth century political landscape characterized by an alliance between Assyria and the Babylonian portion of Karduniaš. Both faced strong rebellion from an Arabian district of Karduniaš that comprised Chaldea and the Sealand, here understood as possibly partly overlapping territories. In the Sealand, a strong dynasty was founded by Yakînu, to which belonged Marduk-apla-iddina (II), who was considered to have extended his rule from the Arabian peninsula into Sumer and Akkad in the late eighth century. The Neo-Babylonian dynasty was seen by Dougherty (*ibid.:* 145) as in continuity, either in direct descent or at least linked ideological-

2 For instance, Dougherty (1932: 25–27) purports nascent monotheistic tendencies in mid-second millennium Sealand, on the basis of the use of *ilum* in royal names.

3 His assumption in fact goes back to very early scholarship, as discussed above. However he extends the territory associated with the Sealand westwards, inside the Arabian peninsula (Dougherty 1932: 8 f., incl. n.23).

ly, with the Sealand dynasty founded by Yakînu. Dougherty hence viewed the Sealand as a nation enduring over two millennia and whose history was reflected almost exclusively in external sources.

1.2 Later research on the Sealand I dynasty

1.2.1 The reassessment of sources pertaining to the Sealand

After assyriologists began distancing themselves from a more literalistic interpretation of sources, in particular literary sources, which characterized scholarship in the nineteenth and early twentieth century, the main conclusions of Dougherty's research were no longer regarded as valid. It is indeed interesting to note that many later considerations on the Sealand do not derive from the discovery of new evidence but from a re-interpretation of sources known for several decades. The assessment of their trustworthiness and historical meaning remains a delicate and contentious exercise.

In his work on second millennium chronology, Goetze (1957: 66) posited that a Sealand king reigned in Babylon, otherwise the first Sealand dynasty would not have been included in Babylonian king lists. He assumed that this occupation of the Babylonian throne by a Sealand ruler took place immediately after the Hittite raid on Babylon, when the Kassites and the Sealanders were both likely contenders. The Sealand kings being however listed before the Kassites, Goetze inferred that a Sealand king occupied the throne first. Basing himself on known synchronisms for previous kings and on the reign lengths provided by the Babylonian King List A, Goetze identified Gulkišar as the most likely candidate. He estimated that, following Gulkišar, the first Sealand dynasty endured another 142 years, here again basing himself on king lists. As for Ulam-Buriaš, known from a chronicle (*ABC* 20B) as the victor over Ea-gāmil, Goetze (1964: 99) argued that he was a (Kassite) king of the Sealand who did not necessarily reign at Babylon but may have conquered the Sealand on behalf of his father Burna-Buriaš.

Landsberger (1954: 70 n.181) proceeded differently and established synchronisms between Sealand I kings and Old Babylonian, then Kassite kings; he suggested that the reign lengths attributed to Sealand kings in the Babylonian King List A were adjusted by scribes to make the first Sealand dynasty match in length its Babylonian counterparts. He also purported that Babylonian scholars had probably fled to the Sealand at the fall of the first Babylonian dynasty, kept alive scribal traditions there, then went back to Babylon under or after Agum II (after almost two centuries in his computation). Hence in his view the scribes responsible for the transmission of Sealand's history in the Babylonian chronographic tradition were in fact Sealand scribes. Going further, Hallo (1983: 12) suggested that the kings of the first Sealand dynasty "aspired to restore Sumerian traditions" in continuity with the first Isin dynasty and that they may have commissioned a first version of King List A to that effect. As for Sealand geography, Roux (1960: 27–38) suggested that Tell Abu Salabikh in the Hammar district may have been the capital of the Sealand kingdom.

In his succinct but informative entry "Meerland" in the *Reallexikon*, Brinkman (1993–97) presented the first summary of all textual sources relevant to the Sealand since Dougherty's book; like the latter, he covered all periods in which the term was used, whether it designated a kingdom, a region, or a province. He reviewed available written sources chronologically, beginning in the second millennium with the first dynasty known from king lists. He considered the Sealand to have been located in the marshy area in the extreme south of Babylonia. This was of importance for Brinkman who considered that the history of the Sealand was strongly determined by its geographical setting, and he identified the two key moments of its history as coinciding with high-water phases that would have made the marshes inaccessible to conquerors: the first dynasty emerging during the Old Babylonian period, and the intense resistance to the Neo-Assyrian empire under Marduk-apla-iddina II. He also emphasized the strong association between the Bīt-Jakīn and the Sealand in that period, as well as a close relationship with Elam. For this review of the Sealand sources, Brinkman drew from his extensive work on the Kassite period; indeed, in *Materials and Studies for Kassite History* (1976), he discussed the textual evidence pertaining to the first dynasty of the Sealand. On the basis of discrepancies found in the Babylonian Dynastic Chronicle (or Babylonian Royal Chronicle), he (1976: Appendix D) assumed that the Babylonian King List A was somewhat more reliable, including for reign lengths. Brinkman (*ibid.*: 104 f.) questioned Goetze's reconstruction of Babylonian history and chronology following the destruction of Babylon, for instance he considered by no means certain that Gulkišar reigned at Babylon; he also believed Goetze's proposed chronology to be too high.

1.2.2 Archaeological evidence and other relevant contributions

Archaeological evidence that we could associate with the Sealand kingdom was until very recently nearly non-existent, there is, therefore, very little literature on Sealand I archaeology. Excavated sites that may have been in Sealand I territory, in southern Mesopotamia, present a discontinuous occupation that points toward abandonment during the time of the Sealand I dynasty (Gasche 1989: 124–32; Stone 1977: 269–71; Armstrong and Gasche 2014: Table 9), with the possible exception of Ur, where Woolley (1954: 197–98; 1965: 1; 77) identified some repairs possibly dating to that period and signs that there could have been continuous occupation in part of the city.[4] For the most part, the southernmost marshes were surveyed only very recently (Gasche 1989: 132; al-Hamdani 2008: 229–30; 2015: 7–8; Hritz et al. 2012; but see also e.g., Roux 1960).

Excavations at Nippur and Qalʿat al-Bahrein each yielded very few texts dated to Sealand I kings—the first and the last of the dynasty, respectively –, but they do not offer enough material to conclude to more than an episode of control over each site (Brinkman 1993–97: 6; Cavigneaux and André-Salvini forthcoming). The site of Tell Khaiber, near Ur, where at least three texts dated to the Sealand I king Ayadaragalama (and probably more that can be attributed to that dynasty) were unearthed alongside architectural and other material evidence, offers great potential. The excavations are still in progress and only preliminary reports (Moon et al. 2014; 2015; 2016), as well as a first analysis of the epigraphic and archaeological finds (Campbell et al. 2017) have been published so far. The extant material evidence has not made it possible to identify a specific Sealand I assemblage with certainty yet. However, there are characteristics that make the Tell Khaiber ware of Sealand I date somewhat different from other second millennium Babylonian assemblages, for instance the absence of the goblet otherwise so typical of the preceding and following periods.[5] Clay plaques, ceramics, and other objects appear generally Old Babylonian in style, with some early Kassite elements. The absence of comparanda in southern Babylonia makes it difficult to situate the pottery in a precise developmental context, and thus to date it (Campbell et al. 2017); the primary occupation of the site appears to fall within the period of de-urbanization of southern and central Babylonia, probably mainly in the later half of it. The ceramics unearthed also appear to correspond to the Babylonian styles observed on Failaka (levels 3 A and B), and to a lesser extent at al-Qalʿat al-Bahrein (level IIIa), confirming Højlund's (1989) surmises of a southern Babylonian influence there in that period; of course, this accords well with the fact that a text bearing a date formula of the last Sealand I king[6] was found at al-Qalʿat al-Bahrein.

The chronology of the second millennium has been and is still extensively discussed by scholars. One contribution certainly stands out: in *Dating the Fall of Babylon* Gasche, Armstrong, Cole, and Gurzadyan (1998) reviewed the availa-

4 It is hoped that the current excavations (A. al-Hamdani, E. Stone, P. Zimansky) will help clarify the transition from the Old Babylonian to the Middle Babylonian periods.

5 I thank D. Calderbank for sharing information and parts of his dissertation on the Tell Khaiber pottery with me.

6 This text is introduced in the next section.

ble archaeological, textual, and astronomical evidence pertaining to the second millennium in Mesopotamia in an attempt to define the absolute chronology of that period on a more comprehensive evidential basis. Site stratigraphies were reviewed, of which none are well-established south of Nippur; however, shorter, incomplete sequences at Isin, Larsa, Uruk, and al-Hibā are documented. Therefore, the analyzed ceramic corpus, in particular the mass-produced goblets whose shape is considered especially time-sensitive, presents a gap in the sequence in the southern alluvial plain, apparently concomitant with a phase of de-urbanization during the late Old Babylonian[7] and the early Kassite periods. The authors (1998: 45) considered, basing themselves on early Kassite goblets from Nippur and Tell ed-Der, that (late) Kassite pottery in southern Babylonia evolved in fact from northern Babylonian ware, not from a parallel local development;[8] Armstrong and Gasche (2014: 99–100; Table 9) remain of that opinion in their recent publication, with a roughly two-century-long period of de-urbanization in the entire southern alluvial plain. Also noteworthy is the fact that the authors considered unfounded Højlund's hypothesis that some of the pottery found on the island of Failaka in the Persian Gulf would reflect early Kassite ware from southern Babylonia (Højlund 1989: 9–14; Gasche et al. 1998: 8). The authors revised the absolute chronology, basing themselves among other sources on texts from Tell Muḫammad mentioning an eclipse and possibly dated with reference to the resettlement of Babylon; they also took into consideration synchronisms with Assyria and Egypt. Their (1998: 91; Appendix) revised chronology resulted in a duration of the first Sealand dynasty well below 200 years, from the beginning of the second half of the seventeenth century to the very beginning of the fifteenth.

The demography and the economy of the Sealand kingdom have not been much discussed since there were until recently no sources available, but it has been assumed by several authors that the Babylonian south was mostly de-urbanized and that significant segments of the population had relocated to the north, including clergies in the context of cult displacement.[9] It was suggested that this came as a result of a drastic shortage of water engineered by Samsu-iluna (Stone 1977: 285). Leemans (1960b: 26–27; 30) saw the collapse of the Gulf

7 The apparent abandonment of urban sites is also discussed by Gasche (1989).

8 Interestingly, a similar theory was proposed for the seal cutting technology by Nijhowne (1999: 66).

9 For evidence on specific sub-groups of refugees, as well as arguments and discussions on the scale of the migration, see for instance: Gasche (1989: 139); Pientka (1998: 179 ff.; 253); Yoffee (1998: 334); Charpin (2004: 345). The relocation of southern cults is reminiscent of King's (1915: 206) early observations on the construction of shrines for southern deities at Babylon.

trade as a logical consequence of this process, which he assumed had begun even before the Old Babylonian period, while others purported that an active trade between the Sealand and Dilmun or Failaka was probably taking place, or at least that a strong Babylonian influence is discernible in the Gulf islands at the time (Høljund 1989; Potts 2010: 22).

Settlement patterns of the mid-second millennium Sealand have not been much discussed. Gasche (1989: 124 ff.) reviewed in *La Babylonie au 17e siècle avant notre ère* the dismally scarce archaeological evidence associated with the late Old Babylonian period in central and southern Babylonia, which mostly point to the (partial) destruction of urban centers at the time of Samsu-iluna, followed by a long period of abandonment. Most recently, al-Hamdani (2015: 149) suggested in his doctoral dissertation that the region south of Uruk, Larsa, and Girsu saw an increase of its marshy area in that period, leading to partial local resettlement of the population. Using satellite images and results of an extensive survey, he identified nearly 500 (almost exclusively unexcavated) sites[10] that could date to the Sealand I period. Most of these are very small, but he (2015: 168 ff.) identified one in the Ur-Eridu region that is quite large and highly urbanized. He (2015: 138 ff.) also assumes occupation on a small scale in formerly large centers. However, his dating of the site occupation is based on a definition of diagnostic Sealand I ceramics[11] that has not been published yet; also problematic is the fact that the ceramics were not found in conjunction with Sealand I textual evidence. Al-Hamdani (2015: 3) contends that the Sealand occupation of marshy areas in that period is reminiscent of other such episodes in the history of southern Babylonia, in which the marshes expanded, thus transforming a place traditionally used for refuge into a permanent living space, and conferring to this polity the status of a shadow state; this is reminiscent of King's and Brinkman's deterministic views on a strong relationship between the power of the Sealand and its physical environment.

---

10 For more results on sites located along the southernmost ancient course of branches of the Euphrates, see also e.g., Alhawi et al. 2017.

11 These ceramics were apparently also found at Tell Sakhariya, near Ur (Zimansky and Stone 2016: 65).

1.3 The new textual evidence

1.3.1 Texts and inscriptions recently published (or identified)

In the previous discussion, I adhered by and large to the denominations used in the reviewed literature to designate the first Sealand dynasty and kingdom. Henceforth, the term "Sealand I" will be used to refer to it.

Dalley's (2009) publication a few years ago of a large group of Sealand I tablets in the volume *Babylonian Tablets from The First Sealand Dynasty in the Schøyen Collection* (CUSAS 9) marked the entry into the field of Assyriology of archival sources from this polity.[12] These 474 unprovenanced texts and fragments, since the 1980s–90s in the Schøyen Collection (M. Schøyen *apud* Dalley 2009: v), can indeed all be attributed to the Sealand I dynasty: several texts are dated to two kings whose names are known from Babylonian King Lists, Pešgaldarameš and Ayadaragalama, and Dalley's philological analysis led her to conclude that the remaining undated texts came from the same period and find spot.[13] The texts are mainly administrative, but there are also a few letters. This archive represents the evidential cornerstone of many results presented in this book and will be introduced in more detail presently.[14] I worked principally from Dalley's (2009) copies and editions, as well as from photographs.[15]

More texts, many of which presumably date to the same period—three date for certain to Ayadaragalama (TK1 3006.17; 3064.67; 3064.135)—have been recent-

12 The few legal texts from Nippur dated to Ilī-ma-ilu are technically also archival texts of Sealand I date but they are essentially the product of mid-Old Babylonian Nippurite scribes, who used a date formula of a Sealand I king for a time, they do not reflect any Sealand specific practices; the texts are BE 6/2 68; ARN 123=Ni 9271; UM 55-21-239=3N-T87=SAOC 44 12; PBS 8/1,89; also the recently published HS 2227=TMH 10 54a (with envelope HS 2226=TMH 10 54b).

13 Dalley (2009: 13–14) noted that the orthography and ductus are related to Old Babylonian with some local peculiarities.

14 Thirty-two additional tablets from the same period and of the same type are now housed in the Musée du Cinquantenaire in Brussels. They are being edited but are still unpublished, and photographs are not available; however, they are abundantly cited by Dalley (2009) who had access to copies. In the present work, they will be referred to as Belgian Collection (BC) and their tablet number, following the references used in Dalley (2009). Attempts to garner additional information on these texts over the past years have remained unsuccessful. The same project will include the edition of two more Sealand I administrative tablets from the Schøyen Collection (MS 4935; 4936); also A. George is currenty editing a letter of the same collection (MS 5009).

15 The tablets not being in regular storage when enquiries were made, it has proven logistically too difficult to get access to selected ones for collation.

ly unearthed at Tell Khaiber,[16] between Ur and Larsa. Most are administrative but there are also a few letters and school texts. Transliterations of a number of them are available on oracc.museum.upenn.edu/urap/corpus, and they were integrated as much as possible in the discussions presented here; also, for a preliminary analysis, see Campbell et al. 2017. Finally, an administrative text dated to the last Sealand I king Ea-gāmil was found at Qalʿat al-Bahrein (text QA 94.46); it is yet to be published (Cavigneaux and André-Salvini forthcoming).[17]

In addition to archival texts, a group of eleven divinatory tablets, two of which are dated to the reign of Pešgaldarameš[18] have been published (CUSAS 18, 22–32), and one previously published text was identified as being of Sealand I origin (AO 7539).[19] George (2013: 131 ff.) attributed them to Sealand I scribes on the basis of a detailed analysis of the orthography, the ductus, and the layout of the tablets, which revealed similarities with the Sealand I archival texts. He also identified a group of eight literary compositions that can be attributed to the same scriptorial tradition (George 2013: 131): an episode of the Epic of Gilgameš, was published in 2007 by the same author (George 2007); a balag to Enlil was published by Gabbay (2014a); an hymn of Ayadaragalama to the gods of Nippur (P431311) is being edited by Gabbay and Boivin (forthcoming); a grammatical list was published by Veldhuis (2017). The remaining four are as yet unpublished (P431313–431314; P431316–431317). In addition, a Königsepos concerning the Sealand I king Gulkišar (HS 1885+) is being edited by Zomer (2016; forthcoming).[20] Some of these texts are also discussed in the present work.

To these texts, one may add the unprovenanced cylinder seal of one Ilī-remeanni[21] who claims in the inscription that he "reveres the king, his lord, Ea-

16 At least sixty-eight tablets or fragments were found (Campbell et al. 2017); many of them probably date to the Sealand I dynasty and the reign of Ayadaragalama, based on the recurrence of personal names in them.

17 I thank A. Cavigneaux for giving me access to the copy and edition of the text ahead of publication.

18 CUSAS 18, 28 appears to be dated to his accession year: mu [king's name] lugal.e (rev. line 15′), but George (2013: 193 n.20) noted that the formula could be an abbreviation for any year of his reign. CUSAS 8, 32 bears a fragmentary date of the year count type which could be his twenty-fourth of twenty-fifth (line 4′). See also Appendix 2 for the date formulae.

19 The text was published by Nougayrol (1971).

20 I thank E. Zomer for sharing with me her transliteration and notes ahead of publication. She also informed me that a small tablet fragment from Nippur, possibly of a hymn of Kassite date, mentions Gulkišar (Ni 13090).

21 Expected would be *rēmanni*, but the form *remeanni* is attested in the Old Babylonian period (Stamm 1968: 167; CAD R, s.v. *rêmu* 1 b 3′). Stamm takes it as a mistake, but the CAD's suggestion that it may have developed by analogy with *ešmeanni* seems plausible. Considering that the in-

gāmil" (Moorey and Gurney 1973: 79, seal no.23).[22] Finally, when this manuscript was nearly ready to go to press, the existence of an unprovenanced seal of the Sealand I king Akurduana came to my knowledge (P455982). Its contents cannot be fully included in this book besides a few short references.

1.3.2 The palatial archive

1.3.2.1 The *Sitz im Leben* of the archive

Because the archive published in CUSAS 9 is unprovenanced,[23] its *Sitz im Leben* had to be deduced solely from internal criteria. The texts are mainly delivery receipts, allocation lists, expenditure records—including for offerings to the gods –, and ledgers;[24] there are also fifteen letters (CUSAS 9, 1–15). The palace (É.GAL) is omnipresent in this archive, not only as an economic and legal body, but as a physical location, since its gates and its roof are mentioned (e.g., CUSAS 9, 69; 87–88). The texts present the palace as a locus of economic, administrative, and diplomatic activity.[25] Therefore, it can be regarded as certain that the archive, notwithstanding its unclear provenance, was the product of a palatial administration.

The question that immediately follows is whether this palace was the main one of the Sealand kingdom at the time when these texts were produced, or rather a provincial palace. Unfortunately, the extant evidence does not allow to decide with certainty on that point. Luxury goods are almost absent from the records, also the economic purview of the administrative records appears to be mainly local (see Chapter 5). Both elements point towards a provincial administration, however, both could result from the chance of discovery, and the fact that an institution was very involved in the local economy does not preclude its playing another role supra-regionally. Other elements could suggest that the palace was the main one in the kingdom. Foreign envoys are present at

stances are mainly from Ur, it may have been a south-western regional variant. Note that there is also one Šamaš-remeanni in the Sealand I palatial archive (CUSAS 9, 426: 16).

22 The seal is housed at Charterhouse School, collection Nr. 2–1956–10. Glyptic will not be discussed in the present work. Several tablets published in CUSAS 9 are sealed: a study of the seal impressions and a discussion of how they correlate stylistically with Old Babylonian and Kassite glyptic is a desideratum.

23 The texts housed in the Musée du Cinquantenaire at Brussels, obviously belonging to the same archive, are also unprovenanced.

24 See Appendix 3 for a functional typology of the administrative texts; for a detailed inventory of tax ledgers, see Boivin 2016b.

25 On the various roles of the palace in this archive, see also Boivin forthcoming.

the court (CUSAS 9, 40; BC 435 in Dalley 2009: 47); the king is mentioned, including in the context of a journey about to begin (CUSAS 9, 101), showing that he would sometimes travel starting from that palace; no title of provincial governor or the like is attested. None of these possible indications is conclusive either, they could in part be the result of occasional sojourns of the royal court at the palace in question, and the absence of a governor identified with that title could result from the nature of the texts that were found. However, the palace seems to have been identified with the king rather than with a provincial governor because there is some slight evidence that the term LUGAL could be used instead of É.GAL in an administrative context (Boivin 2016b: 55; forthcoming). Considering all elements of evidence, I would very prudently suggest that this palace may have been the (or a) main royal palace in the kingdom at the time of Pešgaldarameš and Ayadaragalama; but the texts found by the looters document mostly its local economic affairs.

The lack of information on the context in which the documents were found as well as on the type and size of the palace in question makes it difficult to draw parallels with similar institutional settings. However, the combination of administrative and epistolary texts that we have in the Sealand I palatial corpus is attested in other palaces. Eidem (2011: 12) considered it to be typical of small Old Babylonian palace archives, in particular at Tell al-Rimah, Tell Shemshara, and Tell Leilan, where he noted that such documents were kept closely together, in very few adjacent rooms. But it remains questionable whether a parallel is admissible. Indeed, Eidem (2011: 12–13) remarked that the archival combination of letters and administrative texts in small palaces was typical of the administration of precious resources requiring close monitoring, while administrative texts dealing with agricultural products were kept in a separate location. We do not know whether the Sealand I texts came from different rooms of one building, but the letters certainly do not deal with precious goods. A combination of administrative texts and letters pertaining to the same administrative activities was also observed in a much larger palatial context, namely in specific palace archives at Mari (Charpin 1995: 39). But here again, a parallel is not easy to draw, because at Mari most administrative texts and letters were found in separate locations,[26] the former having been left largely undisturbed by the Babylo-

26 Large administrative archives were found in rooms X; Y; 5; 110; 134; 143; 160. Letters were mostly found in rooms 108 and 115. Room 108 contained both types of texts, but serious uncertainties remain concerning the original recording of the find spot of several tablets attributed to it (Charpin 1995: 35 n.20). It has also been suggested that a few letters found in room 110 had been brought there by Babylonian troops rummaging through the archives after the conquest of the city (Bottéro 1958: 163).

nian conquerors, the latter having been subjected to a selection and probably a relocation (Charpin 1995: 36 n.22; 39).[27]

In the extant Sealand I palace archive, the relationship between some of the epistolary and some of the administrative texts is obvious: the transportation or transaction of various goods, which are the object of administrative texts (most texts in CUSAS 9), are also discussed in letters (beer, grain, oil; in CUSAS 9, 1–2; 4–5; 8; 10; 13–14); also, one letter (CUSAS 9, 14) orders the collection of the *šibšu*, a grain tax otherwise attested in large ledgers (several in CUSAS 9, chapter x). Therefore, it seems not unlikely that such letters and some of the administrative documents were indeed kept together. There may have been a few separate locations involved, corresponding to specialized bureaus of the palace administration. Examination of the administrative practices surrounding book-keeping and of the contents of the texts shows that there was probably a Bureau of livestock, dealing with small and large cattle, including the reception of carcasses, perhaps a Bureau of grain, possibly dealing also with milling, a Bureau of malt and beer, and there may have been others dealing with oil, reed, and other resources (see Chapter 5). There are therefore chances that the texts, when they were still part of a living archive, were kept in separate locations in the palace, and one should thus perhaps rather speak of archives. For the sake of simplicity, I will nonetheless in this book use the term in the singular.

1.3.2.2 The temporal extent and context of retrieval of the archive

Of the 474 archival texts, the large majority, 393, contain a year name. These year names are of two types: some are based on an event, like Old Babylonian year names, others use a simple year count in a fashion similar to the much earlier Early Dynastic and also to the later Kassite practice. The latter formulae almost always lack the king's name:[28] mu (ki) [numeral] (kam). This date type is similar to the year formulae of the lot of tablets from Qalʿat al-Bahrein to which one dated to the Sealand I king Ea-gāmil belongs (Cavigneaux and André-Salvini forthcoming); this shows that this manner of reckoning regnal years endured until the end of the dynasty. Only three texts are dated to Pešgaldarameš, all of which used the year count system:[29] they date to his twenty-seventh and

27 In fact, the very function of certain rooms as archive storage before the Babylonian conquest has been questioned (Charpin 1995: 36 n.22).

28 The name and title of the king appear in texts CUSAS 9, 16; 85; 111; 407, of which the first two are dated to Pešgaldarameš: mu RN lugal.e ki [numeral]. See Appendix 2 for an overview of the year names.

29 This is also the case of the divinatory text CUSAS 18, 32 briefly discussed above.

his twenty-ninth year (years A and C;[30] CUSAS 9, 85; 16; 407), which must have been at the very end of his reign since internal evidence shows that the texts dated to Ayadaragalama followed without a significant interval.[31] All other dated texts in the archive are from the reign of Ayadaragalama. In addition to his accession year (year D: mu Ayadaragalama lugal.e), a number of his year names refer to events (years E, F, G, H, I, J and O can be reconstructed with some level of certainty), while two use the year count system (year L= 7 and year N=8).

Dalley (2009: 11–12) analyzed the year names of the archive, none of which was known before, and attempted to reconstruct their sequence. Nothing in the prosopography and other contents of the texts seems to warrant modifications to the general sequence that she proposes, as long as one keeps in mind that it is neither detailed nor definitive, but rather an arrangement of clusters of years: last years of Pešgaldarameš (A-C), first year of Ayadaragalama (D), middle years of the archive during Ayadaragalama's reign (E-J), later years of the archive during Ayadaragalama's reign (L and N). Taken together, the texts cover a relatively short time span of twelve or a few more years.[32]

Among the uncertainties surrounding the sequence of years is the position of years K and M. They read respectively mu gibil and mu gibil egir, namely "New year" and "The year after the new year," which strongly suggests that M followed K. Dalley (2009: 10–12) proposed to view these formulae as alternative year names that were used alongside other formulae: she equates K with L because both have an intercalary month xii;[33] and since L and N are of the year count type, respectively "year 7" and "year 8" and are thus consecutive, it fol-

30 I follow Dalley's (2009: 11–12) proposed system for naming the years, using capital letters.

31 The matter is discussed in depth in Section 3.2.1.1.

32 For three of the year names attested only once, two of which are very fragmentary, it is not possible to determine whether they represent part of a longer version of another year name (years O, P, and Q). Year R is attested only once and uses the year count system; it is the only one to feature "year 9," and because "year 8" (= year N) is very frequent, it may be a scribal mistake.

33 There were in fact intercalary months in two subsequent years, year L (= year 7) and year N (= year 8); both intercalary months were even added within a few months since we have evidence for an intercalary month xii in year L and an intercalary month ii in year N. Such a measure appears quite drastic and, for it to be justified, one would expect the grain harvest in year L to have taken place rather late in the (by then out-of-phase) lunar calendar, and roughly two lunar months earlier in year N. We have, however, evidence of grain tax collection in month iv for both years (CUSAS 9, 426; 431A; 432). If the relevant year names had not been of the year count type, it would be very tempting to conclude that they were not consecutive and therefore that a two-month correction did not take place between these two grain harvests; for the present this must remain one of the several unanswered questions.

lows that year K=L(=7) and year M=N(=8). There is nothing in the documents that contradicts this reconstruction, but the archive does not offer further indication corroborating it either. If Dalley's surmises are correct, the formulae mu gibil (=K) and mu gibil egir (=M) were certainly not provisional year names since they are both attested for several months,[34] while their purported equivalents (formulae L and N) are both attested as early as in month i. It seems somewhat surprising that the same palatial administration should have used two concurrent formulae for the entire year. A possible explanation could be sought in different administrative habits prevailing in separate bureaus, but the archive presents no convincing evidence for this.[35] It remains therefore uncertain whether years K and M were really identical with years L and N, respectively.

The archive does not offer much evidence enabling a reconstruction of families or administrative careers, which would help in sequencing the documents.[36] But some individuals are attested only for a few years and these years seem indeed to belong together.[37]

If we plot the number of texts per year using Dalley's proposed sequence,[38] considering all texts which bear a legible date, we obtain the distribution shown in Fig. 1.

If we admit the possibility of distinct groups of texts raised above, the archives of the purported "Bureau of livestock (and carcasses)," "Bureau of malt and beer," and perhaps a "Bureau of grain" all show the same distribution pattern with a peak in year N, it is only less marked for the purported Bureau of grain. This could indicate that the texts were all kept together, or that the archives of separate bureaus underwent archival procedures according to the same criteria of elimination and conservation. The curve suggests a living, active

34 Year K is even attested for every month of the year.

35 Grain and beer are more prevalent in documents dating to Year K, whereas livestock is very present in documents of Year L, but there are exceptions, so that this distribution may not be of significance. Also, texts of year M do not feature many livestock deliveries, but the sample is so small that it is impossible to regard this as evidence.

36 One possible exception, though not very convincingly attested, is Tarībātu. He is called once a cook in year J (CUSAS 9, 72) and the overseer of the cooks in all other attestations which all date to year N (perhaps once L), for instance in CUSAS 9, 312; 322–23; 325–27. This apparent promotion to the overseer function would tally with the proposed sequence of years.

37 For instance Arad-Šamaš who delivers sheep in years E and F (CUSAS 9, 18; 21; 22). Other individuals are attested throughout the entire period, for instance Ḫuzālu the maltster-brewer who is attested in over fifty texts (see Index of personal names in Dalley 2009).

38 In this graph, the years K and M are considered coeval with L and N, as per Dalley's suggestion (2009: 10–11). Dissociating them would modify the distribution, but not dramatically, since the number of texts dating to year N is overwhelmingly higher than for any other year.

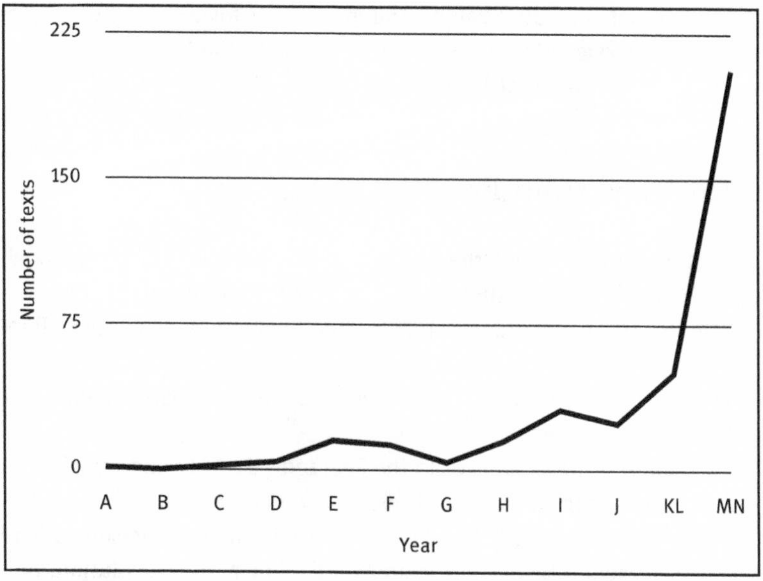

Figure 1: Distribution of texts per year

archive subjected to the pruning of older texts and a sudden, catastrophic cessation of activity (Civil 1987: 46) very late in year N—there are texts dated to the first half of month xii of that year. However, the older texts do not appear to be any different from the later ones, for instance, cumulative records are not more prevalent among the older ones. Choosing to keep a few records for the delivery of a small quantity of malt or one sheep from ten years past seems to defy all archival and administrative good sense. Therefore, the most likely explanation is that it was partly the accident of discovery, in this case in fact the accident of looting, which resulted in this distribution; the contents of storage rooms of the living archive may, for instance, have been mixed with older tablets found in refuse or recycling bins.

As for the provenance of the archive, Dalley (2009: 4–5), followed by George (2013: 131), considered it most likely to be from the vicinity of Nippur. Several looted tablets that had surfaced in Europe and the U.S. in the 1990s were suspected of coming from Nippur because of place names mentioned in them. It appears certain that they were not looted from Nippur directly (Gibson 2012: 118; 2016: 128), but several certainly came for the surrounding area, for instance from Dūr-Abī-ešuḫ and Dūr-Enlilē (several of these tablets are now published or soon to be published e.g., in CUSAS 8; 29; 30; Devecchi forthcoming; for a recent inventory of the known Dūr-Abī-ešuḫ tablets, Földi 2017: 17 ff.). However, in my opinion the contents of the Sealand I archive point toward another provenance, in the south-western Euphrates area, probably in the Ur-Larsa-Eridu triangle. The matter is discussed at length in Section 3.1.3.

1.4 The scope and structure of the present work

The aim of the present work is to write a history of the Sealand I polity—political, religious, and economic—and is thus by and large restricted to roughly two centuries in the middle of the second millennium, and to central and southern Babylonia.

The discussion falls into five chapters. A brief concluding chapter summarizes the key findings of the analysis.

Chapter 2 examines the references to the Sealand I dynasty and kingdom in Mesopotamian historiography. Almost all relevant sources, king lists and chronicles, have been known for several decades, therefore the analysis presented here is mainly a reassessment. The chapter examines the emergence, evolution, and usage of the two names associated with the Sealand I dynasty, Eurukug and *māt tâmti* (Sealand). Then, the royal onomasticon, which combines Akkadian and Sumerian forms, is discussed. The inclusion of the Sealand I dynasty in Babylonian king lists is examined. Finally, chronicles are discussed; because of its relevance for the history of transmission of Sealand I historiographic data, the chronicle *ABC* 20B is given particular attention, including its textual genesis.

Chapter 3 defines the geographical and chronological extents of the Sealand kingdom. Positive, direct geographical evidence, which is scarce because most Sealand I texts were not retrieved in controlled excavations, is reviewed to establish the few cardinal facts of Sealand I geography. Indirect evidence is inferred from textual sources and used to identify additional areas likely to have been under Sealand I control. The provenance of the palatial archive is discussed. Finally, synchronisms between the Sealand I dynasty and other Babylonian rulers are reviewed; among other sources discussed, the reign lengths of BKL A are tested on their accuracy. (Because we have so little solid evidence on the Sealand kingdom, this assessment of geographical and chronological data was kept separate from the writing of its political history; it allows for the discussion in Chapter 4 to go beyond the mere question of availability of evidence, however, at the cost of allowing some repetition when referring to source material in Chapters 3 and 4.)

Chapter 4 presents a political history of the Sealand kingdom from its possible genesis in the southern rebellion early in Samsu-iluna's reign until its conquest by the Kassite rulers of Babylon. Because the extant Sealand I palatial texts are concerned mainly with local matters, most of the sources used to write this political history are external and many have been known for several decades. But their reassessment in conjunction with the analysis of new sources sheds light on some aspects of state affairs, for instance the relations of the Sealand kingdom with its neighbors, and also on specific episodes of territorial control, for instance the question of the occupation and control of Nippur in the mid-second millennium. Due to the uneven availability of evidence, the emphasis is markedly on the first half of the Sealand I dynasty and its turbulent relations with the late Old Babylonian kingdom.

Chapter 5 examines the palatial economy. Because of the nature of the extant documents, the scope of the analysis is mostly limited to the palace and its immediate environment. The procurement, transformation, consumption, and expenditure of resources by the palace is reconstructed. The integration between the palace and temples, main beneficiaries of the palace, as well as between the palace and other institutions involved in the transformation of resources is discussed. The resources documented in the archive are mainly animal and agricultural. Because of the general scarcity of sources for that period, the agricultural resources and products, for instance types of grain or beer, are systematically inventoried in order to build a first reference of what was produced in the Sealand kingdom.

Chapter 6 examines aspects of intellectual and religious history of the Sealand kingdom, in the context of the demographic and social disruptions that characterize its emergence. Elements of two main panthea, the state pantheon and the local-regional pantheon are extracted mainly from archival sources recording the palace-sponsored cult. The onomasticon and the religious *topoi* in year names are also discussed, as well as the few literary compositions attributed to Sealand I scribes. The information thus adduced is used to situate the Sealand I dynastic tradition and ideology within a wider Babylonian context.

Finally, the main findings of the book are summarized in Chapter 7.

2 The Sealand I in Babylonian historiography

Until recently, historians could rely only on Mesopotamian historiographic texts and other secondary records of events as sources of information on the Sealand kingdom. Beyond the undeniable merit of having revealed its existence, these sources have not yielded much detail on its history. Still, king lists and chronicles do offer some information on events, people involved, and their time and place. And this information, however distorted in the process of transmission and interpretation, must be exploited because, at present, Sealand I primary sources and other contemporary records do not offer nearly enough evidence to write a Sealand I history mainly from them. Therefore, with due care, historiographic records will be used as a means of historical reconstruction. But roughly a millennium elapsed between the Sealand kingdom and the compilation of the relevant king lists and chronicles, more than enough time for the memory of actual people and events to fade, interpretation and reinterpretation to occur. We know the result of that long process, we want to deduce from it the starting point, but the intermediate steps are also obscure. When and why did the Sealand I dynasty enter the Babylonian chronographic record? How are the Sealand I dynasty and the Sealand kingdom presented by first millennium chroniclers and how had they been remembered in sources available to them? In order to propose answers to these questions, historiographic documents will also be treated as objects of historical analysis in and for themselves. Their historical context of writing will be examined, as well as the probable sources that the scribes used, how they used them, and what intention they pursued in compiling that information.

One of the key issues when dealing with the transmission of the memory of the Sealand I dynasty is that two different names are associated with it in ancient sources, Eurukug and *māt tâmti*. Moreover, the latter is also the name of a southern Babylonian region and at times province, including at the probable time of compilation of some king lists and chronicles, the Neo-Babylonian period. The occurrences, orthographies, and meaning of both name traditions associated with the Sealand I dynasty need therefore to be carefully examined and, in the case of *māt tâmti*, the possibility of an association—conscious or not—between the second millennium kingdom and later instances of the Sealand must be evaluated. Another important issue is the fact that the Sealand I dynasty was probably for most of its history a power opposed to Babylon, potentially giving it an ambiguous status in first millennium scriptoria at or in the orbit of Babylon.

https://doi.org/10.1515/9781501507823-003

The chronographic records that have kept traces of the Sealand I dynasty and polity are few but diverse in style. Without aiming at revisiting the typology of the Mesopotamian historiographic corpus, for the sake of the present discussion the sources are segmented as follows: I call "king lists" documents whose main object of interest is to establish a royal chronography, whether the rulers are associated with dynasties or not; I call "chronicles" compilations of events and rulers' deeds.

The Sealand I dynasty appears in four king lists that will be referred to using the following abbreviations:

- BKL A = Babylonian King List A = BM 33332[1]
- BKL B = Babylonian King List B = BM 38122[2]
- DynKL = Dynastic King List (= *ABC* 18 = *MC* 3)[3]= K 8532+
- SynKL = Synchronistic King List = A.117

The chronicles and chronicle fragments relevant to the present discussion include:

- BM 96152 = *ABC* 20B = *MC* 40
- BM 26472 = *ABC* 20A = *MC* 39
- Fragments K 2973 and 79–7–8, 36 (probably belonging to the same text) = *ABC* 'Fragment Concerning the Period of the First Dynasty of Isin' (*ABC:* 190–92) = *MC* 41
- Fragments K 10609 and K 14011 (Lambert 1990b) = *MC* 43 and 44
- Fragment BM 29440 (Leichty and Walker 2004: 205–07)
- Fragment BM 29297 (Leichty and Walker 2004: 211–12)
- Fragment BM 38284 = *ABC* 'Fragment Concerning the Sealand' (p. 192 no. 2) = *MC* 42

1 The line numbering of BKL A follows Grayson 1980–83: 91 ff.

2 The line numbering of BKL B follows Grayson 1980–83: 100.

3 I consider this curious text as a king list rather than a chronicle, contra Grayson (1975) but alongside Brinkman (1990: 77 n.21) and Waerzeggers (2012: 289). Finkel (1980: 70) calls it a chronicle but notes its "dependence (...) on the Sumerian King List;" of course, the genre of the latter text may also be debated. My decision of calling *ABC* 18 a king list is based on the fact that the section of the tablet that is of relevance here only lists rulers grouped in dynasties. Henceforth, *ABC* = *Assyrian and Babylonian Chronicles* (Grayson 1975) and *MC* = *Mesopotamian Chronicles* (Glassner 2004).

2.1 The names of the Sealand I dynasty and polity

Two different name traditions are associated with the Sealand I dynasty or with aspects related to its rule: its kings, its kingdom, possibly its capital, and perhaps (part of) its territory. In order to study the distribution of their occurrences, the relevant attestations in the extant written evidence are summarized in Table 1.

Table 1: Names given to the Sealand I dynasty and polity by type of source[4]

	(Near-)contemporary documents		Later 2nd and 1st millennium (chronographic) documents	
Name Tradition	**Sealand I indigenous**	**Sealand I non-indigenous**	**King Lists**	**Chronicles and other documents**
(É.) URU$_x$.KU$_x$ (.GA)(^{ki})	É.URU$_{14}$.KÙ^{ki} (CUSAS 9, 6: 15; P431311: rev. 21′; P455982)			
			URÙ.KU$_6$ (BKL A: I 15′)	
			URÙ.KÙ^{ki} (BKL B: rev. 13 & 24)	
			É.URU.KÙ.GA^{ki} (DynKL: IV 14′)	

4 Included in this table are only the attestations that, in my opinion, did or could refer to the Sealand I dynasty and kingdom. A.AB.BA^{ki} (in the list AN=^{d}Anum) is included because there are chances that the name of the goddess INANA-A.AB.BA^{ki} refers to an aspect of the goddess that emerged in that kingdom, although that reference may not have been understood anymore (Boivin 2016a). Pending the publication of the epic HS 1885+, its likely date of writing remains uncertain. It could be a product of a Sealand I scriptorium of somewhat later date or a Kassite copy; the editor noted possible Kassite features in the ductus (E. Zomer, personal communication); if the text was written during the time of the Sealand I dynasty, this would make it the only attestation of the term A.AB.BA that is indigenous to the Sealand kingdom. The chronicle fragment 'Fragment Concerning the Sealand' in *ABC* p.192 mentions the KUR *tam-tim* but not enough of the document is preserved to establish whether it referred to the Sealand I dynasty (see Section 2.4.2.2). In chronicle *ABC* 20B the term *tam-tì* may also appear without determinative on rev. 5; however, the passage is too fragmentary to allow for a satisfactory reconstruction of the syntax (the term *tam-tì* is immediately preceded by AD$_6^{ME}$-*šú-nu*, their corpses, without any preposition;

Table 1: Names given to the Sealand I dynasty and polity by type of source *(continued)*

	(Near-)contemporary documents		Later 2nd and 1st millennium (chronographic) documents	
Name Tradition	**Sealand I indigenous**	**Sealand I non-indigenous**	**King Lists**	**Chronicles and other documents**
(*māt*) *tâmti*		KUR A.AB.BA (Macehead of Ulam-Buriaš BE6405= WVDOG 4: 7–8)		KUR A.AB.BA (Distanzangabe in *kudurru* BE I/ 1 83: 3 & 6)
				KUR ***tam-tì*** (*ABC* 20B: rev. 12; 14; 16)
				A.AB.BA^{ki} (AN=^{d}Anum: tablet IV, line 129)
(*māt*) *tâmti?*	A.AB.BA(?) (Epic HS 1885+ in the forthcoming TMH 11)	A.AB.BA(?) (OECT 15, 10: 10; OECT 15, 78: 18′; Sem 1278(=Földi 2014: 33 f.): obv. 20; MS 3218/13: 5; CUSAS 29, 3: 10)		

The table shows clearly that king lists and other late documents follow different traditions when naming the Sealand I dynasty or polity. King lists transmitted the Eurukug tradition,[5] a term also found in two contemporary and indigenous Sealand I documents. In contrast, the authors of at least one chronicle (*ABC* 20B) and those of an official legal document of the end of the second millennium followed the *māt tâmti* tradition. The earliest incontrovertible attestation of this term is Kassite, it could therefore be a creation of somewhat later date than

see Section 2.4.1). Without a context suggesting the presence of a toponym, and because Sealand is written with the determinative KUR elsewhere in this text, the passage probably does not refer to the polity, perhaps rather to the sea or a lake.

5 In this regard, Glassner's reconstruction of the missing end of line IV 13′ (in *MC* 3 = DynKL) as [(...) nam.lugal.bi kur a.ab.ba.šè ba.nigin], that is "[(...) its kingship went to the Sealand]" is unfortunate and, for all we know, entirely unfounded since the following line (IV 14′) indicates that the rulers reigned at é.uru.kù.ga^{ki}. The relevant passage is made up of two small fragments, K 16801 and K 16930, respectively published in Lambert 1974 and Finkel 1980: 79 no.4.

the Eurukug tradition. But there are signs that the toponym KUR A.AB.BA has its root in an earlier one, simply A.AB.BA.

Noteworthy is also the fact that Eurukug is never associated with another polity or dynasty except Sealand I, while the term *māt tâmti* is applied to later Babylonian rulers and to an area of southern Babylonia, more or less independently of changes in its political status.

2.1.1 The Eurukug tradition

Table 1 shows that Eurukug was in all likelihood a toponym used in Sealand I indigenous sources, later kept and passed down in king lists. The proposed readings are based on the assumption that all attestations listed in the upper half of Table 1 indeed refer to the same term and are simply orthographic variants. It must be noted that the reading (É.)URU$_x$.KU$_x$(.GA^{ki}) remains uncertain but appears at present the best solution, which can accommodate all known attestations.[6] Alternatively, all instances could be normalized as Eurikug.

The DynKL is the only late source which features É at the beginning of the name of the dynasty, in accordance with the contemporary attestations. The case seems similar to that of the dynasty of (Bīt-)Bazi, written with a preposed É in DynKL (V 12) but without it in BKL A (III 13);[7] the development of this form É + GN could reflect tribal affiliation (Brinkman 1968: 158). If we have the same phenomenon with Eurukug, the reference could be to the place of origin of the rulers, their hometown, not necessarily their capital.

The letter (CUSAS 9, 6) which contains this term does not make entirely clear what it represents but it occurs in what appears to be an appeal to the loyalty of the addressee: (15) É.URU$_{14}$.KÙ^{ki} (16) *i-na lib-bi-ka la i-ba-aš-ši* : "Euruku is not in

6 At the publication of BKL A, Pinches (1884: 194) read the name of the dynasty Šišku, based on a reading KU$_x$ for the sign ḪA, followed by King (1907: vol.I 70). As for the first sign, ŠEŠ, King (1907: vol.I 70–71) suggested that it should be read URÙ and pondered whether Uruk was meant although he concluded that proof is lacking. The reading was still considered uncertain by Dougherty (1932: 17) when he published his work on the Sealand. The case for a reading URU$_x$.KU$_x$, or rather (É.)URU$_x$.KU$_x$(.GA) was strongly reinforced by the publication of a new fragment of the DynKL by Lambert in 1974 in which the name is written É.URU.KÙ.GA^{ki}. He suggested to read it "the house, the holy city" (1974: 209). The passage É.ŠEŠ.UNUG.KÙ^{ki} in CUSAS 9, 6, P431311, and P455982 with the reading proposed above, appears to confirm what Lambert and others before him had suggested.

7 In other documents, the toponym is usually attested without the É but twice with it in *kudurrū* from the late twelfth century (MDP VI 42 = AOAT 51, MAI I 6: I 14 and BBSt XXIV = AOAT 51, NKU I 3: rev. 4).

your heart" or possibly "Is Euruku not in your heart?"[8] It would indeed make sense that the term refers to the seat of power or to the origin of the dynasty, and by extension to the royal dynasty.[9] The Sealand I hymn P431311, also featuring the toponym with the same orthography, is very fragmentary but the relevant passage appears to exalt Eurukug as a royal city of the king Ayadaragalama (Gabbay and Boivin forthcoming: line 21′). The unpublished seal of Akurduana (P455982) probably calls him the king of Eurukug, reinforcing the impression that it was the royal capital.

Considering the morphology of the toponym itself and the orthographical variance found in the available sources, the most plausible explanation is that the hometown (or the capital) of the Sealand I dynasty, Eurukug, was not one of the large, well-known ancient seats of power of Babylonia for which the written tradition had established standard orthographies. But the name may refer to or be a by-name of a well-known town.[10]

2.1.1.1 A probable reference to Ur

The contemporary, indigenous evidence for the term Eurukug points toward a reference to Ur. Indeed, the orthography É.ŠEŠ.UNUG.KÙ^{ki} (see Table 1) appears to correspond to "Urim with epithet" as Dalley puts it (2009: text 6, note to line 15).[11] However, it is unlikely that the toponym designates Ur itself, whose orthography had been long established and remains stable in later periods; integrating the adjective KÙ before the determinative—within the toponym—would represent a surprising departure from it. And indeed, the unstable orthography of Eurukug

8 Dalley (2009: text 6 notes to lines 12 and 16) opts for the interrogative form. She also discusses the negation with *lā*.

9 Dalley tentatively interprets the term as "the house (dynasty?) of holy Ur (?)" She discusses the possibility that it referred to the capital of the Sealand kingdom in 2009: text 6 note to line 15.

10 In addition to Uruk (see note 6 in this chapter), two other possible cities were suggested by early scholars on the basis of their reading of the relevant passage in the then recently discovered BKL A. For the sake of completeness they are briefly presented here. In 1881, Lauth (1880–81: 46 ff.) suggested to read the Sealand I dynastic name "Šešku" and saw in it a reference to Babylon due to a parallel with the term ששך in the book of Jeremiah 25:26. But this term is an athbash cypher for Babylon (בבל), therefore not an Akkadian alternative name for Babylon. The other suggested reading, the one which came to prevail, was "Uruku" and it was understood to represent "most probably, another name of Erech-Warka" (Eastlake 1881–82: 36); this possibility was again considered by King (1907: vol.I 70–71). In addition, the name, Sumerian in morphology, may be an artificial Sumerian orthography given to a purely Akkadian toponym.

11 Dalley discusses Ur as possible royal center of the Sealand kingdom in 2009: 5–6.

in the late sources suggests that the toponym was no longer understood by the scribes. One possible explanation is that it was the name given to a new foundation, perhaps where the cults of Ur as well as part of its population were relocated for a time.

Al-Hamdani (2015: 168–70) recently suggested that the Sealand I capital could be the unexcavated Tell Dehaila, on the lower Eridu branch of the Euphrates, some thirty kilometers from Ur. Satellite photographs enabled him to conclude that it was a highly urbanized city, and he surmises, because of similarities in overall size and in the architectural organization of their main temple precincts, that Tell Dehaila was built as a new Ur, where the inhabitants of the latter resettled following a sudden westward shift of the Euphrates. Should this be the case, Ur would certainly have been dearly remembered among the displaced inhabitants and royal entourage, and one could well imagine such a city bearing a name referring to it. Moreover, since the site was apparently occupied only during one archaeological period, it could explain why the orthography of its name was corrupted in later sources, but as long as Tell Dehaila is unexcavated, this remains a theory.

As for the purported abandonment of Ur itself, archaeological evidence is of limited help. Woolley's excavations reports are contradictory as to the occupation of domestic quarters at Ur between the Old and the Middle Babylonian periods. They offer both examples of continuity and disruption. Above a layer of destruction dated to Samsu-iluna, some houses appear to have been immediately rebuilt without changes to the layout for a prolonged period; on the other side, some Kassite structures do not follow the former layout (Woolley 1954: 174; 197–98; 1965: 77; Gasche 1989: 130–31; Clayden 2014: 34; 42–43). However, late Old Babylonian ceramics are not attested (Armstrong and Gasche 2014: 98), and recent excavations have not uncovered clear evidence of late Old Babylonian occupation (al-Hamdani 2015: 132). While it is difficult to decide to what extent the site was abandoned, it seems clear that it did not function in that period as an important royal city benefiting from the kings' favors (see also Clayden 2014: 23). It is hoped that current and future work at Ur will help lift that uncertainty.[12]

That the city—or the memory of the city—of Ur was important to the Sealand I kings could also find expression in a curious fragment of the Epic of Gilgamesh published by George (2007). The physical appearance and ductus of the unprovenanced tablet have been noted by George to closely resemble those of the

12 Excavations have resumed under the lead of A. al-Hamdani, E. Stone, and P. Zimansky in 2015.

omen and other texts dated to or mentioning Pešgaldarameš and Ayadaragalama, it may thus be considered a product of the same Sealand I scribal tradition (George 2007: 63; 2013: 130). The extant passage recounts the episode of Enkidu becoming acquainted with urban civilization but it contains enigmatic departures from the usual version. Besides featuring ^{d}30 and ^{d}40 instead of the expected Gilgameš and Enkidu, it replaces five times Uruk by Ur (ŠEŠ.UNUG^{ki}),[13] although UNUG^{ki} also occurs once.[14] His thorough comparison of the fragment with other versions of the Epic of Gilgameš has led George to conclude that:

> The wording of the fragment is so close to extant versions of the Epic of Gilgameš that it seems incontrovertible that what we have here is a piece from an edition of the epic in which the names have been changed deliberately. The solitary inconsistency, Uruk for Ur in l. 65, is important in this regard, for it reveals that a text with the expected proper nouns underlies the text on the tablet. (George 2007: 60)

According to George's analysis, this fragment would thus probably not represent the continuation of a minor, heretofore unknown tradition of the Epic of Gilgameš but truly be a Sealand I innovation, a local adaptation.[15] Such an adaptation seems to lend weight to the hypothesis that Ur was an important royal center of the Sealand I dynasty, at least ideologically. George has put forward various interesting hypotheses to explain the strange variations in the Sealand I Epic of Gilgameš: one of them is that the substitutions were mere abbreviations (George 2007: 60), in which case no reference to Ur was intended, but other explanations would indeed present Gilgameš as king of Ur (*ibid.*: 61). The case is further discussed in Section 6.1.1.

Excursus: A less likely possibility: A reference to Girsu or Lagaš

Another, less likely, possibility is that Eurukug refers to the temple district of that name at Girsu, known since Early Dynastic times and also attested during Gudea's reign (Selz 2015). The name É.URU.KÙ.GA is attested in EDIII inscriptions

---

13 Col.I lines 5; 12; 33; col.V lines 3′; 7′. The cases of col.I line 33 an col. V line 7′ are somewhat less certain since the passages are very fragmentary, but the other instances are clear.

14 Col.I line 65.

15 However, he notes that the association between Ur and Uruk, as well as between the royal houses of both cities—including that between the Ur III kings and Gilgameš –, was already well established in the literary tradition (George 2007: 61).

as a by-name of the É.TAR.SÍR.SÍR of Ba'u (George 1993: no.1198).[16] URU.KÙ^{ki} at Girsu is also attested as the location of the Éninnu of Ningirsu and other sanctuaries.[17]

URU.KÙ(G) also appears in association with the town of Lagaš. An inscribed brick concerning the building of the temple of Gatumdu at URU.KÙ was found at al-Hibā (Crawford 1974: 29). Also, in the "Lamentation over the Destruction of Ur," URU.KÙ appears as the location of what was probably a shrine to Ba'u in the É.BA.GARÁ (line 22)[18] and inscriptions unearthed at al-Hibā have shown that the É.BA.GARÁ was located there (Falkenstein 1966: 17; Crawford 1974: 29–30; see also Selz 2015). This has led scholars to identify Eurukug with al-Hibā, either designating the whole town or a temple precinct within it; of course, as an important precinct it could be used as a by-name for the city. On this basis, Lambert (1974: 209–10) considered al-Hibā a likely candidate for the capital of the Sealand I dynasty.

The Sealand I documents pertaining to cultic activity show that while Nazi[19] was prominent in the state-sponsored cult, her circle and other Lagašite deities were remarkably absent or unimportant.[20] This suggests that the ancient city-state did not have a high political weight in the kingdom.[21] Also, excavations at Tello and at al-Hibā have shown no indication pointing towards a role of importance during the late Old Babylonian and early Kassite periods although this absence of evidence should not be considered a positive proof since the excava-

---

16 Lambert (1974: 209) rejects any association between É.URU.KÙ.GA the temple name and the name of the hometown of the Sealand I dynasty. In so doing, he rejects an association between the Sealand I capital or hometown and Girsu.

17 Various sanctuaries are identified as located in that temple district. See George 1993: nos.1085; 1121; 1138; 1198; 1309; 1314; 1323; 1344. A temple of Belili is also called É.ÚRU.KÙ (George 1993: no.1202).

18 URU.KÙ also appears on line 56 of the same text (Römer 2004; Samet 2014). See also George (1993: no.96). (É.)URU.KÙ.(GA) also appears twice as a dwelling place of Ba'u in the "Lamentation over the Destruction of Sumer and Ur", on lines 117 and 161 (Michalowski 1989). In this case, it is unclear whether this refers to the URU.KÙ of Girsu or of Lagaš. See also George (1993: no.1198).

19 For the orthography of the name, see Section 6.4.3.

20 See Chapter 6 for a detailed discussion.

21 It also speaks against an ideological identification of the Sealand I kings with ancient Lagašite rulers, unless one considers Ninurta as a strong indication of Lagašite influence, an interpretation that does not seem warranted (see Chapter 6). This goes for instance against Hallo (1975: 185; also n.26), who, building upon and extending Falkenstein's argument, surmised that references to exploits of Gudea were still understood in Old Babylonian myths concerning Ninurta, despite the fact that Gudea is never mentioned and that Ninurta had indeed replaced Ningirsu.

tions did not cover all areas of the sites and the reports are often lacunary (Gasche 1989: 127–28; al-Hamdani 2015: 130–31).[22]

2.1.2 The *māt tâmti* tradition

Three attestations clearly referring to the Sealand kingdom use the morphology KUR + A.AB.BA or *tâmti*. It is used by the Kassite conqueror in the title he gives himself on a mace-head: LUGAL KUR A.AB.BA (BE6405 recently re-edited in Stein 2000: Ka 1 on p.129). It was found in secondary, Parthian context in Babylon, alongside other stone objects including temple paraphernalia (Koldewey 1911: 46–47; Wetzel, Schmidt, and Mallwitz 1957: 34 ff.) Unless the mace-head was fashioned later to glorify an ancestor,[23] the short inscription shows that the Kassites called the area they had just conquered "the Sealand." The same title, LUGAL KUR A.AB.BA, is given to the Sealand I king Gulkišar in a *kudurru* from the late twelfth or early eleventh century (BE I/1 83 recently re-edited by Paulus in AOAT 51: ENAp 1: obv. lines 3 and 6), showing that, by that time, the kingdom was conceived of as Sealand. In similar fashion, the chronicle *ABC* 20B calls the last Sealand I king Ea-gāmil LUGAL KUR *tam-tì* (rev. line 12); the same text calls also the kingdom or territory taken by the Kassites from him the KUR *tam-tì* (rev. lines 14 & 16).

In addition, there are a number of attestations of the term A.AB.A without the preposed KUR, which may be related to the Sealand kingdom, and may in fact show the origin of the toponym *māt tâmti:* one may be Sealand I indigenous and was probably passed down in the later tradition, three instances probably pre-date the creation of the Sealand kingdom but come from an area that would later belong to it, finally, three others date from the early days of the Sealand kingdom but come from a neighboring area under Babylon's control.[24]

---

22 However, recent data indicate that there was a small Isin-Larsa settlement at al-Hibā, but no evidence for large occupation in the second millennium (C. Reichel, personal communication); see also Pittman and Renette 2016.

23 Because the mace-head was found in a secondary, very late context, it is impossible to establish with certainty whether it was fashioned in the early Kassite period. However, at least one other object found alongside it, a mace-head of Meli-Šipak, could be of Kassite date (Koldewey 1911: 47); other objects found with them date to the Isin II dynasty (*ibid.:* 48). Therefore, it seems certainly possible that the mace-head of Ulam-Buriaš was fashioned in his lifetime, or shortly thereafter, and kept for centuries alongside other votive objects.

24 In addition, in one chronicle fragment the term KUR *tam-tim* is used in an unclear context (Grayson 1975: 192 no.2). Also, a lacunary passage of a chronicle fragment concerning the early Old Babylonian period has been tentatively reconstructed as *tâmti šaplit* and suggested

To begin with the possible indigenous attestation, in the epic HS 1885+ (soon to be published in TMH 11) the goddess Ištar goes to war with Sealand I king Gulkišar and she is given the epithet *narāmti* A.AB.BA (Zomer 2016: 60). Tantalizingly, the term A.AB.BA becomes enshrined in the name of a regional hypostasis of Ištar in the list AN = ᵈAnum, this time also with the determinative KI: line 129 of tablet IV reads ᵈINANNA-A.AB.BA^ki: *ia-bi-i-*[*tu*] (Litke 1998). Given the combined evidence from the epic and from archival texts showing that Ištar was of great importance to the Sealand I kings (Boivin 2016a; also Section 6.4.1), it is very likely that this name somehow refers to the Sealand kingdom, although it may no longer have been understood at the time of compiling this segment of AN = ᵈAnum. While this incarnation of Ištar clearly has a geographical connotation, it is not certain whether the term refers to the entire kingdom or an area within it.

The slightly earlier attestations come from Larsa and Ur. In the two instances presumably from mid-Old Babylonian Larsa, the term A.AB.BA appears without the preposed KUR or the determinative KI. They may date from the time of the southern rebellion, therefore before any other indication that the Sealand I polity existed. Both passages are damaged and their context is unclear. Text OECT 15, 78 is a very fragmentary document, probably concerning land. In it, the phrase LUGAL A.AB.BA appears on line 18′ but the rest of the passage is broken—both before and after this segment –, therefore LUGAL need not be a title, it could be part of a personal name.[25] In the ration list OECT 15, 10, troops of (the) A.AB.BA appear. The text, also possibly from Larsa, is dated to the first year of Rīm-Sîn, whom Dalley (2005: 3) assumes to be the second of that name.[26] On the basis of a parallel with other texts, Dalley (2005: 5) estimates that these troops were prisoners of war who had fought against Rīm-Sîn II either along Babylon's troops or independently. However, in her study of the Old Babylonian *bīt asīrī* texts, Seri (2013) did not include OECT 15, 10 in the group of relevant tablets. And indeed, the Sea(land) does not appear in the contemporary Rīm-Anum archive at Uruk, where several cities and regions are mentioned as provenance of prisoners or allies. However, the term A.AB.BA was apparently used also in a text from Ur, pre-

to refer to "the Sealands" (Leichty & Walker 2004: 212). Both passages are discussed in more detail in Section 2.4.2.2.

25 Dalley (2009: 1) considers that the passage refers to Ilī-ma-ilu who would bear the title LUGAL A.AB.BA. I do not see sufficient proof in the text. The matter is discussed in detail in Section 4.1.

26 Dalley assumes this king to be Rīm-Sîn II because he has the divine determinative before his name whereas Rīm-Sîn I is considered to have adopted it later in his reign. Troops of Elam figure on the same ration list.

sumably of somewhat earlier date during the reign of Samsu-iluna, where it designates a region.[27]

Finally, three slightly later attestations[28] come from administrative tablets from Dūr-Abī-ešuḫ, all dating to the reign of Abī-ešuḫ, therefore in the early days of the Sealand kingdom. In CUSAS 29, 3[29] allotments of grain are given to envoys of A.AB.BA, in another record to "troops come up from A.AB.BA" (Földi 2014: 33, text Sem 1278, obv. 20).[30] Also, an individual who took refuge at the fortress is said to have fled from (*ištu*) A.AB.BA (George 2009: 136; Földi 2014: 37 n.31).

The evidence suggests that, shortly before the emergence of what would be later called the Sealand kingdom, the term A.AB.BA was used to designate a region, presumably in the lower Euphrates since it is attested in sources from Larsa and Ur. The region may have been bordering on the Persian Gulf, a local lake, or may simply have been a marshy area,[31] and, locally, it could be called A.AB.BA

---

27 Al-Hamdani, personal communication. The text was found during recent excavations under his, E. Stone's and P. Zimansky's direction. Additional information on the text or passage could not be obtained at the time of finalizing this manuscript; it is not included in Table 1.

28 These attestations are discussed in more detail in Section 4.3.1.

29 The text was first edited in van Lerberghe and Voet 2010 (text 1); it is re-edited as CUSAS 29, 3 with some corrections; see also on this Földi 2014: 43.

30 For the reading of *e-le* see Section 4.3.1.

31 The semantic field of A.AB.BA and *tâmtu* is rather large. In a geographical context, it may designate "any large expanse of water" (Green 1975: 164), that is, either the sea or large lakes (Horowitz 1998: 303). In addition, Waetzoldt (1981: 168) points out that AMBAR.BI is added as a gloss to A.AB.BA in a Babylonian omen text (CT 41, 13: 10), thus equating marshes with A.AB.BA or adding the marshes surrounding a body of water to the semantic field of A.AB.BA. Also, basing himself on the duration of a journey between Girsu and A.AB.BA in an Ur III text, Waetzoldt (*ibid.*: 164–65) posits that A.AB.BA designated a large lake located in the city state of Lagaš, closer to Girsu than the Persian Gulf. Extending his reasoning to deliveries of fresh fish—hence delivered within a day or two—in Old Babylonian texts, he concludes that this lake still existed in that period and that there were lakes also in the vicinity of Larsa and a few other cities (*ibid.*: 169). Heimpel (1987: 34) refutes Waetzoldt's hypothesis of a large lake near Lagaš and considers that references to the sea and to sea-related work such as the loading of ships indicate that Girsu was home to a sea port accessible from the Persian Gulf via the Tigris from Early Dynastic times into the Ur III period. The deeper branch of the Tigris would have dried out during the Old Babylonian period, blocking the access to the Gulf. Laursen and Steinkeller (2017: Appendix 3) show that GÚ-(A).AB.BA was an important seaport south of Lagaš from pre-Sargonic times until the end of the Ur III period, establishing that A.AB.BA designated the Persian Gulf in that area. The term *tê/âmtu* appears to have been fairly widely used to designate lakes or marshy areas since we find attestations at Mari (Charpin, Joannès et al. 1988: text 358: line 4 and note b), in Assyria (Horowitz 1998: 303; Elayi 1984: 75 ff.) and, from the sixth century, at Borsippa (Cole 1994: 95).

apparently without ambiguity. The fact that the goddess Ištar is called "beloved of A.AB.BA" in a text that was presumably composed by Sealand I scribes shows that the term continued to be used in the Sealand kingdom. The later use of the term A.AB.BA^{ki} in the name of a regional hypostasis of Ištar, which has its parallels in other hypostases like Ištar-of-Kiš, Ištar-of-Uruk, and so on,[32] shows clearly that, eventually, it began to function truly as a toponym. The date of this process is difficult to assess but already following the defeat of the last Sealand I king by the Kassites, we know that the region was called KUR A.AB.BA by the conquerors, as evidenced by Ulam-buriaš styling himself LUGAL KUR A.AB.BA. It was then incorporated into the Kassite kingdom as a province under the same name, with the addition of the prefix NAM: NAM KUR A.AB.BA.[33] It is not the only Kassite province to comprise the term KUR in its name but such a denomination was certainly not the norm.[34] It seems to have been understood by then as belonging more or less obligatorily to that specific toponym.

It appears thus that the local name of a southern Euphrates area, indeed the region where the Sealand kings presumably had their capital (see Sections 1.3.2.1 and 3.1.3), came to be applied to the entire kingdom in a *pars pro toto* fashion, perhaps already by the Babylonian neighbors, at the latest by the Kassite victor. Later, the toponym, still very much alive through its use as a province name, came to be extended and applied perhaps half-anachronistically to the entire Sealand I dynasty and polity, influencing how they were collectively remembered. This process must have happened before the eleventh century since Gulkišar is dubbed "King of the Sealand" in a *kudurru* dated to Enlil-nādin-apli I at the turn of the twelfth to the eleventh century (BE I/1 83 = AOAT 51, ENAp 1: obv. lines 3 and 6). In parallel, the toponym KUR A.AB.BA and (KUR) *tam-tì* would remain in use to designate contemporaneous geographical and administrative realities until the Neo-Babylonian period.[35]

32 They are grouped together on the fourth tablet of the god list AN = ^{d}Anum.

33 This happens at least as early as under Nazi-Maruttaš since the term NAM KUR A.AB.BA is used in *kudurru* L 7072 (for a recent edition, AOAT 51, NM 1).

34 The province names attested in both Kassite and Isin II sources are discussed in Brinkman 1963; for another province name comporting "KUR", namely (KUR) URU *ir-ri-e-a*, see *ibid.*: 235 n.2.

35 See for instance Beaulieu 2002b.

2.2 The names of the Sealand I rulers

King lists remain our main source of information for the Sealand I rulers' names, because only half of them are attested in other documents. The relevant information has already been summarized by others, including Brinkman (1993–97: 7), whose treatment is still fairly accurate. However, the recently published evidence warrants some adjustments to the readings.

Table 2 presents the rulers' names found in king lists. They are preserved for the entire dynasty only in BKL A and B. The contemporary orthography of Sealand I royal names is known for a few of them; the relevant attestations are grouped in Table 3.[36]

The contemporary orthography of Pešgaldarameš and Ayadaragalama shows that the SynKL presents somewhat more reliable spellings of the royal names than BKL B, at least for these rulers.[37] BKL B features in fact orthographies that change how the name was realized and understood.[38] I have thus based my normalization of the royal names on contemporary attestations when-

36 I understand as contemporary all attestations issued from the time of the Sealand I dynasty, even if not necessarily dating to the lifetime of the king in question. Note that Moorey and Gurney (1973) mistakenly transliterate ^d^*e-a-ga-mil* in their edition of seal no.23. I have also included the name Dam(i)q-ilišu, which is Sealand I contemporary but not indigenous since it is found in the year name of a king of Babylon.

37 Indeed the DynKL features the final MEŠ which is also found in all contemporary documents while the BKL B has MAŠ instead. Concerning the SynKL, note that Brinkman (1993–97: 7) wrote erroneously GÁL for GAL. The sign GAL is plainly visible in Weidner's copy (1926: 70); see also Grayson 1980–83: 117. As for Ayadaragalama, the DynKL duly features the double "A-A" at the beginning of the name—as in the numerous contemporary attestations—while BKL B reduces it to a single A.

38 It is interesting to note that the obverse of BKL B, where the names of the Babylon I rulers are listed, also contains one departure from the original orthography which changed how the name was realized, namely *e-bi-šum* for *a-bi-e-šu-uḫ*. That name seems to have caused problems to later scribes; we find it contracted and emended to *a-bi-šu* in a *tamītu*-text (Lambert 2007: text 3c: 27) and written *a-bi-ši* in chronicle *ABC* 20B: rev. 8. But BKL B is the only text in which the vowel /a/ is entirely lost and therefore also the constitutive element *abī*. BKL B does look more faithful to contemporary spelling than SynKL in the case of Ea-gāmil, but the type of discrepancy is not the same: the SynKL spelling of Ea-gāmil results from a simple change in orthography of the theophoric element (^d^*é-a* is equivalenced with ^d^DIŠ), which would not change how the name was realized. Moreover, we have at present only two contemporary attestations of the orthography of Ea-gāmil. In comparison, the orthographies of Pešgaldarameš and Ayadaragalama, taken together, are based on roughly a hundred contemporary instances, and SynKL agrees with them while BKL B does not.

ever possible, then on the SynKL, finally on the attempted interpretation of the name (Section 2.2.2).[39]

Table 2: Sealand I kings in King Lists[40]

Normalized name	BKL A	BKL B	DynKL	SynKL
1. Ilī-ma-ilu	^{m}⸢DINGIR?-*ma?*⸣	^{m}DINGIR-*ma*-DINGIR	^{m}...	
2. Itti-ili-nībī	^{m}⸢KI?-ì?⸣	^{m}KI-DINGIR-*ni-bi*	^{m}⸢KI-DINGIR-*ni*⸣-*bu*	
3. Dam(i)q-ilišu	^{m}⸢SIG$_5$?-DINGIR?⸣	^{m}*dam-qí-ì-lí-šu*	⸢^{m}*dam*⸣-*qí-ì-lí-š*[*u*]	...
4. Iškibal	^{m}⸢*iš?-ba?*⸣	^{m}*iš-ki-bal*	⸢^{m}*iš*⸣-*ki-bal*	^{m} x x x
5. Šuš(š)i	^{m}⸢*šu?-uš?-ši?*⸣	^{m}*šu-uš-ši*	x x x	⸢^{m}⸣*šu-ši*
6. Gulkišar	^{m}⸢GUL?⸣-KI	^{m}GUL-KI-ŠÁR	...	^{m}⸢GUL?⸣-KI-⸢ŠÁR?⸣
7? DIŠ+U-EN?				^{m}DIŠ+U-EN (?)
8. Pešgaldar-ameš	^{m}⸢PEŠ?⸣.GAL	^{m}PEŠ.GAL-DÀRA.MAŠ		^{m}⸢PEŠ.GAL⸣-DÀRA.MEŠ
9. Ayadaragala-ma	^{m}A. ⸢A?⸣-DÀRA	^{m}A-DÀRA-KALAM.MA		^{m}A.A-DÀRA-KALAM.⸢x⸣
10. Akurduana	^{m}É-KUR-⸢DU$_7$?⸣	^{m}A-KUR-DU$_7$-AN-NA		^{m}E-KUR-DU-⸢AN-NA⸣
11. Melamkura	^{m}ME-LÁM-MÀ	^{m}ME-LÁM-KUR-KUR-RA		^{m}ME-LÁM-KUR-⸢RA⸣
12. Ea-gāmil	^{md}BAD-*ga*	^{md}*é-a-ga*-⸢*mil*⸣		^{md}DIŠ-*ga-mil*

39 Contra Brinkman (1977: 337; also in 1993–97: 7) who favored the BKL B versions when normalizing the names.

40 In addition to the evidence of king lists, we find the following names in other chronographic sources: both Ilī-ma-ilu and Ea-gāmil appear in the chronicle *ABC* 20B (rev. 2′?; 7′; 8′; 10′; 12′), where their names are spelled as in BKL B; also, in another segment of DynKL, Dam(i)q-ilišu—who may be the third Sealand I king—is named as the head of a dynasty from which Simbar-Šipak of the later Sealand II dynasty was issued (col.V, line 3′); in this passage his name is spelled SIG$_5$-DINGIR-*šú*, which is close to the spelling of BKL A. Four Sealand I kings are included in the Assyrian list of names VR 44, which also contains interpretations of them: Col. i (14) [x x x]-BAL / (15) [x x x]-ŠÁR / (16) ^{m}A.A-[X]-KALAM-MA / (17) ^{m}A-KUR-D[U$_7$]-AN-NA. The names are fragmentary but the spellings are close to those of BKL B with the exception of Ayadaragalama's. These entries are further discussed in Section 2.2.2.

Table 3: Sealand I kings in contemporary sources[41]

King	Contemporary attestation	Source
1. Ilī-ma-ilu	*ì-lí-ma*-DINGIR	Year names at Nippur: BE 6/2 68; ARN 123; UM 55–21–239=3N-T87; PBS 8/1 89; TMH 10, 54a and b (legal texts)
2. Itti-ili-nībī	-	-
3. Dam(i)q-ilišu	*dam-qí-ì-lí-šu* (less frequent: *da-mi-iq-ì-lí-šu*)	37th year name of Samsu-ditāna; see Charpin 2015a.
4. Iškibal	-	-
5. Šuš(š)i	-	-
6. Gulkišar	GUL-KI-ŠÁR	Part of a divine name ^{d}UTU-ana-Gulkišar-kurub (CUSAS 9, 83: 15′); hymn HS 1885+ (rev. 23)
7? DIŠ+U-EN?	-	-
8. Pešgaldarameš	PEŠ.GAL-DÀRA.MEŠ	Year names in CUSAS 9, 16; 85; 407 (archival documents); also in colophon of CUSAS 18, 32 where PEŠ is partly legible before a lacuna (divinatory text)
	$PEŠ_{11}$.GAL-DÀRA.MEŠ	Colophon of CUSAS 18, 28 (divinatory text)
9. Ayadaragalama	A.A-DÀRA-GALAM.MA	Numerous year names in CUSAS 9 texts, also in TK1 3006.17; 3064.67; 3064.135 (archival documents); and in unpublished CDLI P431311: obv. 11′; rev. 19′; 24′ (liturgical text)
10. Akurduana	[x]-KUR-DU-AN-NI	Unprovenanced seal P455982
11. Melamkura	-	-
12. Ea-gāmil	^{d}*é-a-ga-mil*	Inscription of cylinder seal of Ilī-remeanni (Moorey & Gurney 1973: no.23); also in year name of text QA 94.46 (Cavigneaux & André-Salvini: forthcoming)

I do not count as an attestation of Ayadaragalama's name the inscription on the bronze circlet from Tell en-Nasbeh, which Dalley (2009:1; 2013: 179–80) considers to refer to the Sealand I king. Indeed, given the attestations listed in Tables 2 and

41 I included here the hymn HS 1885+ as belonging to the contemporary sources because internal criteria appear to point towards a mid-second millennium date of writing (Zomer forthcoming), but it could be of later Kassite date. The fragment Ni 13090, perhaps of a hymn of Kassite date, also features the same orthography of the name Gulkišar.

3, her suggested orthography for his name, *a-ia-da-a-ra*, would be entirely at odds with all other second and first millennium sources. Moreover, a reference to this king on such a circlet would be at best surprising historically, since, as far as we know, he did not make his way into the Babylonian first millennium written tradition, unlike Gulkišar for instance.[42]

2.2.1 Additional kings?

The very existence of the seventh king DIŠ+U-EN? is uncertain. His name appears in only one source, the SynKL (col.I: 5′). But since this text appears to be based on a source featuring reliable orthographies, the addition of this king should not be rejected too lightly. Brinkman (1976: 429; 1977: 347 n.8), followed by others, considers in fact that this addition is "not unexpected" since the reign lengths given in BKL A do not quite add up to the total indicated at the end of the section (also, e.g. Pruzsinszky 2009: 100). But several numbers are damaged and are almost certainly, even when considering various possible readings, unreliable (see Section 3.2.1); it is therefore difficult to see confirmation of the existence of an additional king in them. Nonetheless, BKL A may provide another indication that there was an additional king after Gulkišar.

In order to clarify the following argument, the corresponding section of BKL A is presented here. The text indicates first the reign length, then the name of each ruler.[43] The formal arrangement of lines follows Budge's hand copy in CT 36, 24.

Col.I, line	(4)	⸢x+1⸣	^{m}⸢DINGIR?-*ma?*⸣	
	(5)	⸢40(+10)+5⸣	^{m}⸢KI?-ì?⸣	AŠ
	(6)	⸢10(+)+6?⸣	^{m}⸢SIG$_5$?-DINGIR?⸣	
	(7)	⸢15⸣	^{m}⸢*iš?-ba?*⸣	
	(8)	⸢24⸣	^{m}⸢*šu?-uš?-ši?* ⸣	ŠEŠ
	(9)	55	^{m}⸢GUL?⸣-KI	AŠ
	(10)	50	^{m}⸢PEŠ?⸣.GAL	
	(11)	28	^{m}A. ⸢A?⸣-DÀRA	
	(12)	26	^{m}É-KUR-⸢DU$_7$?⸣	

42 The circlet is broken so that probably only the middle of the inscription is preserved. Any reconstruction remains hazardous, but Vanderhooft and Horowitz's (2002: 319 ff.) interpretation certainly appears more plausible since it finds near parallels in other inscribed objects.

43 The values of the reign length are in many cases problematic. The readings presented here are those of Brinkman (1993–97); they are listed again in Table 6, together with other readings, and are discussed at length in Section 3.2.1.

(13)	7	^{m}ME-LÁM-MÀ
(14)	⌜9⌝	^{md}BAD-*ga*
(15)	368	11 LUGAL^{me} BALA URÙ-KU$_{6}$

Between Gulkišar and the following entry, that is between lines 9 and 10, the sign AŠ appears, justified to the right of the column. It has been suggested that it stood for a missing entry, which would therefore tally with the additional name in SynKL (Landsberger 1954: 69 n.177 & n.180). However, if we accept this interpretation of the sign AŠ in BKL A, there must also have been another king between Itti-ili-nībī and Dam(i)q-ilišu since the list features another such sign between lines 5 and 6; this king, the third of the dynasty, would have been ignored in BKL B and DynKL.[44] Also, both kings purportedly represented by the wedge AŠ in BKL A would have been disregarded in the total of "11 kings" given at the end of the section. If there was an historical reality behind this "AŠ" in BKL A, the unknown third king and DIŠ+U-EN may have been rulers who sat on the throne a very short time, perhaps in the midst of a difficult succession.

The reading of the name of the purported seventh(?) king DIŠ+U-EN?, based on only one attestation, is uncertain. Grayson (1980–83: 116–17) has summarized the problems deriving from the low quality of early photographs and from the subsequent deterioration of the tablet. Brinkman's collation in 1971 led to the reading ^{m}GÍŠ-EN (Brinkman 1977: 337, followed by Grayson 1980–83: 117); he later corrected it to ^{m}DIŠ+U-EN (1993–97: 7).[45]

2.2.2 The Sealand I royal onomasticon

The first three kings of the dynasty bore Akkadian names. The name of the first ruler, Ilī-ma-ilu, is somewhat unusual, and Brinkman (1993–97: 7) considered both its reading and its interpretation uncertain. Names with the general morphology DN(-*ma*)-AN are interpreted by Stamm (1968: 222) as "DN ist (wirklich) Gott;" the name of the Sealand I king he normalizes Ili-ma-ilu and renders "Mein Gott ist (wirklich) Gott" (*ibid.*: n.3). That no specific god is named in the nominal

44 Since there is no other trace of that purported ruler, I have ignored him in the numbering of kings in Tables 2 and 3.

45 Weidner's copy from photograph (1926: 70) appears to show much more than DIŠ or DIŠ+U in the damaged section, before the clearly visible EN. This was accordingly read x.KÀD-en by Landsberger (1954: 69). However, later collations have revealed that the copy contained many errors (Grayson 1980–83: 117).

clause is certainly exceptional but not unique; indeed, the name Ya'um-ilum (CT 4, 27a = AbB 2, 94: line 3; Pinches 1915: 126, text 101: line 1) basically makes the same statement, since *ya'um* (mine) and *ilī* (my god)[46] both refer to the speaker's personal god. The enclitic *-ma* usually marks the predicate in such a clause (von Soden 1995: §126), although in the case of Ilī-ma-ilu it is added to the noun in first position, which is usually the subject. The parallel with near-contemporary names of the type DN(-*ma*)-DINGIR[47] suggests that the first element indeed functions as subject, therefore Stamm's interpretation appears justified.[48] The name of the second king, Itti-ili-nībī "My name is with the god," is certainly not common but its morphology does not require comment; it belongs to Stamm's type "Itti-Sîn-milki" (1968: 230 §31).[49] The name of the third king, Dam(i)q-ilišu "The favored one of his god," of a type well attested in Babylonia, seems to be rendered almost exclusively so as to reflect syncope of the vowel in *damiq*.[50]

---

46 That the first element reads *ilī*, with the possessive, is certain because of the syllabic orthography in the contemporary attestations (see Table 3).

47 For instance Dagan-ma-ilum (see Seri 2013: 48–49 for a recent summary of the evidence); Ea-ma-ilum (VS 9, 200: 3); Sîn-ma-ilum (Talon 1997: text 3: 7; and *passim*). There is also one *ì-lí-ma-*DINGIR in an undated text from Qal'at al-Bahrein (text QA 02.11: 5), that was under Sealand I control, at least for a time (see Section 3.1.1); the context makes plain that it cannot be the first Sealand I king and Cavigneaux and André-Salvini (forthcoming) note that the name may have been typical of the Sealand. There is also one *ì-lí-ma-*DINGIR in a fragmentary administrative text from Tell Khaiber dated to Ayadaragalama (TK1 3006.17: 1′). Similar names, namely *ì-lí-ma-a-bi* and *ì-lí-ma-a-ḫi* are present in other Sealand I texts (see CUSAS 9, index). Noteworthy is also the fact that names of the type DN-*ma-ilu* are fairly well attested in Old Babylonian Susa, e. g. Adad-ma-ilu (MDP 22, 61: 29), Sîn-ma-ilu (MDP 23, 190: 13), Šušinak-ma-ilu (MDP 23, 225: 4); similar names that do not specify a deity are also attested: Šu-ma-ilu (MDP 22, 49: 27; MDP 23, 180: 12) and Šunu-ma-ilu (MDP 22, 12: rev. 4; MDP 23, 168: rev. 4; 210: rev. 3′; 311: 9).

48 In Amorite names of the same type, the first element—before the enclitic—is understood as the predicate by Streck (2000: 276), and the second element *'il* as subject. With the substantive case marker *-a*, the element *'ila* in second position, such as in the name of the early Old Babylonian ruler of Sippar Ilum-ma-'ila, can be either the subject or the predicate, but a function as subject appears more likely (*ibid.*: 278–79).

49 In the Old Babylonian period, the term *nību* is attested in the Susean onomasticon (MDP 23, 286: 24).

50 Stamm (1968: 258) even normalizes it Damqi-ilišu; Buccellati (1996: 48) renders it Damqilīšu. By contrast, the name of the last king of Isin is almost always written with the vowel i; the matter is discussed in Charpin 2015a: 55. An orthography reflecting vowel syncope in the element *damiq-* is attested in Old Babylonian Susa, where it co-exists with the more standard orthography (see "Liste des noms propres" p. 187 in MDP 22 and p.205 in MDP 23).

The name of the fourth king, Iškibal, is problematic but may also be Akkadian.[51] One possibility is to read it *Išqi*-BALA(-DN): "The reign/era (of DN) has been exalted." Admittedly, one would rather expect to find *šaqû* in the stative. It was interpreted as Sumerian in the Assyrian name list VR 44 (col. I, line 14). The scribe apparently read it kuš$_7$-ki-bal (Cooley 2016), because he equated it with ^{m}*sa-pi-in*-KUR-*nu-kúr-ti* "The leveler of the enemy land," apparently using an homophone of KUŠ equated with *sapānu* in Aa A= *nâqu* II/7, col.IV, lines 23a′ (MSL XIV: 298). The following king's name, Šuš(š)i, is also atypical, but could be Akkadian as well: indeed, one possibility is that it comes from the Š-stem of *našû* and that only an abbreviated form of the full name has entered king lists.[52]

Starting with Gulkišar, however, all rulers except the last one assumed Sumerian names. Whether the kings who bear these Sumerian names represent a new dynasty is difficult to ascertain. Other dynasties of second millennium Babylonia have a mixed onomasticon without apparent special significance.[53] Gulkišar may be the only king from the middle of the Sealand I dynasty to have been remembered in later sources other than king lists,[54] and he is also the central figure of an epic (HS 1885+). His presence in such sources suggests that his reign was marked by significant deeds which earned him a position in the collective memory and the written tradition. We could therefore imagine that an ambitious ruler, perhaps emboldened by significant victories, decided during his reign to assume a throne name which reflected the magnitude of his deeds in form, by using the ancient Sumerian language, and also in meaning, since GUL-KI-ŠÁR could mean "Raider of the totality."[55] It is how it was understood by the scribe

---

51 Landsberger (1954: 69 n.175) interpreted it logographically with the meaning "Verheerung des Feindeslandes," apparently equating BAL with *gērû*, which may not be correct (*MZL:* III s.v. BAL).

52 Should the orthography of SynKL be indeed the correct one, the name could refer to Susa; indeed, in an Old Babylonian document from Susa (MDP 22, 22: 15), one personal name begins either with *Šu-ši-i*-[...] or with *Šu-ši* followed by DUMU [...].

53 For instance the first dynasty of Babylon (Amorite and Akkadian names) and the Kudur-Mabuk dynasty (Elamite and Akkadian names).

54 To the evidence of Table 2 concerning Gulkišar in king lists, we must add one instance of his name in a non-historiographic text, probably dating to the second millennium: he appears in the colophon of a glass-making treatise (BM 120960; published in Gadd and Campbell Thompson 1936; see also Oppenheim 1970: 59 ff.). It is almost certainly a forgery (see Section 4.7). He also appears in a hymn fragment possibly of Kassite date Ni 13090 (E. Zomer, personal communication).

55 From the verb GUL, to destroy, fall upon, and the noun KI-ŠÁR, the horizon. This interpretation was suggested by Landsberger 1954: 69 n.175, followed by Dalley 2009: 3. Brinkman (1993–97: 7) estimates that the reading requires further study.

of VR 44 who equated it with ^{m}*mu-ab-bit-kiš-šá-ti* (col. I, line 15). If this interpretation is correct, the name certainly sounds programmatic.

Both the names Pešgaldarameš and Ayadaragalama, with the element DÀRA, refer to quadrupeds, perhaps the ibex and/or the stag (the latter if MEŠ is a variant of MAŠ in DÀRA.MEŠ). An oblique reference to Enki, who has the by-name ^{d}DÀRA-ABZU in an Old Babylonian hymn from Ur (UET VI 67: 52 and 55; discussed in Charpin 1986: 373), is possible; also, other by-names built with DÀRA are present in the much later list CT 24 12–17 (Col.II, lines 27–30). The element PEŠ.GAL admits at least two interpretations: either hero, noble, mighty (CAD M, s.v. *mamlu*), which is also attested as epithet of Šamaš (Krebernik 2003–05), or heir (CAD A, s.v. *aplu*, at the end of the lexical section). Dalley (2009: 2) chooses the latter and regards DÀRA.MEŠ as a variant orthography of DÀRA.MAŠ, she thus reads the names respectively "Son of the ibex" and "Son of the clever stag" (*sic* for "Son (PEŠ.GAL) of the stag (DÀRA.MAŠ)" and "Son (A.A) of the clever (GALAM.-MA) ibex (DÀRA)"). She takes both ibex and stag as referring directly to their father(?) Gulkišar (2009: 2–3).[56] While the name Pešgaldarameš could indeed mean "Son of the stag," one can also suggest "The mighty one among the ibexes" if one takes the MEŠ as plural. Ayadaragalama's name seems to be best translated as "Heir (or Son) of the clever ibex."[57] This is based on the contemporary orthography, which consistently uses GALAM, and not KALAM as in BKL B and SynKL.[58] The Assyrian name list VR 44 includes Ayadaragalama and spells it with KALAM, an orthography presumably taken over from a Babylonian king list. The scribe equates ^{m}A-A-[DÀRA(?)-]KALAM-MA with ^{m}IBILA-^{d}*é-a*-LUGAL-*ma-a-ti* (col.I, line 16): "Son of Ea, king of the land." How the scribe arrived at his interpretation is not entirely clear; Cooley (2016) suggests that he equated A-DÀRA with Ea. However, the terms LUGAL and DÀRA are indirectly related in the lexical tradition, they are both equated with *malku* (CAD M, s.v. *malku* lexical section). It

56 The family relation between Gulkišar, Pešgaldarameš, and Ayadaragalama indicated in BKL B is ambiguous: it calls king Pešgaldarameš the son (of Gulkišar) and indicates that Ayadaragalama is "ditto," that is either also the son of Gulkišar or of Pešgaldarameš. BKL B has proved rather imprecise with the orthography of these names but this note on the direct filiation may be true since we find Gulkišar apparently as deified ancestor in an offering list from the palatial archive (see Table 3).

57 Considering that Dilmun is or soon will be under Sealand I control at the time, one cannot help noting that quadrupeds, perhaps including ibexes and gazelles, are omnipresent on (presumably) contemporary seals found there; see for instance Crawford 2001: 23–24; 52ff.

58 With no contemporary orthography of the name available to him, Landsberger (1954: 69 n.175) suggested to read the name "Vater, Steinbock des Landes"; for his predecessor Pešgaldarameš he proposed "Prinzlicher Hirsch," whereas Brinkman (2003–05) did not suggest any interpretation in his RlA entry on him.

seems thus possible that the Assyrian scribe equated *a-a* with Ea, and DÀRA with LUGAL.

The name of the following king, Akurduana, is difficult. We do not have any complete contemporary orthography and the later sources present three more or less homophonic variants. The first two signs are, depending on the source, É.KUR, A.KUR, or E.KUR (see Table 2).[59] It is tempting to read a temple name, especially since the next phoneme is /du/. However, this phoneme is never written DÙ, but twice DU_7 and twice DU. Although an orthographic variant of DÙ cannot be excluded, the overall syntax of the resulting phrase would be very awkward. I would prudently suggest that in this case, the orthography in BKL B A-KUR-DU_7-AN-NA might be the correct one, and it could read "Raging flood of Anu/heaven" (for DU_7, see CAD N, s.v. *nakāpu* A, lexical section; for A.KUR, see CAD M, s.v. *mīlu* A, lexical section).[60] This interpretation may have to be revised once seal P455982 has been fully analyzed.

The name of his successor, Melamkura, seems clear: "Splendor of the land(s)."[61] Finally, the Akkadian name of the last king, Ea-gāmil, "Ea spares," does not require further comment.[62]

This fashion for Sumerian names among the later members of the ruling house stands in contrast with the onomasticon of the known archival documents, where very few Sumerian names appear. Dalley (2009: 13) examines the possibility that individuals with Sumerian names were mostly in high-ranking positions but the evidence is thin and contradictory.[63] As for the Akkadian royal names, it was shown that a number of their characteristics are reminiscent of the Old Babylonian onomasticon at Susa. That these onomastica shared common features agrees with Zadoks's observation that the hypocoristic suffix *-ya'u*

---

59 The list of names VR 44 includes this name (Col.I, line 17) and appears to follow the orthography of BKL B, which begins with the sign A.

60 Note that a hymn for Kurigalzu (MAH 15922: Obv. 11) compares him with a flood, also in the context of Anu's favor (Sommerfeld 1985: 1; 3). Landsberger (1954: 69 n.175) reads the name of this Sealand I king "Bergsohn, Himmelszierde." The scribe of VR 44 gives the Akkadian equivalent as ^{m}IBILA-^{d}*en-líl-ú-su-um*-AN-*e* "Son of Enlil, worthy of heaven."

61 Since BKL B has an orthography ending with -KUR-KUR-RA, the form might be plural. The orthography of BKL A, ME-LÁM-MÀ, is quite at odds with that of BKL B and SynKL. Landsberger (1954: 69 n.175) suggests "Glorie der Welt."

62 For names of the type DN-*gāmil*, see Stamm 1968: 220 n.2, and *passim*.

63 Zadok (2014) undertook an analysis of the Sealand I onomasticon of this archive. Since his aim was to identify non-indigenous vs indigenous names, he did not discriminate between Akkadian and Sumerian ones.

is common to both the Sealand kingdom and the Susiana in the Old Babylonian period (Zadok 2014: 229–32).[64]

2.3 The Sealand I dynasty in king lists

The Sealand I dynasty was included in four of the Mesopotamian king lists that came down to us: the BKL A and B, the DynKL, and the SynKL. The first three have a purview that is restricted to Babylonia, and they group the kings into dynasties; these dynasties are often associated with their main seat of power, which functions as a dynastic name. The latter list, the SynKL is somewhat different in that it does not group rulers in dynasties. Its purpose is one of idealized synchronicity between the kingships of Assyria and Babylonia, ruler by ruler; their names are listed side by side in adjoining columns. Given that half of the Sealand I rulers from king lists are attested in contemporary sources (Table 3), with orthographies more or less respecting the original ones, we can certainly consider that the sequence of rulers presented in these documents is to a certain degree trustworthy.

The scriptoria that produced these king lists shared the same chronographic understanding, which artificially presents dynasties as sequential although they were in fact partly co-eval in Babylonia. The BKL A puts the Sealand I dynasty between the Amorite and the Kassite dynasties of Babylon. This sequence of dynasties (Amorite Babylon, Sealand I, Kassite Babylon) seems to find corroboration in the other lists, as far as their state of preservation allows us to judge. The DynKL positions the Sealand I dynasty after the Amorite dynasty of Babylon; a lacuna follows. On the Babylonian side of the SynKL, Sealand I rulers are preceded by a break; Kassite rulers of Babylon immediately follow the last Sealand I kings. As for BKL B, it associates the Amorite dynasty of Babylon and the Sealand I dynasty in listing them on either side of a tablet.

Only BKL A and the DynKL record reign lengths for the Sealand I kings, although in the latter, the passage is so damaged that no figures can be retrieved. In BKL B, while reign lengths are associated with the Amorite rulers of Babylon, none are given for the Sealand I kings. The SynKL does not record reign lengths at all. This leaves the BKL A as sole historiographic document with legible Sealand I reign lengths, which can be shown to be unreliable; the matter is discussed in Section 3.2.1.

64 This suffix is now also attested in the Tell Khaiber texts dating to the same period, e.g. Iliya'u in TK1 1114.04: 5 and Egiya'u in TK1 3064.053: l.e. ii 5.

The evidence compiled in Tables 1 and 2 shows that the king lists are not uniform in their recording of the Sealand I dynasty. The name of the dynasty presents variations that indicate that there was no received orthography for it in first millennium scriptoria and that the original name was no longer understood (see also Section 2.1.1). As for the rulers' names, BKL A stands out in systematically (and specifically) abbreviating them while the beginning of any name seems fairly close to its original orthography; BKL B displays faulty orthographies for several names; and SynKL adheres closest to contemporary sources (see Section 2.2). This lack of unity suggests a deficient or scattered documentary basis, hinting perhaps at a Sealand I historiographic tradition not solidly established or transmitted.

This raises the question of the documents pertaining to the Sealand I dynasty that were available to the compilers of king lists. It has been suggested that date lists were used to compile king lists, the former being tools of practical clerical use,[65] the latter the produce of antiquarian interest (van Seters 1983: 69) or, as Oppenheim (1977: 145) puts it, an "expression of the consciousness of history." Grayson (1980–83: 90) notes that date lists were primary source material only for the early part of BKL A since they are as yet unattested beyond the Old Babylonian period; he considers the rest of BKL A to be a "running list" that was regularly updated.[66] Hallo (1983: 11–12), with regard to the second millennium, agrees that king lists derived from lists of year names but sees in them the result of an ideological exercise, namely "comprehensive overviews which pressed chronography in the service of ideology."

At least for BKL A, because of its treatment of the Sealand I rulers' names, it seems unlikely that its compilers used date lists:[67] the names are systematically abbreviated, even if there is enough room on the line to write them in full. Comparison with other dynasties in the same document shows that this was not a general principle of redaction. Also, the first two names of the Sealand II dynasty (KUR *tam-tì*)—the dynasty of Simbar-Šipak –, are truncated in the same fashion,

---

65 Glassner (2004: 16–17) opposes to this view that some date lists encompass so many years (up to nearly 170 years) that their purpose must go beyond practical use; he sees in them "the product of genuine chronological inquiry."

66 Grayson's (1975: 5–6) argument roots in the fact that he includes BKL A in his category "A" of chronographic documents. He notes a strong stylistic continuity between date lists and late chronicles of the same category, which suggests a continued compilation of lists with yearly entries. Such lists remain as yet unattested, however. Grayson's reasoning presents BKL A as a by-product of such historical record-keeping practices.

67 Also in the case of BKL B the use of year name lists seems doubtful—at least for part of it –, because some of its orthographies differ significantly from the original ones, e.g. *e-bi-šum* for Abī-ešuḫ.

with one or two signs missing at the end.[68] A possible explanation—and one of historical significance—is that the same, damaged source was used by the compilers of BKL A, that is, a Sealand King List compiling the names of the Sealand I and Sealand II rulers. This hypothetical source would establish a direct relationship between the two dynasties, which suggests a continuous tradition in Sealand scriptoria presenting the rulers of the Simbar-Šipak dynasty as descendants of the Sealand I kings. This would agree with the possible ancestry established between the same Simbar-Šipak and Dam(i)q-ilišu in DynKL (Col.V, lines 2–3), although it is not clear whether the Isin I king or the third Sealand I king is implied. However, a relationship between the Sealand I and II dynasties is certainly not made conspicuous in the compilations of BKL A and DynKL that we know; indeed, they label them by different names, both following the Eurukug tradition for the former, and, respectively, KUR *tam-tì* and KUR A.AB.BA for the latter. Both documents also include another, later Sealand dynasty, in each case comprising only one eighth century ruler, Erība-Marduk in the DynKL (Col.VI, line 6) and Marduk-apla-iddina (II) in BKL A (Col.IV, line 10).[69] Nothing in these king lists establishes a relationship between this Sealand III dynasty and the former two.

The textual relation between the various king lists is unclear, beyond mere typology and general chronography. Hallo (1983: 10) noted that BKL A starts where the Sumerian King List stops. Grayson (1980–83: 117) suggested that BKL A or a similar source was used by the compiler of SynKL.[70] As for BKL B, it has been considered an extract of a larger list, perhaps BKL A (Feigin & Landsberger 1955: 140–41), which may have been lacunary, accounting for mistakes in the lengths of reigns attributed to the kings of the Amorite dynasty of Babylon (Poebel 1947: 111).[71] Poebel (1947: 120) noted that the compiler of BKL A had chronographic material relevant to the Sealand I dynasty at his disposal, allowing him to record reign lengths, while the BKL B scribe did not, therefore, he considered BKL A to postdate BKL B.[72]

68 Col.III, lines 6–9.

69 There is some consistency between both documents because Marduk-apla-iddina calls himself a son or descendant of Erība-Marduk in royal inscriptions (Brinkman 1964: 9), however, without referring to the Sealand.

70 For the Sealand I section the source could not have been solely BKL A since in this document the names are truncated.

71 Poebel (1947: 110 ff.) posited that the faulty figures found on BKL B came from estimates derived from mean values used by the scribe to fill in the lacunary passages in the original.

72 Or at least this section of BKL A would postdate BKL B. His implicit assumption is that both BKL A and B are issued from the same milieu, although apart in time, and that sources becoming available were so to all scribes involved in the compilation of king lists. This appears a somewhat too idealizing and also reductive view of Babylonian scriptoria.

Examining how the compilers of king lists treated information pertaining to the Sealand I dynasty does not solve the problem of their relative date of writing. It does suggest that BKLA was not the source material for this segment in other lists because it contains truncated names. In addition, BKL B presents a few orthographies of the rulers' names that are slightly at odds with the other sources. Therefore, BKL A, BKL B, and SynKL seem to have used different sources. Also, if we accept the hypothesis of a damaged Sealand chronographic record listing the Sealand I and II dynasties in succession, this undermines Brinkman's (1968: 83–84) observation that the *Distanzangabe* given in the *kudurru* BE I/1 83 dating to Enlil-nādin-apli (696 years between Gulkišar and Nebuchadnezzar I) was probably based on canonical king lists containing the reign lengths also found in BKL A. His mathematical demonstration of how scribes may have obtained the sum of years is attractive and—if it is correct—would mean that the Sealand I dynasty had entered king lists in the sequence "Sealand I—Kassite Babylon" with the reign lengths found in the later BKL A before the reign of the Isin II king Enlil-nādin-apli, perhaps as early as the late Kassite period (van Koppen 2017: 76). To complicate matters, the reign lengths of BKL A are almost certainly wrong (Section 3.2.1).

Therefore, for both hypotheses to be correct, that of a Sealand damaged source and Brinkman's explanation of the *Distanzangabe*, one would need to posit that the same source—a Sealand I king list with erroneous reign lengths —was used both by late second millennium compilers of a canonical Babylonian king list and by the early first millennium compilers of a local Sealand king list; the latter, damaged but still containing the reign lengths, would be used by the compiler of BKL A who did not have access to the canonical "forerunner" already containing the information. It is not impossible but appears somewhat unlikely.

As for DynKL, it is probably older than (the last compilations of) BKL A because copies of it were found in Ashurbanipal's library (Grayson 1975: 139; Glassner 2004: 126). But so few Sealand I royal names are preserved in it that it is difficult to decide whether it could have been based on a source that was also used for another list.

The answers to the questions surrounding the exact date of inclusion of the Sealand I dynasty into the sequence of dynasties of Babylonian king lists as well as the sources used by compilers remain by and large unsatisfactory. But it seems that the Sealand I dynasty had been included in the larger Babylonian chronographic tradition at the latest in the early first millennium, and that it was probably present in a number of scriptorial environments.[73] Among them,

73 This is also made clear by the fact that the Sealand I kings were included in the SynKL, an

southern, Sealand scriptoria may have transmitted a local tradition of a continuous Sealand royal chronography that yielded source material for the Sealand I and II segments of BKL A. If this was the case, the compiler of BKL A was fully aware of the syncopated chronology behind this hypothetical Sealand King List.

As for the reasons for including the Sealand I dynasty in Babylonian king lists, the matter remains nebulous. Babylonian king lists present chronography in an idealized geographical-temporal distribution of kingship, in a fashion similar to the Sumerian King List (Hallo 1983: 12). In this Babylonian chronography of power, kingship resides in a locality for a time, then moves to another one; the Sealand I dynasty found its place in this idealized framework and was presented with reference to Eurukug. The very fact that it was included into the Babylonian king lists tradition, in particular in BKL A, has been in turn understood as a sign that the dynasty controlled Babylon for a time (Thureau-Dangin 1927: 184; Goetze 1957: 66; Matthews 1970: 98; Brinkman 1993–97: 6), that it controlled or strongly influenced part of Babylonia (Dougherty 1932: 23), or that it was the most stable power during that period in Babylonia (King 1915: 212). Considering the evidence available, one or all could still be considered viable hypotheses.[74]

2.4 The Sealand kingdom in chronicles

2.4.1 Chronicle *ABC* 20B

The Babylonian chronicle containing most references to the Sealand I kings and related events is a fragmentary chronicle of ancient kings; it was edited by Grayson as text *ABC* 20B.[75] Because of its great relevance for understanding the transmission of the memory of the Sealand I dynasty, it is discussed here at length: I will analyze the structure of the text and its layout, assess the relation of the

---

Assyrian document found at Ashur. Whatever source material the Assyrian scribes used for the Babylonian side, they apparently accepted these kings as being part of the succession of Babyonian kings. The best preserved manuscript we have ends with Ashurbanipal and was probably written just after his reign, at the time of Aššur-etel-ilāni (Novotny 2016).

74 The Sealand I palatial archive published in CUSAS 9 dates from the interval between the Amorite and Kassite dynasties at Babylon, the sole interval in which Sealand I kings could have controlled that city. Nothing in the archive suggests that either Babylon or Marduk were of any great relevance; the city is not mentioned and Marduk holds a very modest rank in the state pantheon (Section 6.4.7). Of course, the texts are mainly anchored in local activities and may not reflect what was happening elsewhere in the kingdom.

75 Grayson calls it Tablet B of the "Chronicle of Early Kings" in *ABC* (1975); Glassner calls the same text "Chronicle of Ancient Kings" (no.40) in *MC* (2004).

chronicle with other texts—including possible source material –, and discuss the date and the intention of that compilation. It will be expounded that the text was probably compiled from written sources pieced together with minimal rewriting by the chronicler; that he weaved a loosely but accurate chronography of events, each of which centers on a legitimate king facing an opponent or contender; that the Sealand I dynasty was given a place among the legitimate dynasties; and that the events related were probably selected in order to keep the scope of the chronicle on central and southern Babylonia.

The chronicle is written on both sides of one tablet, and only one copy is extant. The bottom of the tablet is damaged, leaving a lacuna in the middle of the text. Waerzeggers (2012: 292–94) demonstrated convincingly that this chronicle was compiled at Borsippa, presumably in the last two-thirds of the seventh or the first half of the sixth century. It belongs to a group of chronicles that are characterized by a neutral, annalistic style (*ibid.*: 292–95).

Before further analyzing the text, the relationship between *ABC* 20B and *ABC* 20A needs to be assessed. *ABC* 20A and 20B are considered by Grayson to be adjoining parts of the same text;[76] this is suggested by the chronology of the events recorded and by a number of matching lines near the end of 20A and at the beginning of 20B.[77] However, several elements speak against these tablets being two parts of one and the same text. *ABC* 20A has, after said passage, an additional entry about a synchronism between an Assyrian king and Su(mu)-Abu;[78] this breaks the concept of the identical lines being catch lines linking the tablets.[79] Two further reasons speak for separate texts and have been convincingly presented by Waerzeggers (2012: 292–93): *ABC* 20A contains references to the theology of Marduk and passes moral judgements in its historiographic treatment while 20B is entirely devoid of any religious or moral interpretation; also, the texts have been shown through their acquisition history to belong to different

---

76 Van Seters (1983: 85), starting from Grayson's theory that first millennium chroniclers were writing an official continuous chronicle of Babylonian history in the form of a series, extended the idea to encompass *ABC* 20A and B, placing these tablets as part of the same great endeavor.

77 The relevant passage in *ABC* 20A comprises six lines (lines 31–36 in the edition = rev. 8–13), while its equivalent in *ABC* 20B comprises seven lines (obv. 1–7).

78 It also features an annotation on "various battles" which could be a colophon. It is not given a line number in Grayson's edition but appears after line 37.

79 Moreover, the tablet sizes do not match, and the indentation marking the beginning of sections seems less marked in 20A than in 20B. Therefore, the tablets would at least not belong to the same copy of the text.

sub-groups of the Borsippa chronicle corpus.[80] We can therefore examine *ABC* 20B on its own, not as a part of a longer text.[81]

In order the help the reader follow the discussion, I include here a transliteration of the text (based mainly on Grayson 1975: 155–56[82]; also consulted were Glassner 2004: 272 and the hand copy in King 1907: vol.2, p.121–27).[83]

Obv.

1 [$^{m\ d}$*èr-ra*-ZÀ.DIB LUGAL ^{m}] ^{d}*en-líl*-DÙ ^{lú}NU.^{giš}KIRI$_6$
2 [*a-na* NU NÌ.SAG.GIL]-*e ina* ^{giš}GU.ZA-*šú ú-še-šib*
3 ⸢AGA⸣ LUGAL-*ú-ti-šú ina* SAG.DU-*šú iš-ta-kan*
4 ^{md}*èr-ra-i-mit-ti ina* É.GAL-*šú pap-pa-si im-me-tú*
5 *ina sa-ra-pi-šú im-tu-ut*
6 ^{md}*en-líl*-DÙ *ina* ^{giš}GU.ZA *ú-ši-bi ul it-bi*
7 *a-na* LUGAL-*ú-ti it-taš-kan*

---

8 ^{m}*ḫa-am-mu-ra-pí* LUGAL TIN.TIR^{ki} ÉRIN^{me}-*šú id-ke-e-ma*
9 *a-na* UGU ^{m}AM-^{d}30 LUGAL ŠEŠ.UNUG^{ki} *il-lik*
10 ŠEŠ.UNUG^{ki} *u* UD.UNUG^{ki} *qa-at-su ik-šu-ud*
11 ⸢*bu-šá-šu*⸣-*nu a-na* TIN.TIR^{ki} *il-qa-a*
12 [*u* ^{m}AM-^{d}30] *ina ki-is*-KAP-⸢*pu* ana TIN.TIR⸣^{ki} *ú-bil-la*

---

13 ⸢^{m}⸣*sa-am-su-i*-⸢*lu*⸣-*na* LUGAL TIN.TIR^{ki} DUMU ^{m}*ḫa*-⸢*am-mu-ra-pí* LUGAL⸣
14 [ÉRIN(?)] ⸢$^{me(?)}$⸣-*tú* [*id-ke*]-*e-ma*
15 [...] x ZU NA A ^{m}AM-^{d}30 ⸢ana(?) x x x⸣ GIN-*ik*
16 [...] ⸢ŠU^{MIN}⸣-*su* KUR-⸢*ud*⸣ [-*ma*]
17 [...] x *bal-ṭu-ut-su ina* É.GAL-x [...]
18 [...] x GIN-*ma il-mi* x [...]
19 [...] x UN^{me}-*šú* [...]
20 [...] x [...]
Lacuna

Rev.

Lacuna
1 [...] x [...]
2 [...] DINGIR-*ma* x [...]
3 [x] ⸢ME⸣ E *ib-na* [...]
4 *ṣal-tú a-na* ŠÀ-*šú* DÙ-⸢*ma*(?)⸣ [...]

80 Waerzeggers (2012: 293–95) was able to associate *ABC* 20A with a sub-group of chronicles characterized by a religious judgement of historical facts, the "Rēʾi-alpi group;" she associates 20B with a sub-group containing chronicles of an annalistic style, the "Bēliya'u group."
81 Most recently, Rutz and Michalowski (2016: 19) also consider the texts to be distinct. In contrast, Richardson (2016) treats them as part of the same text.
82 The line count follows the numbering in *ABC* 20B.
83 The formal arrangement on the left-hand side, which is discussed below, reflects that of the cuneiform text on the tablet. The cuneiform text is justified also to the right; this is not reflected in the transliteration for reasons of legibility.

5 AD$_6$^{me}-*šú-nu tam-tì* x [...]

6 *iš-ni-ma* ^{m}*sa-am-su-i-lu-na ana*(?) [...]

7 ^{m}DINGIR-*ma*-DINGIR ZI-*am-ma* BAD$_5$- BAD$_5$ ⸢ÉRIN⸣[^{me}-*šú im-ḫaṣ*(?)]

---

8 ^{m}*a-bi-ši* DUMU ^{m}*sa-am-su-i-lu-na ka-šad* ^{m}DINGIR-*ma*-DINGIR *iš*-⸢*kun*(?)-*ma*(?)⸣

9 ^{íd}IDIGNA *a-na se-ke-ri* ŠÀ-*ba-šú ub-lam-ma*

10 ^{íd}IDIGNA *is-kìr-ma* ^{m}DINGIR-*ma*-DINGIR *ul* [DIB]-⸢*bat*⸣

11 —*ana*—*tar-ṣi*—^{m}20–*di-ta-na*—^{kur}*ḫat-tu-ú*—*ana*—^{kur}URI^{ki}—⸢GIN⸣—[*ma*(?)]—

12 ^{md}*é-a-ga-mil* LUGAL KUR *tam-tì a-na* ^{kur}ELAM.MA^{ki} [*iḫ*(?)-*lik*(?)]-⸢*ma*⸣

13 EGIR-*šú* ^{m}*ú-lam-bur-áš* ŠEŠ ^{m}*kaš-til-ía-àš*(!) ^{kur}*kaš-šu-ú*

14 ÉRIN-*šú id-ke-e-ma* KUR *tam-tì* KUR-*ud* EN-*ut* KUR *i-pu-uš*

---

15 ^{m}*a-gu-um* DUMU ^{m}*kaš-til-ía-àš* ÉRIN-*šú id-ke-e-ma*

16 *a-na* KUR *tam-tì il-lik*

17 ^{uru}BÀD-^{d}50 KUR-*ud*

18 É-GALGA-ŠEŠ-NA É ^{d}50 *šá* BÀD-50 *ú-šal-pit*

2.4.1.1 The layout, structure, and narrative of chronicle *ABC* 20B

The general tone of *ABC* 20B is neutral and factual; it uses simple sentences, left largely unembellished by adverbs or adjectives. The text spans from the Isin I to the early Kassite period. It is organized in sections separated by horizontal dividers, and each section is devoted to a specific king. The text is justified and markedly indented (by roughly two signs)[84] so as to make the beginning of each section's first line visually prominent. And this position is always occupied by the name of a king (with title and/or genealogy) involved in the events recorded in that section. This narrative structure combined with the formal arrangement of the text is very unusual.[85] If it is indicative of the historical understanding of the chronicler, he seems to present the king at the beginning of each section as the legitimate one at the time of the events related. He faces adversity and sometimes comes out victorious, sometimes defeated, from the struggle.

Numerous rulers are omitted but the chronicler loosely threaded a historical narrative respecting chronology. The structure of the text is presented in Table 4.

---

84 This is apparent on the photograph published in King (1907: vol.2, p.iv); the photograph confirms that the spacing in King's hand copy is accurate.

85 Sections in chronicles often begin with MU (e.g. *ABC* 1–5 and many others); and the indentation, when there is one, is usually less marked (e.g. *ABC* 20A; *ABC* 15).

Table 4: Structure of chronicle *ABC* 20B

Section	Dynasty	King	Events related
(1) Obv. 1–7	Isin I	Erra-imittī	The king dies and is replaced by Enlil-bāni in a bizarre succession.
(2) Obv. 8–12	Amorite dynasty of Babylon	Hammurapi	The king vanquishes Rīm-Sîn I, which makes him the conqueror of Ur and Larsa.
(3) Obv. 13 – Rev. 7		Samsu-iluna	The king faces Rīm-Sîn II—(lacuna)—he battles twice(?) unsuccessfully against Ilī-ma-ilu.
(4) Rev. 8–10		Abī-ešuḫ	The king dams the Tigris but does not succeed in seizing Ilī-ma-ilu.
Rev. 11		Mention that the Hittites marched on Babylon at the time of Samsu-ditāna.	
(5) Rev. 12–14	Sealand I	Ea-gāmil	The king flees to Elam and Ulam-buriaš conquers the Sealand.
(6) Rev. 15–18	Kassite dynasty of Babylon	Agum	The king campaigns again in the Sealand, conquers Dūr-Enlil, and destroys its temple.

After the bizarre succession story of Erra-imittī (section 1) come three successive Amorite kings of Babylon: Hammurapi, Samsu-iluna, and Abī-ešuḫ (sections 2–4). Together, their struggles recount the unification of Sumer and Akkad under Babylon's rule and its fragmentation. This is followed by an entry about the Hittites marching on Babylon at the time of Samsu-ditāna. Written in smaller characters on the separating line between sections 4 and 5, it begins with *ana tarṣi*; this puts it visually and stylistically apart from the rest of the text. Grayson (1975: 49) considered that it was a later insertion, and, given its position and phrasing, it is plausible. At any rate, it seems to function as a chronological marker, outside the main narrative. After that, two sections (5 and 6) narrate the re-unification of Sumer and Akkad under Babylon's dominion that was achieved when the Kassite kings of Babylon conquered the Sealand kingdom.

Only the first and the last Sealand I kings appear in the chronicle, Ilī-ma-ilu and Ea-gāmil.[86] But while the founder of the dynasty, Ilī-ma-ilu, is presented as antagonist of Samsu-iluna and Abī-ešuḫ, Ea-gāmil appears at the head of his own section, therefore as a legitimate king. This places the Sealand I dynasty

86 The Sealand I dynasty is the only one whose rise and fall are recorded in *ABC* 20B, they are also the only aspects of its history that are recorded. If Sealand I royal propaganda was available to the compiler, which may have been the case, he discarded any events from the middle years of its existence.

in a legitimate role within this succession of dynasties, making it part of this narrative of Babylonian history—in agreement with king lists.

2.4.1.2 Possible sources and their use by the chronicler

In this section, the sources that may have been used by the chronicler of *ABC* 20B are reviewed and assessed, as well as how he used them. The results of this exercise will help reconstruct the textual genesis of the chronicle.

Having established above that *ABC* 20A and 20B are the products of different Borsippean scriptoria, but considering also that these texts contain (six or) seven identical lines (*ABC* 20A: 31–36 and *ABC* 20B: obv. 1–7), it follows that some common written sources were used by the chroniclers of both groups.[87] The passage in question, represented in both texts, is a curious anecdote about the death of king Erra-imittī sipping hot soup. It has has been suggested that it is based on a legend, which appears likely (van Seters 1983: 85; see also Grayson 1975: 48; Edzard 1957: 140).[88] Be it as it may, if we consider the short Erra-imittī narrative as a segment of the texts into which it was embedded, within *ABC* 20A it appears merely as slightly different in tone from the rest of that chronicle, but within 20B it certainly stands in stark contrast to the balance of the text—a succinct list of war deeds. But the chronicler did not adapt the passage to reduce it to the bare question of succession on the throne and make it more congruent with the style of the rest of the chronicle.[89] In other words, it was treated by the compiler of that annalistic chronicle exactly as it was treated by the compiler of *ABC* 20A, a religious and moral-interpretative chronicle: it was simply copied.

---

87 Oppenheim (1977: 150–51) argued for an oral tradition contributing to the passing down of Babylonian historiographic information, and this evocative passage could be a good candidate for oral transmission. However, both passages are nearly identical, including in the spelling (except for one main difference: in *ABC* 20A, line 34, the scribe apparently tried to cram at the end of the fourth line of the passage some of what corresponds to the fifth line of the same passage in *ABC* 20B, obv. 5).

88 It could also have come from an omen since occurrences that we would consider anecdotic, in particular pertaining to the death of kings, are attested in omens. An example is the story of the stairs of a temple falling on Sîn-iddinam (YOS 10, 1 in Goetze 1947: 265). Cooper (1980: 99) cites other examples of curious kings' deaths in omens. He includes the Erra-imittī episode from *ABC* 20 as "being intimately related to the tradition of historical omens" (*ibid.:* 103 n.2).

89 Glassner (1997: 101–02) interprets this passage and the role of the chronicler in a very different manner. He sees the chronicler as a writer and historian who, via the anecdote on Erri-imittī's death, criticizes the institution of substitute king in reaction to events contemporary to him, and at the same time raises the question of the historical significance of the death of a ruler. However, this interpretation considers this passage alone, completely isolated from the remainder of the texts in which it appears.

It appears therefore that the scribes of both Borsippean chronicling groups were essentially compilers who assembled passages from existing sources with minimal adaptation, in a sense performing "scribal archaeology" (Rubio 2009: 156). This interpretation is supported by the fact that a few passages concerning the Old Akkadian period were taken nearly *verbatim* from omens (Grayson 1975: 46) in *ABC* 20A. Since it has been shown that the same sources could be used for both *ABC* 20A and 20B, and that omens were indeed used for the former, it follows that a compendium of omens could certainly have been source material for the latter.

Another possible source is a putative chronicle, or chronicles, written as early as the first part of the second millennium and recording events contemporary with the first dynasty of Babylon.[90] The existence of such chronicles has been fairly recently even considered proven by Leichty and Walker (2004: 207; 211). They based their argument on documents BM 29440 and BM 29297;[91] they both contain what indeed appears to be excerpts of chronicles about the Old Babylonian kings Sabium and Apil-Sîn. The authors note that that portion of BM 29440 "is full of negative happenings," which certainly suggests a genre other than official royal communication as source material. But the history of

90 In fact, it has also been considered that the chronicle *ABC* 20B itself was partly or entirely written in the second millennium. Cavigneaux and André-Salvini (forthcoming) implicitly suggested a date shortly after the conquest of the Sealand kingdom by the Kassites since, when referring to the fall of Babylon and the conquest of the Sealand, they consider that "the tumultuous and dramatic events were still fresh and known to all." They assume that from the reign of Samsu-iluna onwards, the chronicle is "less dependent" on ancient sources and interpret the chronicle as having been compiled and written with the intention of justifying the current state of affairs, the Kassite control over all of Babylonia. In their analysis, one of the means of historical justification used by the chronicler would be to establish a flattering comparison between the Kassite conquerors of the Sealand and Sargon. But *ABC* 20A and B have been shown to be—in all likelihood—separate texts, which excludes the parallel between Sargon and the Kassite conquerors. Moreover, Cavigneaux and André-Salvini's estimated early date of composition of the chronicle is based on passages in *ABC* 20B only. But with 20A being in fact a separate text, there is no reason to suggest anything extraordinary about its date of writing, which therefore is more likely to lie in the first millennium like the other texts found in the sub-group to which it belongs (Waerzeggers 2012: 293). This in turn would mean that the passage on Erra-imittī's death, present in both texts, would have been treated in exactly the same way in texts whose first redaction lay several centuries apart. This seems far less likely than an integration of that passage in both 20A and 20B roughly in the same period, using the same version of the source text, and applying the same methods and standards of copying with regard to the adaptation of spelling and ductus. For these reasons, a date of redaction of *ABC* 20B during the Kassite period can be rejected with a fair level of confidence.

91 These texts are referred to in Waerzeggers as Fs.Grayson 2 and Fs.Grayson 3. She also published a new copy of BM 29440 (Waerzeggers 2015).

the texts is by no means clear and these passages could have been compiled (from early material) at a much later date.[92] It certainly confirms that sources about the Old Babylonian period were available and of interest to scribes of the same Borsippean scriptorial environment that produced chronicle *ABC* 20B (Waerzeggers 2012: 293). As for the Old Babylonian sections of *ABC* 20,[93] Lambert (1990b: 28) excluded a "chronicle actually compiled during the period" as a possible source because so many rulers were missing. But this is not convincing since it implies that the chronicler necessarily tried to compile a chronological account including all (or most) rulers, as in king lists and some chronicles pertaining to the first millennium.[94] This raises the question of the intention of the chronicler, which will be touched upon in Section 2.2.1.3. All in all, it remains at present unclear whether chronicles were compiled in the Old Babylonian period.

Old Babylonian year name lists, or at least some year name formulae, are frequently suggested as possible sources available to the first millennium chroniclers (recently Waerzeggers 2012: 292; see also Grayson 1975: 195; for a contrasting opinion see van Seters 1983: 81 n.97).[95] This suggestion is based mainly on two passages: one concerns the building of a wall by Apil-Sîn, the other is of direct relevance for the genesis of *ABC* 20B—it is the passage concerning the damming of the Tigris by Abī-ešuḫ.

This passage (*ABC* 20B: rev. 8–10)[96] has been considered to come from a year name list (Glassner 2004: 46; Waerzeggers 2012: 292 n.45)[97] but this interpretation was no doubt strongly suggested by the sources available to us. The damming of the Tigris is also referred to in a *tamītu*-text,[98] a genre that was part of scholarly

---

92 Waerzeggers (2012: 292–93) considers that, besides year names, the source material remains obscure.

93 Lambert regarded *ABC* 20A and B as one text.

94 The chronicler referred to here is the late chronicler (using a hypothetical earlier chronicle as his source).

95 On the copying of "date lists of reigns long past," George (2011: 207) notes that its function "was surely academic." His comment was made in the context of an Old Babylonian copy of an Ur III date list.

96 "Abī-ešuḫ (Abiši in the text), son of Samsu-iluna, set out to conquer Ilī-ma-ilu, he decided to dam the Tigris; he dammed the Tigris but he did not ⸢capture⸣ Ilī-ma-ilu."

97 Grayson (1975: 47) raises the possibility that a year name was the source, without concluding.

98 Lambert 2007: text 3c, lines 22 ff. (= CTN IV 62: IV lines 6 ff.) and text 3d, lines 1–3. The *tamītu*-texts are compendia of oracular questions, which are sometimes very detailed. Therefore, they may reflect historical events about which rulers were consulting the gods. The passage under consideration comprises several lines. The oracular question first enumerates troops of soldiers that "Abī-ešuḫ, king of Babylon" mustered, and asks then whether "on the east side of the Tigris, should they open the water-gate, should they turn it to 90°, by heaping up reed

libraries in the first millennium. But also, there is certainly reason to assume that an undertaking like damming the Tigris could have found its way into other sources unknown to us,[99] perhaps also into oral tradition. Therefore, this reference to the damming of the Tigris cannot be seen as a proof that Old Babylonian year name lists were used by the first millennium chronicler. In addition, the chronicle *ABC* 20B offers a reason for Abī-ešuḫ's hydraulic efforts: it presents it as a military tactic against Ilī-ma-ilu, whereas this information is neither provided by Abī-ešuḫ's year name o[100] nor by the *tamītu*-text. It seems thus likely that other sources were available to the chronicler. The alternative is that he interpreted and edited his material, which was shown above to be unlikely based on his treatment of other segments of the text. The fact that the damming of the Tigris is presented in another chronicle fragment as being commanded by Enlil,[101] while Abī-ešuḫ's year name o identifies Marduk as the god aiding the king in his task, also speaks against the year name as (only) source material for chronicles.[102] It appears therefore that, at least to the chronicler of *ABC* 20B, we have no proof that date lists were a main source of information.

Literary texts and copies of royal donations have been suggested as source material for Borsippean chronicles (Waerzeggers 2012: 294). Concerning the latter, it is interesting to note that the *māt tâmti* name tradition is attested in association with the Sealand I king Gulkišar in a *kudurru* (BE I/1 83); one may wonder whether the use of that term did not enter chronicles through this type of source.

---

bundles and earth should they dam the river;" the question is repeated for the west side of the Tigris.

99 The event may be behind a passage of the late Old Babylonian hymnic-epic CT 15, 1–2 (Römer 1967–68: VIII 5′–9′). For this possible interpretation, see for instance Horsnell 1999: vol.II 260–61 n.94 contra Römer who puts the event during Hammurapi's reign and the damming of the river as a strategy to flood northern arable land against the Subareans (Römer 1967–68: 20). In this passage of the epic, Ištar orders the damming.

100 "The year when Abī-ešuḫ, the king, by the supreme power of Marduk dammed the Tigris." (see Horsnell 1999: vol.2, pp.260–61).

101 *ABC*'s 'Fragment Concerning the Period of the First Dynasty of Isin' B = *MC* 41 B: rev. col.I. The passage is badly broken, but refers undoubtedly to "Ilī-ma-ilu, the ⸢enemy⸣," to "the command of the great lord Enlil," to "the damming," and to "the Tigris."

102 The other passage about Old Babylonian kings that has been suggested to derive from a year name is found in another Borsippean chronicle: BM 29297 (published in Leichty and Walker 2004: 211–12; for the interpretation of the year name as source material, see Waerzeggers 2012: 292 n.45). The passage pertains to the building of a wall by Apil-Sîn, an event also related in the king's third year name. As is the case of the damming of the Tigris, the year name refers only to the construction effort while the chronicle frames the deed within the context of a war. (It will be further discussed below since the enemy of Babylon is possibly identified as Sea or Sealand). This would again put the chronicler in a role different from that of a compiler.

King lists may have been used as source material for chronicles, including for *ABC* 20B, whether one considers them a genre separate from chronicles (van Seters 1983: 68; Glassner 2004: 38) or a sub-type of the same genre (Grayson 1975: 4). They may also be the results of related endeavors of recording the past. Indeed, chronicle *ABC* 20B and king lists BKL A and B (probably) begin with approximately the same historical period (early Old Babylonian). Moreover, the sequence of dynasties associated with the legitimate rulers at the beginning of each section in *ABC* 20B (Table 4), probably corresponds to that of BKL A and a number of other king lists (see Section 2.3).

The tone of the entire chronicle, which presents Babylon in turn as victorious and defeated, suggests that the chronicler of *ABC* 20B had at his disposal sources from all the dynasties involved, which implies that several sources from separate locations had over time been retrieved, copied, and perhaps partly compiled. We know that the chronicler probably combined sources even within individual sections (Samsu-iluna in his section appears both as the victor and at least once as the vanquished). This implies a painstaking piecing together of very short extracts from various sources. Considering chronicle *ABC* 20B as a member of a large sub-group of chronicles—of a "manuscript population"—as demonstrated by Waerzeggers (2012: 297), it appears indeed likely that a rich variety of information had been assembled by the Borsippean chroniclers (*ibid.*: 295). Even if we have no clear proof for any type of source, the odds are that the chronicler of *ABC* 20B had access to a wealth of documents from various milieux.

2.4.1.3 Contingencies and intention in the writing of *ABC* 20B

The eclectic juxtaposition of events recorded in *ABC* 20 A and B has brought van Seters (1983: 85) to suggest that the chronicler copied all that was available to him about the distant past so that "the scope [of his work] was dictated by the kind of information available (...) rather than by any special bias or plan."[103] However, while the work of the chronicler was of course contingent on the availability of sources, I do not think that this evident fact necessarily excludes some plan or systematic selection of information, especially as it was shown above that he probably had at his disposal a variety of sources. How did he select passages among, possibly, omens, *tamītu*-texts, legends, second

103 As noted above, this view is implicitly shared by Lambert (1990b: 28) who considered that there were no Old Babylonian chronicles used for the compilation of *ABC* 20 because of the absence of several rulers.

millennium chronicles, date lists, and king lists? In other words, what type of historiographic endeavor did the writing of *ABC* 20B represent?

Examination of the text suggests that its geographical horizon was deliberately limited to central and southern Babylonia and its thematic purview to deeds of war and royal succession. In fact, especially from the point of view of a first millennium Babylonian scribe, the events related could be considered interior political struggles, namely a problematic succession and episodes of civil war in Sumer and Akkad. This would explain why of all of Hammurapi's campaigns, the chronicler recorded only the war against Rīm-Sîn (I); it would explain why the sole events recorded for Abī-ešuḫ and early Kassite kings pertain to their struggles with the Sealand I kings and kingdom; it would also explain why the Samsu-iluna section is so long; indeed, he waged intense warfare against various southern rebels for the control over these regions.[104] This would also explain why the entry on the Hittites marching on Babylon (rev. 11) was treated differently than the rest of the text, because it was outside its geographical and thematic scope.

Waerzeggers (2012: 296–97) observed that Borsippean chroniclers were "engaged in writing a national history," in other words all in all adhering to a Babylo-centric view. Examination of king lists has suggested that the Sealand I dynasty had probably entered the wider Babylonian historiographic tradition at an earlier date (Section 2.3), allowing it to be present in several sources. Therefore, the compiler of *ABC* 20B probably simply respected a received pattern in modeling his narrative in a way that respected this sequence of legitimate dynasties. Of course, a redaction of *ABC* 20B in the Neo-Babylonian period is quite possible, and the Sealand, the *māt tâmti*, may have been an important province at the time —indeed, its governor, the *šakin tâmti*, stands first amongst local dignitaries in

104 If my hypothesis on the geographical scope of the chronicle is valid, the fragmentary section on Samsu-iluna would omit his activities in northern and peripheral regions and concentrate on his struggles south of the capital. We find indeed mention of Rīm-Sîn II at the beginning of the section (obv. line 15), which must record events in Samsu-iluna's years 8 or 9; the middle part of the section is mostly lost. A passage of five lines follows, perhaps referring to a battle against Ilī-ma-ilu. It is too fragmentary to make a coherent reconstruction possible but it appears likely that it alludes to hostilities against the founder of the Sealand I dynasty. Rev. line 2 probably contains the name Ilī-ma-ilu. Lines 4–5 are damaged but clearly mention a battle, corpses, and the sea while Samsu-iluna appears on line 6, probably in the context of a renewed action (*išni*), perhaps indicating a second attack. The very end of the section pertains to a defeat of Samsu-iluna at the hands of Ilī-ma-ilu (rev. line 7). The war between Ilī-ma-ilu and Samsu-iluna may therefore have been given several lines of text and remembered through at least two major battles, this would tally with the proposed geo-political scope given by the chronicler to the text. On the importance of Samsu-iluna in chronicles, see also Section 2.4.2.1.

the *Hofkalender* (Beaulieu 2002b).[105] This political reality of the scribe may have contributed to presenting the Sealand I dynasty on a par with the dynasties of Babylon, but its inclusion in the sequence of Babylonian dynasties was already accepted in king lists.

As for the trustworthiness of *ABC* 20B as a source for historical reconstruction, it is difficult to gauge. From other sources we find some corroboration for events narrated in it, but not necessarily in the detail. For instance, the (partial?) damming of the Tigris, which seems to have some basis in reality because it is referred to in a year name and in an oracular question, may or may not have been mainly directed against the Sealand kingdom, but it could have be reinterpreted and presented as such in Sealand I sources. It was shown that the chronicler probably worked as a compiler more than a writer, shaping his narrative by selecting sources and piecing passages together within his set scope and structure. Therefore, the trustworthiness of the chronicle probably mirrors that of the sources that he used, passed down through centuries. Accordingly, the evidence it yields will be considered but carefully weighed for the reconstruction of the Sealand I political history (Chapter 4).

2.4.2 Other chronicle fragments

2.4.2.1 Another chronicle on southern Babylonia in the early and mid-second millennium

The period of history covered by *ABC* 20B was obviously deemed a matter of sustained interest by chroniclers since at least another chronicle, of a different style, was written about it. Two fragments, found in Aššurbanipal's library and perhaps belonging to the same large tablet, featured kings of the first dynasty of Isin on the obverse while the reverse of one fragment makes mention of Ilī-ma-ilu and the damming of the Tigris; the reverse of the other fragment is so damaged that no

105 This may or may not result from a Urukean origin of he founder of the dynasty Nabopolassar, which was then almost certainly part of the Sealand province at the time (Beaulieu 2002b; Jursa 2007). This stands in sharp contrast with the apparent stance of Bēl-Iqīša, a prelate of the Esagil, who wrote presumably in the late eighth century to the Assyrian king about the disappearance of the "dynasty of the Sealand" (SAA 17, 24: 24), probably citing from omens and referring to Marduk-apla-iddina (II), who is indeed associated with the Sealand (III) dynasty in BKL A (col.IV, line 10′). See also Dietrich 2003: xxiii for the wider context of the letter.

king's name can be reconstructed (K 2973 and 79–7–8, 36).[106] Lambert (1990b: 29 ff.) suggested that two fragments pertaining to Samsu-iluna, also from Nineveh, may have belonged to the same or to a similar text, K 10609 and K 14011. These fragments are, as Lambert (*ibid.*: 34) put it, "more flowery than the jejune chronicle style"[107] that characterizes *ABC* 20B. Indeed, the tone and language could not be more different. In *ABC* 20B, especially if we exclude the legend-like first seven lines, we find only inornate, matter-of-fact diction: no adjectives are used, no adverbs emphasize the actions described, appositions are used only to identify protagonists (so-and-so, king of...). The fragments from Aššurbanipal's library differ strongly in style: adjectives and (at least one) adverbs enrich the diction, we also find the durative used to narrate past actions, a literary device which is not used in the annalistic style of *ABC* 20B. Noteworthy is also that the Aššurbanipal library fragments are more religious, sacrifices are a subject matter and actions are undertaken at the command of deities. In comparison, the *topos* of divine command is entirely absent from *ABC* 20B.

These fragments are too small and damaged to allow for more analysis. Nonetheless, taken together with *ABC* 20B, they make plain that certain events of the first half of the second millennium in central and southern Babylonia, including events related to the Sealand I dynasty, were of enough interest in first millennium scriptoria to be treated in at least two very different types of chronicling undertakings, one annalistic and one with an underlying religious interpretation. Also, in what has come down to us, Samsu-iluna certainly stands out among the rulers included in such accounts. His presence in a few fragments could, admittedly, be the result of chance, but the fact that his section in *ABC* 20B is by far the longest is also suggestive.

2.4.2.2 Fragments with uncertain or undetermined reference to the Sealand

A fragment dubbed 'Fragment Concerning the Sealand' by Grayson (1975: 192 = *MC* 42) contains a few lacunary lines in which mention is made of the KUR *tamtim* and of an unknown king, Apil-Adad. The historical period and context to which the text refers cannot be reconstructed.

Chronicle excerpt BM 29297 may contain a mention of the sea (or the Sealand) in a very early context, the reign of Apil-Sîn. The passage has been read

106 K 2973 and 79–7–8, 36 correspond to *ABC*'s 'Fragment Concerning the Period of the First Dynasty of Isin' in Grayson 1975: 190–92 and to Glassner's *MC* 41. This text also seems to recount the episode of Enlil-bāni and Erra-imittī.

107 In fact, one may note that they are more flowery than the style of annalistic chronicles such as *ABC* 20B, not of all chronicles.

by Leichty and Walker (2004: 212) as: (1) [^{m}] ⸢*A*⸣-*pil*-^{d}30 A ^{m}*Sà-bu-ú* (2) *tar-ṣú-šú* ⸢*tam*⸣-[*tim*] *šap-lit* (3) ⸢*mim-ma la i-bi*⸣-*el-ši-na-a-tú* : "Apil-Sin, the son of Sabu, during his reign, he did not rule any part of the Sealands." This is followed by a few lines about the construction of the wall of Babylon by the king. The small tablet, inscribed only on its obverse, appears to be a school text from Borsippa (Leichty and Walker 2004: 212; Waerzeggers 2012: 293).[108]

There are several problems with the proposed reading of this passage. The photograph of the tablet[109] shows a much larger lacuna on line 2 than what is suggested by the proposed transliteration.[110] The expression *tar-ṣú-šú* would be very unusual, since the term *tarṣu* is normally used with a preposition rather than the locative-adverbial, both in chronicles and elsewhere.[111] Also, the syntax and the feminine plural complement of the verb on line 3 appear somewhat awkward in the proposed reconstruction.

The date of writing and the historical meaning are also problematic. Leichty and Walker (2004: 211) consider the text to be an excerpt of an Old Babylonian chronicle. It has already been discussed that we do not know whether chronicles were written in the second millennium, let alone at the beginning of it, more than a millennium before any of the known versions were written. The passage is so short and out of context that we do not even know for certain whether it is an excerpt of a chronicle. The genre and date of (first) writing are therefore undetermined. A late date of redaction would open the door to various possible explanations for this "lower sea" region, apparently the opponent of Apil-Sîn.[112] At any rate, it appears unlikely that, should the proposed reading be correct, an anachronistic reference to the later Sealand was made since one would have expected the chronicler to use the (by then) received term to designate it: (KUR) *tam-tim* or (KUR) A.AB.BA. I believe we can reject this interpretation with confidence.

---

108 This fragment is identified as *Fs. Grayson* no.3 in Waerzeggers 2012.

109 From the web site of the British Museum.

110 The only undamaged sign is LIT. The preceding ŠAP is legible. The very first sign on the line could indeed be TAR, but it is by no means certain since only the top part is visible. The other signs are all very uncertain and the reconstructed TAM is problematic since it would look quite different from the same sign plainly readable at the end of the following line.

111 In other cases, it appears in the bound form (CAD T, s.v. *tarṣu* b).

112 There is a remote possibility that it referred to the Borsippean region. Indeed, the control of that branch of the Euphrates, part of the short-lived kingdom of Marad and Kazallu for a time, was hotly disputed until Sîn-iddinam and even later (Charpin 2004: 87–88). The marshy region around Borsippa came to be called *tâmtu*, the Sea, in the sixth century, some time before the end of the period of production of the Borsippean chronicles (Cole 1994: 95 n.76; Waerzeggers 2012: 294).

3 Geographical and chronological considerations

Because of the scarcity of primary Sealand I sources, this polity's geo-political history has been until now mostly defined and written in the negative: its emergence was surmised when a void had been left by others and its location posited more or less because there was nowhere else it could be. To complicate matters, the geography of the Sealand kingdom cannot be described well in terms of control over known, major cities because, so far, the evidence speaks for a dramatic weakening of these southern Mesopotamian centers in that period. They appear to have been (partly) abandoned, and they certainly did not received royal favor for a long time.[1] A widespread geo-demographic movement brought cultic and scribal milieux, and probably part of the population, outside the ancient (and best excavated) cities. Life in the Sealand kingdom took place mainly elsewhere and, with few exceptions, we have not looked for it in the right places yet.

The new textual material which has become available to us, principally with the publication of Sealand I archival and divinatory texts in CUSAS 9 and 18, does not yield much definite, positive evidence on the geography of the kingdom or on the chronology of the dynasty. Nonetheless, there are enough new indications to warrant a reassessment of the sources. Also, the on-going excavations at Tell Khaiber, between Ur and Larsa, offer incontrovertible evidence for a Sealand I control of the site. In addition, a surface survey conducted by the Iraqi Department of Antiquities in 2003–09 and the use of satellite images may bring new evidence for the location and extent of the kingdom by proposing an identification of sites occupied during that period (al-Hamdani 2015: 7 ff.); however, the purported Sealand I presence at these sites is based on diagnostic ware that re-

1 Gasche (1989: 124–31) reviewed the archaeological and textual evidence for the main sites—here of central and southern Babylonia. So far, subsequent archaeological work, publications, or re-analyses have not changed that picture: without aiming at exhaustivity, see e.g. for the Ebabbar of Larsa, Huot 2014; for Ur, Clayden 2014, but there may be soon more evidence as current excavations have brought up texts dated to Samsu-iluna (A. al-Hamdani, personal communication); for Uruk, van Ess 1991a: 91 and 1991b, and Boehmer 1991a: 101 and 1991b; for Lagaš, Pittman and Renette 2016 and personal communication from Steve Renette. The purported small scale occupation of large sites during the time of the Sealand I dynasty posited by al-Hamdani (2015: 137 ff.) remains dubious because it is based on unpublished ceramics; the matter is further discussed in this section.

https://doi.org/10.1515/9781501507823-004

mains as yet unpublished and, without a continuous sequence in southern Mesopotamia, possibly ambiguous.[2]

As will be shown, the Sealand kingdom appears to have occupied large stretches of southern Babylonia, with access to the Persian Gulf, probably controlling the lower portions of the Euphrates hydrographic system as well as of the Tigris. At times, it extended its control as far north as Nippur. Evidence on the geography of the later region called the Sea(land) will not be discussed here since its extent need not correspond with that of the Sealand kingdom (perhaps only part of it did). One may note, however, that the location and the extent of the Kassite province NAM (KUR) A.AB.BA, closest in time to the independent kingdom, would roughly confirm a number of indications on the Sealand I geography: according to a number of *kudurrū*, it lay in the extreme Babylonian south down to the shore of the Persian Gulf, bordering west and east on the Euphrates and the Tigris, and, north, on the province of Isin. It included Uruk and, at times, Larsa and Ur (Paulus 2014a: 193).

3.1 Geographical evidence

3.1.1 Positive evidence of the Sealand I presence in Babylonia

Textual evidence of Sealand I territorial control is very scarce but the little we have does confirm that the kingdom occupied at least part of the territory lost by Babylon under Samsu-iluna. Sources show also that some of it was disputed for more than a generation between the new neighbors, as will be discussed in the next chapter. Our knowledge of the Sealand I geography remains fragmentary because almost all relevant sources are either unprovenanced or of later date, but we have direct proof of Sealand I control from at least three archaeological excavations:[3] five texts and one envelope[4] from Nippur covering a period of slightly over fourteen months are dated to the first ruler Ilī-ma-ilu (from 16.vii.Ilī 1 to 24.ix.Ilī 2); at least three texts dated to Ayadaragalama (probably

2 At Tell Khaiber, where ceramics and Sealand I texts were found in controlled excavations, the ceramic types found so far are judged generally Old Babylonian, without some of the earlier characteristics (Campbell et al. 2017). See also Section 1.2.2.

3 Also, excavations at the site of Tell Abu Thahab, near Ur, is said to have produced a Sealand I archive (al-Hamdani: personal communication and 2015: 139). Photographs or further details could not be obtained.

4 BE 6/2 68; ARN 123=Ni 9271; UM 55–21–239=3N-T87=SAOC 44 12; PBS 8/1,89; and the recently published HS 2227 with envelope HS 2226=TMH 10 54a and b.

years Aa J and K) were found at Tell Khaiber;[5] and one text from Qalʿat al-Bahrein is dated to the last ruler Ea-gāmil (year Eg 4).[6] We know therefore for certain that Sealand I rulers controlled Nippur briefly at the beginning of the dynasty, the southern Euphrates area between Ur and Larsa around the middle of it,[7] and Dilmun at the end of the dynasty—also implying that the Sealand kingdom possessed a maritime access to the Persian Gulf on the mainland. These are the cardinal facts of Sealand I geography as it is known to us from provenanced textual sources available today.

Contemporary evidence also indicates that the town of Udannu was at times part of the Sealand kingdom and was of some importance for it.[8] Indeed, Ammī-ditāna's thirty-seventh year name informs us that he destroyed the wall of EZENxSIG$_7^{ki}$, perhaps read Udinim (Horsnell 1999: vol.II 319 n.176; Groneberg 1980: 244), which had been built by Dam(i)q-ilišu—in all probability the third Sealand I king. The reading of EZENxSIG$_7^{ki}$ and the identification of the town have been much debated;[9] Beaulieu (1992b: 419) suggested that Old Babylonian EZENxSIG$_7^{ki}$, with a double name Kisig(a)/Ud(i)nim, was strongly associated with later Udannu, either being the same town or separate towns, the cults of the former having been transferred to the latter. Udannu, written syllabically, is attested in one Sealand I archival document dated to the reign of Ayadaragalama (CUSAS 9, 101); it is a place which the king is about to visit. If the towns are one and the same, the joint evidence from Ammī-ditāna's year name and from document CUSAS 9, 101 shows that it was of some strategic importance since it was disputed between the neighboring states. The location of Udannu is unknown but Neo-Babylonian evidence suggests that it was probably on the Euphrates, not far from Uruk, possibly also not very far from Larsa (Beaulieu 1992b: 402; 409; 411).[10]

---

5 Texts TK1 3006.17; 3064.67 and 3064.135. See appendix 2 and oracc.museum.upenn.edu/urap/corpus.

6 Text QA 94.46 in Cavigneaux and André-Salvini forthcoming.

7 There are some remains of earlier occupation at Tell Khaiber, but so far only from surface collection, it is thus by no means clear whether the site was occupied continuously. Also, while the large administrative building shows evidence of more than one building phases, there are no signs that much time elapsed between them (Campbell, et al. 2017). Therefore, at present, it seems impossible to decide how long the site was occupied during the time of the Sealand kingdom.

8 Udannu was not the only stretch of land to be disputed between Babylon and the Sealand kingdom since Nippur, taken from Samsu-iluna by Ilī-ma-ilu, was not held long by the Sealand I king(s). A chronology of events is proposed in Section 4.3.1.

9 See Horsnell (*op.cit.*) for a summary of hypotheses and literature.

10 The relative importance of Udannu in the Sealand kingdom and the probable proximity between it and the find spot of the archive are also strongly suggested by the cult of Lugal-irra and

A town called Kār-Šamaš, which is very present in the archive as a palace town, was either the very same which produced the archive, or one located near it. This Kār-Šamaš was, in all likelihood, a town also known from Old Babylonian evidence and very probably located between Larsa and Ur (Boivin 2015; Fiette 2017; see also Section 3.1.3).

In the absence of royal inscriptions[11] or other archives, this is the full extent of the positive evidence for Sealand I territorial control known today. Without a continuous stratigraphy and ceramic types that could be unambiguously identified as Sealand I ware, archaeological evidence alone cannot at present be considered positive evidence on Sealand I occupation.

3.1.2 Indirect evidence on the Sealand I geography

Other sources requiring more interpretation are suggestive of the geography of the Sealand I territory. This indirect evidence, some of which results from the analysis presented in subsequent chapters of this book, includes: (1) the damming of the Tigris by Abī-ešuḫ; (2) the prominence of the goddess Nazi combined with the absence of her entourage in the state pantheon at the time of Ayadaragalama; (3) the reference to Gulkišar in a *kudurru* dating to Enlil-nādin-apli; (4) the capture of traveling Ešnunneans by Sealand I officials at the time of Ayadaragalama; (5) the prominence of Ea in the state pantheon at the time of Ayadaragalama; (6) the importance of (the pantheon of) Nippur in Sealand I religious texts; (7) the possibility of a displaced cult from Uruk; (8) the importance of Larsean and other south-western deities; (9) the possible archaeological evidence for site occupation in southern Babylonia in the late Old Babylonian and the early Middle Babylonian period.[12]

Nin-Eanna in the Sealand I archive as well as the presence of personal names with the theophoric element ^{d}IGI.DU (see Chapter 6).

11 Both the cylinder seals of Akurduana (P 455982) and of Ilī-remeanni (Moorey and Gurney 1973: no.23), “who reveres the king, his lord, Ea-gāmil” and must have been a subject—perhaps a servant—of the last Sealand I king, are unprovenanced. See Section 1.3.1 for the orthography of the name.

12 The fact that a scribe declared himself “scribe of Marduk, man of Babylon” in the glass-making treatise BM 120960 dated to Gulkišar could suggest control of Babylon, but the text is probably of much later date and its colophon a forgery that was aimed at suggesting antiquity of the Babylonian glass-making lore (Oppenheim 1970: 62). See also Section 4.7.

3.1.2.1 Central Babylonia

The presence at Nippur of a few texts bearing date formulae of Ilī-ma-ilu shows that the first Sealand I king occupied that city for a time (Section 3.1.1), however, the recent publication of texts from the fortress Dūr-Abī-ešuḫ (e.g. CUSAS 8) has made plain that the Nippur area was under Babylon's dominion for the larger part of the late Old Babylonian period (the matter is discussed in detail in Section 4.3.1). But evidence from the time of Pešgaldarameš and Ayadaragalama could indicate that the Nippur area was again under Sealand I control, although, at the time, Nippur was probably barely inhabitable (Gibson 1992: 42–45). At any rate, the Nippur pantheon is certainly prominent in the Sealand I palatial archive (Section 6.5.3) and, perhaps more tellingly, Nippur itself and its temples are referred to in a hymn of Ayadaragalama to the gods of Nippur (P431311; see Gabbay and Boivin forthcoming).

3.1.2.2 The lower Tigris

If we accept the account given in chronicle *ABC* 20B, the damming of the Tigris commemorated in Abī-ešuḫ's year name o was directed against Ilī-ma-ilu. This suggests that the nascent polity depended heavily on the Tigris for its water supply. We do not have any other information contemporary with Ilī-ma-ilu to substantiate this, but a later source, a *kudurru*, refers to the involvement of Gulkišar in granting land located along the Tigris. In addition, a few indications pointing towards the Tigris being in Sealand I territory may be found in documents from the middle of the dynasty: the prominence of Nazi in the state pantheon and the capture of Ešnunneans by Sealand I officials.

The *kudurru* BE I/1 83, dating to the fourth year of the Isin II ruler Enlil-nādin-apli at the beginning of the eleventh century, states that a parcel of disputed land located along the Tigris in the province of Bīt-Sîn-māgir had originally been donated by "Gulkišar, king of the Sealand, to Nanše, his lady" (obv. 3–4).[13] This would mean that the Sealand I's jurisdiction extended to an area along the southern Tigris in the period preceding the reigns of Pešgaldarameš and Ayadaragalama. The source dates of course centuries after the alleged donation; in fact a time span—an erroneous one—is given in the text. Notwithstanding the reckoning of years, the question remains why Gulkišar was named in the context of this plot of land. The claim that the land had been taken recently from

13 For a recent edition, see AOAT 51, ENAp 1. Note that the goddess' name is written ^{d}NANŠE in the *kudurru*, whereas it is always written syllabically ^{d}*na-zi* in the Sealand I texts (see Section 6.4.3).

the goddess may not be fictitious (obv. 9–15), but it remains questionable whether an ancient deed naming Gulkišar really existed.[14] Enlil-nādin-apli, in order to give more authority to his confirmation of the land restitution, may have decided to call on the name of a ruler once considered legitimate and still well remembered in that area. Be it as it may, the odds are thus that the Sealand I king indeed ruled over the southernmost stretch of the Tigris, around the junction of what would later become the provinces of the Sealand and Bīt-Sîn-māgir.

The claim made in the *kudurru* seems also cogent with a fairly prominent place given to Nazi in the state pantheon during the reigns of Gulkišar's descendants, when her cult enjoyed significant sponsorship by the palace. However, in these documents the goddess appears alone, without her retinue, which seems to reflect that the Sealand I kings controlled parts of the ancient city-state of Lagaš but that that region was not of foremost importance in the kingdom, at least at the time of Ayadaragalama.[15] In that period Girsu and the environing region received their water from the Tigris. Gasche et al. (2007: 61) established that the old Lagaš branch of the Tigris must have remained active at least into Samsuiluna's reign since Girsu and Lagaš could not have received much water from the Euphrates due to their relative elevation.[16] If we assume that this situation continued in subsequent years, the damming of the Tigris by Abī-ešuḫ could be consistent with a Sealand I presence in the Nina, Girsu, and/or Lagaš area at the beginning of the dynasty. New documents from the fortress Dūr-Abī-ešuḫ suggest that the Babylonians were operating a network of forts in central Babylonia and, if the extant records reflect the situation faithfully, along the Tigris their control did not reach further south than Maškan-šāpir (Abraham, et al. 2017: introduction; and texts CUSAS 29, 39–40); this would also be consistent with a Sealand I presence in the southern Tigris area.

---

14 Paulus (2014a: 118) does not question whether an original donation by Gulkišar took place. Her analysis has shown that most confirmations of donation occurred shortly after an original one (*ibid.*: 117), which could thus still be remembered. It seems questionable whether this applies here.

15 See Chapter 6 for a detailed analysis.

16 We know that an important canal from the Tigris toward the Girsu area had been dug out by Rīm-Sîn I, probably in reaction to Sîn-muballiṭ's damming or diverting water from the Iturungal (Renger 1970: 78); and it may not have been the first time: a feeder canal off the Tigris was apparently built by Lagaš in the Early Dynastic period because of its conflict with Umma (Adams 1981: 134). Textual evidence could also suggest that the Lagaš area was irrigated from the Tigris under Hammurapi: in a letter concerning the collection of taxes (*AbB* 2, 30: 7), an area presumably adjacent to Bad-Tibira was named the "Tigris(-bank)." Naming this area, which must lie east of Bad-Tibira, after the river could indicate that it was dependent on it.

However, depending on how one reconstructs the course of the Tigris, and especially if one adheres to Steinkeller's proposition (2001), a larger area of southern Babylonia may very well have been watered by the Tigris (see also Gasche, Tanret, Cole, and Verhoeven 2002: 541; for a contrasting opinion, see Stone 2003; Hritz 2010). Therefore, Abī-ešuḫ's action need perhaps not only be interpreted as a threat to areas located immediately along the course of the Tigris.

Another element that may indirectly refer to the Tigris with regards to Sealand I territory comes from a letter belonging to the Sealand I palace archive, hence almost certainly dating to the later years of Pešgaldarameš or the early years of Ayadaragalama: CUSAS 9, 3. The missive was sent by the official Nūr-Ba'u to his superior,[17] informing him that Ešnunneans traveling by boat were detained and questioned on their itinerary.[18] The author of the letter concludes by asking for instructions concerning his detainees.[19] Since the two towns—Quppat-ᵈNIN.GAL⁽ᵏⁱ⁾ and Tugi⁽ᵏⁱ⁾—named by the Ešnunneans as their journey's end appear elsewhere in the archive,[20] we know that they were bound for Sealand I destinations, although the location of these towns is unknown. Travelers journeying from Ešnunna by boat must have transited by the Tigris when leaving the Diyala. But whether their journey continued on the Tigris or on a canal branching off it is impossible to say; at some point along these waterways they entered Sealand I territory and were intercepted. Dalley (2009: 21 n.3) suggested that the theophoric element Ba'u in the official's name connects him with Lagaš;[21] the archive does not offer further prosopographical information on this man.[22] What appears

17 Dalley (2009: 21 notes) surmises that the letter was sent from a governor to the king. In this archive, some letters use the Old Babylonian, others the Middle Babylonian opening (Dalley 2009: 19). This letter is of the latter type; lines 1–4 are: *ana di-na-ni be-lí-ia* / *a-na-a-ku lu-ul-lik* / *um-ma nu-úr-ᵈba-ú* / ÌR-*ka-ma*.

18 CUSAS 9, 3: lines 5–9: ⌈giš⌉MÁ.ḪI.A *ša iš-nu-uk-ki-i* / *i-it-ti-qá-ma ak-ta-la-ši-na-a-ši* / *ki a-ša-lu-šu-nu-ú-ši* / ⌈*um*⌉*-ma* ⌈*lu*⌉ *a-na-ku-ú-ma* / *e ša-a te-et-ti-qá*.

19 Lines 18–20: *ki-ša be-lí i-ša-ap-pa-ra* / *šum-ma lu-uk-la* / *šum-ma lu-ma-aš-še-er*.

20 Besides this mention in CUSAS 9, 3: 12–13, the towns appear together in CUSAS 9, 4: 11 & 13. Quppat-ᵈNIN.GAL appears also in CUSAS 9, 77: 6, possibly as a place of offerings. They are apparently otherwise unattested.

21 If this official was based in the area of Lagaš, it would imply that the Ešnunneans had already penetrated far into the southern plain and were then traveling south-west. If they had not been stopped before that stage of their journey, it suggests that they had just entered the territory controlled by the Sealand I kings. But the mere evidence of one personal name is too thin a basis for such an extrapolation.

22 The name may be attested in a tax ledger, CUSAS 9, 441: 5; the passage is damaged. We do not know what his title or function was.

certain is that the Sealand I rulers did not control the Diyala, at least certainly not the area of Ešnunna.[23]

3.1.2.3 The lower Euphrates

Besides the excavations at Tell Khaiber, between Ur and Larsa, and the fact that Udannu and Kār-Šamaš—probably both also located along the Euphrates—were in Sealand I territory in the second half of its history (Section 3.1.1), other elements suggest a control of the lower Euphrates.

As expounded in Section 6.2, Ayadaragalama's year names echo the early Larsean *topos* of invoking Ea—more particularly Enlil and Ea—in year names,[24] which could point toward a Larsean influence on Sealand I kingship. In addition, a cult of Ea (often in conjunction with Enlil) is attested in Sealand I records, which is in itself exceptional in the post-Old Babylonian period and certainly suggests that the extreme south-west of Babylonia was of importance to the dynasty. In fact, the most direct parallel to the close association of Enlil and Ea in the Sealand I cult comes from an Old Babylonian letter from Larsa mentioning a rare "Temple of Enlil and Ea" (Veldhuis 2008: text 10; see also Section 6.4.6). Also, Šamaš is the god associated with what appears to be the deified king Gulkišar, "Šamaš-bless-Gulkišar," in a Sealand I god list (CUSAS 9, 83: line 15′), associating the sun god, and presumably Larsa, closely with the dynasty.[25] In addition, the cities or Ur and Eridu are mentioned in an unpublished Sealand I letter from the Belgian Collection. The information is mentioned in passing by Dalley (2009: 31 notes) without more detail on the context in which these cities occur in the text; pending publication, it seems more prudent to consider this to be merely indirect evidence, but it is certainly suggestive.

The control over the lower Euphrates by the Sealand I kings is further suggested by the fact that an official Urukean cult, that of She-who-dwells-in-Uruk, and perhaps others, may have been observed—in a displaced setting—by the Sealand I kings (Section 6.4.1.1). Uruk appears to have been largely abandoned at the time, and there is no evidence for activity at the Eanna (van Ess 1991b: 204; Boehmer 1991b: 207), but the evidence for that official cult suggests that the Sealand I kings exerted nominal control over the area. However, Uruk and the region north of it may have initially remained for some time in Babylonian

23 The relations between the Sealand kingdom and Ešnunna are discussed in Section 4.4.3.
24 It is surmised that Enlil and Ea have replaced the former triad Anu, Enlil, and Ea (see Chapter 6 for a detailed discussion).
25 A number of other cults, for instance that of nin-é.NIM.ma, point toward the importance of the lower Euphrates in the Sealand kingdom (see Section 6.5.4).

hands because a new text from Dūr-Abī-ešuḫ possibly mentions a fortress of Uruk, although it refers to it indirectly by the name *birti* DU_6 É.AN.NA—perhaps the mound (of ruins) of the Eanna (CUSAS 29, 18: 5 and notes); also, soldiers of Isin and Uruk appear in CUSAS 29, 8: 3.[26] Both texts date to the time of Abī-ešuḫ (year o+1). In addition, a receipt from Dilbat attests of commercial relations between that town and the KAR.UNUG[ki] in the year Ae m (VS 7, 43); it was first interpreted by Pientka (1998: 179 n.7) as a sign that a harbor at Uruk was still functioning and in contact with Babylon. Charpin (1999–2000: 324) observed that the KAR in question was more likely to be a group of merchants from Uruk, incorporated in a *kārum*, in exile in northern Babylonia, but given the new evidence, Pientka's interpretation is not impossible. The fight over Udannu late in Ammī-ditāna's reign probably reflects an episode of redefinition of the border between Sealand and Babylon along the Euphrates.

The analysis of satellite images of southern Iraq has revealed a large number of unexcavated settlements; the area was also extensively surveyed after 2003 (e.g. Hritz, Pournelle, and Smith 2012; al-Hamdani 2015: 121–23). Al-Hamdani (2015: 122; 137; 149) contends that he was able to identify pottery types that are diagnostic to the Sealand I dynasty. Basing himself on his survey results, he dates numerous settlements to the time of the Sealand I dynasty, as well as a limited presence in formerly large cities that were partly abandoned at the time (*ibid.*: 149 ff.). He contends that hydraulic works upstreams had led to a collapse of the irrigation system in central Babylonia, leaving more water in the streams to be carried south, leading to a quasi-desertification of the central plain and a marked growth of the marshy area in the south (*ibid.*: 144). People resettled accordingly, including the transfer en masse from the Ur population to a newly founded urban settlement of similar size further west, on the Eridu branch of the Euphrates, Tell Dehaila, which al-Hamdani proposes to identify as the Sealand I capital (*ibid.*: 168 ff.). This site had been surveyed by Wright (1981: 330; site EP-34). It is also suggested as a potential location for "the palace" mentioned in the Tell Khaiber administrative texts (Campbell, et al. 2017). However, pending publication of the pottery and, hopefully, the establishment of (a) continuous archaeological sequence(s) in southern Babylonia, the precise dating of these sites remains unresolved. The recent (and on going) excavations at Tell Khaiber and Tell Abu Thahab near Ur, which have yielded Sealand I texts and pottery (Campbell, et al. 2017; al-Hamdani 2015: 139), will hopefully contribute towards clarify-

---

26 This text had been published as van Lerberghe and Voet 2010: text 4 and CUSAS 8, 39, with some different readings. See also Földi 2014: 42.

ing diagnostic ceramic types and, perhaps, the chronology of occupation.[27] At any rate, the potential offered by the numerous unexcavated sites is certainly momentous, but only excavations will determine whether they were indeed occupied at the time of the Sealand I dynasty.[28]

3.1.3 The provenance of the archive

Although there is no incontrovertible evidence for it, a number of indications point towards a provenance of the palatial archive published in CUSAS 9 at or very near the town of Kār-Šamaš, presumably in the triangle Larsa—Ur—Eridu. This palace town probably had close economic interactions with the administrative center of Tell Khaiber.

Nearly all geographical names mentioned in the archive are otherwise unattested or, as in the case of Udannu, their exact location is unknown. Although the texts deal almost exclusively with local matters, they do not contain any definite indication that we can use to determine beyond doubt where this all took place. Dalley (2009: 4–5) discussed the question of the provenance of the archive, and whether the town was the Sealand I capital; she reviewed various hypotheses and concluded that it was most likely in the vicinity of Nippur,[29] an opinion shared by George (2013: 131). But very much against a location in the Nippur area is the fact that typical Nippurite names with the theophoric elements Enlil or Ninurta are barely represented in the archive: there is only one name with Ninurta, and one (perhaps two) with Enlil. By contrast, Enlil and Ninurta were extremely prevalent in Nippurite personal names both in the Old Bab-

---

27 The pottery unearthed so far at Tell Khaiber is considered generally Old Babylonian in style, without some characteristics of the earlier ware, and a few "unique forms" are attested (Campbell, et al. 2017). But beyond observing that the assemblage seems consistent with a wider tradition following the late Old Babylonian period—with some specificities –, the lack of suitable comparanda from similar settings and well-established chronological sequences precludes further classification of the Sealand I ceramics of Tell Khaiber (Daniel Calderbank, personal communication); see also Section 1.2.2. Excavations at Tell Sakhariya may have yielded ceramics from that period (Zimansky and Stone 2016); it has not been published yet.

28 One may add to the indirect indicators of the importance of the south-western region in the Sealand kingdom the use of the word *sūtu* in the administration of animals; it seems to echo a practice which was apparently restricted to the territory of the early Old Babylonian Larsean kingdom (see Chapter 5 and Boivin 2016c).

29 Nippur was in fact the suspected origin of a number of tablets retrieved illicitly in the last decade of the twentieth century. Gibson (2012: 118; 2016: 128) was able to ascertain that Nippur itself could not be the origin of the tablets, but they may have come from nearby mounds.

ylonian and the Middle Babylonian periods (Stamm 1968: 68–69; Oelsner 1976: 111–12; 114; Hölscher 1996: 265 ff.). Evidence published more recently suggests that this strong preference for Ninurta and Enlil names was also prevalent in the neighboring area of Nippur, at Dūr-Abī-ešuḫ[30] in the late Old Babylonian period (van Lerberghe and Voet 2009: Index of personal names 243 ff.) and at Dūr-Enlilē in the Middle Babylonian period (van Soldt 2015: Index of personal names 533 ff.). Also, Ea is a popular theophoric element in the onomasticon of the Sealand I palatial archive; he figures in thirty-one out of the roughly 600 PNs represented in it (Dalley 2009: index of personal names); in comparison, the central Babylonian archive of Dūr-Abī-ešuḫ published in CUSAS 8 has only two PNs with Ea out of roughly 300 (van Lerberghe and Voet 2009: index of personal names).

Examination of the CUSAS 9 archive shows that a town of the name of Kār-Šamaš is prominent in it: it appears as a seat of judicial authority (CUSAS 9, 7) and as a palace town, possibly the very same which produced the archive, or one in close vicinity to it.[31] Indeed, records pertaining to beer production refer, apparently interchangeably, to "the palace" and "the palace of Kār-Šamaš" in the same period and with the same personnel involved, therefore, if the palaces were not the same, they were in immediate vicinity to one another. Between the 13.intercalary ii.N and the 12.iv.N, and perhaps also in the months iii and iv of year L,[32] a large majority of records related to beer production bear the mention of Kār-Šamaš. It stands either after the list of maltsters or brewers (*ša* KAR-^{d}UTU$^{(ki)}$, e.g., in CUSAS 9, 215; 218), or in the phrase É.GAL / *ša* KAR-^{d}UTU (e.g. CUSAS 9, 213; 216; 220). Prosopography shows that the maltsters and brewers involved are the same (see also Section 5.3.4.1). But this holds true only for receipts and delivery records for barley and malt; the beer deliveries dated to the same period do not make mention of Kār-Šamaš. For instance, Dannū-mūšu, "the brewer of Kār-Šamaš" received malt on the 30.iii.N (CUSAS 9, 214) and delivered beer "to the palace" on the same day (CUSAS 9, 268).[33]

There are two possible interpretations which can account for these facts. The most likely seems to be that Kār-Šamaš is the name of the town where the archive comes from, or a district in it, and the expressions "the palace" and "the palace

---

30 I refer here to the fortress located at the outflow of the canal; see Section 4.3.1.

31 Also, there are indications in the palatial archive that the sun god had a temple of some importance there, which would tally with the town's name being Kār-Šamaš (see Section 6.2.4).

32 This is less certain; CUSAS 9, 192 is slightly damaged so that the numeral of the year name may be "7" (year L) or "8" (year N). CUSAS 9, 190 appears to be dated to year L but it could very well be the only exception to the time span otherwise identified; therefore, an error by the scribe who could have forgotten one wedge can not be ruled out.

33 There are similar examples for other brewers, we can thus exclude a case of homonymy.

of Kār-Šamaš" are interchangeable, perhaps the result of a change in scribal personnel or recording habits. The fact that Kār-Šamaš was also a place of judgement is cogent with the interpretation that it was indeed of some importance. If Eurukug was the capital—this capital—at the time, Kār-Šamaš may have been indeed a district in it. The other possibility is that there were two palaces in close proximity, one in an unnamed palace town—this would be the palace that produced the archive –, and one at Kār-Šamaš, in its immediate vicinity.

There were a few Babylonian towns of the name of Kār-Šamaš in the Old Babylonian period, and the Kār-Šamaš of the Sealand I archive need not be one of them. However, there is one previously existing Kār-Šamaš that could very well be the same; it was part of the ancient kingdom of Larsa, probably between Larsa and Ur (Boivin 2015; Fiette 2017). A find spot of the Sealand I archive in this area would tally with the Larsean influence on the Sealand I panthea (see Section 6.5.2), but also with new evidence from Tell Khaiber.

Indeed, there might be prosopographical connections between the Sealand I texts unearthed at Tell Khaiber, between Ur and Larsa, and the CUSAS 9 archive since a number of craftsmen appearing in the palatial list of personnel CUSAS 9, 381 may be attested also at Tell Khaiber. The leather-worker (AŠGAB) Bēlī-iddina appears in CUSAS 9, 381: 21 as well as in TK1 3064.57: 11 and TK1 3064.83: 10; another leather-worker whose name is fragmentary, may be attested in both archives, as r[i? x x]-*ši-im*-DINGIR in CUSAS 9, 381: 31 and as [...]-*im*-DINGIR in TK1 3064.57: 13, in the latter case not identified by the profession but following closely on the above mentioned leather-worker. The carpenter (NAGAR) Aḫī-illika appears in CUSAS 9, 381: rev. 27′ and in several texts from Tell Khaiber, e.g. TK1 1096.48: 21′ and TK1 1096.47: rev. 24; another carpenter, Uṣi-ana-nūr-Adad, may be attested in both locations since he appears in CUSAS 9, 381: rev. 20′ and perhaps in TK1 3064.57: 17.[34] Also, yet another carpenter known from the palatial archive (e.g., CUSAS 9, 426: 10) bears the rare name Ēgi-ana-mēšū; this name occurs also at Tell Khaiber (TK1 3064.33: obv. 6; 3064.136: obv. 4; and probably 1124.01: obv. 4). Moreover, two individuals identified as *iššiakkū* appear in both corpora: Habbil-ilu in CUSAS 9, 442: 14 and in a number of Tell Khaiber texts, e.g. TK1 3064.33: rev. 37 and TK1 3064.107: 4; Ilī-iqīša in CUSAS 9, 415: 16 and in TK1 3064.123: rev. 23. Finally, one Arad-Šamaš called a shepherd (SIPA) in TK1 3080.04: 10 and TK1 3064.51: 17 may be the same who delivers sheep in CUSAS 9, 18; 21 and 22.

34 The name is fragmentary and has been transliterated [...]-*nu*-NI-PA?-^{d}IŠKUR. There are chances that NI-PA should be read in fact *úr*.

In addition to these possible connections,[35] one document from Tell Khaiber (TK1 1114.45) mentions that a *ḫazannu* brings back (lines 5–6) "that of the Sibitti, from the city" (*ša* ᵈIMIN.BI *i-na a-li*). A cult of the Sibitti, sponsored by the palace, is attested in the palatial archive, a rare occurrence in that period (see Section 6.4.9 for more detail). This reinforces the overall impression of geographical proximity between Tell Khaiber, and hence Ur and Larsa, and the palace town where the CUSAS 9 archive was found: the "city" referred to in letter TK1 1114.45 could indeed be that palace town, and thus the palace mentioned in the Tell Khaiber texts (e. g., TK1 3064.76; 3064.107) the one that produced the archive published in CUSAS 9. Campbell, et al. (2017) also identified signs that Tell Khaiber acted as a small administration center interacting with "the palace," e. g. sending agricultural goods there. They suggest Ur, Larsa, or Tell Dehaila[36] as potential locations for this palace town.

3.2 The chronological conundrum

Positioning the Sealand I dynasty in time is also fraught with difficulties. A number of sources make it possible to anchor its chronology with that of other Babylonian dynasties, however never with absolute certainty. The greater number of attested synchronisms, and the most precise ones, are with the first dynasty of Babylon, but a margin of error always remains—even if only one of very few years in one case. The latter part of the Sealand I dynasty was contemporary with the obscure early Kassite rulers, with whom the only known synchronism attests at the same time of the demise of the Sealand kingdom. Also, the local dynasts at Tell Muḫammad must have been concurrent with Sealand I rulers.

The following synoptic table gives a general overview of the relative chronology of the Sealand I dynasty and other contemporary Babylonian dynasties. Sources and detailed synchronisms are discussed hereafter.

---

35 There are many more common names between both corpora, but without additional corroboration like the name of the father or the profession, those were not considered reliable evidence. However, it should be noted that, as in the case of the CUSAS 9 archive, the theophoric elements Ninurta or Enlil are not frequent in Tell Khaiber personal names; moreover, the hypocoristic suffix *-ya'u* is attested in both corpora, whereas it is not attested, for instance, in late Old Babylonian Dūr-Abī-ešuḫ(canal) (van Lerberghe and Voet 2009: Index of personal names 243 ff.); for the CUSAS 9 archive, see Zadok 2014: 229–32; for the Tell Khaiber texts, see e.g. TK1 1114.04: 5 and TK1 3064.53: l.e. ii 5. (For a divergent interpretation of *-ya'u*, see most recently Keetman 2017).

36 They refer to it as site EP-34 in Wright (1981: 330).

Table 5: Overview of the chronologies of the Sealand I and neighboring dynasties[37]

Tell Muḫammad	Babylon I	Sealand I	Kassite
	Samsu-iluna	Ilī-ma-ilu	
	Abī-ešuḫ		
		Itti-ili-nībī	
		Dam(i)q-ilišu	
	Ammī-ditāna		
	Ammī-ṣaduqa	Iškibal	
		Šušši	
	Samsu-ditāna	Gulkišar	
		DIŠ+U-EN?	
Ḫurbaḫ(?)			
		Pešgaldarameš	
Šipta-ulzi			
		Ayadaragalama	:
		Akurduana	Agum II
		Melamkura	Burna-buriaš
		Ea-gāmil	Kaštiliaš III
			Ulam-buriaš
			Agum III

3.2.1 Problems with BKL A and synchronisms with Babylon I

The BKL A, because it records reign lengths, appears as an obvious source for the chronology of the Sealand I dynasty. It has proved quite reliable for later periods, but whether this can be extrapolated to the Sealand I section has remained a moot point. The surface of the tablet is in a bad state of preservation, which has gradually worsened since the first edition (Grayson 1980–83: 90); some of the reign lengths are thus difficult to read and various collations have been of limited help. Table 6 shows the readings that have been suggested (Grayson 1980–83: 91; Brinkman 1993–97: 7).[38]

37 I do not attempt to establish a synchronism with the kingdom of Hana since we have no clear evidence at present. In her recent presentation at the 62nd RAI (2016), Podany, basing herself on textual sources, including year names of the Late Old Babylonian king Kaštiliašu of Terqa, showed that the latter resided at Terqa and was apparently exclusively concerned with local affairs; therefore, she rejected her previous opinion that he was identical with a king of Babylon, Kaštiliašu I (Podany 2002: 51). On this, see also van Koppen 2017: 54.

38 Also, in his reconstruction of lost passages of DynKL, Glassner (2004: text 3, col.iv, lines 14′ ff.) suggests reign lengths that must be mainly based on his readings of the BKL A; I include these values in the comments column.

Table 6: Reign lengths of Sealand I kings in BKL A

	Grayson	Brinkman	Comments
1. Ilī-ma-ilu	[x] + ⸢1⸣ (?)	⸢x+1?⸣	There appears to be only the sign DIŠ on the tablet. Poebel (1947:121) reads 60, considering that the scribe added the reign lengths of Samsu-iluna and Abī-ešuḫ. Glassner reads 60(?) in his reconstruction of the corresponding passage in DynKL.
2. Itti-ili-nībī	x	⸢40(+10) +5⸣	Grayson (1980–83: 93 n.I 5) considers that the number is 45, 46, 55, or 56; Glassner reads 56(?).
3. Dam(i)q-ilišu	26(?)	⸢10(+)+6?⸣	Glassner reads 36(?).
4. Iškibal	15	⸢15⸣	
5. Šuš(š)i	24	⸢24⸣	
6. Gulkišar	55	55	
7? DIŠ+U-EN?			This king does not appear in BKL A; he is attested only in SynKL.
8. Pešgaldar-ameš	50	50	
9. Ayadaraga-lama	28	28	
10. Akurduana	26	26	
11. Melam-kura	7	7	
12. Ea-gāmil	9	⸢9⸣	

New evidence can now be adduced from the Sealand I archive to put BKL A to the test; in addition, a detailed examination of the attested synchronisms between the later kings of the first dynasty of Babylon and their early Sealand I counterparts yields milestones that can be used as criteria in determining the reliability of the reign lengths in BKL A.

3.2.1.1 The problem with the reign length of Pešgaldarameš

The archive published in CUSAS 9, the first to emerge from the Sealand I dynasty, yields an important argument against the trustworthiness of the reign lengths attributed to Sealand I kings in BKL A. It offers very strong indications that the reign of Pešgaldarameš was of 29 (or only a few more) years, a much shorter rule than the 50 years of BKL A. The few texts dated to Pešgaldarameš all use the year count system and date to his years 27 and 29: mu peš.gal.dàra.meš lugal.e ki.[27 or 29](.kam).[39] We know that these years almost immediately preceded the first years of his successor Ayadaragalama because Nanna-mansum, the GÌR official for a delivery of sheep in text CUSAS 9, 16 dated to Pe 29, had the same function in texts dated to two different years in the reign of Ayadaragalama (CUSAS 9, 18; 21; 22). Also, several individuals listed in ledger CUSAS 9, 407 dated to Pe 29, including individuals with rarer names, occur in documents dated to the following king, in particular in CUSAS 9, 413 in which the concentration of names identical to those of CUSAS 9, 407 is quite high (see also Dalley 2009: 10 on the same topic). Dalley (2009: 11) interpreted this immediate continuity between Pe 29 and Aa 1 with the assumption that Pešgaldarameš used an era-type reckoning of years referring to an event that occurred during his reign. The system which she surmises for Pešgaldarameš would be similar to the one attested for Rīm-Sîn I in the second half of his reign, when his year names stated the time elapsed since his conquest of Isin. She assumes therefore that an event, unknown to us but "of maximum importance," took place in the twenty-third (*sic* for twenty-first) year of Pešgaldarameš's reign; this would equate his twenty-ninth year as recorded in the archive with a purported year Pe 50*, and thus match the reign length of fifty years attributed to him in BKL A.

However, the year count system used by Sealand I kings was probably not referring to an event, but rather to the reign length of a given king (in other words to the event of his accession). Indeed, the documents found at Qalʿat al-Bahrein, which we know was under the control of the last Sealand I king because one tablet bearing his date formula was among them, all use formulae either of the type ki + [numeral] or of the type [numeral] + kam, with the exception of only two year names apparently referring to a new year.[40] It appears, therefore, that a system of year count without reference to a specific event was well established in the later days of the Sealand kingdom, and we have no reason to assume that it was not already the case a few generations earlier since several of the texts published in CUSAS 9 use exactly the same formulae without referring to an event: ki +[numeral] and [numeral] + kam, in addition to ki + [numeral] + kam.

The most likely explanation that reconciles the distribution of year names and the prosopographical evidence in the CUSAS 9 archive is that Pešgaldarameš

39 One year name of Pešgaldarameš of the same type is attested outside the administrative archive, in a divinatory text (CUSAS 18, 32); it reads mu RN lugal.e ki.24(25?).kam. See also Appendix 2.

40 mu ne(.ne) (Cavigneaux and André-Salvini forthcoming: texts QA01.5 and QA 94.421).

reigned twenty-nine years, or if longer certainly not by many years. At any rate, the reign length of fifty years given in BKL A is grossly inflated, a view shared by van Koppen (2010: 456–57).

3.2.1.2 Synchronisms with Babylon I and more problems with BKL A

Other sources give us precious information on the relative chronology of the Sealand I and the Babylon I dynasties. The following events and sources yield synchronisms:

The Ilī-ma-ilu texts at Nippur. At Nippur five legal texts were found that use Ilī-ma-ilu's date formulae: three appear to be of his first year, unless it is an abbreviated formula (mu *ì-lí-ma*-DINGIR lugal.e); the others seem to mark the following year: (mu gibil/ús.sa mu *ì-lí-ma*-DINGIR lugal.e). These texts cover a period of slightly over fourteen months from 16.vii.Ilī 1 to 24.ix.Ilī 2[41] and were found in fairly unspecific Old Babylonian context. The synchronism with the first dynasty of Babylon corresponds to the moment when Nippurite scribes went on from dating documents with Samsu-iluna's year formulae to using Ilī-ma-ilu's, reflecting the change in rulership over the city.

The damming of the Tigris. We know from Abī-ešuḫ's year name o (and from the *tamītu*-text Lambert 2007: 3c and d) that he dammed the Tigris, and chronicle *ABC* 20B (rev. 8–10) claims that this happened at the time of Ilī-ma-ilu.

The destruction of the wall of Udannu. Ammī-ditāna's thirty-seventh year name informs us that he destroyed a city wall which had been built by (Sealand I king) Dam(i)q-ilišu, giving us a *terminus ante quem* for the accession of the latter.

The epic of Gulkišar. The royal epic HS 1885+ recounts that Sealand I king Gulkišar went to war against the last king of the first dynasty of Babylon, Samsu-ditāna, presenting them as contemporaries (Zomer 2016; forthcoming).

The evidence is discussed at length and compared with the chronology of BKL A in Appendix 1; the main results are summarized here. (1) Examination of the documentary sequence at Nippur shows that the first year of Ilī-ma-ilu probably corresponds to Si 29[42] or a little later; however, should the reckoning of regnal years in BKL A recognize previous years of rulership of Ilī-ma-ilu outside Nippur, his accession year in this reckoning could be somewhat earlier. (2) The damming

41 The earliest text is SAOC 44 12=UM 55–21–239, the latest PBS 8/1 89. The others date respectively to: 19.ix.Ilī 1 for TMH 10 54a and b; 18.x.Ilī 1 for ARN 123=Ni 9271; and 26.viii. Ilī 2 for BE 6/2 68.

42 See Appendix 1 for the possibility that Si 30 texts are extant at Nippur.

of the Tigris almost certainly occurred in Abī-ešuḫ's middle years, in all likelihood Ae 19–23, or perhaps Ae 13–18 (less probable but also possible), which in turns means that Ilī-ma-ilu reigned at least until Ae 13. (3) In order for Dam(i)q-ilišu to have built the wall destroyed by Ammī-ditāna, he must have acceded to the throne at the very latest in Ad 36, and almost certainly earlier. (4) If we can trust the epic which presents Gulkišar and Samsu-ditāna as protagonists, they must have had at least one coeval year of reign.

Using these few synchronisms,[43] one can put the Sealand I chronology as purported in BKL A against the gauge of the fairly well established chronology of the Babylon I, Amorite dynasty. The result is that the Sealand I reign lengths of the king list are almost certainly incorrect. They can only be accurate if the following, necessary conditions are met: (1) the compilers of BKL A had access to material documenting that Ilī-ma-ilu reigned somewhere else before his thrust into central Babylonian territory and they accepted this information as relevant for their compilation;[44] (2) this in turn makes it necessary to posit that the scribes at Nippur, shortly after its conquest by the Sealand I king, used shortened or alternative local forms for the year names of Ilī-ma-ilu; (3) the damming of the Tigris took place earlier in Abī-ešuḫ's reign than what is considered most likely by Goetze and Horsnell on the basis of the distribution of year names in two archives, that is before Ae 19 (summarized in Horsnell 1999: vol.I 71–76); (4) Ilī-ma-ilu died (almost) immediately after the damming of the Tigris by Abī-ešuḫ; (5) Dam(i)q-ilišu acceded to the throne late in Ammī-ditāna's reign, undertook immediately to construct or finish construction of the city wall of Udannu, which was as soon destroyed by Ammī-ditāna; (6) Gulkišar became king at the very end of Samsu-ditāna's reign and set out immediately to campaign against him; (7) the reign lengths of Ammī-ṣaduqa and of Samsu-ditāna cannot be shorter than what is indicated in BKL B; (8) the correct reading for all damaged Sealand I reign lengths in BKL A must be—without exception—the lowest possible one, which also implies that the compiler made a mistake in computing the total duration of the dynasty (see Section 3.2.1.3).

In other words, mathematically the reign lengths recorded for the first six kings in BKL A could be correct, but historically the balance of probability is very strongly against it. The numbers are almost certainly too high.

---

43 See Appendix 1 for detailed computations.

44 This in itself is not unlikely, especially if we consider the possibility that the BKL A compiler used a Sealand king list as source material (see Section 2.3).

3.2.1.3 Another problem with BKL A and final remarks

The total number of years inscribed at the end of the Sealand I section in BKL A, 368 years, is curious. It appears to be even higher than the sum of the reign lengths listed above it, which have already been shown to be (almost certainly) too high.[45] Brinkman (1976: 429) explained this discrepancy by the fact that the seventh king DIŠ+U-EN, who appears in SynKL, was omitted in BKL A, thus leaving in the latter document a number of years unaccounted for. In order to match the total of 368 years, he attributed 12 or 22 years to him, which means that he assumed at the time a reading based on the highest possible value for Ilī-ma-ilu and Itti-ili-nībī, respectively 60 and 56 years;[46] such values have been shown above to be untenable with the known synchronisms between the Sealand I and Babylon I chronologies.[47] This comes in addition to the fact that the reign length of 50 years for Pešgaldarameš, considered correct in Brinkman's reckoning, was also shown in Section 3.2.1.1 to be too high by far.

Evidence shows thus that there is no or very little value in the reign lengths attributed to the Sealand I kings in BKL A. This could tally with the hypothesis that the source used by the compiler was damaged (see Section 2.3): it would explain that the names are curiously truncated and that the reign lengths apparently rather fancifully estimated.[48] At any rate, for chronological purposes, BKL A is of no use whatsoever in that period.

---

45 The reign lengths and the total in BKL A are both higher than what was considered likely by Gasche, et al. (1998: 67; 91; appendix) in their low chronology.

46 Following collation of the document in 1987, he revised his readings of reign lengths (Brinkman 1993–97: 7). The values indicated in Table 6 are based on his revised readings.

47 Of course, independently of the historical accuracy, there could be some theoretical consistency in the numbers used by the scribes. For instance, using Poebel's (1947: 110 ff.) work on BKL B's reign lengths, one could imagine that also the compiler of BKL A used mean values or approximations resulting in "round numbers" (finishing in 5 or 0) for reign lengths which were not available to him. This could have applied to the reign lengths of Itti-ili-nībī (probably 45 or 55), Iškibal (15), Gulkišar (55), Pešgaldarameš (50), perhaps also to Ilī-ma-ilu if we assume that the sign DIŠ stands for 60 and was not preceded by any other sign. However, for this theory to have some substance, one would expect the total number of years associated with the dynasty to match the sum of individual reign lengths listed, since the scribe, if venturing into mathematical speculation, would probably have made sure that his construct was coherent. Using various combinations of readings for the damaged entries does not yield any obvious solution for the numbers to match. It looks rather as if the scribe had used different sources or estimation methods for the individual reign lengths and the total.

48 See also Section 2.3 and Brinkman (1976: 427).

3.2.2 Other (possible) synchronisms

3.2.2.1 At the time of the fall of Babylon

The latest synchronism available between the Sealand I and Babylon I dynasties is a literary one: the conflict between Gulkišar and Samsu-ditāna recounted in HS 1885+. The text does not appear to contain any indication that the Sealand kingdom was directly involved in the ultimate defeat of Samsu-ditāna, we can therefore not establish that Gulkišar was still on the throne when Babylon fell, but if he himself wasn't, then his successor must have been.

This is also the time when it might be possible to establish a first synchronism with a Kassite ruler, although this exercise proves difficult. The role played by the Kassites in the fall of Babylon is unclear. The Gandaš inscription, known from a later copy (BM 77438) which may have been a forgery, could refer to conquering Babylon: the end of line 4, after a mention of the Ekur of Enlil, contains a passage that has been read by some *i-na ka-šad bà-bà-lam*, and by others *i-na ka-mat bà-bà-lam* (Stein 2000: text Kb 1; 149 incl. n.84 for a brief summary of the problem).[49] If the inscription is genuine and if a conquest of Babylon is implied, Gandaš could have been involved in the attacks against Samsu-ditāna, which would thus secure a synchronism between him and either Gulkišar or his successor. But the uncertainties surrounding the source and the reading of the passage are important and such a synchronism can certainly not be considered established at present.[50] Another early Kassite candidate for an involvement in the fall of Babylon, and therefore for a synchronism with Gulkišar or his successor, is Agum-kakrime. The case was made by van Koppen (2010: 460–61) who considered likely that the Kassite king seized the throne of Babylon either directly from Samsu-ditāna and from other contenders shortly thereafter.[51] More recently, he (2017: 65–70) revisited the question and proposed to identify Agum-kakrime with one Agum, a military leader of Samḫarû extraction under Samsu-ditāna; he posits that he quietly took over after the demise of the Amorite dynasty.

Both the case for the involvement of Gandaš and that of Agum-kakrime in the fall of Babylon need to be treated with prudence. They are both (partly)

---

49 See also a brief discussion by Brinkman (1976: 127); George (1993: 117 no.679) opts for the reading *ka-mat*, which results in saying that a temple called the Ekur of Enlil was located outside Babylon.

50 Even if the source is genuine and the reading is indeed *ka-šad*, the historical interpretation remains problematic (we could be dealing with an episode of infighting amongst the powers that had ousted Samsu-ditāna). But the inscription gives Gandaš the title "king of Sumer and Akkad," which suggests control over southern Babylonia; this appears improbable at the time.

51 See also Paulus 2014b: 67.

based on later inscriptions, and the textual evidence requires a good dose of interpretation. At present, the case for Agum certainly seems promising, but the history of these early Kassite rulers remains obscure and, thus, their chronological relationship with the Sealand I dynasty highly uncertain.

3.2.2.2 After the fall of Babylon

Also for the period following the fall of Babylon the evidential situation is rather dire, notwithstanding the presence of Sealand I archival texts. These documents offer limited help in matters of chronology: as seen above, we learn from them that Pešgaldarameš reigned at least twenty-nine years and certainly not many more, also that Ayadaragalama reigned at least eight years[52]—but there is no reason to assume that he did not reign longer—and finally that Ea-gāmil reigned at least four years. The documents do not yield any useful synchronisms:[53] the Elamite ruler who despatched an envoy to the Sealand I court is not named and the Kassite ruler or leader Buragindar who also sent one is otherwise unattested (CUSAS 9, 40; BC 435; both cases are discussed in Section 4.4).

King lists do inform us that Ayadaragalama was followed by two other kings before the last ruler of the dynasty Ea-gāmil ascended the throne, but we do not know how long they ruled since, as it was shown above, the reign lengths of BKL A cannot be trusted.

The texts from Tell Muḫammad

The excavations at Tell Muḫammad in the 1970s and 1980s have also yielded material relevant for the transition between the late Old Babylonian and the early Kassite periods, but neither the pottery nor the dating formulae used in the administrative texts unearthed in levels III and II are easy to interpret. The texts have not all been published yet, but a number of them were edited in an MA thesis (al-Ubaid 1983). Among these, a handful of texts are from level III; they fea-

52 The minimum reign lengths of Pešgaldarameš and Ayadaragalama are based on date formulae attested in the archive published in CUSAS 9; see Appendix 2.

53 Dalley (2009: 31 notes) briefly discusses an unpublished letter (BC 423) in which one Burra-x-riaš appears alongside two other individuals, one of whom may be attested in the CUSAS 9 archive. Concerning Burra-x-riaš, she notes that "an identification with a king of Babylon cannot be excluded." Also van Koppen (2017: 76 n.146) refers to it briefly. Pending the publication of the text or at least of more detail on its contents, there is no basis to assume that this was a (future) Kassite king, reigning at Babylon or not. Therefore, this information is at present of no help for the relative chronology of the Sealand I dynasty.

ture date formulae based on events in which the name of various individuals appear, one of whom is called a king, Ḫurbaḫ(?).[54] The texts from level II are more numerous and also more varied in the dating system(s) they use: a few bear year names based on events like the older texts from level III; most texts feature two date formulae, one of the usual type and one of the era type (MU.[numeral].KÁM (.MA) *ša* KÁ.DINGIR.RA^{ki} *uš-bu*); finally, a few bear only a year formula of the era type. In the event-based year names, one individual is identified as king, Šiptaulzi. As expounded by Gasche, et al. (1998: 84–87) the older dating system must reflect the local tradition, while the era year names represent a novel way of naming years; documents featuring both types of year names should be transitional. The historical implications of the contents, the formulary, and the sequence of these year names are of importance and the date of this site has been much debated.

Both levels III and II, in which texts were found, were considered Old Babylonian (Gasche, et al. 1998: 83 n.334), level III has also been dated to the Isin-Larsa period (Metab 1989–90: 129; 149).[55] But the dating is moot since the individuals named in the texts are not known elsewhere (except for the possible presence of two rulers in SynKL),[56] and the pottery sequence in the lower Diyala or in north-eastern Babylonia is not well established for that period.[57] Any attempt at dating the levels using pottery has to be based on comparison with ceramics from the Babylonian plain; this is the best means available at present and

---

54 The reading is problematic. It is almost certain that the same individual appears in the date formulae of level III documents (IM 90602 and IM 90606), as well as of level II documents (IM 92725 and IM 92721); in the later documents, he appears as the father of an unnamed son. In particular the last sign seems to vary in shape, according to al-Ubaid's hand copies (1983: 121 ff.) She read them as two different names (1983: 114; 118–19), followed by Gasche, et al. (1998: 86). Also Sassmannshausen (2004a: 302–04) read the names as two different ones, namely *ḫu-ur-ba-aḫ* and *ḫu-ur-ba-tum*. They were read as one and the same by van Koppen (2010: 458 n.12), namely *ḫu-ur-ba-aḫ*. Boese (2008: 204), followed by Paulus (2014b: 67), read the name of the king in the level III texts as *ḫu-ur-ba-zum*.

55 Hamza (2011: 414) mentioned that the artefacts from level III display a stylistic affinity to various periods from the late third millennium until the time of Hammurapi; he noted, in agreement with Gasche, et al. (1998), that some pottery from level II could have lasted from the end of the Old Babylonian into the early Kassite period. He adds that the transition and relationship between level II and level I, the latter being clearly Kassite, are not well understood (Hamza 2011: 415–16).

56 Boese 2008: 205; the matter is discussed at the end of the present section.

57 In the upper Diyala the sequence at Tell Yelkhi is fairly well established but it is probably of no relevance for Tell Muḥammad since most of the pottery from this site is not typically Babylonian (Armstrong and Gasche 2014: 11–12).

several parallels were established.[58] Unfortunately, the Tell Muḥammad pottery has not been published with systematic reference to the level in which it was found.[59] All in all, the transition from level III to level II—both of uncertain date—and that from level II to level I—the latter of Kassite date—remain nebulous.[60]

This leaves the interpretation of the enigmatic date formulae of the type MU.[numeral].KÁM(.MA) *ša* KÁ.DINGIR.RA[ki] *uš-bu* without a clear temporal or political context. Gasche, et al. (1998: 85) looked at instances of the combination "toponym + *wašābu*" in omen compendia and found that the expression was used to express the resettling of a place following its abandonment or destruction. That the date formula referred to the resettlement of Babylon, following the raid that probably sealed the fate of the Babylon I dynasty, is certainly a plausible interpretation to which, following Gasche, et al., a number of scholars have adhered (Sassmannshausen 2004a: 302ff. and 2004b: 64; Boese 2008: 202–03; Paulus 2014b: 67).[61] Gasche, et al. (1998: 89) consider that the use of such date formulae reflects the allegiance to a new king, unnamed in the Tell Muḥammad texts but whom they assume to be Agum-kakrime (= Agum III in their opinion), reigning at Babylon over a re-unified Babylonia. This dating of the Tell Muḥammad texts is considered too late by Sassmannshausen (2004b: 64), and also by Boese (2008: 202–03); the latter assumes that Ḫurbaḫ and Šipta-ulzi—the kings named in date formulae that are not of the era type—were in fact kings reigning at Babylon, which had been quickly resettled after the raid. Van Koppen's (2010: 460) interpretation differs completely: he considers that the ambiguous wording of the era-type date formula precludes any historical interpretation from it, arguing that translation is only possible when informed by a presupposed historical context. His analysis led him to conclude that the Tell Muḥam-

---

58 Recently, Armstrong and Gasche (2014: *passim*) established parallels between some of the Tell Muḥammad pottery published in Metab (1989–90) as well as in Metab and Hamza (2003–04) and second millennium Babylonian pottery types. These references are found in the sub-section "Comparanda" of each relevant pottery group. A correlation with the sequence of Tell ed-Der in the northern alluvial plain remains difficult as long as the Tell Muḥammad pottery is not published with full reference to the stratigraphy.

59 But even if it had been the main problem remains: using pottery sequences from the Babylonian plain is probably inadequate for any precise assessment of the Tell Muḥammad material. Some of the ceramic found does correspond to Kassite period pottery in the Babylonian lowland, and perhaps in the Diyala (in particular groups 205 A_2 and 215 A_2 in Armstrong and Gasche 2014).

60 See also Hamza 2011: 415–16.

61 Charpin (2004: 383) seems to consider this a likely scenario.

mad texts date to the late Old Babylonian period,[62] both kings named in their date formulae being contemporary with Samsu-ditāna. He added that Šipta-ulzi, an ally of Babylon, was probably defeated by Agum-kakrime (= Agum II) while Samsu-ditāna was still in power; although he revised his interpretation on this last point recently (van Koppen 2017: 61), it had no consequences on his proposed dating of the Tell Muḫammad texts. The era-type year names are interpreted by him as a reference to an unspecified subject, probably a Kassite prince or garrison taking up residence at Babylon because the privilege of guarding the city had been granted to them (van Koppen 2010: 461–62); he puts the beginning of this era late in the reign of Ammī-ditāna (Van Koppen 2017: 62). This translation of the date formula with the suppressed subject and the corresponding interpretation appear somewhat forced.[63]

The translation proposed by Gasche, et al., which is more direct and is based on parallels in the divinatory literature, seems more plausible. Such a reading, which refers to the resettlement of Babylon, makes it thus very likely that the texts from level II were roughly contemporary with the Sealand I archive published in CUSAS 9, therefore Šipti-ulzi's reign at Tell Muḫammad may have been coeval with that of Pešgaldarameš or Ayadaragalama. This remains uncertain because we know neither whether and how long Gulkišar reigned after the fall of Babylon, whether there was an additional king between him and Pešgaldarameš, nor how long Babylon remained (partially) unoccupied (although this would probably have been a short time).[64]

It was also established convincingly that the two kings named in the Tell Muḫammad date formulae probably correspond to Kassite kings 7 and 8 in SynKL, whose readings are uncertain (Boese 2008: 205, followed by others, e.g., Paulus 2014b: 67; van Koppen 2017: 65). If these two kings are indeed the rulers attested in the Tell Muḫammad texts, their position within king lists would certainly be compatible with a post-Old Babylonian dating for them,[65] or at least for the

62 His interpretation was critically received by Paulus (2014b: 67 n.18). See also Gentili 2002: 211–12 who dates the texts even earlier within the Old Babylonian period and translates the era-type year dates as "when Babylon was established (in the region)." Another translation is offered by Dalley (2009: 8 n.70), who considers "inherently unlikely" that the resettlement of a city would be commemorated for many years; she translates "Year that (the king) stayed (in) Babylon." She does not specify to what king the formulae would refer and to what period they date.

63 See also Paulus (2014b: 67 n.18).

64 According to van Koppen (2017: 72–73), the city was not abandoned, and not long neglected.

65 But contra van Koppen 2010; 2017.

later one, since other sources suggest that king 11, perhaps even 10 were contemporary with the last Sealand I ruler Ea-gāmil.

3.2.2.3 At the time of the fall of the Sealand I dynasty

From the texts found at al-Qalʿat al-Bahrein we learn that one Agum (e.g., in year formula of QA 94.49), presumably Agum III, probably reigned shortly after the last Sealand I king, without more indications on the exact temporal relationship between them, neither from the archaeological context[66] nor from the prosopography. The other two Kassite rulers named in year formulae in this corpus are otherwise unknown: Kadašman-Saḫ and Urra-?-iaš (e.g. QA 94.44; 01.18).[67]

The chronicle *ABC* 20B informs us that Ulam-Bur(i)aš and Kaštiliašu (III) were contemporary with Ea-gāmil since the first episode of the conquest of the Sealand kingdom is said to have been accomplished by "Ulam-Buraš, brother of Kaštiliaš" (rev. 13), after Ea-gāmil had fled. If we accept this relation of events, we may assume that there was no significant interval between the departure of Ea-gāmil from his land and the Kassite conquest; it seems in fact more than probable that the events were linked.[68] The chronicle adds that "Agum, son of Kaštiliaš" (rev. 15), therefore nephew of Ulam-buriaš, also marched on the Sealand. This Agum (III) must be the one attested at al-Qalʿat al-Bahrein.[69] How much time elapsed between these campaigns is unclear but the family relationship between Ulam-buriaš and Agum III limits the interval, probably to about the length of one generation.

Ulam-buriaš is known from two inscriptions: one on a diorite mace head and one on an agate weight (both were (re-)edited in Stein 2000: 129–30, Ka 1 and 2), in which he identifies himself as Ula(m)-burariaš[70] and his father as "Burna-burariaš, the king." The mace head inscription also adds that the former is "king of the Sealand." The brother of Ulam-buriaš could be identified with the

66 The stratigraphy apparently suggests that the texts covered a short period but does not yield any more precise information (André-Salvini and Lombard 1997: 166; Cavigneaux and André-Salvini forthcoming).

67 Van Koppen (2017: 75) considers that both rulers were included in SynKL, as 13th and 14th kings, after Agum III.

68 The documents found at al-Qalʿat al-Bahrein suggest at least administrative continuity between the time of the document dated to Ea-gāmil and the documents dated to Agum and to other Kassite rulers or governors.

69 Note that André-Salvini and Lombard (1997: 168), followed by van Koppen (2017: 76), consider that Agum is the first Kassite ruler to have gained control over Dilmun.

70 The varying orthography of the element bu(ra)riaš is discussed in Balkan 1954: 104; the longer form is older. The matter is also briefly discussed in Brinkman 1976: 12 n.17.

Kaštiliašu of a newly published royal inscription concerning the digging of a canal; indeed, in this inscription the latter identifies himself and his ancestry as follows: "I am K⸢aš⸣tiliašu (...) / son of Burna-burariaš / grand-son of Agum (II)" (Abraham and Gabbay 2013: 184 obv. 1–3).

This gives us the following (approximative) relative chronology:

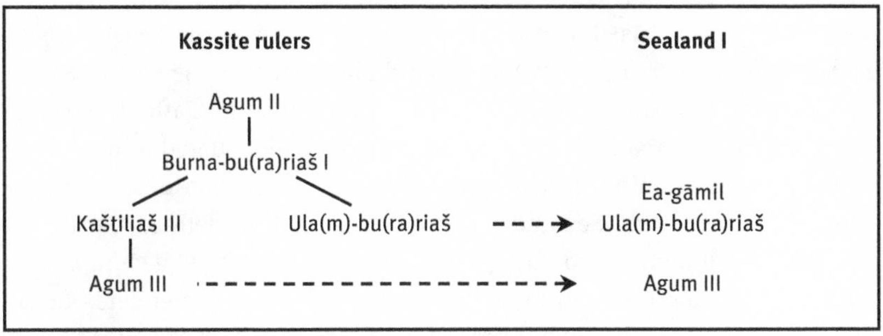

Figure 2: Kassite-Sealand I synchronism at the end of the Sealand I dynasty

This diagram is certainly no comprehensive reflection of the political landscape in Babylonia at the time. It merely indicates the synchronism between Ea-gāmil and the Kassite rulers of the family of Agum II (probably Agum-kakrime) involved in the conquest of the Sealand kingdom, as well as a chronology of the transition of power in Sealand I territory, from the Sealand I to Kassite rulers. The other rulers with Kassite names who are attested in the texts from al-Qal'at al-Bahrein would have to be inserted in this chronological scheme, at least locally, but we don't know where exactly.

Whether all the Kassite kings named in this diagram reigned at Babylon is uncertain; this section of SynKL, should it be taken as an indication of it or not, is badly damaged. Abraham and Gabbay (2013: 187–89) have summarized the main reconstructions[71] suggested by scholars in the last few decades; these reconstructions do not affect directly the synchronism expounded above, which is based on chronicle *ABC* 20B and on royal inscriptions.

71 In particular, for diverging opinions on the inclusion of Ulam-buriaš in SynKL, see Abraham and Gabbay 2013: 187–89 and van Koppen 2017: 75; see also Paulus 2014b: 68 n.28.

4 A political history of the Sealand kingdom

4.1 The southern Babylonian revolts: genesis of the Sealand kingdom?

Although the earliest positive evidence for a Sealand I king dates to the later part of Samsu-iluna's reign—as shown in the previous chapter –, the general historical backdrop of the emergence of the Sealand kingdom must be sought earlier, in the widespread rebellion against Babylon. A mere generation after the constitutive conquests of Hammurapi, texts gradually ceased to be dated to his successor Samsu-iluna, beginning in southern Babylonia, then soon also in central Babylonia. While the early Sealand I polity can indeed be defined partly as a complementary counterpart to the waning Amorite kingdom, geographically and politically, it may have had to vie for power with other contenders, Kassite and indigenous, at least for a time. Indeed, although only Rīm-Sîn (II) of Larsa[1] and Rīm-Anum of Uruk figure prominently in our records,[2] the rebellion of the years Si 8 – 9 apparently resulted in and was also fueled by the formation of a number of short-lived, more or less independent fiefs and kingdoms. That the secessionist movement was highly fragmented shows in the fact that both Samsu-iluna and Rīm-Anum enumerated several enemies in year names of that period. The Babylonian king alone identified in his date formulae between Si 9 and Si 13 —beside the generic Sumer and Akkad—the Kassites (met in combat at Kikalla), Ida-Maraṣ, Ešnunna, Emutbalum, Uruk, Ur, Larsa, Isin, Kisurra, and Sabûm as his opponents.[3] While later inscriptions of the Babylonian king may have reinter-

1 Larsa is the city in which texts temporarily ceased to be dated with Samsu-iluna's year formulae at the earliest date: in the last month of Si 7 (TCL 11, 215). Rīm-Sîn II was considered king of Larsa by Samsu-iluna (Frayne 1990: text E4.3.7.7 lines 93–97). However, he seems to have also claimed the title of king of Ur (in his year name a; see Stol 1976: 54) and been remembered as such in the chronographic tradition (*ABC* 20B: obv. 9). Towards the end of his short reign, Rīm-Sîn appears to have added another capital to his secessionist realm, or transferred it, since his third and last year name—year formula b—proclaims that he was raised to kingship by the Kešite mother goddess Ninmaḫ at Keš (Stol 1976: 54). See also Charpin 2004: 338–39 and Richardson 2010: 16 n.60.

2 Newly published correspondence of Iluni of Ešnunna shows that good relations with Babylon preceded or alternated with the conflict evidenced in Samsu-iluna's year names that are discussed forthwith, but the chronology of events remains unclear (Guichard 2016: 27–29).

3 In his Kiš cylinder inscription, he puts the number of his foes, besides Rīm-Sîn II, at twenty-six (Frayne 1990: text E4.3.7.7, lines: 101–02). It is unclear to what period exactly the inscription refers; Charpin (2004: 341) suggested that a very high fragmentation of rebellious leadership may have immediately followed Rīm-Sîn II's death in Samsu-iluna's ninth year.

https://doi.org/10.1515/9781501507823-005

preted the events,[4] the year names can probably be considered fairly trustworthy at least in the identification of opponents. The list of insurgents makes plain that the Babylonian king was facing troubles in southern and central Babylonia, as well as in the Diyala; even northern Babylonia was probably the stage of some turmoil early on, although in that case the troublemakers were not the local population but the newly arrived Kassites.[5] Despite Samsu-iluna's efforts to counter the secessionist movement—his ephemeral success is evidenced by a brief return to his year formulae in a number of cities –,[6] Babylon's hope of reestablishing its rule in the southernmost region must have dwindled rapidly.

The third year name of Rīm-Anum, which corresponds to Samsu-iluna's ninth or tenth year,[7] makes plain that Babylon played by then no major political role in southern Babylonia anymore:[8]

> The year in which King Rim-Anum, the (forces of) the land of Emutbalum, the armies of Eshnunna, Isin and Kazallu, as if all together (with him), having presented themselves at Uruk for war, inflicted a defeat upon their troops. Since time immemorial Uruk had never experienced (such) a dust storm (raised by a foreign army), but after the dust storm settled, he slaughtered (all of them) and by his power ejected (them all) from the homeland. (Michalowski and Beckman 2012: 427)

---

4 For instance, the events could have been presented within the literary trope of Naram-Sîn's Great Rebellion (Glassner 1986: 58–59).

5 Kikalla was probably located near Kiš (Pientka 1998: 368). On this, see most recently van Koppen 2017: 53. Kassite groups were hostile also to Rīm-Sîn II, as per the second clause of his year name b, his second, probably promulgated in Si 9 (Stol 1976: 48; Seri 2013: 35 f.): "the enemy, the evil Kassites from the barbarous country, who could not be driven back to the mountains" (Stol 1976: 54).

6 Texts dated with Samsu-iluna's date formulae resume at Larsa at the very beginning of Si 10 (YOS 12, 314), followed later in the same year by other cities, for instance Ur (UET 5, 243), Nippur (OECT 8, 11), and Lagaš (TCL 1, 129). See also Charpin 2004: 342.

7 The events recalled in Rīm-Anum's third year name would have occurred in his second. To the relative chronology between Samsu-iluna and the rebel king: Rositani, followed by Charpin, puts the proclamation of Rīm-Anum's first year name as coeval with Si 8 (Rositani 2003: 16; Charpin 2014: 129); in fact, Charpin's reconstruction differs slightly from Rositani's since he suggests that the first two year names of Rīm-Anum were versions of the same one used for a period of about seventeen months, but the resulting chronology is the same. In contrast, Seri (2013: 35) considered that there was a delay between the revolt at Uruk and Rīm-Anum's assuming kingship, she puts the latter first year's proclamation in Si 9. This would make the situation described in Rīm-Anum's third year name either coeval with Samsu-iluna's ninth or tenth regnal year.

8 Seri (2013: 36) suggests that Rīm-Anum may at the time have become for a brief time an ally of Babylon. If that is the case, the Babylonian troops were possibly not significantly involved in the conflict since this alliance found no mention in the year name, at least in the extant versions.

After that Babylon still fought over the south but its actions, as reflected in its year names,[9] appear to have been essentially war campaigns, probably leaving little opportunity for any serious attempt at stabilizing the area: three years of military campaigns from Si 11 until Si 13 were followed by Babylon's final disengagement from the southernmost region. That Babylon was then ineluctably losing ground during that period is perhaps reflected in its year names. Seri (2013: 33) aptly noted that the language of the twelfth and the fourteenth year names was kept vague, in contrast to the formulae of the preceding years: Samsu-iluna did not name his enemies anymore, he referred only to "assembled (foreign) countries," "the army of Sumer and Akkad,"[10] and "the rebellious enemy kings."[11] This suggests that the entire area had slipped from his control to the point where it had entered the realm of the unnamed, generic outside world. In fact, the textual record appears to stop altogether in southern Babylonia in that period: the last extant texts from several cities are dated between his tenth and twelfth years.[12] Indeed, by Samsu-iluna's twelfth regnal year (the events are recorded in his thirteenth year name), the front line[13] apparently moved towards central Babylonia, around Kisurra and Sabûm. The restoration of the city wall of Isin celebrated in his fifteenth year name confirms that the area had seen fierce battle and suggests that the Babylonians were probably establishing the retaken city as a stronghold of their new southern border area. That border was not long stable since documents dated with the date formulae

9 The relevant year names are: Si 12 "The year: Samsu-iluna, the king, against whom the foreign countries had again revolted, defeated the army of Sumer and Akkad by the supreme power which Marduk gave him;" Si 13 "The year: Samsu-iluna, the king, at the command of Enlil (and with the pure weapon which Enlil gave <him>), brought (the region of) Kisurra and (the land of) Sabum into submission;" Si 14 "The year: Samsu-iluna, the king, by his great power slaughtered the rebellious enemy kings who had caused Akkad to revolt with their own weapons (...)" (Horsnell 1999: vol.II 197 ff.).

10 In the twelfth year name: kur gú-si-a and ugnim ki-en-gi ki-uri (Horsnell 1999: vol.II 197).

11 Fourteenth year name: lugal im-gi$_4$ gú-bar-ra (Horsnell 1999: vol.II 199).

12 To my knowledge the latest text dated to Samsu-iluna in southern Babylonia is from Ur and dates to 3.viii.Si 12 (UET 5, 868); this may change with the current excavations led by A. al-Hamdani, E. Stone, and P. Zimansky. The texts recovered will be published by D. Charpin. Note that Rochberg-Halton and Zimansky had tentatively identified Larsa as the provenance of a text dated to Si 29 (Rochberg-Halton and Zimansky 1979: text 15; the tentative location is indicated on p.129); Charpin noted on archibab.fr that it is impossible.

13 I am using this term in a loose sense since the nature of the rule exerted by the Babylonian state and by the rebellious leaders was probably not one of ubiquitous control in a continuous territory, which would have resulted in well defined front lines between the belligerents. On the patchy nature of Mesopotamian state control, see Richardson 2012: 17–18; 24–25.

of the Babylonian king ceased in the years Si 28–30 at Isin, Lagaba, and Nippur[14] (Charpin 2004: 360).

What happened in southern Babylonia after the definitive disengagement of the kings of the first dynasty of Babylon and why major urban settlements then appear to have been abandoned is unclear. That the Sealand I state eventually thrived—or at least emerged—among the rubble left by the violent clashes between secessionist and Babylonian troops is evidenced by later archival texts. Although the modalities of this development remain uncertain, it is certainly a likely place and time to look for the first Sealand I ruler Ilī-ma-ilu; indeed, he must have successfully mustered numerous troops by the time he was able to take Nippur in Si 29 (or shortly after), notwithstanding the lack of solid evidence for his involvement alongside the other rebels in Si 8–10.[15] Dalley (2009: 1) argued for his presence in a very fragmentary document probably concerning land, perhaps from Larsa (Ash 1922–353 = OECT 15, 78). While "LUGAL A.AB.BA" indeed appears on line 18′, the rest of the passage is broken. The only visible sign preceding LUGAL could be NI; Dalley's suggestion that the passage referred to Ilī-ma-ilu, whose name she reconstructs as Ilum-ma-ili, is thus based on only one fragmentary sign and implies that a spelling was used in this text which is

14 For the regnal year of the last texts dated to Samsu-iluna at Nippur, see Appendix 1.

15 Jacobsen did not hesitate to establish Ilī 1 = Si 8 based on the fact that he saw in the southern and eastern rebellion the general context, and more specifically in the Kassite invasion the occasion, for the rise of the Sealand I king. The Nippur texts with a Ilī-ma-ilu year formula that were known at the time are dated to his second year; Jacobsen (1939: 195, in particular n.15) considered that this was coherent with the absence of Si 9 texts. Most recently, Seri counted him among insurgents whom Samsu-iluna would have included in his statement that he faced twenty-six rebel kings in the Kiš cylinder inscription (Frayne 1990: E4.3.7.7, line 101; Seri 2013: 239). This inclusion raises the question of the date and the chronology of the events related in this inscription, which probably commemorates the rebuilding of the city wall mentioned in the king's twenty-fourth year name. If Seri's sequence of events is correct and Ilī-ma-ilu was one of the twenty-six rebels, he would have been actively part of the rebellion and defeated by Babylon between the death of Rīm-Sîn II and that of Iluni; the moment of the latter event is unknown, estimates ranging from Si 10 (Charpin 1998: 33) and Si 20 or 23 (Charpin 2004: 340; Jacobsen 1940: 200). Identifying Ilī-ma-ilu with one of the twenty-six rebel kings would also imply that the Babylonian king did not kill all rebel leaders since we know that Ilī-ma-ilu survived him, but such a sweeping hyperbole would not be surprising in a royal inscription. It is at present impossible to decide whether Seri was right in seeing Ilī-ma-ilu as one of the rebel kings of Samsu-iluna's inscriptions; but the only basis for her assumption is the circumstance that Ilī-ma-ilu also fought against Babylon on Babylonian soil at some point during Samsu-iluna's reign. This is certainly no positive evidence that Ilī-ma-ilu was part of the early days of the southern rebellion.

otherwise not attested for the name of this king.[16] This interpretation must thus be regarded as unlikely.[17] In fact, the evidence appears even insufficient to conclude that a king of a political entity called A.AB.BA existed at the time. Another text, also presumably from Larsa and possibly dating to Rīm-Sîn II, mentions troops of A.AB.BA (OECT 15, 10). This may or may not refer to a distinct political entity. If it did, its significance must have been still very limited since it does not appear at all, either as foe or as friend, in the *bīt asīrī* texts from Uruk. The term probably rather designated a geographical area at the time.[18]

Another possibility for a trace of Ilī-ma-ilu in documents dating to the time of the rebellion could be in the distribution of flour to messengers that Rīm-Sîn II sent to Uruk, one of whom is one *ì-lí-ma* (Nisaba 4, I.25).[19] Since the (later) Sealand I king's name is also attested elsewhere in abbreviated form without the final DINGIR there is a remote possibility that this Ilī-ma was the future king, who would have started his career in the diplomatic service of Rīm-Sîn II. A Larsean origin of the founder of the dynasty would indeed be in agreement with signs of a Larsean influence that are discernible in the Sealand I archive.[20] It would also agree with the fact that Eurukug, possibly the capital of the kingdom (or origin of the dynasty) probably refers to Ur; indeed Rīm-Sîn II himself claimed the title of "King of Ur" in his year name a (Stol 1976: 54).[21] One could therefore imagine that a continuator of Rīm-Sîn II's short-lived kingdom was or came to be associated with Ur,[22] but this remains highly hypothetical.

---

16 In the attested year names at Nippur, as well as in king lists, in chronicle *ABC* 20B and in other chronicle fragments, the spelling either finishes on the sign AN or drops it entirely. See Tables 2 and 3. In addition, the contemporary evidence (Table 3) indicates that it is the first element of the name which bears the possessive marker -ī, therefore the reading must have been Ilī-ma-ilu, not Ilu(m)-ma-ilī.

17 In fact, one can not exclude that LUGAL was the last sign in a personal name instead of a title. Another possibility is that the name refers to the deity attested later as LUGAL-A.AB.BA but which may have its origin as LUGAL-AB.A attested in the Old Babylonian god list TCL 15, 10 (see also Krebernik 1987–90).

18 Both possible early references to A.AB.BA are discussed in Section 2.1.2.

19 The text is also discussed in Seri 2013: 73; it is dated to the second year of Rīm-Anum.

20 See Section 6.5.2.

21 Seal impressions from the seal of one Sîn-ibīšu "servant of Rīm-Sîn (II)" were also found at Ur (Frayne 1990: E4.2.15.2001). Rīm-Sîn II seems to have been associated with more than one seat of power but the available evidence does not permit us to fully grasp how he established his rule. Sources associate him with Larsa, Ur, and Keš (Charpin 2004: 338–39)

22 Gasche (1989: 135) considers Ilī-ma-ilu to have taken up the cause of the fight against Babylon begun by Rīm-Sîn II twenty years earlier. Other individuals in contemporary texts originating from Uruk bore the name Ilī-ma-ilu but were very probably simply homonyms since nothing in their role points towards one of them becoming a king some years later (they appear respec-

The search for the origins and the early days of the Sealand I dynasty yields meagre results. There remains mainly a balance of probability based on later geographical evidence and on the imperatives of war: we know that the first ruler Ilī-ma-ilu would soon conquer Nippur and that Babylon's counteroffensive by Abī-ešuḫ would target the southern Tigris. But this need not imply that the Sealand I rise to power unfolded or even began before Samsu-iluna's repression of the rebellion. Indeed, there is no solid evidence for the presence of Ilī-ma-ilu at the time of the great southern and eastern upheavals, merely a very slight possibility that he started in the diplomatic service under Rīm-Sîn II.

4.2 Ilī-ma-ilu's northern ambitions: the struggle for central Babylonia begins

Our earliest incontrovertible evidence of Sealand I rule is at Nippur, but it does not mean that it was the hometown or the main power base of the first king of the dynasty, Ilī-ma-ilu. In fact, some indications suggest otherwise. The lacunary passage of the chronicle *ABC* 20B: rev. 2–7 may indicate that before Ilī-ma-ilu successfully attacked Samsu-iluna at Nippur, at least another violent encounter had taken place between both kings, perhaps close to a sea or lake.[23] If we posit that the success registered to the credit of Ilī-ma-ilu at the end of the passage refers to his conquest of Nippur (line 7), it would imply that the scene of their first important battle was elsewhere, possibly in the south, where Babylon was not longer exercising power.[24] Be it as it may, there are good chances that Ilī-ma-ilu's authority had its roots further south and that it is where he was able to build up his military power. Samsu-iluna may have reacted to that by strengthening his defenses both along the Euphrates and the Tigris, by rebuilding the city wall at Isin (as per his fifteenth year name) and in the Emutbalum (his seventeenth year name celebrates the rebuilding of fortresses there), probably the area of Maškan-šapir (Charpin 2004: 347).

---

tively as a cook, a scribe, and an owner of slaves in Sanati-Müller 2000b: no.269; BM 88447; BM 88515; Seri 2013: no.35).

23 This interpretation is highly uncertain and is based on the reconstruction AN-*ma*-[AN] on rev. 2, as suggested by Grayson in *ABC* 20B, followed by Glassner in *MC* 40. Also the term *tam-tì* here is not preceded by KUR in the text (rev. 5′), as is the case when referring to the Sealand polity/territory in this text.

24 Moreover, if the dynasty had originated from such a prestigious city as Nippur, one would have expected this fact to be remembered in association with it.

Ilī-ma-ilu's successful conquest of Nippur certainly suggests that the Sealand I ruler had gathered significant support, resources, and troops beforehand. Indeed the city was in all likelihood no easy target: as part of his strategy for defending the southern border of central Babylonia Samsu-iluna had probably just rebuilt Nippur's fortification wall, an undertaking known from a building inscription (Frayne 1990: E4.3.7.2).[25] And if the Babylonian king considered it necessary to strengthen the defensive infrastructure of the city, it was probably manned accordingly. When Ilī-ma-ilu conquered Nippur, he must have been at the head of a large and well-armed group. However, no signs of destruction were found. Archaeological evidence suggests rather that large stretches of the city were abandoned during the Old Babylonian period (Gasche 1989: 124–25, and n.341; Gibson 1992: 42–44), for which a natural cause, namely insufficient water supply, was at least in part, perhaps even mainly, responsible (Stone 1987: 27–28; Gibson 1992: 43).[26] It may have been due to a westward shift of the Euphrates system (Adams and Nissen 1972: 39; Cole and Gasche 1998: 27; Gasche, et al. 2002: 534; 538–39). The recent study by Van Lerberghe, et al. (2017), which uses a vegetation model and climate parameters to estimate anomalies, also suggests that the period was characterized by a marked decline in precipitations. This seems to leave the Nippur archaeological record without any traces of its conquest by the Sealand I ruler. It would seem that, by the time Ilī-ma-ilu marched on Nippur, Samsu-iluna's grip over the central Babylonian town had weakened enough—perhaps because of reduced demographic and economic conditions partly linked to the availability of water (Stone 1977)—to make it possible for the Sealand I king to take it without major battle or opposition.[27] Or

25 We do not know when these works were carried out; the period following the reconquest of the town from Rīm-Sîn II, which took place late in Samsu-iluna's tenth year (Charpin 2004: 342), is a possibility. It may have been part of a larger program of improvement of city fortifications in central Babylonia since similar works are attested for Isin and are commemorated in the year name Si 15 (fortification works are also attested in northern Babylonia; see Pientka 1998: 13–14).

26 Such an explanation is difficult to reconcile with the rebuilding of the city wall mentioned above. A water crisis severe enough to cause the (partial) abandonment of an important city would probably have developed gradually and its consequences would therefore have been in part foreseeable, especially since a large territory upstream was in Babylonian hands; it seems uneconomic to invest in rebuilding the defenses of a city about to be evacuated or abandoned, even if the religious importance of the Ekur could have played a role in such a decision. Based on changing patterns in land transactions, Stone (1977: 285–86) suggested that Babylon had in fact cut off the water supply to southern Babylonia in Si 10, affecting Nippur, but that the situation began to improve roughly ten years later.

27 Another scenario that could reconcile the facts is that part of the population had fled in front of the approaching Sealand I army, leaving a half-empty city for the conquerors to enter and occupy, after which the Babylonian king cut off the water supply from the north.

else, he was favored by such popular support that he did not have to take the city by force, an eventuality for which we have no indication.[28]

If we accept that the Sealand kingdom had its core area in southern Babylonia, the conquest of Nippur was not necessarily its founding event but it came early in its history, and the city appears to have been important ideologically in the later Sealand I scriptoria and palace-sponsored cult (see Chapter 6). Although no texts dated to him have been found in other central Babylonian towns, it is not unlikely that Ilī-ma-ilu's attack on Nippur was part of a larger offensive in that area since evidence of destruction in the Old Babylonian period was found at Isin, where the last texts using Samsu-iluna's year names may date to Si 28.[29] This destruction layer is covered by sediments, suggesting that at least part of the city was then abandoned for a few centuries (Gasche 1989: 126). The date of the latest texts found in a context of destruction shows that there was another attack on Isin some years after the events to which Samsu-iluna referred in his fifteenth year name;[30] nothing indicates that Sealand I troops were responsible for that later attack but their attested presence at Nippur at about the same time certainly makes them likely candidates.

It appears that the turmoil which characterizes that period of Samsu-iluna's reign also affected north-eastern Babylonia, where texts dated to Samsu-iluna ceased in Si 30 at Lagaba (Charpin 2004: 360), which was probably located between Babylon and Kutha (Tammuz 1996: 24). If we use these data as positive evidence, it could mean that, by the end of his reign, Samsu-iluna had lost southern and central Babylonia, and also a portion of north-eastern Babylonia.[31] It is, given the absence of evidence of (Sealand I) occupation of these towns, impossible to determine whether this was all the doing of Ilī-ma-ilu: the action of the nascent Sealand I polity is inextricably mingled with the destruction and the abandonment of entire or parts of long-established cities, the shrinking of the Babylonian kingdom, and a generalized ebbing of textual and archaeological

---

28 Pientka (1998: 11) saw in the southern rebellion a popular uprising, but there is no evidence for this.

29 Charpin 1981: 518 n.3; also Charpin 2000: 201. The most recent text found in a layer containing the rubble of destroyed Old Babylonian houses (in the *Nordabschnitt II*) dates to Si 26 (Gasche 1989: 126 n.347). A provenanced, but not further specified text dating to Si 27 is also mentioned in von Soden 1976: 108. An unprovenanced text dated Si 29 has been suggested to come from Isin (Gasche 1989: 126).

30 In this year name he commemorated the rebuilding of "(...) the wall of Isin, which had been destroyed" (Horsnell 1999: vol.II 201).

31 His later year names also suggest that, after losing Nippur, he turned his attention to the middle Euphrates and the Diyala regions.

evidence. In this complex context, it is difficult to make out cause, co-factor, coincidence, and consequence.

4.2.1 Establishing a viable kingdom: the need for water

However widespread Ilī-ma-ilu's campaign in central Babylonia was, we know that he took at least Nippur. One possible explanation for this northward thrust by the new ruler is that he wanted to secure a sufficient water supply further downstream. The question of water was probably crucial to the Sealand kingdom's viability because its territory lay mostly downstream from the area still controlled by Babylon, all the more so if river levels were low (Van Lerberghe, et al. 2017; Gasche, et al. 2002: 534). Renger (1970: 77) observed that the Old Babylonian Larsean kings had an obvious interest in extending their kingdom northward because it translated in a control of the water supply, and Charpin (2002: 559) justly noted that this was in fact the reality faced by all southern rulers.

There are indeed good chances that the Sealand I kings found themselves in the uncomfortable position of depending upon their counterparts in Babylon for water; they may even have faced chronic water shortage in some areas, which were made worse by excessive intervention against seasonal flooding of the Euphrates in northern Babylonia early in the reign of Samsu-iluna (Charpin 2002: 555–56).[32] Therefore, besides the appeal due to the religious significance of the city, Ilī-ma-ilu's conquest of Nippur could have been partly motivated by a need to ensure water supply, either through the control of the Hammurapi-nuḫuš-nišī canal or of the Nippur branch of the Euphrates; since we do not know the course of the Hammurapi-nuḫuš-nišī, this remains a moot point. George (2009: 139) even suggested that the canal did not really water the cities listed by Hammurapi in his year name celebrating its construction, his thirty-third (Nippur, Eridu, Ur, Larsa, Uruk, and Isin),[33] and that the assertion was pure hyperbole. His reconstruction of the course of the canal would make Nippur entirely irrelevant to its control. However, there may be some truth in Hammurapi's claim since the list of cities named shows a certain amount of geographical and hydrological coherence: they are all south-western locations on the Eu-

32 This is in opposition to al-Hamdani's (2015: 144) theory that hydrological intervention in the north led to an increase in the water volume reaching the extreme south.

33 Horsnell 1999: vol.II 146.

phrates water network, especially if we consider that also Larsa probably received water from it, in addition to the Bad-Tibira channel (e.g. Stone 2003).[34]

Because of these uncertainties, it remains difficult to establish with confidence whether the conquest of Nippur by the first Sealand I king was indeed part of a plan to ensure sufficient water supply to the southern core of his kingdom but it is a likely possibility.[35] This would accord well with a reconstruction of the course of the Hammurapi-nuḫuš-nišī canal linking the Tigris and the Nippur branch of the Euphrates above Nippur, possibly in fact a re-excavation of the KA.SAḪAR canal known from Ur III times (Steinkeller 2017; 2001: 56 ff.; Abraham, et al. 2017: introduction), and perhaps with the damming of the Tigris by Abī-ešuḫ and the construction of fortresses in the area.

4.3 Abī-ešuḫ tries to contain the damage

After the conquest of Nippur by Ilī-ma-ilu, which was the last of a long series of reductions of its territory, Babylon tried at least to contain the expansionist ambitions of its hostile southern neighbor, among other threats. Abī-ešuḫ inherited from his predecessor a severely reduced kingdom, curtailed from its southern plain, from parts of north-eastern Babylonia, and perhaps from stretches of the Diyala valley. The Babylonian king appears to have tried to reduce or contain the damage early in his reign but the enemies were many; from his year names we learn that he fought against Kassite troops (year name d = Ae 3), Elam (year name f = Ae 5 or 6),[36] and Ešnunna (year name dd).[37] Too little is known of the

34 The fact that they are enumerated starting with the northernmost city, then the southernmost, and finally in naming successively the remaining cities along a northward axis is somewhat puzzling and could be construed as artificial, but the sequence can also simply be a logical way of first establishing the impressive hydrographic range of the canal, before systematically naming the main cities included in it.

35 A recently discovered year formula, considered a variant of Ad 22 by Richardson (2015b), seems to indicate that Ammī-ditāna later (perhaps only partly) re-excavated the Hammurapi-nuḫuš-nišī canal. If his reconstruction of the fragmentary formula is correct, this probably happened in conjunction with Babylon's renewed control over Nippur (see Section 4.3.1). Ensuring an adequate water supply for Nippur was also a task on which, later, Kassite kings set upon early, as attested in an inscription of Kaštiliašu (III) (Abraham and Gabbay 2013).

36 This year name recording another military clash between Babylon and Elam was discussed recently by van Koppen (2013). He suggests that an Elamite raid by Kutir-Naḫḫunte may be behind it and that it would have resulted in the abduction of Nanaya, which is alluded to in the annals of Ashurbanipal (*ibid.*: 380). He follows Beaulieu who suggested that this may have taken place at Kish (Beaulieu 2003: 185; van Koppen 2013: 381).

37 For the year names, see Horsnell 1999.

geo-political situation to decide whether there was some cooperation or infighting among Babylon's foes but the period certainly appears to have been one in which no new equilibrium had been found yet.

Official communication does not explicitly mention that Babylon endeavored to militarily regain southern territory, but we learn from at least three sources[38] that Abī-ešuḫ dammed the Tigris. And if we accept the version of events given in chronicle *ABC* 20B, the damming of the river was done in a failed effort to vanquish Sealand I ruler Ilī-ma-ilu. Abī-ešuḫ may also have had non-military reasons to divert (some of) the Tigris water, although such a project certainly seems very radical compared to the usual digging of canals and de-silting of sluices. The dam may have fulfilled a double function: besides being aimed at drying up the marshes against the Sealand foe,[39] it redirected water into the Euphrates system via the Hammurapi-nuḫuš-nišī canal (Van Lerberghe, et al. 2017: 7–8; Van Lerberghe and Voet 2016: 559).[40] Whatever hydraulic effects may have been desired upstream, their corollary is a severe reduction in the availability of water downstream;[41] whether the latter was a primary objective of the king of Babylon in damming the river is uncertain but likely.[42] The great attempt failed[43] and Abī-ešuḫ celebrated only the damming of the river in a year name, but the event had enough resonance to be retained also in the divinatory and historiographic tradition.

---

38 This event is recorded in the king's year name o (Horsnell 1999: vol.II 260), in a *tamītu*-text (Lambert 2007: text 3c, lines 22ff. and text 3d, lines 1–3), and in the chronicle *ABC* 20B (rev. 8–10). See Section 2.4.1.2 for a discussion of the sources and their possible interrelations.

39 This view was adopted be others, e.g., Charpin (2002: 558). Van Lerberghe, et al. (2017: 2) add that the effect was probably increased by a period of reduced precipitations.

40 Steinkeller (2017) suggests that the damming may in fact have been effected with the intention of flooding the Sealand troops, which would have had to be still in the area of Nippur. The chronology of Abī-ešuḫ's reign does not support this view; we know that the area had been retaken by Babylon very early in his reign (see Section 4.3.1). Of course, the Babylonian king could have tried to slow down the progress of troops preparing another attack.

41 As seen above, al-Hamdani (2015: 144) contends on the contrary that more water reached southern Babylonia, following shifts in the river bed.

42 Charpin (2002: 558) sees in it a military strategy: drying out the marshes to capture the enemy. Van Lerberghe and Voet (2016: 559) agree with this view, adding that the Babylonian king also wanted to gain more water for the Euphrates system.

43 Pientka (1998: 268 n.67) surmised that the damming of the Tigris may in fact have been a success for Abī-ešuḫ, this operation allowing him to oust Ilī-ma-ilu from Nippur and force him to retreat further south. However, the chronology of events suggests that Nippur had already returned under Babylon's control when the damming of the river took place (see Section 4.3.1).

4.3.1 The fortresses, the dam, and the control of Nippur

There are also signs that, after his predecessor had apparently neglected his southern border in the latter part of his reign, Abī-ešuḫ decided to redirect Babylon's attention towards it and invest heavily in militarizing the area. We know that the Sealand kingdom had lost Nippur to Babylon by year e of Abī-ešuḫ—probably very early in his reign –,[44] because an administrative text from Dūr-Abī-ešuḫ mentions troops from the *birti* EN.LÍL^{ki} "the fortress of Nippur," among other beneficiaries, receiving barley at Dūr-Abī-ešuḫ (CUSAS 29, 41: 31); three other texts from the same archive contain a similar reference, one whose date is broken off (CUSAS 29, 39), one from Ae m (CUSAS 29, 40), and one from Ad 6 (CUSAS 29, 34). Moreover, this fortress of Nippur—which was presumably located very near the city itself—appears to have been one among a chain of fortified posts and military detachments positioned in the area, from Maškan-šāpir on the Tigris across to the Euphrates, perhaps as far down as Uruk (Abraham, et al. 2017: introduction; and texts CUSAS 29, 1–40 documenting distributions of barley to troops from various fortresses and locations).[45] Given this level of militarization in and around Nippur, the city must have been in Babylonian hands at the time.

As part of this chain of fortresses, two were called by the same name, Dūr-Abī-ešuḫ.[46] This is shown incontrovertibly in texts CUSAS 29, 25 and 27, which

---

44 Year e corresponds to year 4 or 5 (van Koppen 2013: 378–79). Until recently, the eighth year of Ammī-ṣaduqa was the earliest for which we had proof that Babylon had recovered control of Nippur because in that year sacrificial animals were sent there from Dūr-Abī-ešuḫ (CUSAS 8, 23). That in itself was quite a novelty. Before the publication of texts from Dūr-Abī-ešuḫ, sources remained silent about the fate of Nippur following the Sealand I conquest until the rebuilding program by Kassite kings (Bartelmus 2010). A date list and a later copy of an inscription of Ammī-ṣaduqa were found at Nippur (Frayne 1990: E4.3.10.1 and commentary), but this evidence had been considered insufficient to conclude to a reconquest of the city (Charpin 2004: 368). Other evidence concerning Nippur found in the Dūr-Abī-ešuḫ archive published in CUSAS 8 is discussed in the introduction (Van Lerberghe and Voet 2009: 3–4).

45 In particular, for the possibility of a fortress at Uruk, see CUSAS 29, 18: 5 referring to troops of a *bi-ir-ti* DU_6 É.AN.NA, perhaps the "fortress of the (ruin) mound of the Eanna" (see also the corresponding note in the edition). Troops from Uruk and Isin also appears in CUSAS 29, 8: 3 (this is a new edition of the text previously published as CUSAS 8, 39; on the same passage, see also Földi 2014: 42 with another suggestion). Both texts are dated to the year Ae o+1.

46 Until recently, it was believed that there was only one fortress called Dūr-Abī-ešuḫ, and that it was probably also the fortress whose construction on the Tigris is commemorated in Abī-ešuḫ's year name m. Its location has been the object of conjectures, some of which are now obsolete. Arnaud (2007: 42) considered that the fortress was located immediately south of Nippur, Van Leberghe, and Voet (2009: 6) put it at some distance north of it—near the putative location

refer to travels between both locations, in the latter case more specifically by boat. The waterway between them must have been the Hammurapi-nuḫuš-nišī canal dug out by Hammurapi in his thirty-second year,[47] since one fortress is called BÀD *a-bi-e-šu-uḫ*^{KI} *ša* KUN$_8$ ^{I7}*ḫa-am-mu-ra-bi-nu-ḫu-uš-ni-ši* "Dūr-Abī-ešuḫ-of-the-outflow-of-the-Hammurapi-nuḫuš-nišī"[48] and the other BÀD *a-bi-e-šu-uḫ*^{KI} *ša me-eḫ-ri-im ša* ^{I7}IDIGNA "Dūr-Abī-ešuḫ-of-the-barrage-of-the-Tigris" (e.g., CUSAS 29, 25: obv. 9–12).[49] The matter was also recently discussed by Charpin (2015b: 145–50). In the following discussion I will refer to them, respectively, as Dūr-Abī-ešuḫ$^{(canal)}$ or fortress$^{(canal)}$ and Dūr-Abī-ešuḫ$^{(Tigris)}$ or fortress$^{(Tigris)}$.

Dūr-Abī-ešuḫ$^{(canal)}$ is the site where the archive published in CUSAS 8 and 29 comes from. Its exact location is unknown, but it cannot have been located very far from Nippur since several texts show that Babylon resettled part of the cultic (including the Ekur) activity there (van Lerberghe and Voet 2009: 1–3), while still maintaining some activity at Nippur itself, at least for a while.[50] Also, the letter CUSAS 29, 205 referring to an attack on Nippur probably indicates that Nippurites fleeing their city took refuge at Dūr-Abī-ešuḫ$^{(canal)}$—their place of refuge is called KUN$_8$-ÍD.DA^{ki} "the outflow of the river," which sounds like an abbreviation of the name of the fortress. On the other side, administrative notes from Dūr-Abī-ešuḫ$^{(canal)}$ show that extispicy was often performed about safe travel between the fortress and Nippur, and that troops accompanied the convoy (Abraham, et al. 2017: introduction; and most texts among CUSAS 29, 44–63). Apparently, the travel distance was sufficient for the Babylonians to judge that enemies may think it worthwhile to attack travelers—this is somewhat more probable at some distance from well-manned fortresses. At any rate, and whatever role

---

of Lagaba –, while George (2009: 141) considered that it was "about twelve kilometers east-northeast" of Nippur.

47 Its construction was celebrated in Hammurapi's thirty-third year name, as discussed in Section 4.2.1. However, no traces of a canal joining directly Nippur and the Tigris are indicated in Hritz' reconstruction of the hydrographic network (2010: map).

48 The sign KUN was originally read GÚ, (river-)bank (Van Lerberghe and Voet 2009: 58, note to line 11 of text 25); see also George 2009: 139 n.1 for a summary of the debate, including the fact that the sign could also be KUN$_8$.

49 I thank K. Van Lerberghe for generously sharing his transliteration of these texts with me, ahead of publication.

50 For instance, travels from the fortress to Nippur in order to perform sacrifice there are documented during the reign of Ammī-ditāna (most texts among CUSAS 29, 44–63 dating to the years Ad 11–13). The oldest attestation of the *nešakkum* priest Enlil-mansum at the fortress is found in the texts CUSAS 8, 2 and 55 dated to Aṣ 5, but grain for the gods of Nippur is received by unspecified *nešakkum* priests in year Aṣ 2 (CUSAS 8, 54). Sacrifice at Nippur itself continued for a time, because sacrificial animals were went there from the fortress, for instance in Aṣ 9 (CUSAS 8, 24).

the "fortress of Nippur" mentioned in CUSAS 29, 39–41 may have played in the defense of the city, the letter CUSAS 29, 205 shows that Dūr-Abī-ešuḫ$^{\text{(canal)}}$ had an important role to play in defending it and its citizens. The construction of that fortress, probably in the very first years of Abī-ešuḫ's reign, must have followed immediately the recapture of Nippur from Sealand I control and been part of Babylon's strategy to defend it against the new southern polity.

As for Dūr-Abī-ešuḫ$^{\text{(Tigris)}}$, it must be the fortress whose construction is commemorated in Abī-ešuḫ's year name m, since they are both said to be located on the Tigris, and more so, near a barrage or weir.[51] Moreover, it is very likely that this barrage of the Tigris is the same that was built when Abī-ešuḫ claims that he dammed the river in his year name o,[52] and the fortress may well have served to protect it (George 2009: 138–39; Van Leberghe, and Voet 2009: 5).[53] The project to dam the Tigris was very carefully planned and heavily militarized because we learn from an oracular question in preparation for it that Abī-ešuḫ had consulted about it already and that he mustered numerous troops (Lambert 2007: text 3c).[54] In addition, one omen text from Dūr-Abī-ešuḫ$^{\text{(canal)}}$ (CUSAS 18, 4) puts a dam (the dam on the Tigris?) in a military context, and more generally seems to associate it with the fortresses. It is dated to 2.ii.Ae m—the year celebrating the construction of the fortress$^{\text{(Tigris)}}$—; the diviner asks about the well-being of the fortress$^{\text{(canal)}}$ (obv. 4–5) and of troops at the dam, as well as about the intentions of the enemy (rev. 23′ ff.). This certainly bespeaks a period of troubles, and the enemy presumably included the Sealand kingdom, which had most to lose from the dam and had successfully campaigned in central Babylonia in the past.

---

51 George (2009: 138f.) made a convincing case that term GIŠ.GI$_4$.GI$_4$ in the year formula Ae m, which states that a fortress was built "above the GIŠ.GI$_4$.GI$_4$ of the Tigris," should be translate "barrage;" the term must correspond to *meḫrum* used in the passage above (see also CAD M, s.v. *miḫru* A4). George (2009: 141) saw in the fortress a means of defending Nippur and the area from a Sealand invasion. A fragmentary cylinder found at Kiš contains the epithet "king of the Tigris" (Ash 1924–616); if Frayne (1990: E4.3.8.1001, commentary and line i 4′) is correct in his suggestion to attribute it to Abī-ešuḫ, we would have a striking piece of evidence that the Babylonian king put much emphasis on controlling that river.

52 "The year: Abieshuh, the king, by the supreme power of Marduk dammed the Tigris" (Horsnell 1999: vol.II 261).

53 The chronology of most of Abī-ešuḫ's reign is uncertain. It was suggested that year name o commemorating the damming of the Tigris corresponded to Ae 19 (Horsnell 1999: vol.II 260f.) and that the year name m commemorating the construction of the fortress (on the Tigris) is equivalent to Ae 21 (*ibid:* 262). It is generally assumed that the fortress was built after the dam (Horsnell 1999: vol.I 79; George 2013: 14; Abraham, et al. 2017: introduction).

54 Also, the effective damming of the Tigris may very well have taken place at the end of month v since this *tamītu* states that it would take place on the thirtieth day of the month of Abu (line 29).

The political climate may have changed rapidly following (or during) the construction of the fortresses and the dam. Indeed, there are possible signs of interactions between the Babylonian fortress(canal) and the Sealand kingdom, but such an interpretation depends on how one understands the term A.AB.BA, which appears at least three times in texts from Dūr-Abī-ešuḫ(canal). One text dated to the year n of Abī-ešuḫ (CUSAS 29, 3: 9–10) records that grain was put at the disposal of envoys (DUMU.MEŠ *ši-ip-ri*) of A.AB.BA. The term also occurs in a text dated to Ae 28 (Földi 2014: 33, text Sem 1278, obv. 20) in the phrase ÉRIN *e-li* A.AB.BA, probably to be read ÉRIN *e-le* A.AB.BA "troops come up from A.AB.BA."[55] The context is one of grain allotments handed out to troops. While nothing suggests that these soldiers were prisoners, they are treated differently than the others troops in the same and in similar texts (CUSAS 29, 1–40) : the soldiers "come up from A.AB.BA" are few, they are named individually, and they don't appear to have a commanding officer, whereas other soldiers in these texts usually appear simply as troops under the command (NÍG.ŠU) of their officer. In fact, the "Sealand" soldiers could be defectors from the south.

If A.AB.BA is to be understood as a term designating the Sealand I polity, these two texts, or at least the former, could indicate that there were sporadic official relations between the two neighbors. But the evidence is ambiguous and does not allow yet for a clear understanding of the situation. Also, because the chronology of Abī-ešuḫ's reign is poorly understood, these putative contacts cannot be put into a clear sequence of events: that the year Ae 28 was indeed the last one of this king seems almost certain (Horsnell 1999: vol.I 76), but his year n has not been positioned satisfactorily yet.[56] At any rate, if we admit the presence of official Sealand I delegates at the fortress, in particular if this happened before the construction of the fortress(Tigris), it would seem that a complex game of negotiations and threats took place between the two states.

Of more anecdotal interest is the fact that an individual dubbed a refugee (*munnabtu*) is said to have fled to the fortress(canal) (*iš-tu* A.AB.BA *in-na-bi-ta-am*), from the Sea(-land?); this happened in the very year following the construction of the fortress on the Tigris (MS 3218/13: lines 4–5).[57]

---

55 For the interpretation of *e-le* as the infinitive of *elû*, see Brinkman 1976: 411 ff. This appears a more likely reading that Földi's "on the sea."

56 Horsnell's reconstruction of Abī-ešuḫ's chronology draws heavily on other previous studies, in particular Goetze's work; all are cited abundantly in Hornsell 1999: vol.I 65–81. This reconstruction puts tentatively year n before that commemorating the construction of the fortress(Tigris) (year m).

57 The year name is well legible on the photograph on cdli. The text is as yet unpublished but is briefly referred to in George (2009: 136) and Földi (2014: 37 n.31). In addition, another unpublish-

While Dūr-Abī-ešuḫ(canal) may have witnessed changes in the relations between Babylon and the Sealand kingdom, it probably stayed continuously in Babylonian hands well into the reign of Samsu-ditāna since the texts found there, published and unpublished, roughly cover the entire period from its construction until probably Sd 15 (in particular CUSAS 8 and 29; Sigrist, Gabbay, and Avila 2017: text 5).

The situation was clearly less stable at Nippur: it had fallen into the hands of Ilī-ma-ilu in or shortly after the twenty-ninth year of Samsu-iluna, and had probably been reconquered by Babylon either later in Samsu-iluna's reign or very early in his successor Abī-ešuḫ's. It appears that cultic activity at Nippur had been disrupted in that period because we find, besides other signs of a transfer of cult to Babylon and Sippar (Pientka 1998: 190–95), that an incantation singer from Nippur, Taqīš-Gula, probably became a courtier of Abī-ešuḫ (Charpin 1999–2000: 324). But a number of texts from Dūr-Abī-ešuḫ(canal) show that some cultic activity remained in Nippur. During Ammī-ditāna's reign, convoys were sent from the fortress to Nippur to offer sacrifices (several texts among CUSAS 29, 44–63); also, the court record CUSAS 10, 17, known from later copies, shows that one Gimil-Marduk went to Nippur to sacrifice a lamb in Ad 16 (lines 21–23). In fact, sacrificial animals were sent to Nippur as late as in the reign of Ammī-ṣaduqa, as recorded in texts from Dūr-Abī-ešuḫ(canal) (CUSAS 8, 23 in Aṣ 8 and CUSAS 8, 24 probably in Aṣ 9).

However, these must have been turbulent times considering that Nippur and the Ekur were attacked with horses and hundreds of men in the eleventh year of Ammī-ditāna (as per the letter CUSAS 29, 205). This episode cannot be associated with archaeological evidence since no signs of destruction of the Isin-Larsa Ekur, on top of which the Kassite temple was built, were found.[58] However, a leveling of the ground seems to have taken place before the construction of the latter, apparently accompanied by a thorough clearing of debris resulting in a low elevation of the Kassite temple (McCown, et al. 1967: 12); this may have obliterated traces of the conflict.

---

ed texts from Dūr-Abī-ešuḫ(canal) apparently mentions a traveler coming to the fortress from Ur (Arnaud 2007: 43 n.119). If the text refers not only to his origin but truly to the place where he set out on his journey, this means that merchants were able at the time to travel from south-western to central-eastern Babylonia. However, pending the publication of more detail on the text we do not know whether this merchant was acting in a usual trading context.

58 Also, the archaeological evidence does not speak for a reconstruction of the Ekur in the interval. However, building work on the É.KUR could be the referred to in one fragmentary year name of the Sealand I king Ayadaragalama (year P; see Appendix 2).

The archaeological record also suggests that the city was largely abandoned for a time in the late Old Babylonian period (Gasche 1989: 124–25), although Gibson (1992: 44) noted that the abandonment may not have been total, suggesting that a "skeleton staff at Ekur after Samsuiluna's time" may have remained. George (2009: 137) considers that a period of abandonment began during Ammī-ṣaduqa's reign, more precisely in the years following the texts CUSAS 8, 23 and 24 from the Dūr-Abī-ešuḫ$^{(canal)}$ archive, which record sheep deliveries to Nippur (whereas later such deliveries of the same archive are all directed to the fortress). He even suggests to narrow down the moment of abandonment of the city between Aṣ 9, the year of the last attested delivery of sheep to Nippur, and Aṣ 15[59], the year in which a tablet was sealed at Dūr-Abī-ešuḫ with a cylinder-seal bearing the inscription ^{d}NANNA-ME.ŠA$_4$ *ka-ri-ib* ^{d}AMAR.UTU *ud-du-uš* É.KUR *ù* NIBRU^{ki} *li-mu-ur* : "May Nanna-meša, who renders homage to Marduk, (live to) see the renovation of Ekur and Nippur" (seal B on text CUSAS 8, 16; George 2009: 137).

The chronology of events at Nippur is presented in Table 7.

Table 7: Chronology of events at Nippur

Date	Source and contingencies on dating	Event at/Control of Nippur
Ha 32	In the year name Ha 33	Excavation of the Hammurapi-nuḫuš-nišī canal bringing water to Nippur and other southern cities
Si 9	Corresponds to RSII 2. At least 1.iv – 25.x. (OECT 8, 14 and 8, 19)	Occupation by Rīm-Sîn II
Si 10	Month i? (TIM 4, 6)	Reconquest by Babylon
In or after Si 10?	Building inscription (Frayne 1990: E4.3.7.2)	Reinforcement of the wall (by Babylon)
In or after Si 29	For at least 1.5 year, from 16.vii.Ilī 1 to 24.ix.Ilī 2 (ARN 123; PBS 8/1 89)	Occupation by Sealand I king Ilī-ma-ilu
In or after Si 29?	See Pientka 1998: 190–95; Charpin 1999–2000: 324	Transfer of some clergies and cultic activity to Babylon and Sippar?
Between Si 31 and Ae e (=4?)	Troops from a "fortress of Nippur" are mentioned in a text from Dūr-Abī-ešuḫ$^{(canal)}$ dated ix.Ae e (CUSAS 29, 41)	Reconquest by Babylon

59 This period corresponds also to the construction of a fortress apparently at the intake point of a canal branching off the Euphrates, according to the year name Aṣ 11.

Table 7: Chronology of events at Nippur *(continued)*

Date	Source and contingencies on dating	Event at/Control of Nippur
Ad 11	19th and 24th days of month xi (letter CUSAS 29, 205)	Unsuccessful attack by unidentified enemy who nonetheless can penetrate briefly in the Ekur
Ad 11 – Aṣ 8	Several texts among CUSAS 29, 44–63; CUSAS 8, 23; CUSAS 10, 17: lines 21–23	Sacrifice can still take place at Nippur (sent from Dūr-Abī-ešuḫ$^{(canal)}$)
Ad 21	In a variant of the year name Ad 22(?)	Re-excavation of the Hammurapi-nuḫuš-nišī canal (related to the occupation of Nippur?)
After Aṣ 9	Latest delivery of sheep to Nippur recorded in the Dūr-Abī-ešuḫ archive, on the 20.vii. Aṣ 9?(CUSAS 8, 24); perhaps before Aṣ 15 (inscription of seal B expressing hope for renovation of Ekur; on CUSAS 8, 16)	Abandonment and transfer of remaining cultic activities to Dūr-Abī-ešuḫ$^{(canal)}$?
Sd 15	Sigrist, Gabbay and Avila 2017: text 5. The text mentions a number of (Nippur) temples, including the Ekur, the Ekiur and the Ešumeša in a receipt for grain; it does not make clear whether the original temples at Nippur are meant or perhaps a displaced cult	Residual activity in the temples of Nippur?
Time of Ayadaragalama	Hymn of Ayadaragalama (Gabbay and Boivin forthcoming): the hymn is dedicated to the main gods of Nippur and mentions Nippur.	Sealand I control over the city?

Without more evidence, the circumstances surrounding the (brief?) Sealand I occupation remain in the dark. Whether the Sealand I kings were involved in any further episode(s) of turmoil is unclear. The possibilities were many in this volatile period; Kassite groups[60] or Elam for instance could also have had their hand in the struggle for Nippur. Also shrouded in uncertainty is the question of the abandonment. That the city was partially abandoned seems certain according to archaeological evidence and it must have lasted some time since ero-

60 The Kassite ruler Ḫašmar-galšu (Brinkman 1976: 325–27), known from a few Sumerian inscriptions referring to some building work on temples at Nippur, is a possibility.

sion even created stable sloping surfaces in the area TA on Tablet Hill, which the Kassites did not level when they reoccupied it (Gibson et al. 1998–2001: 562). At any rate, the chronology of events presented in Table 7 suggests that the Sealand kingdom may not have been directly involved in the abandonment of the city.

4.4 Other allies, foes, and neighbors of the Sealand kingdom

The emergence and early growth of the Sealand kingdom appears to have been a struggle against Babylon over territory and water, a series of (re-)appropriation of what had been for a while under Babylonian control. While it has proved impossible to ascertain whether an embryonic Sealand political entity or Ilī-ma-ilu himself were already involved in the rebellion of Si 8–9, its repression by Babylon in the years Si 11–13 must have reduced—at least momentarily—the number of potential contenders for the control over southern Babylonia. At some point during the following decade and a half Ilī-ma-ilu apparently seized his chance, established his credibility as leader, and built up a power base sufficient to attack Nippur some years later, in or shortly after Si 29. In fact, Samsu-iluna's elimination of some of the rebellious leaders must have unintentionally helped him in this. Nonetheless, the Sealand polity certainly did not grow in a power vacuum: the eastern neighbors Elam and Ešnunna may have played a role, as well as the newcomers in the Babylonian lowland, the Kassites.[61]

4.4.1 Elam

One factor which may have played a role in the emergence and establishment of the Sealand kingdom is a possible political or military involvement of Elam. We know that Babylon and Elam clashed fairly early in Abī-ešuḫ's reign. Indeed, new evidence from Sippar has revealed that his year name f contains a reference

61 This discussion does not include, for instance, the kingdom of Hana, since we have no information whatsoever on the contacts that it may have entertained with the Sealand kingdom: in the first half of the latter's history Babylon lay between them, but in the second half there are chances that they had at least commercial connections, however, there is no evidence for this at present. The fact that the Haneans are named in the *kudurru* of Kadašman-Ḫarbe I as having participated in causing Babylon to fall suggests that they may have been on the same side as the Sealand I king (see Section 4.7). For a recent summary of sources from the kingdom of Hana and its chronology, see Podany 2014; also most recently Podany 2016; van Koppen 2017: 68–70.

to the Elamite army (van Koppen 2013). This year name is one of the few of that monarch that are partly preserved on a date list, making it certain that it was in the early years of his reign.[62] This bellicose episode could be associated with a putative Elamite raid, perhaps on Kiš, which resulted in the removal of the goddess Nanaya.[63] However, the purported abduction of Nanaya by the Elamites is based on a passage of the annals of Aššurbanipal recording the return of the cultic statue into the Eanna; with no source nearer in time, the veracity, let alone the date of the event are impossible to assess.[64] But what can certainly be adduced from year name f is that Babylon and Elam were at war again. The involvement of Elam in the Babylonian lowland may have been advantageous for the Sealand kingdom in diverting its opponent's military attention, although we do not know what stance Elam took towards the rising southern Babylonian power at the time. We may have an indication that open conflict between Elam and Babylon continued in the fact that Elamite slaves came on the Babylonian market in the first decade of Ammī-ṣaduqa's reign (van Koppen 2017: 61). Finally, Elamite troops are included by Samsu-ditāna among potential enemies threatening a city when he consults the omens, presumably in the later years of his reign (Lambert 2007: no.1 lines 33 ff.). It seems thus that the relations between Babylon and Elam remained bellicose to the last.[65]

---

62 Horsnell (1999: vol.I 74) suggests that year f = Ae 5. Van Koppen (2013: 378–79) raises the possibility of one additional line in the preceding lacuna of Date List B and concludes that year f could be equated with Ae 5 or 6.

63 Van Koppen (2013: 381) using previous works by Beaulieu (2003: 185).

64 This episode was first associated with a raid on Uruk during Samsu-iluna's reign (Leemans 1968: 217; Glassner 1993; see also Beaulieu 2003: 185 and Charpin 2004: 342 n.1785.) According to the annals, the statue would have resided a very long time in Elam. Concerning the date of the event, Glassner (1993) saw a possible connection between the passage in the annals and the fact that the term SUKKAL.MAḪ appears in a chronicle fragment referring to Samsu-iluna (MC 43). But the passage is very fragmentary; it was discussed by Lambert (1990b: 31 n.9) in his edition of the text.

65 We know that Elamites were integrated into Babylonian society in northern, central, and southern Babylonia during the entire Old Babylonian period (Van Lerberghe 1986: 152; Seri 2013: 134–35) but that is no reliable indicator of the official relations between the states. A few Elamites are also present in the Sealand I archive, some of them identified as such (Zadok 2014: 224–26; 232; Dalley 2009: 3). They appear as payers of agricultural taxes of Kār-Šamaš (CUSAS 9, 428 and perhaps 441) and craftsmen, some of whom received rations (Zadok 2014: 224–25). Nothing in their interaction with the palace distinguishes them from other individuals besides the fact that they were sometimes identified as Elamite. The same appears to hold true for the Tell Khaiber texts (e.g. TK1 3064.135: rev. 7′). Dalley mistakenly identifies one messenger Ugin-Saḫ in CUSAS 9, 455 as an Elamite (2009: 3 and 41, note to line 9 of text 29): he has in fact a Kassite name (Zadok 2014: 225).

A bit later, after the fall of Babylon, the Sealand kingdom and Elam apparently maintained diplomatic relations; this is shown in CUSAS 9, 40 (dated to Ayadaragalama) which records a messenger from Elam[66] as the intended recipient of ewes delivered to the palace. An Elamite envoy was therefore present at the time at a Sealand I palace, presumably the royal court.[67]

The historiographic tradition may also indicate that the relations between the last Sealand I king and Elam were friendly, but this interpretation depends on the reconstruction of a lacunary passage of the chronicle *ABC* 20B. The penultimate section[68]begins with the line:[69] ^{m} ^{d}*é-a-ga-mil* LUGAL KUR *tam-tì a-na* KUR ELAM.MA^{ki} [....]-*ma*. King (1907: II 22, line 11) reconstructed the passage as [*il-li-ku*]-*ma* and translated it as "Ea-gamil, king of the Country of the Sea, [set out] against the land of Elam." Basing himself on the same reconstruction of the passage, Weidner (1926: 69 incl. n.1) translated it more neutrally as "[ging] nach Elam" but added that Ea-gāmil was probably brought as a prisoner; this brings an entirely new light on the passage but still implies that the states were at war with one another. However, both interpretations are based on a reconstruction which was probably erroneous; it appears indeed problematic in terms of space needed, if we can trust King's hand copy (1907: II 127). Grayson (1975: 156, rev. 12), after collation, suggested to reconstruct the verb *i*[*ḫ-liq*]-*ma*, translating it "f[led] to Elam."[70] If we accept this reconstruction, Elam and the Sealand kingdom were perhaps still on friendly terms at the time. It appears therefore that at least from the middle of its history, the Sealand I kings had established lasting diplomatic ties with the eastern power.

This would agree with the generally friendly stance that Elam seems to have held towards southern Babylonian small polities against Babylon, following the

---

66 LÚ KIN.GI$_4$.A *ša* ELAM.MA^{ki} (lines 3–4).

67 It is likely that travel between Sealand I territory and Susiana could take place unhindered since it was not contingent on the possibility of safe passage in the Diyala or via Der. Indeed, it has been shown that Girsu, Lagaš, and other southern cities were directly connected to Susa by waterway in the Early Dynastic and Ur III periods via the Karkheh or the Karun river (Lafont 2010: 174; Gasche et al. 2007: 51 n.234; Leemans 1960a: 175; Laursen and Steinkeller 2017: Appendix 3). The chances are that such itineraries were still used.

68 See Section 2.1.1 for a transliteration of the text. The structure of the chronicle is discussed in Section 2.4.1.1.

69 *ABC* 20B: rev. 12′.

70 Glassner's (2004: 272–73, rev. 12′) reconstruction agrees with Grayson's. This reconstruction matches for instance the passage in *ABC* 1: col.I line 3 in which Marduk-apla-iddina II is said to have fled (ZÁḪ) to Elam.

formidable expansion under Hammurapi.[71] Elam and Rīm-Anum of Uruk appear to have entertained friendly relations for a short time since we find that an overseer of Elamites received a group of young prisoners from the *bīt asīrī* in Rīm-Anum's first year (Nisaba 4 II.3; Seri 2013: 134; 240). However, these relations may have soured rapidly since in Rīm-Anum's third year Elamites were brought as prisoners to Uruk (VS 13, 13; Seri 2013: 128). Elam may also have backed a coalition formed by Rīm-Sîn II of Larsa, Dagan-ma-ilum (probably of Mutiabal), and Rīm-Anum, before the latter turned against his allies to side with Babylon, also against Ešnunna, as reflected in his third year name (Seri 2013: 240–41).

For Elam, supporting southern opponents to Babylon was in a sense reviving the alliance with early Old Babylonian Larsa, and it seems indeed not too far fetched to posit that it looked favorably upon the Sealand I continuators of this opposition against the same foe.

4.4.2 The Kassites

Although Kassites were certainly present before,[72] it is during the southern rebellion that they entered the Babylonian political record, as the enemies both of Babylon and of the rebel king Rīm-Sîn II: Samsu-iluna's ninth year name claims that he defeated them at Kikalla, while Rīm-Sîn II, probably in the same year, mentions the "evil Kassites from the barbarous country, who could not be driven back to the mountains" (Stol 1976: 54). It is difficult to decide whether there was concerted action on the part of the Kassites, that is, whether they attacked lowland settlements in an organized military fashion, but sources certainly do not suggest that they were unified under one leader. They may simply have migrated massively onto the northern and central Babylonian plains, in separate groups, presumably entering the lowland from the Diyala valley.[73] The exertions of

---

71 The conquest of Larsa by Hammurapi may have been felt by Elam as the last of several blows dealt by Babylon against its base of power in the lowland (Durand 2013: 337–38). We do not know whether Elam still had any velleities of direct presence on the Mesopotamian plain at the time of the rebellion during Samsu-iluna's reign, therefore how interested its support to smaller southern polities was. At any rate, the Elamite ruler probably preferred smaller neighbors to a large, powerful one.

72 It seems that a Kassite individual is attested in a text from late in the reign of Rīm-Sîn I; possible earlier attestations are uncertain (Sassmannshausen 2000: 410).

73 Rīm-Sîn II's date formula certainly seems to point to this scenario. See also van Koppen (2017: 59–61).

Samsu-iluna and Rīm-Sîn II to repel the Kassites[74] were to no avail, they were ineluctably becoming part of Babylonian society; and the process did not run smoothly, since, according to his year name d, Kassite groups caused problems also to Abī-ešuḫ early in his reign. Despite these conflicts, many among the newcomers integrated very rapidly; indeed Kassite troops are attested at Dūr-Abī-ešuḫ somewhat later in Abī-ešuḫ's reign (Arnaud 2007: 43; several texts in CUSAS 29).[75]

The Kassites may have been a factor to reckon with in Ilī-ma-ilu's plans, especially when he pushed into central Babylonia, where they were presumably more numerous than in the south. But we have no evidence that they had much influence, favorable or detrimental, on the emergence of the Sealand kingdom, besides the fact that they apparently, at times, mobilized some of Babylon's troops and resources.[76]

A number of Kassites certainly migrated into Sealand I territory, since by the middle of the dynasty, we find evidence of their presence in the texts dated to Pešgaldarameš and Ayadaragalama. However, only a limited number of individuals bear Kassite names in the CUSAS 9 archive (Zadok 2014: 227–28).[77] The onomasticon is of course a deficient method of analysis for Kassite demographics because most individuals identified as Kassite in Old Babylonian texts had adopted Akkadian names (Sassmannshausen 2000: 411). However, it is the only means at our disposal for the Sealand I corpus because people are never identified as Kassite in it.[78] Individuals with Kassite names appear in various functions: plowman (CUSAS 9, 386: 5), leather-worker (CUSAS 9, 448: 16), worker (CUSAS 9, 396: 12), leader of a group of workers (CUSAS 9, 387: 12), GÌR official

74 According to van Koppen (2017: 53), the arrival of Kassite groups was not threatening. They integrated the Babylonian army, and clashes erupted only as a result of adjusting from their pastoralist lifestyle in their new environment.

75 Already at the end of Samsu-iluna's reign, Kassites appear in economic texts, for instance receiving agricultural tools (OLA 21, 19: in particular line 13; the text is discussed in Van Lerberghe 1995: 382).

76 A number of late Old Babylonian letters bear witness to the sense of insecurity which prevailed both around towns and in the back country due to what Pientka (1998: 260) incisively described as "plündernden und mordenden Völkergruppen." Among these minatory hordes of wanderers, Bimatites and Samḫarites are sometimes named, who may have been affiliated with the Kassite ethno-linguistic group (Pientka 1998: 261–62); for a recent study concluding against their identification with Kassite tribes, see van Koppen 2017: 78–79.

77 The situation appears to be more or less similar at Tell Khaiber, with very few Kassite names; we find for instance one Burrašu in TK1 3064.83: 11.

78 This differs from Elamites who are sometimes specifically identified as such, for instance in CUSAS 9, 444: line 37.

(CUSAS 9, 74: 8). Some received grain allotments and ewes (CUSAS 9, 25: 5–6; 49: 1–2; 451: 2 and 7), others had probably been allocated a *miksu*-field since they paid such royalties accordingly (CUSAS 9, 410: 27; 448: 16; probably 413: 21 and 35).[79] These individuals had obviously integrated the local economic life quite seamlessly.[80]

The social integration of Kassites is more difficult to gauge. One letter refers to Kassite houses or a Kassite house, É *ka-aš-ši-i* (CUSAS 9, 7: 17′ and 20′), which seems to indicate that they tended to live in separate settlements, perhaps organized according to tribal affiliation, as was apparently the case around late Old Babylonian Sippar and Dilbat (Van Lerberghe 1995: 380); van Koppen (2017: 49–50) considers them military settlements—land attributed to Kassite soldiers. But the context of the passage is unclear; it follows a break and the preserved text uses the ambiguous verb *gummuru:* ⸢*a-na* x x⸣-*ni* / *a-na* É *ka-aš-ši-i* / *gu-um-mu-ri* / *iš-ta-pa-ar* / *ù šu-nu aš-šu* É *ka-aš-ši-*⸢*i*⸣ / *gu-um-mu-ri* / *il-li-ku-ú-ni* (CUSAS 9, 7: 16′–22′). The term "É" appears here to refer to actual dwellings[81] but the plurality of meanings of the verb makes it difficult to decide whether their completion or their destruction is alluded to.[82] Van Koppen (2017: 51) considers that the context is military and that "the Sealand army comprised an important Kassite component." I do not find confirmation for this in the extant Sealand I record. But a deity called "The-One-who-dwells-in-the-Kassite-Houses" may have received offerings sponsored by the palace (CUSAS 9, 59: 16; perhaps in 82: 26′), which certainly suggests royal acknowledgement that this group was welcome in Sealand I society.

In addition, one unpublished text shows that Ayadaragalama entertained diplomatic relations with a Kassite lord or ruler:[83] a lamb was delivered to the

---

79 See Boivin 2016b: 54–56 for a detailed discussion on *miksu*-fields and the related tax; see also Section 5.2.1.1.

80 The only role in which Kassites appear which could distinguish them from the mass of individuals bearing Akkadian names is as recipients of textiles and copper; this will be discussed forthwith.

81 See on this Sassmannshausen 2004a: 290–91.

82 Dalley (2009: 25 n.21′) opted for the former interpretation, but also noted the other possible reading.

83 Year name F of Ayadaragalama might refer to enmity between the Sealand I ruler and Kassites but the interpretation of the formula is uncertain: mu a.a.dàra.galam.ma lugal.e bàd zag (.gar) (íd) ḫar gu.la^{ki} lú.kúr KAL ŠU Ú mu.un.na.dù.a (the long version is used in the texts CUSAS 9, 156; 409). Dalley (2009: 11) suggested a reading "Year when A. the king built the wall of the shrine (...) Great Ring, (against?) the Kalšû-enemy(?)." She notes that a reading /*kaš*/ of the sign KAL is problematic, as would be the hypothesis of a dissimilation *šš* > *lš*, and therefore an interpretation of "Kalšu" as Kassite appears unwarranted. However, since

palace for the messenger (DUMU *šipri*) of one Buragindar (text BC 435 cited by Dalley 2009: 47),[84] a ruler otherwise unknown. This attestation shows that a Kassite leader was on diplomatic terms with the southern kingdom shortly after the fall of Babylon. Buragindar did not necessarily reign on a large area but he was important enough to have his messenger received at a Sealand I palace. Other texts from the archive suggest that these good relations were either facilitated by gifts or perhaps by trade. Indeed, although this "messenger of Buragindar" is not identified by name, another individual bearing a Kassite name, Ugin-Saḫ, is also called a messenger—in that case KIN.GI_4.A—in the same archive (CUSAS 9, 455: 4–5). The text records that he received garments and copper in moderate but non-negligible quantities, a transaction which was apparently no exceptional event because we find Ugin-Saḫ receiving the same goods also in CUSAS 9, 460: 1–3; in the latter text, he is not identified as messenger but the complete similarity of context suggests that we are dealing with the same person. He may also be the same Ugin-Saḫ who twice received ewes (CUSAS 9, 25: 5; 49: 2)[85] and once grain allotments (CUSAS 9, 451). Whether there was one or more individuals by the same name is impossible to say,[86] but at least one Kassite messenger received items fit for trade or for presentation as a gift.

The recipients of copper and garments in the archive may in fact all have names that are neither Akkadian, nor Sumerian, and at least some of which are Kassite.[87] The quantities handed out appear rather modest for trade and none of these individuals are identified as merchants. However, the context of the few relevant records is unknown, and trade can not be excluded. What these few documents tell us for certain is that moderate quantities of imported

---

the Akkadian form of the gentilic *kaššû* derives from galzu, perhaps also *kalzu (Balkan 1954: 131), such an orthography may not be completely impossible.

84 This took place only a few days before a messenger (LÚ KIN.GI_4.A) of Elam received two ewes (CUSAS 9, 40: 3–4). The lamb for the Kassite messenger was apparently required for the 8.iii of year N, the ewes for the Elamite messenger on the 12.iii of year N. There may have been political reasons for the presence of a Kassite and an Elamite envoy at the same time at the Sealand court. Noteworthy is also that the Kassite messenger received fewer animals than the Elamite one.

85 If he is the same, and if he was sent by a neighboring Kassite leader, he was present at least in four different years at the Sealand I palace (years I; J; L; and N).

86 Ugin-Saḫ appears alongside one Šigin-Saḫ in CUSAS 9, 25 and 451.

87 In CUSAS 9, 456: 2 and 4 garments were given to two individuals whose names are broken but perhaps Kassite: one begins with Kutta-, an element attested at Nuzi (Purves 1943: 231; Oppenheim 1937–39: 34; Ebeling 1939: 56) and one with Burra- (Balkan 1954: 48). The other recipients of copper and garments in CUSAS 9, 460 are probably also non Akkadian but their origin is unclear: Inbassati on line 6, Kunakki on line 8 and perhaps Šupal on line 10. Zadok (2014: 229) considers that Kunakki is "unexplained (non-Semitic)." Šu-pa-al is reminiscent of Kassite names attested at Nuzi (Purves 1943: 195; 259).

goods (copper) and goods that were probably produced locally (textiles) were handed out to individuals with foreign names—including Kassites—sometimes more than once on the same day (CUSAS 9, 460). We know from a few records that Kassites were involved in trade in northern Babylonia during the late Old Babylonian period (Van Lerberghe 1995: 383 and 386),[88] one can thus wonder whether some Kassite groups and settlements acted as trading agents between the Sealand kingdom and its northern neighbor(s).

4.4.3 Ešnunna

We do not know much about the political history of the Diyala, in particular of Ešnunna, in the late Old Babylonian period. Babylon's hegemony in the region after Hammurapi's conquest must have been short-lived or at least unstable, since newly published letters to and from the Ešnunnean king Iluni suggest that he entertained close diplomatic relations with his eastern neighbors but that he was only distantly friendly with Babylon (Guichard 2016: 33; 38–39). In his tenth year name, Samsu-iluna celebrated a victory over Ešnunna; after that episode, the situation is unclear but the relations were certainly at times acrimonious (Charpin 2004: 347),[89] although one text from Babylon informs us that, by the time it was on the eve of its demise, Babylon maintained at least commercial relations with the eastern city (VS 22, 37).[90] All the while, Kassites (or perhaps

88 Van Lerberghe (1995: 387 f. no.1) refers in particular to texts BM 97292, 97252, and 97206 dated to Abī-ešuḫ, and to text BM 78378 for which he offers an edition.

89 The period of distant diplomacy between Iluni and Babylon may pre- or post-date Si 10 (Guichard 2016: 27–29). At any rate, Samsu-iluna's twentieth year name celebrating a victory over Ešnunna shows that Babylon was still trying to keep or regain control over the city, after which we are in the dark as to Ešnunna's fate. It appears that Samsu-iluna had not given up controlling the Diyala since he built a fortress at Khafadje—commemorated in his twenty-fourth year name—probably to ensure control over its lower plain (Charpin 2004: 347–48). Also, towards the end of his reign, he may have been for a time in control of the Hamrin Valley in the upper Diyala, although we have only year names attesting to Babylon's involvement in the area (*ibid.*: 363; Pientka 1998: 263). Conflict with Ešnunna perdured during Abī-ešuḫ's reign, but trade also took place with other locations in the Diyala (Pientka 1998: 263; Charpin 2004: 369).

90 This contract from Babylon is dated to the fourteenth year of Samsu-ditāna and records a loan to fund a commercial expedition to Ešnunna (Klengel 1983: 34–35). The text is also discussed in Charpin 2004: 383 n.2003, where it is erroneously identified as VS 22 34. See also Pientka 1998: 296. In the very few other texts of this period in which Ešnunna is mentioned, the context and relationship between Babylon and Ešnunna is even less clear; see Pientka 1998: 296. She apparently assumed that trade took place because, in her discussion of the text VS 22,

more precisely Samḫarû) apparently settled in the Diyala, as may be evidenced in changes in the slave trade and personal names (van Koppen 2017: 61–63).

In the period following the fall of Babylon, the Sealand kingdom and Ešnunna—or whatever power controlled the latter—seem to have entertained strained relations. Indeed, the letter CUSAS 9, 3 informs us that Ešnunneans traveling by boat to Sealand destinations were detained by one of its officials (see also Section 3.1.2.2). The incident recorded in the letter shows that traveling into Sealand territory did not appear impossible to Ešnunneans, however, they were probably not very numerous to undertake such a journey, because the official who detained the travelers needed to ask his superior for instructions.[91] His hesitation on his course of action could also be indicative of a recent, sudden change in the relations between both polities, perhaps related to instabilities and uncertainties following the fall of Babylon.

4.5 A second wave of expansion under Dam(i)q-ilišu?

Sources available to us are silent on Sealand I activity following the clashes between Babylon and Ilī-ma-ilu surrounding the latter's thrust into central and perhaps even part of northern Babylonia, and Babylon's response to it. Whether the Sealand kingdom had a stake in further turbulent episodes at Nippur—the only city that we know for certain had fallen under early Sealand control—is unclear, and it was shown that there are at present no indication that the southern kingdom was directly involved in the (partial) abandonment of that city. In fact, we do not know whether open conflicts occurred at all in the period between Abī-ešuḫ's failed attempt to defeat Ilī-ma-ilu and a raid of Ammī-ditāna's on Udannu late in his reign. If we take this absence of sources as positive evidence, it could suggest that the second Sealand I king, Itti-ili-nībī, positioned himself differently than his predecessor and tried to make peace with Babylon. Surmises drawn from the absence of evidence are always a perilous exercise but this purported scenario would certainly match the indications—admittedly very slight—found in texts from Dūr-Abī-ešuḫ[(canal)] that diplomatic relations may have taken place between the Sealand I state and Babylon during Abī-ešuḫ's reign (on this, see Section 4.3.1).

84, she mentions that certain goods were bought there; however, the letter is probably referring to the private property of someone who moved his household (Kraus and Klengel 1983: 52–53).

91 Van Koppen (2010: 457; 2017: 76) sees in that letter evidence that Ešnunna was "still a political factor of importance." I don't see proof of this in the letter; the origin of the travelers need not imply that Ešnunna itself was a seat of political power.

At any rate, by the reign of the following king Dam(i)q-ilišu, the situation had certainly deteriorated.

4.5.1 Ammī-ditāna's campaign and the control of Udannu

The next open conflict between Babylon and the Sealand kingdom known to us was recorded in Ammī-ditāna's thirty-seventh year formula (Horsnell 1999: vol.II 319–20). This year name informs us that Babylon destroyed the wall of EZENx-SIG_7^{ki}, probably corresponding to the town of Udannu.[92] The chronology of events suggests that Udannu was of some strategic importance: the third Sealand I king Dam(i)q-ilišu fortified the city, Ammī-ditāna took it—or at least could reach it and cause some destruction –, then the town was certainly rebuilt by a Sealand I ruler because text CUSAS 9, 101 shows that by the reign of Aya-daragalama Udannu was (again) part of his realm and a place that the king could visit.

Considering that Udannu was almost certainly located on the Euphrates, and very probably north of the main seat of power of the dynasty,[93] it probably belonged at the time to the border region between both kingdoms. Ammī-ditāna's attack on it, which could be effectively contained, shows also that Babylon had by then shifted its theater of action against the southern state from the Tigris to the Euphrates area. It may also indicate that the Sealand kingdom was now beginning to threaten the Euphrates fortresses that Abī-ešuḫ had operated and probably controlled the area along the river as far down as Uruk, probably not far north of Udannu.

4.5.2 Dam(i)q-ilišu makes a name for himself

Ammī-ditāna's attack on a Sealand I fortified city may have been the culminating event in a series of otherwise perhaps mainly defensive measures by the Babylonian king, as reflected in a number of year names concerning a military conscription and the construction of fortifications between his third and his thirty-fifth year.[94] The Babylonian king was certainly justified in this, considering

92 For a discussion of the name of the town, see Section 3.1.1.

93 On this, see Section 3.1.3.

94 The most relevant years are his third (military conscription); his eleventh, sixteenth, eighteenth, thirty-second, and thirty-fifth (fortification works). Richardson (2017) considers in particular the years Ad 11 to Ad 22 to have been a "crisis decade."

that Nippur was attacked in his eleventh year (see Section 4.3.1). Although the identity of the attacker in that case is unknown, there are a few indications that Ammī-ditāna's measures were, at least in part, a response to an increased threat from his southern neighbor the Sealand, during the reign of its third king Dam(i)q-ilišu.

In the year name Ad 37, the builders of the city wall of Udannu are called either ÉREN *dam-qí-ì-lí-šu*-KE$_4$ "troops (people) of Dam(i)q-ilišu," or simply *dam-qí-ì-lí-šu*. The Sealand I king is personally acknowledged in a fashion that is not very common in an Old Babylonian year name.[95] There is apparently a will to associate this military deed with that particular foe: Babylon did not only destroy the city's wall, it did it against Dam(i)q-ilišu.[96] This may have arisen from the wish to record at least that success—however small—against this enemy, because no decisive victory against the entire polity appeared possible anymore.

The DynKL calls Simbar-Šipak, who is listed as the first king of the Sealand II dynasty (col. V line 8′), a soldier of the BALA of Dam(i)q-ilišu (col.V lines 2′–3′).[97] If the latter is the third Sealand I king (and not the Isin I king), this not only presents him as the remote ancestor of Simbar-Šipak, but also as the head of his dynasty, therefore bypassing his two predecessors as per king lists. We do not know what sources were used by the chronicler but they seem to have presented Dam(i)q-ilišu in a fairly prominent position. This would be cogent with active leadership and probably war exploits by this Sealand I king.

Finally, it is possible that Dam(i)q-ilišu was remembered in another late text, probably from the seventh century and found at Nineveh, in which his name is dubbed eternal (K 3992: line 10).[98] The text is very fragmentary and does not make clear in what context these rulers are referred to, but it seems to give weight to the fact that Dam(i)q-ilišu left his imprint in local historiographic and perhaps literary tradition.

---

95 In the same period, other enemies identified by name in the year formulae of a king of Babylon are Araḫab(u) in Ad 17 (Horsnell 1999: vol.II 292–93) and Aḫušina, king of Ešnunna in year dd of Abī-ešuḫ (Horsnell 1999: vol.II 258–59); in the latter case, the king was taken captive, which certainly explains why he was named in the formula.

96 As opposed to a formula like "destroyed the walls of Ur, Larsa, and Uruk and defeated the army of Akkad" in Si 11 (Horsnell 1999: vol.II 195).

97 Glassner (2004: 132–33) interprets the passage differently; he considers that the ancestor of Simbar-Šipak, Erība-Sîn, was a soldier who died during Dam(i)q-ilišu's reign.

98 A transliteration and a translation are given in Winckler 1893–97: 516. See also Brinkman 1976: 96. One Agum, probably one of the early Kassite kings, is also mentioned in it (line 8).

4.6 A fragile equilibrium

On the whole, sources suggest that open conflict between Babylon and the Sealand kingdom took place only sporadically. Late Old Babylonian evidence from northern Babylonia does not identify southern Babylonia—or the Sealand kingdom—as a source of slaves or prisoners at any time during that period (van Koppen 2004; Richardson 2002: 304–05). Also, since the year names and inscriptions of the later kings of Babylon remain, with only one exception, stubbornly silent on the Sealand kingdom, some equilibrium of sorts probably developed between the neighbors.[99] The basis for such a situation may have been a reciprocal dependency: while the southern state probably needed a certain measure of good will from Babylon to ensure sufficient water supply downstream,[100] one may surmise that Babylon was interested in keeping some access to the gulf trade, even if only indirectly; the latter was probably best attained through peaceful trading relations with the Sealand kingdom. We have proof for Sealand control over Dilmun—and hence political involvement in the Gulf trade—only for the end of the dynasty, but, given the southern anchor of early Sealand geography discussed in the previous chapter, it seems likely that a direct access to the Persian Gulf was ensured very early in Sealand I history. As for the water supply, we can only observe that hydraulic undertakings became less numerous in year formulae of the kings of Babylon after they lost the southern plain, and after Abī-ešuḫ's damming of the Tigris (Pientka 1998: 224). The location of the canals dug by the late Old Babylonian kings is unknown (*ibid.*: 225), therefore we do not know whether and how they affected Sealand I territory.[101]

This suggested interpretation of a pragmatic balance of interest between Babylon and the Sealand kingdom is speculative; there is only little and indirect evidence for it. The sources available at the moment suggest in fact that Babylon and the Sealand kingdom had no direct economic interactions. Babylon's atten-

---

99 However, the number of royal inscriptions decreases sharply after Samsu-iluna, leaving us for historical purposes with one fewer type of source to work with.

100 Perhaps the Sealand I rulers were also interested in safe passage upstream on the Euphrates for commercial purposes; a few archival records show that aromatics from the West were used in the Sealand kingdom (see Section 5.2.1.3). However, such goods may also have been bought through intermediaries.

101 Most recently, Richardson (2015b) suggested to identify a canal dug by Ammī-ditāna as the already existing Hammurapi-nuḫuš-nišī canal, probably delivering water to Nippur and perhaps further downstream. If his interpretation is correct, this deed would be recorded in a variant of his twenty-second year name.

tion mostly followed the Euphrates upstream,[102] including Hana (Podany 2002: 55), and we have seen that there were interactions with Ešnunna. The Sealand I rulers were probably maintaining trading relationships mostly south in the gulf area,[103] since evidence shows that they later controlled Dilmun, and perhaps Failaka,[104] and also east with Elam, with which it was shown that they entertained good relations.[105] As discussed in Section 4.4.2, they may also have traded through Kassite groups, if so, presumably with northern areas. But the Sealand I archival texts available to us yield very limited information on diplomatic and commercial matters; their purview is for the most part restricted to palatial involvement in the local economy, they are therefore not the best witnesses of the geo-political reality of the kingdom.

Richardson (2017) suggests a different analysis of this period of equilibrium: he sees in the late Old Babylonian evidence, mainly year names and edicts, signs of an active, programmatic courting of southern Babylonian political and cultural loyalties by the kings of Babylon who positioned themselves as the true heirs to the ancient Sumerian kingship, vying for it with their Sealand counterparts. His argument is attractive, there are, however, some problems with his proposed chronology of events. The very identification of a "Sumerianizing" in Babylon's year names *after* Samsu-iluna is somewhat problematic because many elements considered diagnostic by Richardson are already present in the early date formulae of Samsu-iluna.[106] Also, we do not know whether the early Sealand I kings positioned themselves as champions of whatever Sumerian sense of identity there might have been in southern Babylonia; one cannot but observe that nearly

---

102 No records of commercial contacts with Sealand I agents have been found in northern Babylonia. Silver loans for commercial expeditions do not necessarily specify the destination; but when they do they indicate that late Old Babylonian merchants from northern Babylonia traded along the Euphrates (see Skaist 1994: 185 for a list of texts; also Richardson 2002: 340 ff.).

103 On the basis of a parallel with proto-Canaanite alphabetical scripts Hamidović (2014: 146) has prudently suggested that the linear inscriptions found on the edge of four Sealand I tablets could indicate trade contacts across the Arabian peninsula. Similarities between some of the symbols scratched on the edge of tablets CUSAS 9, 67; 134; 149; 435 and symbols found on pottery on Failaka and Dilmun (Laursen 2016: 6) can also be observed, although the repertoire used on the Sealand I tablets appears definitely larger, and its origin is probably indeed to be looked for in the western semitic early scripts.

104 See Section 3.1.1.

105 See Section 4.4.1.

106 Some "diagnostic" terms are already attested in the early years of Samsu-iluna, for instance: in Si 6 (ALAN(.A.NI); ŠÙD; ^{d}LAMMA), in Si 7 (^{giš}TUKUL; ŠU-NIR), and in Si 8 (^{urudu}KI.LUGAL.GUB(.BA))

all the Sealand I rulers who were contemporary with the late Old Babylonian kings at Babylon probably bore Akkadian names (see Section 2.2.2).

4.7 Gulkišar and the final strife against the first dynasty of Babylon

An unpublished fragmentary royal epic (HS 1885+) in which the Sealand I king Gulkišar is the main protagonist evokes a battle between him and the last ruler of the first dynasty of Babylon Samsu-ditāna (Zomer 2016; forthcoming). The best preserved portion of the epic presents Gulkišar haranguing his troops, describing how he will utterly defeat Samsu-ditāna's armies. The exact archaeological context of the tablet is not known but it is considered to be from Nippur; the script and ductus suggest either a late Old Babylonian or perhaps rather a Kassite date of writing,[107] therefore possibly relatively close in time to the purported battle. If we accept that the epic has its origin in actual events, then an episode of war of some historical moment took place. Of course, the purported original occurrences probably underwent first propagandistic inflation before being recycled into epic literature. Nonetheless, the very existence and tone of the epic seem to suggest that Gulkišar came out as the victor of a conflict with Samsu-ditāna, and the question which immediately presents itself is whether it was part of Babylon's final downfall. But because reign lengths in BKL A have proved unreliable, we cannot even be certain that Gulkišar was still on the throne at the end of Samsu-ditāna's reign.

An oracular question posed by the hard-pressed Samsu-ditāna suggests a conjunction of enemy forces menacing one of his cities, but the Sealand or Eurukug is absent from that list (CTN IV 63: i31 ff. = Lambert 2007: no.1 lines 31 ff.), an absence qualified of "noteworthy" by Lambert (2007: 144). He considered that this attack failed, which could have prompted the Hittite king Muršili I to march from Anatolia "to do the job properly and finish off the First Dynasty of Babylon;" his surmise implies that he assumed Babylon was the endangered city. Charpin (2004: 382), for his part, suggested that the city in question was rather one whose citizens' loyalty was doubtful because the question also inquires about the possibility of residents conferring with the enemies and letting them

107 E. Zomer, personal communication. I also thank her for sharing with me her transliteration of the text prior to publication. The text apparently does not present the typical Sealand I ductus; there may be a regional aspect to that difference, should other known Sealand I tablets all have originated in south-western Babylonia.

in (lines 78 ff.).[108] At any rate, the last Babylon I king knew that he was threatened by many enemies—in that particular episode coming at least from the east and the north—and he apparently expected them to attack together in a very organized fashion, with siege engines (lines 54 ff.) and allied foreign troops (line 34 and *passim*).[109] The Sealand kingdom is not mentioned either in other documents referring to this episode.[110]

Although it may not have been recorded as a participant in the downfall of the first dynasty of Babylon, the following facts are nonetheless suggestive of Sealand I involvement: it has been shown that Elam and the Sealand kingdom entertained good relations, and Elam is named as an enemy threatening Babylon in the oracular question discussed above; also, and perhaps more significantly, the Sealand I dynasty was able to maintain itself for many years after foreign powers intruded deep onto the Mesopotamian lower plain, when they dealt the fatal blow to Babylon. This strongly suggests that the Sealand kingdom was part of this coalition of sorts. The battle between Gulkišar and Samsu-ditāna can therefore probably be viewed as an episode of a broader scheme.

As one of the victors over Babylon, it would seem likely that the Sealand I king gained something by it, part of the spoils or control over some areas. This is the time when a ruler of that dynasty may have reigned at Babylon, although there is no evidence for it. But if a Sealand I ruler did, Gulkišar could certainly be a good candidate since his reign may have extended after Samsu-ditā-

---

108 Richardson (2016: 117 and n.82) considers that it is Babylon.

109 The list of powers involved in the fall of Babylon has given rise to much discussion and speculation; the oracular question, cast by the party which was attacked, identifies the Elamite army, the Kassite army, the Idamaras army, the Hanigalbat army, the Samharite army, the Eda-šuštu army and their foreign allies (Lambert 2007: no.1 lines 31–40). See also Richardson 2015a for a recent addition to the interpretation of this passage. Babylon probably could not have stood long against such an onslaught, especially since the loyalty of "important citizens" *a-šib* URU DUGUD and "foreign speakers" KA! *na-kar-tum* (lines 78 and 85) within the city seemed ready to shift to embrace the cause of Babylon's opponents. Therefore, the oracle question was probably put late in Samsu-ditāna's reign, whether it pertained to an attack on the city of Babylon itself or not. For a recent and comprehensive assessment of the extant sources, see Richardson 2016.

110 The *kudurru* of Kadašman-Ḫarbe I, therefore written by the descendant of one of the victors, lists the Amorites, the Haneans, and the army of the Kassites (Paulus 2014a: document KḪ I 1, lines i 5–7). The Edict of Telepinu states that when Muršili (I) destroyed Babylon, he also fought Hurrians (Hoffmann 1984: 18–19 § 9 lines 29–30); if we are to trust the historiographic information contained in this document, it remains unclear whether these Hurrians were defending Babylon or also fighting it (they were perhaps the Hanigalbat army of the *tamītu* text cited above?).

na's, at a time when Babylon could have been easy to occupy.[111] Also, he accomplished a feat which only few Sealand I kings achieved: he was remembered in later sources, although never as king of Babylon.[112]

Indeed, Gulkišar appears in the colophon of a glass-making treatise known from a tablet (BM 120960) probably dating to the Kassite period (Oppenheim 1970: 60; 62).[113] The treatise explains a recipe for making "red-stone glass" and concludes with the name of the scribe, his filiation, the additional information that he is a "scribe of Marduk, a man of Babylon," É.MAŠ ^{d}AMAR.UTU LÚ.NUN^{ki} (lines 39–41), and a date formula giving the year as mu.ús.sa gul-ki-šár lugal.e (line 43), thus apparently very early in Gulkišar's reign. The insistence on the Babylonian origin is surprising; it does not belong to the usual formulary of colophons (Hunger 1968: 1). The scribe gave as the name of his father Uššur-ana-Marduk, who is attested as the ancestor of a fourteenth century scribal family that saw members of the second and third generations enter in the service of the royal houses in Aššur and Babylon (Wiggerman 2008: 205). Whether this was his true ancestry is doubtful, but the reference to Uššur-ana-Marduk—be it as his father or as a famed ancestral name in scribal circles—proves that the document was not written during Gulkišar's reign, unless we have a case of homonymy. The dating of the tablet was dismissed as a forgery early on (Landsberger 1954: 68 n.174; Oppenheim 1970: 62–63), an interpretation now confirmed by Wiggerman's analysis (2008: 225; see also George 2009: 149). If we accept that the tablet is no copy of an ancient original, for which there are no indications, the central question is why of all Babylonian rulers the scribe chose Gulkišar for his falsified date formula. Oppenheim (1970: 62–63) suggested that the scribe used an archaizing syllabary and the name of Gulkišar perhaps to "demonstrate the antiquity of the native glass lore." George (2009: 149) pointed out that the

111 Note that van Koppen (2017: 72–73) considers that there was no significant hiatus at Babylon.

112 Of course, the inclusion of the Sealand I dynasty in king lists could be based on other criteria: the scribes may have preferred a local, after all Babylonian, dynasty to fill in that period of confusion in which a number of foreign powers had a hand.

113 Oppenheim (1970: 60) considers that the ductus is fairly unspecific and can only be associated with the second half of the second millennium or the first two centuries of the first millennium. It is the onomasticon, in particular the orthography of the name of the scribe, which he considers more typical of the period between the fourteenth and the twelfth century, as well as the use of the expression *ša qāt* to introduce the name of the scribe (*ibid.*: 62). A number of peculiarities in the orthography of this text are also found in the prologue of the *kudurru* of Kadašman-Ḫarbe I (YBC 2242 = AOAT 51, KḪ I 1). Paulus (2014: 300) notes these parallels in the commentary of lines i 2; i 4(!); i 11; note that she identifies the glass-making treaty as BM 120690 instead of the correct BM 120960.

scribe, when trying to give an impression of antiquity to the document, unwittingly built in an anachronism in bringing together the names of Uššur-ana-Marduk and Gulkišar, but more importantly that the reference to this king "can now be taken as explicit recognition by later Babylonian scholarship that the Sealand kings (...) presided over a realm in which scholarship was active."[114] This scholarship is indeed now evidenced by divinatory and literary texts produced in Sealand I scriptoria (George 2013: 129–31; Gabbay 2014a; Gabbay and Boivin forthcoming). While this certainly seems a cogent explanation, a memory of this specific king as a great patron of scholarship remains to be proven by more solid documentary evidence. At any rate, although it is impossible to reconstruct the intention of the scribe when forging the date formula of his text,[115] his reference to Gulkišar certainly suggests that this king was well remembered a few centuries after his reign, which agrees with the fact that he was also made the stuff of epic literature. A small hymn fragment from Nippur (Ni 13090), possibly of Kassite date, also mentions Gulkišar, indicating that his memory was transmitted in Babylonian scribal milieux in the second half of the second millennium.

That the name of Gulkišar was well-remembered at least until the beginning of the eleventh century is evidenced by his mention in the *Distanzangabe* of the *kudurru* BE I/1 83 (obv. 3 and 6)[116] dated to Enlil-nādin-apli. Again the central question is why Gulkišar was chosen by the Isin II king to establish that a parcel of disputed land had very long ago[117] been donated to the goddess Nazi. It may

---

114 George also refers to Hallo (1975: 199–201) who had, with little textual evidence, posited that the Sealand I kingdom had been a refuge for Sumerian scholars after the fall of Babylon, making it the *locus* of production of what he called post-Sumerian literature.

115 The juxtaposition of the statement of the scribe's origin as Babylonian and of the name of Gulkišar is puzzling. Even if Gulkišar or perhaps his successor(s) did rule for a time at Babylon, it probably never was at the center of their kingdom; the archive published in CUSAS 9 and dating to Gulkišar's two successors points towards a modest importance of the god Marduk in the palace-sponsored cult. But after the northwards movements of groups of individuals which marked the beginning of the late Old Babylonian period, one can certainly imagine refugees still cherishing and passing on to the next generations a sense of belonging to southern and central Babylonian culture. The reasons for migrating are complex and refugees need not have been staunch opponents of the southern kings, especially not in the following generations. Conversely, some northern scholars may have fled into Sealand I centers for a while after the fall of Babylon (Hallo 1975: 201), at a time which could indeed be that of Gulkišar.

116 For a recent edition, AOAT 51, ENAp 1. See also Section 3.1.2.2.

117 The number of years covering the span of time between Gulkišar and Enlil-nādin-apli's father Nabuchadnezzar I is given as 696 years, a figure that is blatantly wrong since it puts Gulkišar's reign in the late nineteenth century. Brinkman (1968: 117), considered that an original of the time of Gulkišar has indeed been found, and he suggested an ingenious explanation for the

simply be that an ancient real estate document from Gulkišar was indeed found and that the later king saw fit to refer to it. But it may very well be that Enlil-nādin-apli and his administration simply used the well-remembered(?) name of Gulkišar to confer legitimacy to a claim over land, as it was used for specialized knowledge in the case of the glass-making treatise.

The evidence for Gulkišar's relationship with Babylon is meagre and ambiguous; without more positive sources, one can neither conclude to nor exclude a rule of this Sealand I king there. But it seems fairly certain that events and tradition conferred to him a special stature since he was remembered long after his time. The evidence from the reign of his two successors, in particular from the reign of Ayadaragalama, suggests that the Sealand kingdom came to control the Nippur area: the texts show that the Nippur pantheon was then of importance in the Sealand I state pantheon—and perhaps that they controlled its official cults.[118] Therefore, it is possible that the final collapse of the late Old Babylonian state resulted in the Sealand I kings, perhaps already Gulkišar, either occupying Nippur on a very modest scale in order to carry on cultic activity, and/or taking over parts of its official cults in a displaced setting at Dūr-Abī-ešuḫ (see Section 4.3.1; Gabbay and Boivin forthcoming).[119]

4.8 The redesign of the Babylonian political landscape

We know very little of the period following the fall of the first dynasty of Babylon. The prologue of a *kudurru* dating to Kadašman-Ḫarbe I (YBC 2242 = AOAT 51, KḪ I 1) suggests that the land went through a major disruption, which of course probably began before the final blow to Babylon. The text is known from an exemplar probably dating to the eleventh century (Brinkman 2015), but which may have been based on an original from ca.1400.[120] It mentions that land plot borders were no longer recognizable (col. I, 1–13), which bespeaks a period of abandonment or at least severe disorganization in parts of Babylonia.[121] If there was

figure of 696 years, based on reign lengths in king lists and an oversight by the scribe (see Section 2.3).

118 See Section 6.5.3.

119 Van Koppen (2017: 71) considers that central and northern Babylonian cults could have been taken over in a displaced setting, from Ḫursaĝkalama.

120 Brinkman (2015) does not take position.

121 The *kudurru* is unprovenanced; the plot of land discussed in the document lay along the Tigris (col.II 1–4). However, the prologue has probably no direct bearing on the legal object of the *kudurru*, therefore no specific area can be associated with the claims of obliteration of the

an original of the time of Kadašman-Ḫarbe I, beyond any hyperbolae used by the ruler to exalt his own exertions[122] the reference to neglect in land management probably contains some truth, at least enough to make the allusion understandable and therefore effective. This suggests that in some areas no state was managing land rights properly.

As seen above, the Sealand kingdom was probably involved in the events surrounding the final years of the Babylon I dynasty and may have been in a position to partake in whatever spoils the victory brought with it. We have no evidence that an important northern expansion of the Sealand kingdom ensued, but at least a nominal control of Nippur appears likely. The CUSAS 9 archive, which dates roughly to that period—one or two generations after the fall of Babylon—pertains by and large to local matters and is not very helpful for determining whether the geo-political situation of the kingdom had changed in the recent past. The use of imported aromatics[123] does suggest access to western trade routes; these may have been more easily accessible to the southern kingdom with the Babylon I kings and their grip over the middle Euphrates gone. The great similarity between the documents found at al-Qalʿat al-Bahrein, which include one tablet dated to Ea-gāmil, and the Sealand I archive dating two to three generations earlier could suggest that Dilmun had been a dependency of the southern Babylonian kingdom for some time.[124] It has been shown in Section 4.4.3 that relations with Ešnunna were probably strained (or perhaps had changed recently), but that the Sealand kingdom entertained diplomatic relations with its Elamite neighbor (Section 4.4.1) and with at least one Kassite group (Section 4.4.2). This latter ally of Ayadaragalama, Buragindar, may have belonged to a Kassite house competing with the one that finally installed itself at Babylon, since his name does not appear in king lists. This could in the end have put the southern kingdom on the wrong side of friendships among the aspiring contenders to the Babylonian throne. Be it as it may, while Tell Mu-

---

borders; indeed, the prologue mentions sweepingly the borders of "KUR *šu*$_4$*-me-rim* / *ù ak-ka-di-i*" (I 2–3).

122 Baker (2011: 301) noted that Kassite and Isin II rulers "actively sought to promote themselves (...) as guardians of fairly established boundaries."

123 See Section 5.2.1.3.

124 The formulary of a number of documents is the same, for instance: the "MU.DU *ana* É.GAL" in delivery records QA 94.55; 94.56; 94.66; etc. (for the same use in the Sealand I archive, see Section 5.1); the use of Ì.SÁ in ledger QA 01.4 (for the same in the Sealand I archive, see Boivin 2016b: 47 n.13). Also there are similarities in the ductus: for instance the ligature *a+na* (in QA 94.56: 5 and many other instances), the position of the *Winkelhaken* in RI as an additional vertical wedge at the bottom of the last vertical (in QA 94.394: 2 and many other instances); for a description of these features as characteristic of the Sealand I script, see George 2013: 131–32.

ḫammad apparently came under renewed overlordship by Babylon—or belonged to the same early Kassite state –, as suggested by the era-type year formula appearing in level II (Section 3.2.2.2), the Sealand kingdom maintained its independence for a few more generations, probably a sign of vigorous leadership and, at least for a time, wisely chosen friendships.

This need not mean that all went on peacefully in the southern kingdom: one year name of Ayadaragalama (year O; see Appendix 2),[125] points to a rebellion of his land (kalam.ma.a.ni mu.un.bal.e). We don't know when during his reign this happened but the overall time horizon of the archive puts it within the first eight years or little more following his accession. Two other of his year names suggest that troubles also came from outside: two enemies, on whose identity we have no information whatsoever, are alluded to in year E, and one enemy, the identification of which is uncertain, is mentioned in year F.[126]

In the end, neither Kassite nor Elamite allies could help the last Sealand I king Ea-gāmil defend his kingdom, although Elam may have at least offered him refuge, if we can trust the account given in *ABC* 20B (see Section 4.4.1). His kingdom was conquered by the Kassite rulers of Babylon and incorporated into Karduniaš, their growing realm.[127] There was probably some resistance to this conquest since chronicle *ABC* 20B records that, after Ulam-buriaš,[128] also Agum (III) had to march against the Sealand, on which occasion he destroyed a temple[129] at Dūr-Enlil, written ^{uru}BÀD-^{d}50 (rev. 15–18). Tantalizingly, a town of almost the same name, BÀD-^{d}EN-LÍL-LE-KE$_4$, is referred to in year name H of Ayadaragalama, which probably commemorates the (re)building of a temple.[130] It is tempting to establish a parallel between Dūr-Enlil and Dūr-Enlilē and suggest

---

125 It is attested only once, perhaps twice; for that reason, Dalley (2009: 12) suggested that this may be a clause within a longer year name.

126 For year E, Dalley (2009: 11) suggests the Kassites and the Elamites. We have no indication for it. In fact, at least in the case of Elam, we have indication that relations were friendly as seen in Section 4.4.1. As for the Kassites, they were probably a very scattered and divided group—or rather a collection of groups—at the time, therefore the diplomatic ties with one of their leaders was certainly no guarantee of peace with other Kassite groups. The reading of KAL ŠU Ú in year F is discussed in n. 83 in the present chapter. See also Dalley 2009: 11.

127 Van Koppen (2017: 76) suggests that the name applies to the unified Babylonia.

128 Van Koppen (2017: 75–76) suggests that the Sealand kingdom was in fact bequeathed to Ulam-buriaš by his father, who split his kingdom between his two sons, Kaštiliašu receiving the northern portion.

129 The É.GALGA.URÙ.NA, which is not attested in other sources. It is listed as no.336 in George 1993.

130 The name of this temple is transliterated by Dalley (2009: 12) as É.UNÚ$^{(ki)}$ LIBIR.RA.

that they were one and the same town; indeed one can well imagine that local resistance to the new overlords crystallized around a center which had enjoyed the favor of its past kings. However, they may be two different locations: one Kassite ledger recording tax payments lists separately the towns BÀD-^{d}EN-LÍL and BÀD-^{d}EN-LÍL.ḪI.A (BE 14, 5: respectively lines 5 and 10).[131] Identification (or dissociation) between those two locations remains thus uncertain.[132] At any rate, Agum III's raid probably sealed the fate of the Sealand kingdom.

The Kassites presumably immediately occupied the land conquered, including Dilmun; this shows in the seamless continuity that characterizes administrative activities and recording procedures at al-Qalʿat al-Bahrein in the period ranging at least from the time of Ea-gāmil until Agum (III) (Cavigneaux and André-Salvini forthcoming).[133] It appears also that the Kassites went actively to work on the southern mainland: Kurigalzu I, and before him to a lesser extent Karaindaš, rebuilt several temples in southern Babylonia, and after them Kadašman-Enlil I and Burna-buriaš II at Larsa (Bartelmus 2010: 163–65). It would seem, therefore, that one or two generations following the Kassite conquest of the Sealand kingdom the new rulers embarked on a large sacral building program in their newly annexed territory.

This extensive program may be in part responsible for the dearth of Sealand I archaeological evidence: no building inscriptions were found and, as yet, no structure explicitly built by Sealand I kings in any of the ancient cities. Heavy Kassite repairs and reconstruction may have obliterated much of the traces left by their predecessors. But the evidence for destruction and abandonment of

---

131 Nashef (1982: 90–91) also lists two towns: he normalizes as Dūr-Enlilē the toponyms in which the orthography of the theophoric element is ^{d}EN-LÍL.ḪI.A, ^{d}EN-LÍL(.LE).MEŠ, or ^{d}EN-LÍL-LE-E; recently published texts of the late Kassite period, presumably from Dūr-Enlilē, also feature orthographies with ^{d}EN-LÍL.ḪI.A and ^{d}EN-LÍL.MEŠ (van Soldt 2015); under the entry Dūr-Enlil in Nashef 1982: 90, the theophoric element is always written ^{d}EN-LÍL, with the exception of the instance that is of interest to us in *ABC* 20B, written ^{d}50.

132 The interpretation of the writing ^{d}50 used in the chronicle seems straightforward and must correspond to Dūr-Enlil. The also otherwise unattested orthography in the year name, ^{d}EN-LÍL-LE, is somewhat less clear; the year name is attested only once since other instances of it are either abbreviated or damaged (Dalley 2009: 12). One of the towns could correspond to the former(?) Dūr-Abī-ešuḫ where the illicit archive was found since Enlil was revered there (Van Lerberghe and Voet 2009: 3); moreover, the texts from Dūr-Enlilē, recently published, show that there were regular interactions between it and Nippur (van Soldt 2015: 29–30), which would agree with it.

133 The text dating to Ea-gāmil is QA 94.46; the texts dating to Agum are QA 94.42; 94.47; 94.49; 96.26. There is evidence that a Kassite governor was present at Dilmun in the fourteenth century, suggesting a fairly long occupation of the island by mainlanders (Potts 2006: 115 f.); this presence in the Persian Gulf may have included Failaka (Potts 2010: 22).

parts of the large urban centers cannot be entirely explained away; the built environment and the living space of the Sealand kingdom remain a largely unanswered question. The CUSAS 9 archive seems to confirm that the Sealand I state did not thrive (only) in the former urban and institutional setting. The palace-centric provisioning of temples showing in the records of its administration (Section 5.5) suggests that Sealand I rulers had (re-)established this palace, and sponsored cults in an environment devoid of well-functioning temples and clergies. Either this town was a new foundation or the Sealand I rulers occupied a town deserted by its clergies, a phenomenon which we know affected a number of urban centers.

The demographic trend that partly emptied cities has been explained by political factionalism: Yoffee (1998: 334) suggested that Sealand I leaders could have driven urban populations into the countryside because it was what they controlled, whereas cities remained pro-Babylonian. But the conquest of Nippur by Ilī-ma-ilu, and presumably of Dilmun including its fortress al-Qalʿat al-Bahrein at some point in Sealand I history, suggests that the southern rulers were very much able to take over well defended cities; moreover, the fact that the dynasty endured several generations makes it unlikely that Sealand I kings maintained themselves only by controlling stretches of land interspersed by hostile fortified enclaves; the duration of the dynasty suggests some measure of stability. That the political landscape was fractioned has also been suggested for northern Babylonia towards the end of its first dynasty (Richardson 2005: 284 and *passim*), a symptom of the rulers' waning grasp,[134] which would have been less sudden than in southern Mesopotamia but running along somewhat similar lines.

Environmental causes have also been considered to be behind the socio-economic and demographic changes in both north-Babylonian and Sealand I territory: repeated inundations appear to have plagued northern Babylonia in the late Old Babylonian period (Gasche 1989: 141–43; Cole and Gasche 1998: 53; Charpin 2002: 555), and hydraulic measures certainly had an effect downstream, probably reducing the water availability (Gasche 1989: 141; Charpin 2002: 555–56);[135] this probably worsened the effects of a general reduction of precipitations in that period (Gasche, et al. 2002: 534; Van Lerberghe, et al. 2017). The result was the partial abandonment of the large urban centers, which were most extensively excavated. The population probably resettled there only when the Kassite kings began reviving these centers with hydraulic and building works.

---

134 This could also be visible in the marked diminution in the number of royal inscriptions.
135 Al-Hamdani (2015: 143) considers that more water reached southern Babylonia because of a general abandonment of the field irrigation infrastructure in central Babylonia.

5 The Sealand I palatial economy

The evidence available to us so far does not warrant anything approaching the writing of a Sealand I economic history: we know nothing of the private sector; supra-regional state administration and economy, temple economy, and trade are also barely reflected in the extant documentation. Only the palatial economy,[1] whose apparatus produced the archive published in CUSAS 9, discloses itself to us in these tablets. The palace, written É.GAL, appears in the archive as an economic and administrative body managing resources for its own household and for a number of temples. The best documented resources in the extant texts are agricultural and animal: the records allow us to reconstruct, at least tentatively, how the palace procured and probably partly produced these resources, stored them, transformed them or commissioned their transformation, and consumed or spent them. Contemporary administrative texts recently unearthed at Tell Khaiber do not, so far, extend our understanding of Sealand I economy, rather, they corroborate elements of evidence found in the palatial archive by documenting the palatial procurement of agricultural resources from the outside perspective.

Accordingly, this chapter proposes a reconstruction of the Sealand I palatial economy, at least the portion of it that transpires through the recording of its resource management. In addition, ample space is given to an inventory of the resources—raw or transformed—found in these texts, as well as to the types of transactions described. Because the extant Sealand I texts are witnesses of a period for which we have very little information in general, be it on the crops grown, the types of dishes offered to gods, or the administrative jargon, it appears relevant to assess and present the little we now have in some detail.

5.1 A functional inventory of sources

The flow of goods between the palace and other economic actors, or between services within the palace, is documented in over 400 texts, a large subset of the extant palatial archive. An inventory of the tablets pertaining to the handling of goods reveals that most of them are delivery records, followed by receipts, then various types of expenditures. Delivery records were highly standardized and deliveries were overall subjected to more administrative measures of control

---

1 What I understand under "palatial economy" here is not a state economy dominated by the palace, but simply the economy of the palace itself as an institution.

https://doi.org/10.1515/9781501507823-006

than other transactions.[2] They were almost exclusively recorded from an external point of view (MU.DU PN *ana* É.GAL : delivery or delivered by PN to the palace). Apparently, only delivery records were issued in two copies: the copy was identified as *me-eḫ-rum* and stored in the palace, where it was apparently found by the looters. Similarly, with one exception,[3] only delivery records were sealed (presumably by the receiving palatial service), and they were probably the only records sometimes encased in an envelope. All these administrative operations applied to the same sub-group of tablets. They show that great care surrounded the recording of incoming goods, and that methods were in place for the palace to trace whether the delivering parties had fulfilled their obligations, and also for the latter to prove that they had. In addition, an official was very often recorded as being involved in the transaction, even two officials for certain types of deliveries; this confirms the keen interest of the palace administration in monitoring incoming goods (see also Boivin 2016c: 6–8). To the corpus of palatial texts, we can now add a number of records from Tell Khaiber, as yet unpublished, which document how grain was collected "for the palace" (Campbell et al. 2017).[4] This palace may very well have been the same (see also Section 3.1.3).

In contrast, outgoing goods were recorded in various manners, sometimes from the point of view of the palace, sometimes from the point of view of the recipient since both receiving and issuing formulae were used with no apparent consistency.[5] In general, the recording of outgoing goods seems to have been subjected to less standardized rules and less control. They are often identified only by the type of expenditure (salary, supplies, etc.). Officials are by far less present in expenditure records than in delivery records.

All relevant texts are grouped in the following table,[6] based primarily on their function (incoming, outgoing, etc.), and secondarily on their main administrative key word (MU.DU, ŠU.TI.A, *ana*, etc.). The grouping according to key

---

2 For a detailed examination of the formulary of Sealand I delivery records and a discussion of administrative procedures surrounding the procurement and the expenditure of goods, see Boivin 2016c.

3 Exceptionally, one list of *ḫargalû*-grain, presumably expenditures, is sealed (CUSAS 9, 369).

4 The authors also note a number of common features between the Tell Khaiber administrative texts and those published in CUSAS 9.

5 For instance one Dummuqu, a jeweler, received twice rams and other foodstuffs towards the end of the same year, once in a ŠU.TI.A receipt (CUSAS 9, 103), once in an expenditure record using the key word *nadānu* (CUSAS 9, 105: 1–8). The archive offers no indication that there was double recording (one receipt matching one record of expenditure), and the overall lack of standardization of records of outgoing goods speaks against this possibility.

6 Table 8 gives the quantity of texts for each group and category; the corresponding text numbers are given in Appendix 3. In the table, the numbers in brackets include the uncertain cases.

words on the right-hand side of the table derives directly from the terms used by the scribes; in only a few uncertain cases was it necessary to rely on a certain amount of interpretation based on the reconstruction of damaged passages and on the comparison with similar tablets from the archive. As for the functional grouping on the left-hand side of the table, it is interpretative because it is based on the meaning inferred from the records, not only on the terms used. This is particularly true for records without any key words. This interpretation is the result of a thorough study of the entire archive, combining functional, historical, and philological analyses of the material, several aspects of which are presented in this chapter.

The types of expenditure are so varied—including several kinds of allotments, supplies, and gifts—that they are not discriminated in Table 8; also, they all present the same basic functional aspect of recording outgoing goods. They will be discussed in detail in Section 5.4.

Table 8: Functional typology of sources pertaining to the movement of goods[7]

Function	Aspect of the transaction	Nr of texts	Main key word	Number of occurrences
Incoming goods	Delivery (to the palace)	230 (234)	MU.DU	227 (231)
			wabālu	1
			ana	3
	Purchase	1	*šâmu*	1
Incoming goods & material outgoing/ transferred for transformation	Delivery (to the palace) & reception	8 (9)	MU.DU & ŠU.TI.A	7 (8)
			MU.DU & *maḫāru*	1
	(Delivery) to the palace & expenditure	1	*ana* É.GAL & (a type of expenditure)	1
Material outgoing /transferred for transformation	Reception	51 (52)	ŠU.TI.A	50 (51)
			maḫāru	1
	-	1	-	1
	Expenditure & reception	2	*nadānu* & ŠU.TI.A	2

7 See Appendix 3 for corresponding text numbers. This table is a slightly modified version of the compilation presented in Boivin 2016c.

Table 8: Functional typology of sources pertaining to the movement of goods *(continued)*

Function	Aspect of the transaction	Nr of texts	Main key word	Number of occurrences
Outgoing goods	Reception	37 (40)	ŠU.TI.A	19 (22)
			maḫāru	18
	Expenditure & reception	3	*nadānu* & ŠU.TI.A	2
			nadānu & *maḫāru*	1
	Expenditure	73 (74)	ZI.GA	3
			nadānu	21 (22)
			SUM	1
			ZI.GA & *nadānu?*	1
			naqû	2
			ana	10
			-	37 (38)
Other or unclear		7		7

We see that the available archive gives us insight into the following economic processes in which the palace was involved:

(1) the procurement of several largely non-luxury resources by the palace, mostly animal and agricultural; this is documented in records of delivery to the palace, almost always with the key word MU.DU;

(2) the transformation of some resources either by the palace or commissioned by it; the most direct indication for this comes from texts recording both the reception of raw materials by workers (or a separate institution) and the delivery of transformed products to the palace. Also, some expenditures and receipts record materials handed out for transformation, either through a note to that effect on the record, or because such a context can be reconstructed from other texts of the archive concerning the same goods and individuals;

(3) the expenditure of several raw and transformed goods (mostly foodstuffs) for extispicy, cultic purposes, various rations and supplies to temples and individuals, some of whom were palace dependents. Outgoing goods were recorded either in expenditure records or in receipts, without an apparent system; due to the fairly free formulary of these records, it is not always clear

whether expenditures were indeed outgoing or whether they were for palace-internal consumption.[8]

5.2 The procurement of resources

As will be shown, the means used by the palace to procure resources included:

(1) levying taxes on the production of grain and various vegetables, as a share of the harvest; this applied apparently to more than one type of land ownership or use;[9]

(2) requesting the delivery of small cattle (probably palace-owned);

(3) imposing the delivery of dead cattle, including that of large cattle that was (probably) not palace-owned, either as a quota or for all carcasses;

(4) buying from merchants (leeks; bitumen; certainly also aromatics and means of production such as grinding stones).

The mechanisms for the procurement of dates, sesame, and live large cattle are unclear, as is the harvesting of wild-growing products (e. g., reed). Texts recording these transactions were probably not found by the looters. The same holds largely true for metals and other luxury resources.

5.2.1 Agricultural and other vegetal resources

This section reviews vegetal resources found in the Sealand I archival documents, mainly from the angle of their procurement by the palace. However, in order to present a comprehensive overview of the species attested in the archive, some plants found only in expenditure records are also surveyed here. However, malt and beer, also delivered to the palace, will be treated in the section on the

8 For that reason, internal and external expenditures are not treated in separate categories, which would have rested on moot criteria. In addition, some goods counted as outgoing may have been in reality for product transformation; the context does not always make it easy to determine what was intended.

9 In addition to regular tax levying, other deliveries of agricultural products may have been requested by the palace. Text CUSAS 9, 91 records the delivery to the palace of leeks and coriander by a merchant and by gardener(s), respectively; this delivery is called *erištu*. Dalley (2009: text 91 n.1) noted that the term probably had a meaning different from the more frequent *mēreštu*. The most apparent difference in use in this archive is that *erištu* is a delivery to the palace while *mēreštu* always appears in expenditure records. I would therefore suggest that the former was a request *by* the palace, the latter a request *to* the palace (see also Section 5.4.2).

transformation of raw materials because there is evidence that the palace did not simply procure them as (semi-)finished products but was greatly involved in their production.

5.2.1.1 Cereals

Cereals are omnipresent in the palatial archive. The production itself is not directly documented, since field work is never referred to.[10] Eighteen ledgers[11] record the payment of agricultural imposts to the palace in the form of a splitting of the crop following a fixed rate; these imposts were applied on a few crops, but cereals—barley in particular—make up the bulk of the produces registered. These ledgers show that the *šibšu* and the *miksu* were the main types of agricultural imposts, usually amounting to one third of the harvest. The *šibšu* may have applied to communal ground, while the payment of the *miksu* seems to have been related to the function or profession of the tax payers, perhaps for fields attributed to them for a royal service or as emolument. The payers of agricultural taxes are generally called *muškēnū* although the archive does not make it possible to determine what this term represented socially and economically.[12] One list shows that the *miksu* could be remitted (CUSAS 9, 384). For a detailed analysis and discussion of the Sealand I agricultural taxes, including the smaller imposts *kiṣru* and the barley of the *bāb/babti āli*, see Boivin 2016b.

The relevant documents in the palatial archive show that the collection of agricultural taxes was managed locally, at the town level: ledgers recording imposts delivered to the palace were drawn up for a given town (Boivin 2016b: 47; 52; 56), and the letter-order CUSAS 9, 14 shows that grain was—at least sometimes or partly—stored locally first, before being requested by the palace (for a discussion of this letter, see Boivin 2016b: 53). Tell Khaiber appears to have been one of the towns delivering agricultural imposts to the palace. Among the tablets found there, a few fragmentary texts seem to correspond to the recording of agricultural imposts, probably tallying quantities received with quan-

---

10 There is one exception: letter CUSAS 9, 13 refers to workers in a field. The Tell Khaiber texts unearthed so far do not appear to contain much information on this either (see also the comments to that effect in Campbell et al. 2017).

11 CUSAS 9, 410; 411; 413; 415; 426; 428; 429; 430; 431A; 432; 434; 441; 442; 443; 445; 446; 447; 448. Ledger CUSAS 9, 444, which appears to record quantities of cereals, is too fragmentary to be included in this category.

12 The term *iššakku* also occurs occasionally in the Sealand I ledgers; for its occurrence in the Tell Khaiber texts, see also Campbell et al. 2017. Both terms in the context of field tilling are discussed in Leemans 1973: 283–84.

tities expected (e.g., TK1 3064.12; 3064.18; see also Campbell et al. 2017). In addition, the letter TK1 3064.93 records instructions to "let the grain move on/cross over,"[13] perhaps referring to its transport to the palace.

The main crop figuring in the Sealand I documents is barley (ŠE), followed by small barley (ŠE TUR.TUR) and emmer-wheat (*kunēšu/kunāšu*); a variety of large barley (ŠE GAL.GAL) also seems to be at least marginally cultivated as well as *kibtu*-wheat.[14] *ḫargalû*-grain and *terru*-grain also figure in the archive but may not be types of crop.

5.2.1.1.1 Barley

We find in the Sealand I texts mainly barley (ŠE), but also small barley (ŠE TUR.TUR) and large barley (ŠE GAL.GAL).

Neither small nor large barley are well attested in Mesopotamian texts. They do not appear on Tablet XXIV of UR_5.RA = *ḫubullu*; this does not necessarily mean that they were rare varieties since the ŠE entries of UR_5.RA were "not a classified list of species" (Powell 1984: 50), most entries in fact recording various qualities and products of processed barley. They are attested together in a bilingual prayer to Šamaš (Cooper 1972: 72–73 line 18) in which types of barley are listed: "'large' grain, 'small' grain, white grain, black grain" (Cooper's translation);[15] to the Sumerian[16] še gal-gal-la še tur-tur corresponds the Akkadian ŠE-*am ra-ba-a* ŠE-*am ṣi-iḫ-ra*.[17] This text, I believe, offers enough evidence to reject Dalley's hypothesis (2009: 59 and n.3 to text 124) that GAL.GAL and TUR.TUR may have applied to the standard used for measuring the grain.

Archaeobotany is of limited help to interpret these terms. As noted by Potts (1997: 59), the Akkadian lexicon does not seem to make the distinction between hulled and naked or two- and six-row barley, all varieties that are attested archaeologically. According to archaeobotanical evidence, the barley cultivated in the southern plain in that period may have all been of the six-row variety,

13 ŠE.GUR *le-ti-iq*. The passage is also discussed in Campbell et al. 2017.

14 GIG or *kibtu*-wheat appears to be the only type of cereal not represented in the *šibšu*-ledgers. It appears in the list CUSAS 9, 408 and in the record CUSAS 9, 92.

15 Stol (1985a: 127) does not interpret this as a simple enumeration; he considers it possible that ŠE GAL.GAL is a general term for major crops including white and black barley and that ŠE TUR.TUR stands for minor crops including pulses which are enumerated after the cereals in the same passage. This interpretation, which accepts ŠE TUR.TUR as a variant of ŠE NÍG-TUR.TUR and extends the idea to ŠE GAL.GAL, is not compatible with the Sealand I evidence.

16 The orthography given here is that of the Nippur manuscript (Cooper 1972: 72)

17 For two other instances of ŠE.GAL, see CAD Š, s.v. *še'u* 1a 3′.

or a mix of six-row and two-row varieties although in the latter case the evidence is inconclusive.[18] But even if we had proof of the presence of both main varieties of barley, we have no way of assessing whether these varieties were reflected in the epithets TUR.TUR and GAL.GAL,[19] let alone understanding what ŠE without epithet would be when listed alongside other types of barley.[20] When appearing alone, for instance in a ration list, ŠE was probably understood as a generic term for grain including all types of barley and probably also emmer. Also, we do not find large or small barley in Sealand I palatial documents other than ledgers: the distinction, either of quality or variety, may have mattered less in contexts other than tax-paying.[21]

According to ledgers recording the payment of the *šibšu*-tax, and assuming that TUR.TUR and GAL.GAL do designate varieties of barley, a same individual could cultivate in the same location more than one type of cereal. When this was the case, the quantity of common barley was usually the largest and listed first. Other cereals, small or large barley or emmer-wheat, follow in smaller quantities.[22] This indicates that the choice between the cereal varieties was not only a question of soil condition and climate. While the preference clearly went for common barley, small barley is quite well attested. Table 9 shows which crops appear together in *šibšu*-payment ledgers.

Table 9: Crops in *šibšu*-ledgers[23]

Month	Text CUSAS 9,	ŠE	ŠE TUR.TUR	*kunāšu*	ZAG.ḪI.LI. SAR (*saḫlû*)	ŠE GAL.GAL	Additional crop/comment
v?	411	●	●	●			
v	415	●	●	●	●		

18 Charles (1984: 27) and Renfrew (1984: 39), both basing themselves on works by Helbaek; see also Potts 1997: 57 ff.
19 Similarly, a type(?) of emmer called zíz GAL appears in the Sargonic Mesag archive (Bridges 1981: 250).
20 I will adopt the following designations in the present discussion: ŠE GAL.GAL = large barley; ŠE TUR.TUR = small barley; ŠE = common barley when discussed as a crop listed along other types of barley, otherwise barley. In general discussions, 'barley' includes all varieties.
21 Note that it is now also attested in a Tell Khaiber text (TK1 3064.33).
22 For instance CUSAS 9, 426: 3–4; 6–7; 10–11; 12–13. One tax-payer apparently produced no common barley: CUSAS 9, 431A: 14–18.
23 Text CUSAS 9, 443 is called a *miksu*-ledger but is much more similar in format and contents to the other *šibšu*-ledgers (Boivin 2016b: 55); *miksu*-ledgers usually contain only common barley.

Table 9: Crops in *šibšu*-ledgers *(continued)*

Month	Text CUSAS 9,	ŠE	ŠE TUR.TUR	*kunāšu*	ZAG.ḪI.LI. SAR *(saḫlû)*	ŠE GAL.GAL	Additional crop/comment
iv	426	●	●	●	●		*dalû?*
iv	428	●		●			
v	429		●				no ledger; single payment
v	430	●	●	●			
iv	431A	●	●	●	●	●	*kāšu?;* GÚ?
iv	432	●		●	●		
⌜iv⌝	434	●	●			●	very fragmentary
-	441	●		●			*tatarru?*; very fragmentary
-	442	●					
iv	443	●	●	●			very fragmentary
-	446				●		
-	447	●	●				

On the basis of the *rēš makkūri*-entries in the *šibšu*-ledgers, which I understand to be harvested quantities, we can endeavor to evaluate the average size of the fields on which crops were produced. The figures vary greatly.[24] Small harvests of barley can be partly explained by the fact that some individuals also grew (and delivered) various crops, but we have nonetheless to conclude that these individuals either harvested more barley which we do not see in the extant records (which is extremely likely), or that they partly relied on allocations for their subsistence.

Stol (2004: 840 ff.) has summarized the discussion surrounding the estimation of barley yields in the Old Babylonian period, concluding to a maximum of 30 *kurru* per *buru*. The area of a subsistence field in the Old Babylonian period is estimated at 18 *ikû* (Stol 2004: 844).[25] I assumed an average yield of 20 *kurru* per

24 For instance, within one ledger, CUSAS 9, 415, we find values ranging from 274 *qû* to over 21 000 *qû!*

25 Among the literature reviewed by Stol, note Renger 1995; in this contribution, he estimates the average size of a subsistence field for a "person of low rank" in the Old Babylonian period at approximately 17 ikû (p.300).

buru, corresponding to 333,3 *qû* per *ikû*, and posited that this average yield would apply to common, small, and large barley.[26]

The resulting average field area[27] is very low for some ledgers, for instance 1,5 *ikû* in ledger CUSAS 9, 432 or 4 *ikû* in CUSAS 9, 442. This could point toward a communal type of organization in which each individual was responsible only for a small area for the cultivation of barley, but it would mean that individuals had other resources. In other ledgers, the average field size lies much higher, around the estimated area of Old Babylonian subsistence fields: for instance 15,7 *ikû* in CUSAS 9, 426, 18 *ikû* in CUSAS 9, 443, and 20 *ikû* in CUSAS 9, 431A. In a few exceptional cases, fields were larger: as much as 41 *ikû* in CUSAS 9, 429 (recording only one delivery) and 34 *ikû* in CUSAS 9, 411.[28]

Barley appears extremely frequently in the archive. Besides the evidence of its procurement by the palace through the payment of taxes, we find it given for milling and for malting, and allotted as wages and allocations. Transformation and expenditure of barley are treated in Sections 5.3.2, 5.3.4, and 5.4.

5.2.1.1.2 Emmer-wheat

Emmer-wheat,[29] written syllabically (ŠE) *ku-ni-(e)-šu* / *ku-na-(a)-šu*, is very present in the *šibšu*-ledgers (Table 9). This is rather surprising because the cultivation of wheat is considered to have been barely present in southern Mesopotamia after 1700 and probably entirely abandoned in some areas (Neumann and Sigrist 1978: 240–41). Already during the Ur III period, only an estimated 1.7 % of the cultivated area around Girsu was used for emmer (Potts 1997: 62 using data by

---

26 One text mentions "a field of 1 *ikû*, 1 *kor* of barley" before stating a name, patronym, and date (CUSAS 9, 126). No context is offered but it may be the estimated yield associated with this parcel of land.

27 For all following average field areas, I have excluded uncertain entries, either when the quantity was incomplete or when the last column of the ledger did not allow me to determine whether the crop was barley. This has resulted in the fact that for some ledgers, no estimate could be computed.

28 The ledger is fragmentary so that this value is based on only a few entries.

29 Probably Triticum dicoccum Schübl. The discussion surrounding the identification of *kunāšu* with emmer is well summarized in Powell 1984: 51 ff. The Sumerian ZÍZ(.AN) is never used in the Sealand I texts. Powell's hypothesis that originally unprocessed emmer was called *zīzum* and processed emmer *kunāšu*, and that during the Old Babylonian period *kunāšu* came to have both meanings can neither be proved nor disproved with the Sealand I evidence. What it shows is that shortly after the end the Old Babylonian period, *kunāšu* was used both for processed and unprocessed emmer by the Sealand I scribes and that they did not use the Sumerian logogram.

Maekawa). The archaeobotanical evidence also points towards an abandonment of emmer in the Old Babylonian period in southern Babylonia (Renfrew 1984: 39; Potts 1997: 60 f.), but data are scarce for that region (van Zeist and Bottema 1999: 29), which weakens conclusions based on the absence of evidence.

Emmer-wheat was not cultivated by all Sealand I producers; when it was, the corresponding *šibšu*-payment was recorded in second or third position, after barley. Based on the harvest quantities recorded, when a producer grew both common barley and emmer, the volume of the latter represented in average 9 % of the former.[30] Emmer-wheat is associated with at least four localities[31] and, therefore, as far as the archive shows, appears to have been cultivated more or less wherever barley was, which speaks for rather good soil conditions in that area. The harvest time was apparently around the same time as the barley's.

5.2.1.1.3 *kibtu*-wheat

kibtu-wheat,[32] written GIG(-*tum*), also syllabically in the plural *ki-ba(-a)-tum,*[33] appears occasionally in the Sealand I texts, but never in a context linked to its cultivation. We find it among seized goods (CUSAS 9, 92) or given as supplies or allocations. It may have been processed into groats (see Section 5.3.2.4.5).

This variety of wheat is not attested in the archaeobotanical record for Old Babylonian southern Babylonia (Potts 1997: 61; Renfrew 1984: 39). It seems that already in the Ur III period, it was cultivated in very small quantities with a mere 0.15 % of the cultivated area around Girsu alloted to it (Potts 1997: 62 using data by Maekawa). The Sealand I texts, without offering direct evidence for its cultivation, at least show that this cereal was still marginally present shortly after the Old Babylonian period in southern Babylonia.

---

30 It is based on eight instances, only those in which both harvest yields were well preserved. The proportion emmer-barley varies from 2% to 20 %. I chose not to compute the proportion of emmer with regard to the entire harvest associated with a given individual because sometimes several crops are listed (up to five) which increases the risk of finding lacunae in one of the quantities and would have further reduced an already extremely limited sample.

31 Kiribti-Enlil, Nūr-šarri, Kār-Šamaš, and Kār-šeduanni.

32 For the identification of GIG/*kibtu* as wheat, probably "some type of free threshing wheat," see Powell 1984: 56 ff.

33 It is unusual but not unheard of to find this term in the plural (see CAD K, s.v. *kibtu*).

5.2.1.1.4 *ḫargalû*-grain(?)

We find several occurrences of *ḫargalû*-grain, mostly written (ŠE) *ḫar-ga-lu-ú*,[34] but never in the context of grain production. The term is also associated with flour, in phrases such as ZÍD.DA *lìb-bi ḫar-ga-lu-ú* (CUSAS 9, 370).[35] In the Middle Babylonian period this term of obscure meaning was associated with flour, although Sassmannshausen (2001: 251 n.5) noted that it was probably a type of grain.[36] The Sealand I evidence does not necessarily corroborate that it was a type of grain, but it does confirm that it applied to both grain and flour. If it was not a variety of grain, it may have qualified its quality or condition. Dalley (2009: 192) suggested an etymological connection with large millstones.

Another possibility, suggested by the writing *ḫar-gal-lu*, is that we could be dealing with a word related to the Sumerian loanword *ḫargu/allu*, a lock. This grain, perhaps because it was of special quality, would have been kept under lock? This seems a little far-fetched, but not impossible. It is interesting that one list (presumably of distribution) of *ḫargalû*-grain (CUSAS 9, 369) is sealed. In this archive, it is probably the only sealed document recording an expenditure and one of only two dealing with grain.[37] But then one would expect to find this special grain or flour perhaps in offerings to the gods rather than in allocations to workers as is the case in this archive (as well as in the Tell Khaiber records). The meaning remains elusive.

See also Section 5.3.2.3 on *ḫargalû*-flour which shows that its production was apparently separate from that of other flours.

---

34 Also once *ḫar-gal-ú* or ḪAR.GAL-*ú* (CUSAS 9, 374), once *ḫar-gal-lu* (CUSAS 9, 368A) and once *ḫa-ar-ga-lu-ú* (CUSAS 9, 377). On the basis of the latter orthography, Dalley justly noted (2009: 192) that in this archive, the normalization should be *ḫargalû* and not *ḫirgalû*, which seems to be the later form of the word (CAD Ḫ, s.v. *ḫirgalû*). The term ḪAR.GAL-*ú* to qualify grain and flour is also attested in texts from Tell Khaiber, e.g. in TK1 3064.48 and 3064.52.

35 Dalley's reconstruction of the word [*ḫar-ga-lu*]-*ú* at the beginning of text CUSAS 9, 373 would imply that *tappinnu*-flour and regular flour are to be considered sub-types of *ḫargalû*-flour, but the beginning of the line is entirely lost so that the reconstruction is based on only one sign. Moreover, it appears from the photograph that this sign may be in fact KAL. The evidence from this text appears therefore too uncertain to be considered for defining *ḫargalû*.

36 The term occurs also a few times in the recently published Middle Babylonian texts CUSAS 30, 256–58. The context does not offer new insight into the meaning of the term and van Soldt (2015: 34) refers to Sassmannshausen's remarks on this.

37 The other is CUSAS 9, 395.

5.2.1.2 Vegetables, spices, fruits, and pulses

5.2.1.2.1 Cress

The cultivation of cress[38] (*saḫlû*), written ZAG.ḪI.LI.SAR,[39] is attested in four ledgers recording the payment of the *šibšu*-tax, three times along other crops and once alone (see Table 9). Its presence in Sealand I texts is not surprising since it was "an important ingredient in the daily diet" in Babylonia (Stol 1983–84: 26). It appears mostly along cereals and was delivered by the same individuals who also paid their imposts on grain, therefore, we may assume that cress was grown on fields.[40] It indicates also that the harvest took place in or before the months iv and v. The list of cress seeds CUSAS 9, 407, probably a distribution list, is dated to the beginning of month xi. If these seeds were intended for sowing, the date of the text suggests a harvest roughly at the same time as the harvesting of cereals,[41] which agrees well with the recording of cereals and cress on the same *šibšu*-ledgers. The Sealand I evidence does not agree with Stol's (1983–84: 26) suggestion that cress was mainly harvested in the month vii, but there is other evidence that cress was also harvested as a winter crop early in the year (months ii and iii: *ibid.:* 26 n.16; at the time of the barley's harvest: Jursa 1995: 178).[42]

The ledgers show that the *šibšu*-tax rate was the same for cress and for grain (one third for the palace)[43] and that the same standard GUR measure (of 300 *qû*) was used. The smaller imposts (*kiṣru* and *bāb āli*)[44] seem to behave differently than for grain but the sample is too small to establish a rule. Quantities harvested (*rēš makkūri*) vary between 0,0,4,0 and 2,3,3,0 with an average just over one

38 The identification of the *saḫlû*-plant as cress remains uncertain. See Stol 1983–84 for a detailed discussion of the evidence and the etymology. Dalley (2009: 87 n.1 to text 89) discusses the problem, reviews more recent hypotheses and leaves the term untranslated. Among the recent hypotheses, Haas (2003: 349) suggested for the Hittite plant written ZAG.AḪ.LI(.SAR) that it may have belonged to the family of parasitic plants cuscuta; Dalley already noted that there may be a climatic incompatibility with southern Mesopotamia; I believe there is another argument against this hypothesis in the fact that the *saḫlû*-plant was cultivated as a crop (Stol 1983–84: 25 and the Sealand I evidence), something for which a parasitic plant would probably not be suited. This plant belongs to the MUN-GAZI species (Maekawa 1985: 99 ff.; Potts 1997: 66).

39 Once written ZAG.ḪI.LI.A.SAR in CUSAS 9, 92; see comment by Dalley (2009: n.4 to this text).

40 According to Stol (1983–84: 25), it was cultivated both in gardens and fields.

41 This concords also with a Neo-Babylonian list of cress seeds CT 55, 386 dated to the 29th day of month x (Jursa 1995: 178).

42 This also appears to agree with the evidence from Astronomical Diaries (Slotzky 1997: 36).

43 With one exception (CUSAS 9, 432).

44 See Boivin 2016b: 56–58; incl. n.94.

kor. Quantities of seeds distributed vary between 0,0,0,2 and 0,0,2,0 with an average of 11 *qû*.

The archive does not contain any information on the processing of cress, nor much insight into its consumption and distribution.[45]

5.2.1.2.2 Leek

Leek, written *kar-šum*SAR,[46] appears only once in this archive in a short list also featuring coriander (CUSAS 9, 91), both in modest quantities. It was delivered by a merchant, while the coriander was delivered by a gardener.[47] The presence of a merchant is exceptional in this corpus. If the mention of his profession is here meaningful as to his role in the transaction, which appears likely since it figures in the header of the document, it ensues that leeks were not readily available to the palace, at least not in sufficient quantity[48] and had to be bought.

5.2.1.2.3 Coriander

Coriander,[49] written ŠE.LÚSAR, is also only marginally present in the extant Sealand I texts. Like cress, it belongs to the mun-gazi plants (Maekawa 1985: 99 ff.), which include pulses, herbs, and spices. It appears along leeks in the already discussed list CUSAS 9, 91 but was delivered by a gardener while the leeks were delivered by a merchant. The quantities registered are modest.

5.2.1.2.4 Dates

The only fruit attested in the extant Sealand I documents is the date, always written ZÚ.LUM.[50] We never find the specific UḪIN for green or fresh dates,[51] and nei-

---

45 It was probably recorded as an expenditure in CUSAS 9, 89, and among seized goods(?) in CUSAS 9, 92.

46 *karšum* is probably the common Middle Eastern leek, less frequent in sources than the "bulb-leek" (Stol 1987: 62).

47 Coriander is delivered by a gardener on line 5. On line 6 the profession of another individual also delivering coriander is not legible.

48 There is proof that during the Old Babylonian period leeks were imported by merchants based in northern Babylonia (Veenhof 1991: 291 ff.).

49 Meissner (1891: 294) identified the Akkadian *ki/usibirru* as coriander. See also Potts 1997: 66.

50 This is not surprising since other fruits are very rare in Old Babylonian documents (Postgate 1987a: 125; also only briefly mentioned in Stol 2004: 857).

51 Most texts recording dates are dated to the fall and winter (or the very beginning of spring). Indeed, most are dated to the months vii through xii, while one dates to month vi and one to

ther their cultivation nor their procurement is reflected in the extant documents. We find dates as expenditures, mostly as offerings to the gods,[52] also as supplies to individuals.[53]

5.2.1.2.5 Other crops

Cumin(?),[54] written *ka-mu-nu*, is another mun-gazi plant marginally represented in the archive, as part of seized goods (CUSAS 9, 92). There is no quantity[55] associated to it, which is unusual. It may also appear, written logographically TIN.TIR.SAR in CUSAS 9, 98. Onions,[56] written SUM.SIKIL.SAR, probably appear only once in a damaged passage of a list of foodstuffs offered to the gods (CUSAS 9, 99). A crop probably beginning with *ka-a-* figures in the *šibšu*-ledger CUSAS 9, 431A: 16 but the end of the line is damaged. Dalley suggested for the last sign *-ši?*; a *kāšu*-plant is, I believe, otherwise unattested.[57]

Another crop probably appearing only once features in a damaged passage in ledger CUSAS 9, 441: 19. Dalley reads it *ta-ta-ar?ri?* and suggests that it could be a type of garlic *tatturru*, a term otherwise attested only in the first millennium (CAD T, s.v. *tatturru*).[58]

---

month i. Since the harvest was in the fall (months vii to x in Charles 1987: 15; months vii and viii in Slotsky 1997: 29 and Stol 2004: 855), it is not surprising to find records of dates at that time of the year, but fresh dates could certainly not conserve long into the winter. Slotsky (1997: 30) suggested that there may have been a second picking in months xii and i or that fresh dates were delivered from elsewhere.

52 For instance in CUSAS 9, 61; 65; 66; 67; 70; 71; 73.

53 For instance in CUSAS 9, 88; 97; 98; 101.

54 The identification with cumin is uncertain (Maekawa 1985: 99).

55 The entry is on the lower edge of the tablet and the space where the quantity should stand is strongly tapered, however the level of preservation is very good and there definitely appears to be no numeral there.

56 Probably the common onion (Stol 1987: 60).

57 There is a *kasû* spice (cuscuta?) (Stol 2004: 857) which would be a possibility if the last, damaged sign was misread but that would not explain the long /a/. A thorny plant *kalû* (CAD K, s.v. *kalû* D), if the last sign is to be read *-lim*, would also be possible but it does not seem to be attested as a crop.

58 The date for harvesting garlic (months xii, i, and ii: Stol 1987: 58) could be compatible with a recording of garlic following the somewhat later barley harvest. However, garlic was normally cultivated in gardens, not in fields according to Stol (1987: 65), which makes it slightly less likely to be found alongside barley and emmer-wheat, the produces otherwise recorded in this ledger.

Pulses are barely represented in the Sealand I archive.[59] GÚ, perhaps an unspecified type of pulse,[60] may appear in *šibšu*-ledger CUSAS 9, 431A: 11. Most pulses being harvested in the spring (Charles 1985: 56–57), it would indeed be possible to find it in a ledger dated to the month iv. With only one possible instance, neither the cultivation nor the use of pulses can be considered to be documented with certainty in the Sealand kingdom.

5.2.1.3 Oil plant and aromatics

5.2.1.3.1 Sesame(?)

The oil plant ŠE.GIŠ.Ì,[61] almost certainly sesame (Kraus 1968; Stol 1985b; Bedigian 1985: 164 ff.), appears in a few Sealand I texts. None of these documents refer to its cultivation.[62]

We learn from them that sesame seeds could be given by the king as a gift (?)[63] (CUSAS 9, 121;[64] 129; 139). Sesame seeds also figure in a receipt (CUSAS 9, 135) and in a short list (CUSAS 9, 440), possibly recording a distribution to the individuals named in the document. The quantities vary, from 5 *qû* to 1 *kor.*

5.2.1.3.2 Aromatics

Cedar, written ^{giš}EREN, figures only as an aromatic in the extant Sealand I documents. It appears in two forms: crushed (CUSAS 9, 68; 101) and as resin (CUSAS 9,

59 In a few ledgers, Dalley reads GÚ as a column header (CUSAS 9, 409; 418; 420; 422; 424; 428; 436), with the interpretation that it was an abbreviation for GÚ.UN, the *biltu*-tax. However, Cavigneaux and André-Salvini (forthcoming) suggested, convincingly, that it should be read LÁLx-NI, arrears. See also Boivin 2016b: 47 n.13, and now Campbell et al. 2017 for similar evidence in texts from Tell Khaiber.

60 Read GÚ(?) by Dalley (2009: text 431A n.11) and tentatively interpreted by her as an abbreviation for GÚ.GAL, which she translates as chick-peas. The identification remains problematic and will not be further discussed here since it is not even certain that this crop is attested in the archive, and if so only once. For a brief summary of the problem, see Stol 2004: 857–58.

61 Once ŠE.Ì.GIŠ.

62 Sesame is a summer crop, harvested between the months v and viii, and not very salt resistant (Charles 1985: 48–49; Potts 1997: 68; Stol 1985b: 119 and 2004: 854; it is rated "sensitive" in a report by the Food and Agriculture Organization of the UN: Tanji and Kielen 2002: Appendix 1). The other candidate for identification with ŠE.GIŠ.Ì is flax, which is a winter crop (Renfrew 1985: 63). The fact that the Sealand I archive contains several ledgers recording the payment of the *šibšu*-tax on various winter crops but that the oil plant ŠE.GIŠ.Ì never figures in them reinforces slightly the case—if needed be—that we are indeed dealing with sesame rather than flax.

63 On the interpretation of the term NÍG.BA, see Section 5.4.5.

64 This text will be further discussed in Section 5.3.5.1.

143). Cypress, written ^{giš}ŠU.ÚR.MÌN, appears once in a damaged passage (CUSAS 9, 99). Both aromatics are well attested in Mesopotamian perfumery (Brunke and Sallaberger 2010: 49). Even if very few, these occurrences of aromatic wood in the Sealand I material are evidence that the southern Mesopotamian kingdom had access to products from the West (Leemans 1960a: 126–27; Middeke-Conlin 2014: 19; Van De Mieroop 1992b: 158 ff.), at least for a short period.[65]

5.2.1.4 Reed

Reed is not directly mentioned in the archive but we find the term AD.KID: reed worker.[66] Also, reed bundles or bales may be recorded in text CUSAS 9, 425. In this text, the commodity is not specified but the header of the document identifies it as the ÉŠ.GÀR AD.KID.MEŠ, adding that it was a delivery to the palace. The ambiguity of the term ÉŠ.GÀR, often loosely translated "assignment," combined with the absence of further information on the commodity recorded, is problematic.

The term ÉŠ.GÀR in the context of reed is attested at Old Babylonian Ur (Van De Mieroop 1992a: 147). There, it appeared in the phrase "ÉŠ.GÀR of day X" on records of quantities of reed associated with workers; in this context, ÉŠ.GÀR probably meant the bundles of reed harvested by the reed cutters (*ibid.*) or the quotas assigned to them (*ibid.*: 153 n.2). In our case, quotas can be excluded since the document is a delivery record; we are either dealing with the work requisites or the finished products of the reed workers. The fact that one entry includes a fraction seems more compatible with a record of raw material requisites,[67] probably bales,[68] than with finished objects. This interpretation suggests that supplies had been requested and were delivered for the reed workers attached to the palace; however, the evidence is at present far too limited to suggest that an *iškāru*-system of state service, as in the Neo-Assyrian empire, was in

65 Two texts are dated to year J (CUSAS 9, 68; 101), one has no year (CUSAS 9, 143). Cypress is attested in a text dated to year I (CUSAS 9, 99). Cedar and cypress were imported at Old Babylonian Ur and Larsa (Van De Mieroop 1992b: 158; 160).

66 The AD.KID is not the reed cutter but the craftsman, maker of reed objects (CAD A, s.v. *atkuppu*).

67 This interpretation of "raw material requisites" would tally with the Middle Babylonian evidence in which only this meaning of ÉŠ.GÀR may be attested (Sassmannshausen 2001: 259); this agrees also for instance with the evidence in CUSAS 30, 219–21, where grain for the miller is called by that term. However, see Section 5.3.2.1 for evidence of another possible meaning of ÉŠ.GÀR.

68 A bundle was probably much too small to be fractioned (for quantities, see Streck 2009–11: 184–85).

place (Postgate 1987b: 268). No information on the harvesters or the place of harvest are given.

5.2.2 Animal resources

5.2.2.1 Ovine and caprine livestock and products

Deliveries of ovine and caprine livestock are recorded on very standardized delivery records (key word: MU.DU),[69] which indicate the animals delivered, their purpose or end recipient, the name of the source/deliverer, the primary destination—nearly always the palace (*ana* É.GAL) –, and the date. Sheep are overwhelmingly more numerous than goats[70] in the extant record and are sometimes delivered alongside small quantities of wool.[71]

The individuals delivering the animals are sometimes identified as shepherds (SIPA). The prosopography indicates that this occupation was passed down within the family. The shepherds received grain allotments from the palace[72] and they also figure as *miksu*-tax payers,[73] which very probably means that some shepherds received a field for their service.[74] Also, ownership marks or further precisions on the source of the animals delivered are never mentioned. It seems therefore fair to assume that the animals came from palace-owned flocks that were entrusted to shepherds employed by the palace. One Arad-Šamaš, who delivers sheep to the palace at least three times (CUSAS 9, 18; 21–22), could be the same who figures as shepherd in two Tell Khaiber documents dealing with grain (TK1 3064.51: 17; 3080.04: 10).

Since the purpose for the animal delivery is usually added, the procurement of the animals appears to occur at the request of the palace, for specific needs.

---

69 There are forty-two delivery records of ovine (and caprine) livestock: CUSAS 9, 16–26; 26A; 27–50; 52–54; 56–58. The formulary of such records is analyzed in Boivin 2016c.

70 In delivery records for live animals, the proportion is as low as one goat for c. 240 sheep.

71 For instance ten shekels in CUSAS 9, 30 and 31; half a mina in CUSAS 9, 29; two minas in CUSAS 9, 26. According to Dalley's reading, there would be another, in that case very large, delivery of wool recorded in CUSAS 9, 461. However, her reading SIG_7 on the first line is dubious; moreover, this would be the only instance of this orthography for wool in this archive since it is always written SÍG-*tum*. Also, the quantity given is in capacity measures, not in weight. Based on a collation from the photograph I suggested in 2016c: n.20 the reading ESÍR: bitumen.

72 They received *ḫargalû*-allotments at least in CUSAS 9, 371: 3, 18, 29, 38 & 48; 374: rev. 14′ & 21′; 376: obv. 18 & rev. 23′.

73 CUSAS 9, 384: 30; 413: 29; 448: 34.

74 For the ownership model behind fields on which the *miksu* was paid, see Boivin 2016b: 55–56; 59.

Most animals were destined for offerings or extispicy but the purposes recorded are varied, and several intra- and extra-palatial ones were sometimes recorded on the same tablet: this suggests the existence of a palatial bureau or service responsible for the reception of livestock, acting as a point of entry for the animals into the palatial economic body. The transaction was recorded with an outward-looking perspective because it recorded a delivery (MU.DU) and named the individual responsible for providing/delivering the animal. Great care was given to this book-keeping: most delivery records of livestock were identified as *meḫrum* (copy) and were sealed; some are still or had been encased. This points toward an obligation of delivery to the palace by the shepherds which was carefully monitored by the palace. An official (or officials), the GÌR, was sometimes involved and his name recorded. His exact role is not clear but his function seems to be on the receiving side and may be related to the use of the animal.[75] For an in-depth discussion of the palatial management of animal husbandry, including the role of the officials involved in it, see Boivin 2016c.

Only a few texts record the delivery of ovine carcasses.[76] The prosopography shows that the same shepherd could deliver ovine and caprine carcasses and livestock.[77]

5.2.2.2 Bovine livestock and carcasses

For bovine livestock we have only three delivery records of the MU.DU type (presented in the preceding section).[78] A large, fragmentary ledger (CUSAS 9, 449) may also record live cattle deliveries,[79] perhaps summed up over a period of time. However, neither the term delivery nor palace are mentioned or preserved on it, therefore its interpretation remains uncertain,[80] but enough names are still

75 For instance, diviners acted as GÌR officials in the delivery of a lamb for extispicy in CUSAS 9, 22.

76 CUSAS 9, 309; 311; 316; 326; 350; 365.

77 Ilūni, son of Arad-Enlil, delivers live and dead sheep and goats (CUSAS 9, 26A; 36; 42; 311).

78 CUSAS 9, 51; 52; 55. The deliveries were also to the palace.

79 There are no indications that the animals counted were carcasses (RI.RI.GA). It seems therefore that we are dealing with live cattle.

80 The column headers indicate that the book-keeper discriminated between various types of animals (male calf, female calf, etc.), summed the quantities entered, and associated these with individuals whose names stand in the last column. The tabular format is reminiscent of the large ledgers recording the payment of taxes on agricultural produce. However, nothing in the preserved portions of the document indicates that the animals were paid as a levy. The economic mechanism of procurement of live large cattle by the palace remains without further evidence unclear.

legible on it to show that several of these individuals figure also in delivery records of cattle carcasses as providers (deliverers).[81]

In this archive, most documents pertaining to large cattle are by far delivery records of carcasses.[82] These tablets are cast as MU.DU records to the palace, like the delivery records for livestock; however, instead of indicating a purpose for the animal delivered they usually add information about its provenance and sometimes the (accidental) cause of its death (e.g., killed by a lion or a wolf). The records almost always specify that the dead animal bore an ownership mark (*šimtu*), often without further precision. However, several records comprise an additional "*libbu* (*ša*) X" clause, probably indicating who owned or herded the animals. We find, among others, cattle "of the queen,"[83] "of Šamaš,"[84] and "of the ox-drivers."[85] This clause shows an interest of the palace administration for the provenance of the animals and probably indicates that some of the cattle was not palace-owned, or at least that the herding of large cattle was less centralized than that of sheep. The fact that the carcasses of animals were delivered to the palace suggests that it was mandatory to deliver some or all of them to the palace to be processed.

Delivery records of cattle carcasses were usually copied and sealed, and sometimes encased in an envelope like the delivery records of (mostly ovine) livestock. Officials were often involved in the delivery of cattle carcasses, more so than for ovine livestock. The GÌR function,[86] introduced in the preceding section, was in this case almost always assumed by the cooks (MUḪALDIM.MEŠ), which reinforces the assumption that the function was related to the processing of the received goods by the receiving party. A *pīḫatu*-official was often involved,[87] apparently individuals issued from the ranks of the herders, according to prosopography. Unlike the shepherds, the cattle herders are never identified as

81 For instance Ṣilli-Šamaš, son of Ili-išmeanni who appears in CUSAS 9, 449: 10 & 11 and in CUSAS 9, 347; also Pirḫi-Amurru, son or Erību who appears in CUSAS 9, 449: 46 and in CUSAS 9, 352. There are seven other such cases.

82 There are fifty-six (perhaps fifty-seven) such records: CUSAS 9, 310; 312; 314–15; 317–22; (323); 324–25; 327–42; 342A; 343–49; 350A; 351–53; 353A; 354–55; 355A; 356–64; 365A; 366–67.

83 CUSAS 9, 312; 321; 333; 337; 345; 351. It is written *lìb-bu (ša)* UN.GAL. See Dalley 2009: 163 n.2 of text 312 for the reading of UN.GAL.

84 CUSAS 9, 349; 363.

85 CUSAS 9, 314; 366.

86 GÌR-officials are recorded fifty or fifty-one times. For instance in CUSAS 9, 310; 314–15; 331–40; 353.

87 Thirty or thirty-one times. For instance in CUSAS 9, 312; 317; 320; 324; 331–340. Another official, the NÍG.ŠU, appears only twice, along with a GÌR-official, in CUSAS 9, 353 and 357. He is also discussed in Boivin 2016c.

such, which could reinforce the hypothesis that much of the cattle was not palace-owned. The prosopography suggests that the profession was inherited within families. Some herders, like shepherds, may have received grain allotments (rations) from the palace but, without a professional designation, the evidence is based in this case only on clusters of names in such lists that seem to correspond to individuals known to deliver cattle (carcasses). For a detailed discussion, see Boivin 2016c.

5.2.3 Other resources

Few documents pertain to goods other than those issued from agriculture and animal husbandry. The acquisition of millstones by the palace is recorded in CUSAS 9, 421, which lists transactions by two individuals.[88] The millstones appear to have been paid for in silver and in grain.[89] They may have been purchased for the *nupāru*-workhouse or for grain milling by servants of the palace (see Section 5.3.2). Six millstones are also mentioned in a letter (CUSAS 9, 4) in which various goods are said to have been sent to a high official.[90] Metals, copper and silver, are very scarcely represented. A delivery of copper to the palace is recorded in CUSAS 9, 458; the other few attestations are probably expenditures.[91] Bricks are delivered, presumably to the palace, by several individuals in ledger CUSAS 9, 420.[92] We also find the delivery of a large quantity of bitumen by mer-

88 For each purchase, the millstones are recorded in two columns. The header of the first column, ^{na_4}ḪAR, may either designate the complete set of millstones or specifically the lower millstone (Stol 1979: 91–92). The header of the second column is problematic: Dalley suggested ^{na_4}DA (?).BAR as an alternative spelling of ^{na_4}AD.BAR, that is, basalt. If correct, millstones of basalt were listed separately from those in the first column, then presumably made of a different stone.
89 To the recorded quantities of acquired millstones two entries are associated: KÙ.BABBAR SUM-*nu* and ŠE SÁM, therefore “silver given” and “price (in grain).” The sign following the quantities in silver has been read MA as an abbreviation for MA(.NA) by Dalley, which would result in the extremely large quantities of 13 MA.NA for the first purchase and 4 2/3 MA.NA for the second. (The fraction was read 1/3 by Dalley but collation from the photograph shows that it is 2/3). I would suggest that the sign MA may perhaps be read as GÍN. Another observation is that the quantities of barley and silver are in proportion since they present between line 1 and 2 the same ratio. (It is impossible that we are dealing with an equivalent barley/silver because we would have a course of 60 SILÀ of barley per MA.NA or GÍN of silver, depending on the reading of the quantities in silver.)
90 Perhaps the king (Dalley 2009: text 4 notes).
91 For some evidence of copper being given for trade or diplomatic gift, see Section 4.4.2.
92 The header of the second column reads *ma-ḫi-ir-tum*, which Dalley translates as “boat coming upstream(?).” I would suggest the translation: “received.” The feminine of the adjective

chants (CUSAS 9, 461),[93] one of the very few attestations of merchants in this archive.

5.3 Storage and transformation

5.3.1 Storage of grain

We have evidence that the palace stored grain from the expenditure record CUSAS 9, 100: an offering took place at the occasion of the opening of a granary (GUR_7).[94] This does not come as a surprise since we know that the palace procured significant quantities of grain through the payment of taxes and gave out grain as well as transformed products from grain for allotments and offerings.

5.3.2 Production of flour

There is evidence that the palace produced flour, some of which was milled by palace servants and some probably by workers in a workhouse attached to the palace.[95] We have evidence also that flour and flour-based products were given as offerings to various deities by the palace.

5.3.2.1 The *nupāru* as workhouse for cereal-milling?

We have in receipt CUSAS 9, 85 evidence that barley was delivered "for grinding" *ana samādi* to a *nupāru*-workhouse. This institution is attested in the Old Baby-

---

would not be surprising since bricks are the commodity recorded (*libittu* written SIG_4-*tum*). The ledger appears indeed to balance between an expected quantity in the first column (SAG.NÍG.GA), the received quantity in the second (*maḫirtu*), and arrears (LÁLxNI) in the third, which features repeatedly the entry Ì.SÁ "it is equal, balanced."

93 This is based of my suggested reading ESÍR for the last sign on line 1 (see Section 5.2.2.1).

94 The letter CUSAS 9, 14 also refers to granaries, however, these granaries were probably not attached to the palace since the aim of the letter is to request the payment of the *šibšu*-tax of a town, Dūr-Ninurta. There was therefore storage of grain at the municipal level as well.

95 Pieces of grinders were found in the public building at Tell Khaiber, including parts of a large quern. However, the excavators cannot yet determine whether flour production took place "on a large or a purely domestic scale" (Campbell et al. 2017). Therefore, it cannot at present be determined whether the flour production taking place there was for the palace.

lonian period mainly at Mari, Chagar Bazar,[96] and Sippar, where school letters were found which attest that the term could be used instead of *ṣibittu*/prison (Kraus 1964: 27 ff. letters p and q). It has been considered, like the *ṣibittu* and other institutions such as the *bīt asīrī*, to be an *ergastulum* where distrainees, prisoners for debt, prisoners of war, and common criminals were put to forced labor, often involving flour production (van der Toorn 1986: 250; see also Seri 2013: 11 ff.).[97]

Other documents of the Sealand I archive may be related to the *nupāru*. The ledgers CUSAS 9, 419; 422; 424; 436 (and probably 409; 416; 418)[98] record quantities of flour (of various qualities) which appears to have been ground by workers in an institutional context. Indeed, the main header of these documents states that flour (ZÌ.DA), namely the ÉŠ.GÀR (LÚ.)EN.NU.UN(.MEŠ)[99] "ÉŠ.GÀR of the guards," was delivered to the palace.[100] The term ÉŠ.GÀR precludes that it was an allocation:[101] we must be dealing, as discussed in Section 5.2.1.4, either with the requisites or the finished product of the listed workers.[102] The latter interpretation, flour as the finished product, is the more likely explanation here because the last column of these ledgers (before the names) records "barley received" ŠE ŠU.TI.A, probably grain received for milling.

If we consider (1) that *nupāru* is equated with *bīt maṣṣarti* in the first tablet of *malku* = *šarru* (Kilmer 1963; line 97 of the composite);[103] (2) that barley grinding took place at the *nupāru*;[104] (3) that quantities of flour are associated in several ledgers with the EN.NU.UN (*maṣṣartu*); and (4) that this flour was delivered to the palace: the most likely explanation is indeed that a guarded workhouse, the *nupāru*, produced flour for the palace from which it received grain to be ground.

---

96 CAD N, s.v. *nupāru* A b.

97 Seri (2013: 253) found no evidence for flour production in the Old Babylonian *bīt asīrī* at Uruk. Charpin (2014: 131 incl. n. 56) notes that a servile status of some sort and the grinding of flour are often associated in the second millennium.

98 The ledger CUSAS 9, 450 presents a very similar structure but bears neither a main header nor column headers. As for CUSAS 9, 413A, it is considered by Dalley to be a delivery of flour but it has a very fragmentary header and her reading [ZÌ].⌜DA⌝ is by no means certain.

99 Once with the plural form ḪI.A.

100 CUSAS 9, 416 and 418 make exception: they have no main header.

101 This is the interpretation chosen by Dalley (2009) in her edition.

102 The other possible meaning of ÉŠ.GÀR, a work quota, probably does not apply here since the documents record deliveries. See also Deheselle 2004: 274 for a brief diachronic survey of the meanings of the word.

103 It has been shown that this list is partly based on Old Babylonian forerunners (Kilmer 1963: 423).

104 Probably for the palace since receipt CUSAS 9, 85 was presumably, like the rest of the archive, drafted by the palace administration.

Book-keeping took the form of small ledgers in which the flour produced was recorded as the work produce that the guards of the *nupāru*-workers delivered to the palace.

Most *nupāru*-workers were women and the same names tend to recur in all ledgers. The lists begin with two or three men,[105] followed by several women.[106] Some of the quantities recorded appear too high to be the product of one person-day of labor if we trust Ur III production-rates (Powell 1984: 55), but what recording principle was at work is not easily elicited from these ledgers.[107] In general, quantities associated with men are larger and some types of flour, ZÌ.KIN.SIG and ZÌ.KUKKUŠ,[108] are only associated with them. The records are dated to at least three separate years (F, J, and K).

5.3.2.2 Types of flour milled at the *nupāru*

According to the ledgers probably recording the *nupāru*'s output (CUSAS 9, 419; 422; 424; 436; and probably 409; 416; 418), several types of (barley) flour were produced in this institution.

5.3.2.2.1 ZÌ(.DA) : flour

The most common term used for flour in the archive is ZÌ.DA, sometimes written only ZÍD, and often used as a generic term for flour. It stands in the main header of the ledgers while specific types of flour are named in the column headers. It sometimes appears in apposition to a specific type of flour in expenditure records, for instance in CUSAS 9, 60 where we have (lines 1–2):

---

105 Mainly Ātanaḫ-Šamaš, Dayyān-ilum, Atta-ilamma; once Kalbu and Tarībātu.

106 Among them, Amat-Šimut, Ūmāyutu, Waqartu, and Alānitu always appear in prominent position.

107 In the most complex ledgers, the first column called SAG.NÍG.GA (*rēš makkūri*) is followed by various types of flour, after which comes a first ŠU.NIGIN column (a sub-total?), followed by (ŠE) *ti-rum*(?), then another ŠU.NIGIN, the LÁLxNI column (arrears?), and finally, before the last column with the personal names, a ŠE ŠU.TI.A column. In general, the following principle applies for the quantities recorded, with some exceptions:

SAG.NÍG.GA = ŠU.NIGIN (1) = ŠU.NIGIN (2) = ŠE ŠU.TI.A

The column (ŠE) *ti-rum* has always only NU as entry, apparently meaning that no such grain or flour was recorded. The column LÁLxNI always features Ì.SÁ "balanced."

108 In CUSAS 9, 419; 422 and 436. Dalley read this header TÚG.IŠ. I suggest to read it ZÌ.KUKKUŠ (see Section 5.3.2.2.4).

0.0.1.0 ZÌ.DA One *sūtu* of flour,
ZÌ.MA.AD.GÁL *maṣḫatu*-flour

It also appears alone in several records of expenditure,[109] in which case it either meant that the flour was of common quality or that it was not necessary to specify its type.

5.3.2.2.2 ZÌ.SAG : best quality flour

This quality of flour is attested a few times in the archive. We mostly find it in the ledgers associated with the *nupāru*, as a column beside other types of flour.[110] It was apparently not produced by all workers, only by the men and very few women.

5.3.2.2.3 ZÌ.KIN.SIG : flour for the meal

We can probably consider that this phrase indeed designates a quality of flour[111] because it figures among other types of flour in ledgers. The evidence suggests that it was produced only by men.

5.3.2.2.4 ZÌ.KUKKUŠ : *kukkušu*-flour

We probably find *kukkušu*-flour, a sort of groats (Milano 1993–97: 26), among the types of flour recorded in a few ledgers (CUSAS 9, 419; 422; 436). Dalley consistently read this column header TÚG.IŠ. She based her reading on the assumption that, in this archive, ZÌ has four horizontals and TÚG three (Dalley 2009: text 419 n.2) But collation from photographs and comparison with other texts do not, in my opinion, sustain her assertion. ZÌ has often three horizontals.[112] In addition, since these ledgers have ZÌ.DA in the main header, one expects flour or at least cereal-related products in the document, ZÌ.KUKKUŠ appears thus a better reading. Also, I would suggest that the column header read TÚG.IŠ AŠGAB by Dalley in

109 For instance: CUSAS 9, 65–67; 70–73; 103; 138. It appears also in a few Tell Khaiber records, e. g. TK1 1114.06.

110 We also find it in expenditure records, for instance CUSAS 9, 414. It was given to the *Egirmaḫ*, perhaps for the preparation of food offerings (CUSAS 9, 131): see Section 5.3.3.

111 Dalley (2009: text 8 n.6) considers that it may have been used only for ritual meals. Expenditures of this type of flour seem to confirm her hypothesis, for instance: CUSAS 9, 86; 109. It was also given to the *Egirmaḫ* (CUSAS 9, 131): see Section 5.3.3.

112 On the shape of this and other signs in Sealand I texts, see Gabbay and Boivin forthcoming.

ledger CUSAS 9, 436 could be read ZÌ.KUKKUŠ SA "roasted *kukkušu*-flour." There is no definite evidence that the signs SA and AŠGAB were differentiated in this archive, even if the sign SA appears to be usually written with horizontals; we find AŠGAB both with horizontals (CUSAS 9, 410: 11) and with obliques (CUSAS 9, 72: 5). According to the ledgers, *kukkušu*-flour was produced only by men.

5.3.2.2.5 ZÌ.UŠ : second-rate flour

This second-rate flour[113] is attested only in ledgers. It was apparently produced by all workers and may have been the main type of flour produced in the *nupāru*.

5.3.2.3 Production of *ḫargalû*-flour at the palace

The uncertain meaning of *ḫargalû* has already been discussed in the *ḫargalû*-grain section (5.2.1.1.4). There is evidence that flour was produced from that type(?) of grain at the palace: document CUSAS 9, 372 is a list recording the assignment of *ḫargalû*-grain to several GEMÉ É.GAL "servant-girl(s) of the palace," 3 *pānū* each,[114] for grinding (*ṭênu*).[115] The women named in this document do not appear to belong to the group of women well represented in the flour ledgers recording the output of the *nupāru*.[116] This type of flour was also delivered to the palace according to records CUSAS 9, 368 and 370,[117] from an unspecified source, and nothing in these records allows us to establish a relation with the production of *ḫargalû*-flour by the palace servants. However, *ḫargalû*-flour is also attested in three records found at Tell Khaiber (TK1 3064.48; 1114.40; 1114.48); the first two could be expenditures, but the latter probably refers to flour production and appears to mention "servant-girls of the palace," as in CUSAS 9, 372. This could indicate that the public building at Tell Khaiber and the palace interacted in the production of *ḫargalû*-flour.

---

113 It is considered *minderwertig* by Sassmannshausen (2001: 452).

114 This quantity would probably be too much for one work day, according to Ur III production rates (Powell 1984: 55).

115 The fact that *ḫargalû* grain was ground (also?) by palace servants speaks against Dalley's suggestion that the term *ḫargalû* refers to a communal mill (Dalley 2009: 192).

116 Only one name is identical although CUSAS 9, 372 dates to month x of year K, a period in which we have two *nupāru*-ledgers (month viii and month xii intercalary of the same year in CUSAS 9, 422 and 424).

117 In this record, one Pirḫi-Sîn acts as GÌR; he may be the same who appears in connection with emmer-flour (CUSAS 9, 148).

5.3.2.4 Other types of flour

There are several other types of flour whose production is not documented in the extant archive, but they were either produced or acquired by the palace because they appear in records of expenditures. Some of these appellations refer to the intended use and may in fact be of one of the qualities discussed above. Although these types of flour are attested only as expenditures in the archive, they are listed here in order to complete the inventory of flour types.

5.3.2.4.1 ZÌ.GU.SAG : best powdered(?) flour

This type of flour is attested twice in the archive. Once it qualifies a type of bread used by diviners—it is its main ingredient (CUSAS 9, 111) –, and once it figures in a letter among other foodstuffs probably sent to a high ranking person (CUSAS 9, 8). The meaning of ZÌ.GU is elusive, "a very common sort of flour made of barley," perhaps very finely crushed (Milano 1993–97: 26).[118] The epithet SAG could be an orthographic variant of SAG_{10}; indeed, ZÌ.GU SAG_{10} is a well attested type of fine flour in Ur III times (Brunke 2011: 91–92 and *passim*).

5.3.2.4.2 ZÌ.MA.AD.GÁL : *maṣḫatu-flour*

This flour appears a few times in this archive. It is written sometimes logographically, sometimes phonetically *ma-aṣ-ḫa-tum* (CUSAS 9, 76), also in the plural *ma-aṣ-ḫa-ta-a-tum* (CUSAS 9, 111). We find it used in divinatory (CUSAS 9, 111) and in ritual context (for instance CUSAS 9, 60; 62; 65), which confirms previous Old Babylonian evidence (Milano 1993–97: 25; 28). In CUSAS 9, 84, quantities of *terru?*-cereal and of *maṣḫatu*-flour are recorded for several deities. The additional mention of "26 bread loaves" on the left edge may indicate that these were ingredients used to make bread.

5.3.2.4.3 ZÌ.ŠE : *tappinnu*-flour

We find only one mention, written logographically, of this coarse barley flour or barley "grits" (Milano 1993–97: 25) in CUSAS 9, 373. The beginning of the text is broken off but it seems to record foodstuffs received by a messenger.

---

118 Dalley (2009: text 8 n.6) equated it with ZÌ.KUM (contra Charpin 1986: 314 and Milano 1993–97: 26), and suggested a normalization as *i/ašqūqu*.

5.3.2.4.4 Ground emmer

We have only slight evidence of the processing of emmer-wheat in the archive. Text CUSAS 9, 148, cast like a list but containing only one entry, begins with the header ŠE *ku-ni-šu* ḪAR.RA "ground emmer." A small quantity is associated with an individual; the undated text does not make it clear whether he received or delivered it.

5.3.2.4.5 NÍG.ḪAR.RA : *mundu*-groats?

This foodstuff, portioned in measures of dry capacity, appears twice in the archive (CUSAS 9, 65: 26; 100). Dalley chose to read it NINDA.ḪAR.RA and translated it as bread of *samīdu*, a type of coarse flour or groats usually written syllabically (CAD S, s.v. *samīdu* B). NÍG.ḪAR.RA is probably a better reading: it is a well-attested type of groats (Brunke 2011: 34),[119] always written logographically in earlier periods. It starts being written syllabically, *mundu*, from the Middle Babylonian period on.

It seems to have been produced mostly from barley[120] (CAD M, s.v. *mundu*) but it has been shown that it could also be made out of wheat, as in the Assyrian medicinal text AMT 42,2: NÍG.ḪAR.RA GIG.BA, interpreted "Weizenfeinmehl" by Haussperger (2012: 222).[121] In CUSAS 9, 65: 26, NÍG.ḪAR.RA is followed by a fragmentary passage *ša ki*-X-X-X? Dalley reads the sign following *ki*- as *-na-* and considers it certain; she reconstructs: *ša ki-na-*⌜*a-ti?*⌝.[122] Collation from the photograph is difficult but the *-na-* does not appear entirely certain; I suggest as another possible reconstruction *ša ki-*⌜*ib-ti*⌝, therefore, "wheat groats."

5.3.2.4.6 ZÌ.SUR.RA : flour for magic circles

We find three occurrences of flour for magic circles, written ZÌ.SUR.RA in the archive. It appears twice in record CUSAS 9, 73 listing offerings for Ninurta and Šamaš—once for each god—and once among other offerings for "when the silo is opened" (CUSAS 9, 100). It is usually considered to be (barley) flour used to draw ritual or magic circles (CAD Z, s.v. *zisurrû*). Whether this flour was in fact

---

119 Or on the contrary "Feinmehl" according to AHw.

120 See also Postgate 1984: 108.

121 Englund (1990: 87–88) discusses the quality of this flour. Hartman and Oppenheim (1950: 19) translate it as groats.

122 She suggests "of the servants(?)" (Dalley 2009: text 65; see also n.26).

of one of the types previously discussed is not known.[123] It has also been interpreted as a paste made of flour and water and used to draw magic lines (Schramm 2001: 9 f.).

5.3.2.4.7 ZÌ *si-ir-qí* : flour for scattering

This phrase occurs twice in record CUSAS 9, 73 listing offerings for Ninurta and Šamaš, once for each god. The name refers to the strewing and scattering of foodstuffs and aromatics in cult and ritual. It is in both cases listed alongside flour for magic circles. (See also n.123 for the evidence of UR_5.RA = *ḫubullu*).

5.3.3 Preparation of breads and other flour-based products

We have no direct evidence pertaining to the making of bread and other cereal-based dishes but we find various types of such products in records of expenditures. They must therefore have been either acquired or prepared by the palace. One text may indirectly suggest where they were produced there: the receipt CUSAS 9, 131 records that two types of flour to (or for) the *Egirmaḫ* (*ana* É.GIR_4.MAḪ) were received by the cooks (MUḪALDIM.MEŠ). Whether these cooks are the same MUḪALDIM.MEŠ who appear often as GÌR officials when livestock and carcasses are delivered to the palace is not entirely certain but if it is the case, it would mean that the *Egirmaḫ* functioned within the palatial economy, apparently as the service responsible to prepare the ritual foodstuffs that we find in expenditure records for deities and temples. In other words, the *Egirmaḫ* is probably the palace kitchen, which is also suggested by the term itself ("house of the great oven"). The *Egirmaḫ* also appears twice as the end recipient of rams (CUSAS 9, 34 and 37) and once of lambs (CUSAS 9, 44)[124] delivered to the palace.

---

123 In tablet XXIII of UR_5.RA = *ḫubullu,* it is indirectly equated with ZÌ.DUB.DUB.BU and a few Akkadian expressions, in particular (*qí-me*) *si-ir-qí*, all in relation with ritual and cultic purposes: col.V, lines 8–11:

[ZÌ.DUB.DU]B.BU*qí-me ma-aq-qí-tum*
[ZÌ.DUB.D]UB.BUMIN *si-ir-qí*
[ZÌ.SUR].RAMIN MIN
[ZÌ.SUR].RAŠU-*u*

In CUSAS 9, 73 we find it listed after ZÌ *si-ir-qí.*

124 In this case, it is written syllabically *gi-ir-ma-a-ḫi.*

5.3.3.1 NINDA : bread

Common(?) bread, written NINDA, is attested four times in cultic context (CUSAS 9, 63; 84; 86; 109). In text CUSAS 9, 84, the quantity appears to be given in discrete units, 26 bread "loaves." It is written on the edge of a tablet containing quantities of grain and flour given to several deities, these may thus be ingredients used to make the loaves. In other texts, the bread quantities are given in measures of dry capacity. In two cases (CUSAS 9, 86; 109), the bread is part of the supplies[125] for a ritual night meal given on the fourteenth day, probably the full moon, of month viii.[126]

5.3.3.2 NINDA Ì.DÉ.A : *mersu*-dish

The best attested NINDA-dish in the Sealand I texts is the *mersu*-dish, written mostly logographically NINDA (Ì).DÉ.A, once syllabically *me-er-si*. It always appears in ritual (CUSAS 9, 63; 68; 69; 86; 100; 109), or once in divinatory context (CUSAS 9, 111). The *mersu*-dish was a compound of ground cereals and fat to which various aromatic ingredients were added, such as leeks, onions, and honey (Vincente 1992: 334; 344), but also dates, spices, and others (Brunke 2011: 203–08; Bottéro 1995: 22ff.; Sigrist 1977: 175). The mixture was apparently not solid[127] and had to be served in appropriate containers (Brunke 2011: 209; Maul 1994: 51ff.).

5.3.3.3 NINDA ZÌ.GU.SAG : bread of best powdered(?) flour

We find one occurrence of bread made of the previously discussed ZÌ.GU.SAG-flour (Section 5.3.2.4.1). It appears in a divinatory context (CUSAS 9, 111).

5.3.3.4 NINDA ZÌ *šu-mi* : garlic powder bread?

A type of bread appearing in CUSAS 9, 69: 6 is of problematic reading: Dalley reads NINDA *šu?-šu-mi* and leaves it untranslated.[128] However, collation from the photograph suggests that the sign following NINDA is ZÌ, hence: NINDA ZÌ *šu-mi*. The term ZÌ, while mostly used for flour of cereals, is also attested with vegetables, fruits, and pulses (AHw *qēmu* 8; also CAD Q, s.v. *qēmu* b); it is

125 Called *isiḫtu* in CUSAS 9, 109 (see Section 5.4.3).

126 Both records are for the 14.viii, in one case of year D, in the other of year K.

127 For this reason I prefer the term "dish" over "cake" chosen by Dalley.

128 She discusses possibilities in her note to that line.

then considered a powder. If this reading is correct, we could have a bread aromatized with(?) powdered or crushed garlic.

5.3.3.5 Other types of bread

Text CUSAS 9, 100, which lists food offerings for "when the grain silo is opened," contains two other types of bread. On line 8 the type recorded is unclear; Dalley transliterates it NINDA ḫi im bu bu *a-za-a-tum* and leaves it untranslated.[129] In particular the first signs seem very clearly written; it is portioned in measures of dry capacity. On line 9, we find ^{NINDA}*ti-il-pa-na-a-tum* "bow(?)-shaped bread" (CAD T, s.v. *tilpānu* f 4′; "Bogen-Brote" in Maul 1994: 369 and 371 line 12′).[130]

5.3.4 Malting and brewing

Beer brewing has a long and well attested tradition in Mesopotamia and is also abundantly represented in the Sealand I texts. Indeed, the transfer of raw material, semi-processed, and finished products of barley malting and beer brewing has produced, with over 150 records, a large subset of the Sealand I palace documents that have become available to us. These delivery records and receipts are standardized and fairly repetitive and, without being rich in detail, they do offer valuable information about the actors and institutions involved in these activities.

The brewing of beer in Mesopotamia has been shown to involve two separate series of operations to process barley, one aimed at ensuring fermentation, resulting in a so-called "beer-bread" or perhaps rather sourdough (BAPPIR_x or BABIR_x),[131] and one aimed at sweetening the beer by means of malting, resulting in

129 She suggests possibilities in her note to that line. Also, knowing that NINDA GÍD.DA "lange Brote," given in measures of dry capacity, are attested in *namburbi*-rituals (see Maul 1994: 235 and 244 line 6), one could suggest to read GÍD.GÍD reading instead of BU BU.

130 See also Dalley's comment in 2009: text 100 n.9. It is not clear whether a quantity is specified; one expects specially shaped bread to be counted in loaves. This is the case in the *namburbi*-ritual referred to here and in which "7 *til-pa-na-ti*" are used.

131 For the reading BABIR_x and the interpretation as sourdough, see Sallaberger 2012: 308–10. This preparation is usually not considered to have been produced from malted barley, although there may be contrary evidence (Stol 1987–90: 325–26). Powell (1994: 96 ff.) discussed whether it was indeed a baked bread; it may have been simply dried (Sallaberger 2012: 309–10; 325).

a prepared malt mash.[132] Both ingredients were then mixed in order to brew beer (Sallaberger 2012: 325; a slightly different process was reconstructed by Stol 1971: 169, followed by Van De Mieroop 1994: 314; see also Stol 1987–90: 325 ff.). Of all the ingredients and semi-finished products involved in this brewing method, only barley (including barley for malt) and malt appear in the Sealand I archive.[133] A few types of beer are also recorded.

It appears that the palace where the archive was found was actively involved in beer production. We learn from the records that malt was produced from barley for the palace and that beer was brewed at an institution called the *Egipar*, which may have been attached to the palace; if it wasn't, then beer was also brewed at the palace. The same palatial administration—the same Bureau of malt and beer—tracked the circulation of barley for malt, malt, and beer between maltsters, brewers, the palace, and the *Egipar*. We have no indication that tablets were encased in an envelope, and only very few appear to have been drawn up in two copies[134]—unless the mention that is was a copy (*meḫrum*) was usually omitted in this bureau—, as opposed to the book-keeping practices observed for livestock and animal carcasses deliveries. Several delivery records, especially of beer jars, were sealed.[135] This suggests a careful but somewhat looser tracking of the movement of goods than for the procurement of livestock and carcasses. It would tally with a malt and beer production probably largely controlled by the palace:

132 According to Stol (1987–90: 325), this would have been the TITAB, a Malzkuchen or Malzbrot; and it may have been mostly associated with dark beer (Powell 1994: 101). According to Sallaberger's reconstruction (2012: 316–17; 325), this was coarsely ground malt mixed with water.
133 A small quantity of *agarinnu*, beer mash or perhaps rising sourdough (Sallaberger 2012: 312), appears exceptionally in CUSAS 9, 92: 3 among other foodstuffs; the context does not seem related to beer brewing. Also in the Old Babylonian beer archive at Tell Leilan we find that the sweetening/malting operations are better attested than the fermentation: in that archive all the semi-finished products for this procedure are attested, barley for malt and malt being by far the most common (Van De Mieroop 1994: 314–15).
134 The malt delivery records CUSAS 9, 216; 226; 230. These copies were also sealed.
135 In addition to the malt deliveries CUSAS 9, 177; 216; 226; and 230, the following beer delivery records are sealed: CUSAS 9, 258–59; 262; 268; 270–71; 273–74; 280–81; 283–85; 287; 289–90; 297–301; 303–04. In addition, one damaged delivery record involving brewers was sealed (CUSAS 9, 193). The sealing habits appear to have differed from those used in the recording of livestock and animal carcasses. In the administration of malt and beer, the iconographic part of the seal appears to have been very important, and it was often applied on the top edge of the tablet (e.g., CUSAS 9, 262; 268; 274). When the inscription was rolled on the edges, it was applied perpendicularly, therefore, only the middle of it is visible (e.g., CUSAS 9, 297); when it was rolled on the obverse or reverse of the tablet, the orientation seems to have been freer than on livestock and carcass records (e.g., CUSAS 9, 289 where it is almost perpendicular to the text).

the goods involved in the brewing process may have circulated mostly inside the palace economic system.

Beer was given out by the palace as offering to deities, there is also some evidence that it was given out as supplies or gift of the king to various individuals although no beer allotments (or rations) are attested. Curiously, the types of beer brewed do not seem to correspond to the common Mesopotamian beer types. They are reviewed in Section 5.3.4.4.

5.3.4.1 Maltsters, brewers, and the men in charge of(?) the *Egipar*[136]

Examination of the relevant administrative records shows that the activities surrounding the malting of barley and the brewing of beer involved two professional groups: the maltsters written (LÚ).MUNU$_5$(.MEŠ),[137] and the brewers written (LÚ).ŠIM(.MEŠ). The maltsters received barley, sometimes with the additional precision that it was for malt,[138] and delivered malt to the palace.[139] Brewers received malt, a few times also barley, and delivered beer to the palace; in delivery records they are usually identified only by name, not by their professional title, but the co-occurrence and recurrence of personal names leaves no doubt on their identity. In addition to maltsters and brewers, we find that *bēlū pīḫati ana Egipar* were involved as well, a phrase which alternates with *bēlū pīḫati* LÚ *Egipar* and *bēlū pīḫati ša Egipar.* These "men in charge of/for (men of) the *Egipar*" also received malt, and exceptionally barley, like the brewers. In fact, we also find the phrase "brewers *ša Egipar*" in one receipt (CUSAS 9, 223) and "brewers *ana Egipar*"[140] in another (CUSAS 9, 187). Clearly, these appellations were interchangeable, especially since the individuals involved were the same,[141] as is shown in Table 10 (I have included the individuals delivering beer in the brewers' column).

Whether all brewers were attached to the *Egipar* is more than the texts allow us to say with certainty but the correlation appears quite strong,[142] especially since the same men were recorded in both capacities during the same period.[143]

136 The orthography of this institution's name varies in the archive: *gi-pa-ru* and É.GI$_6$.PÀR.
137 The sign MUNU$_5$ is written PAB—ŠExPAB in this archive.
138 The phrase is usually "ŠE *ana* MUNU$_5$."
139 And a few times with the additional mention that it was for the palace of Kār-Šamaš; the matter is discussed below.
140 The same indifferent use of *ana* and *ša* must apply to "brewers *ana* É.GAL" found in CUSAS 9, 207; 235; 244, whose meaning, therefore, must be "brewers of (as well as for) the palace."
141 We also have once only *bēlū pīḫati* (CUSAS 9, 156).
142 Only two brewers do not appear explicitly as "men in charge at the *Egipar*": Rabût-Adad, who is only marginally present in the documents with only three occurrences, and Ṣābī-(E)-Ulmaš.

Table 10: Title distribution of individuals involved in barley malting and beer brewing

Maltsters	***bēlū pīḫati*/(Brewers) (LÚ/*ana*/*ša* Egipar)**	**Brewers**
Qišti-Marduk	Qišti-Marduk	Qišti-Marduk
Ḫuzālu	Ḫuzālu	Ḫuzālu
Ṣābī-(E)-Ulmaš		Ṣābī-(E)-Ulmaš
	Dannū-mūšu	Dannū-mūšu
	Māšu	Māšu
		Rabût(i)-Adad
Ḫabbil-ilu		
Ilīyatu		
Erību		
Šamaš-dumqī		
Amurru-naṣir		

Table 10 shows also that a number of individuals cumulated the functions of brewer and maltster, in the same period of time. But when barley or malt was received or delivered, these maltsters-brewers always appeared in the records in the corresponding capacity, either as maltster or brewer.

That the palace was certainly directly involved in the process of beer production shows in record CUSAS 9, 232, which probably identifies the palace as the obligatory *locus* of transit for malt, that is, a semi-transformed product. In this text, we find on the same record a delivery of malt (MU.DU) by a maltster to the palace, followed by the reception (ŠU.TI.A) of almost the same quantity of malt (merely with an additional 5 *qû*) by the brewers.[144] The most likely explanation is that malt was delivered to the palace and was almost immediately reached further to the brewers, after topping up an incomplete *sūtu*.

Beer brewing is also characterized by a strong economic and organizational relationship between the palace and the *Egipar*. This shows in texts CUSAS 9, 151 and 161: both record that a quantity of malt for the *Egipar* (Qty MUNU_5 *ana*

143 For instance receipts of malt CUSAS 9, 219 and 223, listing the three same individuals, in one case as brewers, in the other as "brewers of the *Egipar*" are dated respectively to the 10th and the 22nd of the same month (month iv of year N).

144 The second quantity (line 6) is erroneous in Dalley's transliteration, but correct in the autograph copy.

É.GI$_6$.PÀR) was delivered to the palace (MU.DU ... *ana* É.GAL). Also, one delivery record of beer—although they do not usually identify the brewers by their titles—does mention the *bēlū pīḫati* LÚ[145]*Egipar* (CUSAS 9, 253), without specifying the end destination. But since MU.DU records in this archive are as a rule deliveries to the palace, it is a fair assumption that this delivery by the men of the *Egipar* was also intended for the palace, that is, that the *Egipar* brewed beer for the palace.

We therefore have a situation in which some maltsters-brewers could divide their time between malting for the palace and brewing for the *Egipar* as part of the palace, or perhaps separately brewing for the palace and the *Egipar*. If the brewers split their time between (at least) these two institutions,[146]these activities were still monitored by the same administrative body.

The alternative is that all brewers' titles were completely interchangeable and that the *Egipar* was organizationally within the palace,[147] functioning as its brewery. There is some slight evidence speaking for it. That a *gipāru* can have an economic function as storage for foodstuffs is suggested for instance in TCL 16, 70 (lines 30–31), a religious text dedicated to Ištar, in which *gipāru* is equated with a storehouse (É.UŠ.GÍD.DA). It can also designate a part of a private house, separate from the living quarters (CAD G, s.v. *gipāru* 2). It seems thus likely that the Sealand I *Egipar*/*gipāru*, functioning as a brewery, was an extension of the latter meaning of the term, a part of a house (here the palace) with an economic function pertaining to foodstuff.

Moreover, in the list of professions of the Old Babylonian "Sargon Ur Letter" (UET 7, 73), in the section pertaining to food preparation, the entry LÚ.GIPAR$_X$.RA follows immediately a fragmentary entry beginning with KAŠ, obviously a profession related to beer brewing (Westenholz 1997: 160–61, lines 108–09).[148]

---

145 The sign LÚ was mistakenly read MÍ by Dalley.

146 This is known for instance for prebendary brewers at Nippur in the first millennium, an organization which may have had its roots in the Old Babylonian period (Beaulieu 1995: 94ff.). Also, in a text from Dūr-Enlilē dated to Šagarakti-Šuriaš, beer appears to be destined to Nippur (CUSAS 30, 283: 6).

147 Be it as it may, maltsters and brewers do not seem to be attested in allotment (or ration) lists or *miksu*-ledgers. Therefore, although they certainly appear to be employed by the palace, we have no information on their remuneration.

148 It has been suggested that beer may have been brewed at the *Egipar* of Ur, mainly because of the identification of an oven(?) that may have been used to bake "beer-bread" (Breniquet 2009: 189). While there is indeed no question as to the presence of ovens and a well in the *Egipar* at Ur, there is no archaeological evidence that the installations were particularly appropriate for the brewing of large quantities of beer, nor is there any indication in the texts found *in situ* that the *Egipar* functioned as a brewery beyond producing for its own need. There is therefore no

5.3.4.2 The palace administration of beer brewing

The reconstructed organization of beer production can be schematized like this:

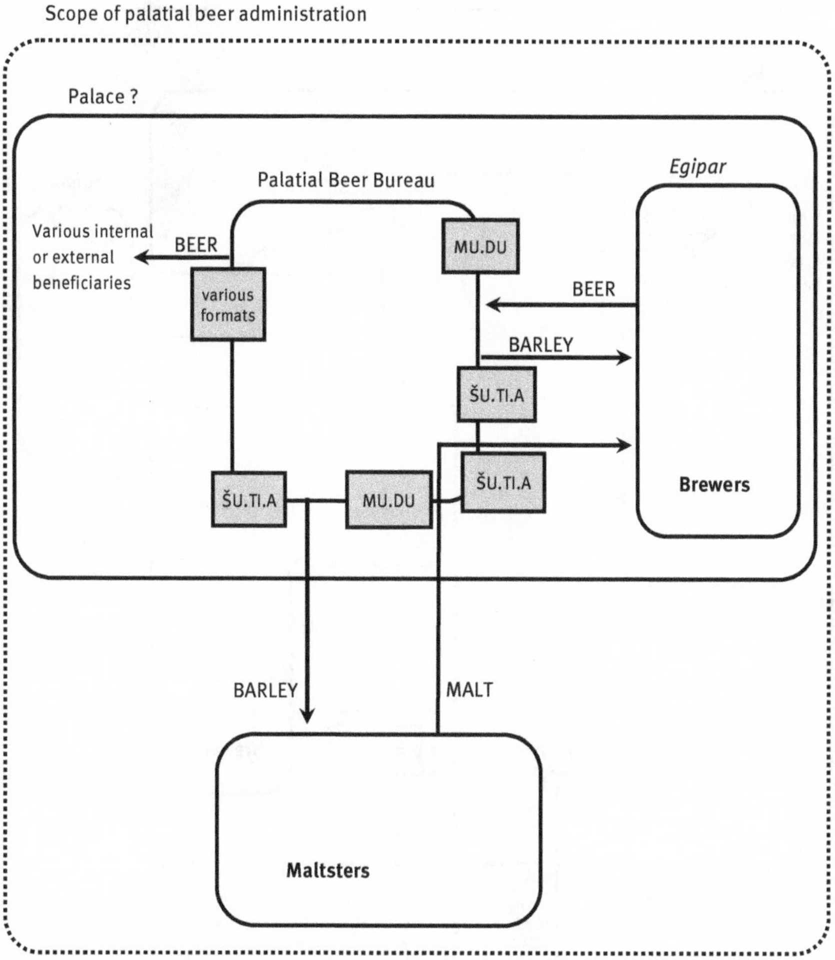

Figure 3: Palatial administration of beer production (scenario A)

conclusive association of the *Egipar*-institution at Ur with a special vocation in beer brewing. However, the evidence seems to show that there was initially a physical separation between the temple of Ningal, the É.NUN, and the actual *gipāru*—that is, the residence of the *entu*-priestess—and that they were merged only in Ur III times (Charpin 1986: 210–19; Weadock 1975: 123–24). The *gipāru* may have had a mainly economic function.

or, less likely, like this:

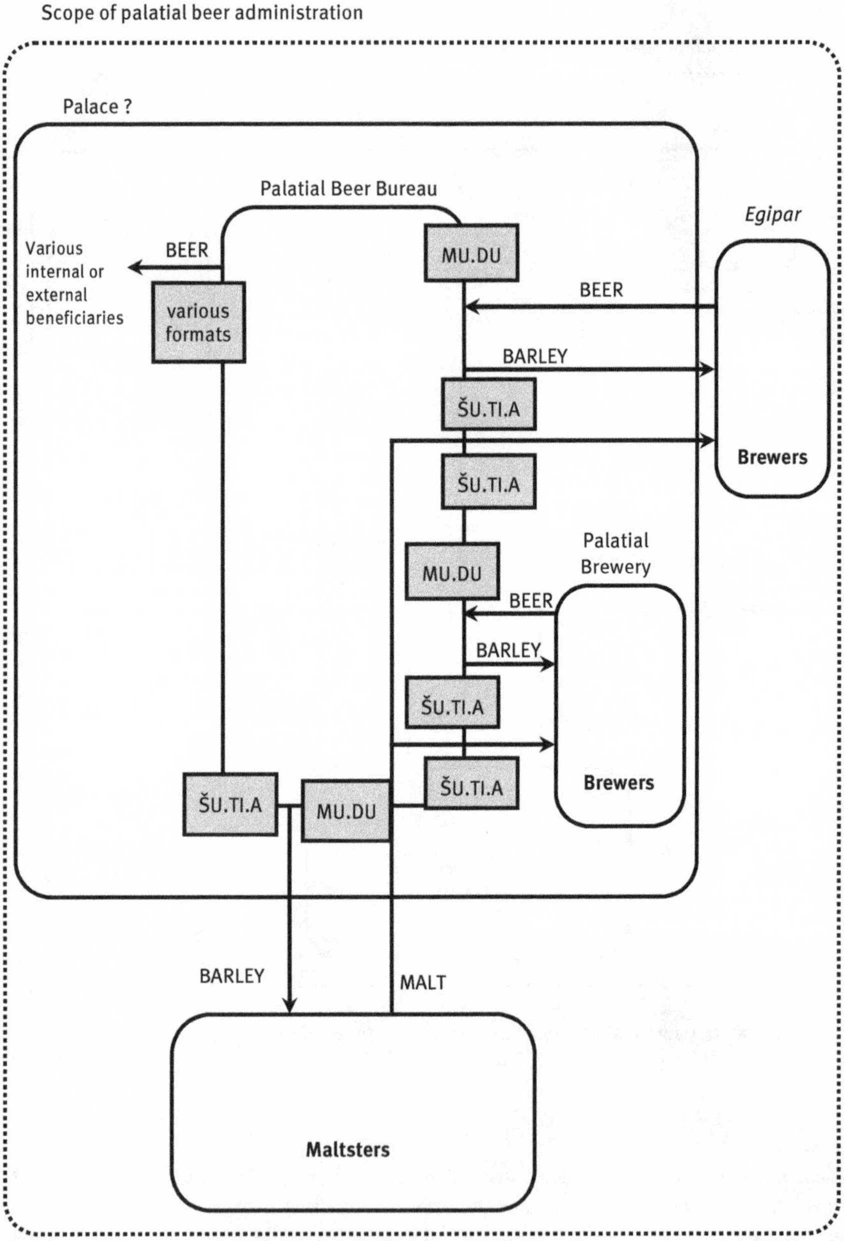

Figure 4: Palatial administration of beer production (scenario B)

5.3.4.3 Malt

Several receipts and delivery records are concerned with malt (MUNU_5), also with barley for malt (ŠE *ana* MUNU_5). As discussed above, malt was produced by maltsters (LÚ.MUNU_5.MEŠ), delivered to the palace, and received by brewers. We find once in CUSAS 9, 188 a direct reference to the process of malting, that is, to one step of the process: the quelling caused by germination which follows steeping. The verb used to describe this step is *rabû* D : "aufgehen lassen" (Stol 1987–90: 324), therefore "to let grow, quell." Since it appears in the context of a delivery of barley to a maltster in the phrase ŠE (...) *ana* MUNU_5 *ru-ub-bé-e*, the intended meaning is probably simply "barley for malting."[149]

Malt is also delivered once to the palace as fodder for horses (CUSAS 9, 203). Residues of the malt production, the malt rootlets and the draff (or spent grain) are considered good animal fodder (Stol 1971: 169–70); this may have been what was delivered here.

5.3.4.4 Beer

A few types of beer are attested in the Sealand I records. Beer was delivered almost always to the palace and quantities are always given in numbers of *pīḫu*-jars, a type of jar widely attested in the Old Babylonian period.[150] The phrase following the number of jars is written (KAŠ) *pí/pi-ḫu* (.ḪI.A)[151] and is sometimes followed by a specific variety of beer.

---

149 Dalley translated the passage "for increasing malt" and suggested that it was to stimulate fermentation (n.1 to text CUSAS 9, 188).

150 Its capacity was sometimes two *sūtu* but could be different (CAD P, s.v. *pīḫu* a). See also Van De Mieroop 1994: 338 for a discussion on the capacity and the value of the *pīḫu*-jar as standard measure for beer; see also Sallaberger 1996: 116. In the Sealand I palace archive, the statement of quantities and beer types (there are one or two types of beer per record) is always followed by *maḫ-ru-(ú)-tum*. As noted by Dalley (2009: 142 n.2), the term does not seem to apply to the type of beer since it always appears only once, at the end, even if more than one type of beer is listed. It may apply to the jars. Jars of beer "received" (*maḫrūtum*) seems improbable because they are recorded as being delivered (MU.DU). The reading is probably rather *maḫrûtum*. As for its interpretation, we may be dealing with delivery records drawn up after the delivery, and referring explicitly to "earlier jars;" this remains uncertain but seems slightly more probable than "first jars" because no later or subsequent deliveries are attested.

151 The use of PI is rather typical of southern Babylonian use (Goetze 1945: 146). In this archive PI is the usual orthography for /pi/, although it is less common in this word.

5.3.4.4.1 KAŠ : beer

Jars of beer without any other specification of its type were often delivered. Besides being present in several delivery records (for instance CUSAS 9, 247–54), this unspecific beer figures in letter CUSAS 9, 4 in which goods sent to a high official are listed. It also appears as food offering to the gods (e.g. CUSAS 9, 63; 65: 4, 15, 23, and 32), as gift of the king (e.g., CUSAS 9, 138: 1–5), or as payment or other type of allotment to individuals, always along other foodstuffs (e.g., CUSAS 9, 103; 112; 114).

The term is usually considered generic for all types of beer, when no specification was required (Röllig 1970: 28). While this explanation seems easily tenable when examining the Sealand I evidence, for instance in the specific context of cultic offerings in which the type and quality of beer was implicitly known by the involved parties, it is more surprising to find it often in delivery records. It may have come to designate a particularly common type of beer, however, it is never found alongside another specific type of beer.

5.3.4.4.2 *marsānu*-beer

This term does not belong to the usual Mesopotamian beer names; it is written *mar-sa-(a)-nu* on the line following the statement of quantity and (KAŠ) *pi/pí-ḫu* (ḪI.A).[152] As noted by Dalley, it is attested once in a Middle Babylonian text (Dalley 2009: text 255 n.2; Sassmannshausen 2001: text 302: III 10). Sassmannshausen suggested that the name referred to a type of container known from Old Akkadian and Middle Assyrian texts. Dalley's explanation that the word derives from *marāsu* "to stir into a liquid" seems more plausible. I would suggest that it may refer more specifically to a type of beer[153] in which malt mash (SÚN : *narṭabu*) has been stirred into. Indeed, the verbal adjective *marsu* is equated in tablet XXIII of UR_5-*ra* = *ḫubullu* with SÚN.ŠU.AKA.A (AHw, s.v. *marsu*; Hartmann and Oppenheim 1950: 24 Col.III 24; 50 n.75). We could also be dealing with a "stirred beer," perhaps simply unstrained, as opposed to strained(?) beer (*našpu*-beer). They are indeed often delivered together, for instance in CUSAS 9, 255–57 (see also Section 5.3.4.4.3), but it was also sometimes delivered alone (for instance CUSAS 9, 264; 296). Another possibility is that the term simply derives from *rasānu* "to brew beer" (CAD R, s.v. *rasānu* 2).

---

152 There is one instance, probably an error of the scribe, in which we have the syntax "Qty *mar-sa-nu* / *mar-sa-nu*" (CUSAS 9, 308: 3–4).

153 The fact that it is attested not only in the phrase "Qty *pi/pí-ḫu*.(HI.A) *mar-sa-(a)-nu*," the most common syntax in this archive, but also when the specific KAŠ stands before *pīḫu* (CUSAS 9, 300; 295?), excludes that a type a semi-finished product was delivered.

5.3.4.4.3 *našpu*-beer

Another type of beer found in the archive is the *našpu*-beer;[154] the word is written *na-aš-pu* on the line following the statement of quantity and (KAŠ) *pi/pí-ḫu* (ḪI.A). The term is known to apply to various types of beer and beer ingredients (CAD N, s.v. *našpu*) but the meaning is not immediately apparent. Powell (1994: 105–06) discussed various possibilities and prudently suggested a meaning related to a light color of the beer, perhaps "golden." However, the verb *našāpu* means "to blow away, winnow,"[155] and it has been suggested that, for beer, the meaning would be "von Rückständen gereinigt" (Röllig 1970: 37). Therefore, it would probably equate with "strained beer"(?) If this is correct, this could indeed be the opposite of the *marsānu*-beer (stirred? beer). It is often delivered alongside *marsānu*-beer, but also features alone in a few delivery records (e.g., CUSAS 9, 262; 307).

5.3.4.4.4 Beer for the meal

In only two delivery records (CUSAS 9, 298; 301), dated two days apart, we find a delivery of a quantity of *pí-ḫu*.(HI.A) KIN.SIG.[156] It is not clear whether the intended purpose for the beer or its type (or both) is implied by that term. In both texts, this delivery was not the only one on that day, there was another delivery, in one case of (unspecified) beer, in the other of *marsānu*- and *našpu*-beer. The expression is reminiscent of the "flour for the meal" (see Section 5.3.2.2.3).

5.3.4.4.5 KAŠ.SIG$_5$: fine beer(?)

This type of beer, otherwise so well attested in Mesopotamia, may appear once in this archive, in a small ledger of outgoing (beer?) jars (CUSAS 9, 269). The header is damaged and only the sign SIG$_5$ is partially visible. Since it would be the only

154 Translated "sweet beer" by Dalley.

155 With that meaning, it could only refer to a treatment of the grain used in the preparation of the beer, as suggested by Powell 1994: 105.

156 In CUSAS 9, 298, it is followed by an obscure phrase (line 3). Dalley transliterates it *a-na? ša ki-*⌈*te?-e*⌉ and suggests the translation "for the one of the flax(?)" However, collation from the photograph shows that the beginning of the line could be read either ŠÀ KAŠ *ša ki-*... or ŠÀ-*bi ša ki-*... Also, since CUSAS 9, 299 has on line 3: ŠÀ-*bu ša ki?-*...., the latter transliteration must be correct, therefore "from among..." The remainder of the line remains obscure.

occurrence in the corpus, the reconstruction should be considered very uncertain.[157]

5.3.5 Oil production and transformation

5.3.5.1 Ì.GIŠ : sesame(?) oil

We have no direct information on oil pressing. A few records suggest that oil was not produced by the palace itself but its production may have been commissioned by it. Sesame[158] appears alongside sesame oil (Ì.GIŠ) in one text (CUSAS 9, 121): it records that sesame seeds were given by the king, apparently to one Narbu who is named on the following line, and that oil was delivered[159] to the palace.[160] The fact that both outgoing sesame and incoming oil were recorded together by the palace administration suggests that sesame oil was pressed on behalf of the palace and that this individual was (or acted for) an oil-presser. The quantities involved are modest (5 *sūtu* of sesame seeds and 1 *sūtu* of oil) but by no means unheard of.[161] It remains unclear what exactly the sesame seeds represented in the transaction. If they were the raw material—the seeds that had

157 The document is peculiar in other respects: it is the only ZI.GA record in the whole beer archive and one of very few among the Sealand I documents; the quantities recorded are higher than in other beer delivery records; finally, it refers to the "quay of Dūr-Ninurta," a town known from a letter (CUSAS 9, 14) but never otherwise mentioned in the context of beer production. In addition, the offering record CUSAS 9, 76 may feature two other types of beer, of uncertain reading (lines 3–4).

158 See Section 5.2.1.3.1 for the discussion on the identification of ŠE.GIŠ.Ì. In addition, see Stol 2003–05: 33 for the identification of Ì.GIŠ with sesame oil in most contexts in Mesopotamia.

159 There is no verb but the phrase *ana* É.GAL and the presence of GÌR officials, very often found in combination with deliveries to the palace in this archive, makes it almost certain that the oil was indeed delivered to the palace.

160 The obscure line following Narbu, probably qualifying him, does not help clarify the transaction. Dalley (2009: text 121: 4) reads it *ša* nar un ḫi. Based on the photograph, I would suggest that NAR could be in fact GAL although Dalley's comment that the signs are clear certainly speaks against it. But if my suggestion is correct, we could have here a GAL.UN official. If the ḪI is an abbreviated plural(?), we would have "Narbu of the GAL.UN officials"(?) This would be surprisingly late evidence for this office otherwise not attested after the Ur III period, unless we equate the GAL.UN official with the *mu'erru*, as does Selz (1989: 85 Anm.3:4); for an opposite opinion, see Bauer 1989–90: 81–82.

161 In a late Old Babylonian contract from Dilbat (YOS 13, 444), 5 *sūtu* of sesame seeds were given for pressing for which ten days were allotted. For comparison, 10 *kurru* are given for oil pressing in another late Old Babylonian contract CT 8, 36c discussed in Pientka 1998: 221 and Stol 2004: 942.

been pressed—the ratio "sesame seeds : oil" of 5:1 corresponds indeed to those known from third millennium sources (Waetzoldt 1985: 81) for sesame oil extraction. This seems hard to reconcile with the fact that the sesame is qualified as "NÍG.BA of the king." However, the meaning here may not be best conveyed by the term "gift" chosen by Dalley; "honorarium, compensation" would probably be more adequate (CAD Q, s.v. *qīštu* 3a). It may thus have been that the palace supplied sesame, presumably as raw material and salary to oil-pressers. Payment in sesame seeds suggests that (at least some) oil-pressers were independent from the palace and made business with other customers; this would tally with the fact that they are not attested in allotment (or ration) lists.[162]

Common sesame oil appears only a few times in this archive. We know that it was sometimes measured by the bronze *sūtu* (CUSAS 9, 90; 120).[163] We find it at least twice delivered to the palace (CUSAS 9, 120; 121), and the transaction involved at least one official, a GÌR.[164] One of the GÌR officials present in the delivery record CUSAS 9, 121, namely Arad-Amurru, also acts in the same function in two expenditure records involving sesame oil: CUSAS 9, 128 and 143. It appears thus that the GÌR function for oil included responsibility both in its reception and its expenditure by the palace. It was not given as offering to deities,[165] who received only scented (or fine) oil, but it was handed out as supplies to individuals (CUSAS 9, 90; 128; possibly 150).

5.3.5.2 Ì.DÙG.GA : scented oil

Scented oil,[166] Ì.DÙG.GA, used in offerings to the gods, may have been produced for the palace by perfumers. We find it delivered twice (CUSAS 9, 94;[167] 107) and in one case there is a possible mention of perfumers in the transaction: MU.DU / *ra-qí-i?* (CUSAS 9, 107: 3–4). A perfumer, one Ilānutum whose profession is writ-

---

162 Two oil-pressers are attested in the Tell Khaiber texts (TK1 3064.33: rev.18 and TK1 1114.40: rev.17).

163 The term *sūtu* is implied (only ZABAR is written). The bronze *sūtu* was also used once for barley in the context of malting, although its occurrence there is exceptional (CUSAS 9, 200).

164 One of them, Ardijû, was a barber in CUSAS 9, 120 (for the reading of the name, see Zadok 2014: 229). For a detailed discussion of the GÌR function, see Boivin 2016c: 11–13.

165 It may be used in a ritual related to a journey of the king (CUSAS 9, 101: 6); however, it is followed in the record of expenditure by cedar pieces, possibly to perfume the oil.

166 Middeke-Conlin (2014: 13) pleads for Ì.DÙG.GA as designating processed or worked oil, therefore perfumed, whereas Ì.SAG would indicate the quality (see also his review of other opinions on p.12 n.49). Brunke and Sallaberger (2010: 52–54) also consider Ì.(GIŠ) DÙG.GA to be scented oil.

167 Here Dalley transliterated erroneously DUG_4.

ten logographically Ì.RÁ.RÁ, figures in a list of craftsmen (CUSAS 9, 381: 11′), which suggests some form of employment by the palace. In this document he is listed with the physicians, which agrees with the association of herbalists with physicians in the Mesopotamian tradition (Middeke-Conlin 2014: 16).

In what relationship exactly the perfumers stood to the palace is unclear but one text suggests that the palace supplied them with the ingredients they needed to prepare the scented oil: CUSAS 9, 143. It records a quantity of oil and one of cedar resin for the anointing of doors, probably as an expenditure, and may therefore list the raw materials needed by a perfumer. The text also seems to indicate that common sesame oil Ì.GIŠ was used to prepare scented oil. The evidence is thin[168] but since sesame oil can be of very fine quality (Stol 1985b: 120) and is adequate as "a vehicle for fragrances" (Middeke-Conlin 2014: 11), there is no reason to assume that the Ì.DUG.GA in the Sealand I texts used another oil as base.[169] It would agree with Ur III evidence (Brunke and Sallaberger 2010: 52).

Scented oil features only four times in the archive and the quantity is never given in standard measures of capacity, always in specific containers, namely: *pīlu*(?) "limestone jar(?)"[170] in CUSAS 9, 65: 7; DUG(?) "jar" in CUSAS 9, 94; and [dug]*namandu* "*namandu*-measuring vessel"[171]in CUSAS 9, 107. In CUSAS 9, 68, it is not clear from the syntax whether the scented oil, to be poured with the *mersu*-dish, is also measured in a [dug]BUR.ZI.GAL "large *pursītu*-bowl" with the *mersu*-dish or whether there is no quantity specified for it.

5.3.6 Transformation of other resources

We have limited information on the transformation of other resources by the palace. The large number of delivery records for animal carcasses strongly suggests that they were processed by the palace. The GÌR function for these deliveries being almost always fulfilled by the cooks (MUḪALDIM.MEŠ),[172] it appears likely that this professional group was responsible for the processing of the incoming

168 As noted above, we also find sesame oil and crushed cedar listed together in CUSAS 9, 101: 6–7; but because this document includes other items, the context is less clear.

169 In fact, Middeke-Conlin (2014: 12) entirely excludes linseed oil in perfume production in Mesopotamia.

170 CAD P, s.v. *pīlu* d.

171 CAD N, s.v. *namaddu* A.

172 See Section 5.2.2.2.

carcasses. In this archive the cooks are associated with the *Egirmaḫ*—the palace kitchen –, therefore, the animal carcasses were probably processed there.

We know that leather-workers (AŠGAB) were employed by the palace: in one record two of them received barley as wages (CUSAS 9, 378: 16–17), and *miksu*-ledgers show that they could be attributed such fields by the palace (CUSAS 9, 410: 11; 443: 16; 448: 16). We also find a leather-worker probably receiving an allotment of ghee (CUSAS 9, 72: 5). Given the large number of animal carcasses that were almost certainly processed by the palace, there is no surprise in its employing leather-workers to take care of the hides. One of the leather-workers attested in the palace records, Bēlī-iddinam, could be the same who appears also in an *ḫargalû*-list from Tell Khaiber, where he precedes a carpenter who is also attested in both corpora (TK1 3064.83: obv. 10).

There is no direct information on textile weaving or garment making in the extant documents. Wool was sometimes delivered to the palace by shepherds (alongside sheep; see Section 5.2.2.1), we also find a few mentions of garments, presumably in expenditure records, probably in the context of trade or diplomatic gifts (see Section 4.4.2). But we have no textual basis to relate directly these elements of information to one another. However, we know from *ḫargalû*-lists and a list of workers that clothiers (LÚ.TÚG) and stitchers (LÚ.TÚG.KAL.KAL.LA) were employed by the palace (CUSAS 9, 371: 5 & 11; 377: 19; 381: rev. 12′). Stitchers are attested at Tell Khaiber, also in *ḫargalû*-lists (TK1 1114.05: l.e. 2; 1114.40: rev. 6; 1124.04: obv. 6).

Reed-workers (AD.KID) were employed by the palace.[173] Text CUSAS 9, 452 probably records the receipt of raw material for them to manufacture reed objects. They apparently received *ḫargalû*-allotments (CUSAS 9, 376: rev. 29′) and may have been endowed with *miksu*-fields (CUSAS 9, 410: 23). Reed-workers also appear in a few Tell Khaiber texts, including in one *ḫargalû*-list (TK1 1114.04: obv. 7–8; 1114.40: obv. 19; 3064.57: obv. 28).

Several minas of copper are recorded as having been given to and received by a smith (CUSAS 9, 459),[174] certainly for transformation. That the palace employed smiths (SIMUG; URUDU.NAGAR) is also shown by their presence in one *ḫargalû*-list (CUSAS 9, 371: 42) and in the list of professionals (CUSAS 3, 381: 2ff.). Smiths are also attested in Tell Khaiber lists apparently mostly dealing with grain (TK1 1096.47: rev. 22; 1096.48+49: obv. 24′; 1096.53: obv. 2; 1114.04:

173 See Section 5.2.1.4 for a discussion on the procurement of reed by the palace.
174 The smith was apparently attached to an institution whose name is partly damaged and difficult to read (line 3). It seems to end with $É.NA_4$: "house of stone." Dalley suggests that this was the smith's workshop.

obv. 10; 3064.33: rev. 19); but copper is not attested in that corpus yet, as far as I know.

Carpenters (NAGAR) are also attested, however never in the context of their actual work; they either pay taxes or receive emoluments, including *ḫargalû*-grain (CUSAS 9, 144; 371: 34; 378: 7; 410: 20; 413: 38; 423: 10; 426: 10). Several also figure in the list of workers CUSAS 9, 381: 17′ff. At least one of them, Aḫi-il-lika, appears in the Tell Khaiber texts (e.g. TK1 1096.48: 21′ and TK1 1096.47: rev. 24). Other carpenters who may be represented in both corpora are discussed in Section 3.1.3.

Silversmithing could be attested indirectly in one expenditure record (CUSAS 9, 453): a small quantity of silver was handed by the palace to a woman as well as a jeweler (KÙ.DÍM). But we do not know whether it was for transformation, and if it was, whether this took place completely outside the palace. At any rate, some jewelers seem to have had a close economic relationship with the palace, they appear in the list of workers CUSAS 9, 381: rev. 5′–10′, as well as in documents showing that some received supplies and a *miksu*-field (CUSAS 9, 105; 384: 10; 457).

5.4 Expenditures

The goods acquired, stored, and sometimes transformed by the palace were used and expended for external and internal purposes. The palace sponsored several cults and temples, and the records pertaining specifically to these cultic expenditures are discussed in detail in Chapter 6. The palace gave emoluments, probably both to external workers and palace-dependents, in providing barley allotments as salary (ŠE.BA, ŠE.ŠUKU) or wages for hired work (*idu*).[175] It also gave out work materials, travel provisions, gifts, and other supplies to various individuals, including messengers, some of whom were apparently on diplomatic missions.

The main types of expenditures that we can identify in the archive are: the *mēreštu*-requested supplies(?), the *isiḫtu*-allotment(?), the *aširtu*-pious gift(?), the NÍG.BA of the king, ritual offerings, and barley allotments (ŠE.BA, ŠE.ŠUKU, and distribution of *ḫargalû*-grain). In several cases, the document does not state what type of expenditure is recorded, only what goods were handed out. The at-

175 I follow here Steinkeller's proposition (2015: 26–30) to translate še.ba as barley allotment (or allocation) instead of the widely used term "ration" since the latter conveys the notion of purely alimentary sustenance, while it was rather a regular salary. Also, some individuals who were in the employment of the palace were probably assigned a *miksu*-field of whose produce they could keep two thirds (see Boivin 2016b).

testations are grouped in Table 11 according to the type of expenditure, not the book-keeping key word pertaining to the transaction (ŠU.TI.A, etc.). The table does not include the records of grain given for milling or brewing, already discussed in Sections 5.3.2 and 5.3.4.

Also, because the present section deals only with records of expenditures, the table does not include the numerous animals delivered to the palace and identified as being intended for extispicy or offerings: this diminishes drastically the apparent importance of the divinatory and ritual portions in outgoing goods.

Table 11: Types of expenditures

Type of expenditure	Texts CUSAS 9,...	Number of occurrences
mēreštu-requested supplies(?)	74; 87; 90; 99; 105; 110; 113; 116; 118; 128; 133; 138; 437	13
isiḫtu-allotment	65; 73; 75; 99; 101; 109; 110	7
aširtu-pious gift(?)	88; 95; 96	3
NÍG.BA of the king	102; 106; 117; 119; 121; 123; 129; 134; 136; 138; 139; 457	12
ŠE.BA-allotment	386–88; 431	4
ŠE.ŠUKU-allotment	127; 379–80; 383	4
ḫargalû (allotment?)	368A; 369; 371; 373?; 374–77	7 or 8
Barley given as wages	149; 378	2
Allotments to workers (?)	389–94; 408; 412; 423	9
ṣidītu-travel rations	433	1
Other expenditures of foodstuffs and others to individuals	89; 93; 97?; 98; 103–104; 108; 112; 114–15; 122; 125; 130; 135; 137–38; 140; 144–145; 147?; 455–56; 459–60	22 to 24
ZI.GA expenditures	77; 269; 414; 417	4
Other sacrificial and ritual expenditures	59–71; 76; 79; 82–84; 86; 100; 124; 132	22
Other divinatory expenditures	111	1
Undetermined	72; 407; 438–40; 451	6

When recipients of palace expenditures are individuals, their profession is sometimes recorded. Several of these professions are also known from the fragmentary list of professionals CUSAS 9, 381. Comparison of these documents reveals some principles of remuneration put in place by the palace administration for its workforce. The payment of the *miksu*-tax must be included in this analysis since it was, in all likelihood, related to the provision of a field as a type of remuneration by the palace.

The relationship between the profession and the types of supplies and emoluments given by the palace is presented in Tables 12a and b;[176] the tables include only cases in which the profession was explicitly stated in the records. Most recipients of palace expenditures are identified only by name; in order to avoid any mistakes due to homonymy, no speculations based solely on prosopography were attempted. (Cases in which the identification of the profession or the type of remuneration was based on a fragmentary passage are indicated in gray.)

The evidence from Tell Khaiber is not included in these tables; the processes behind the administrative records and the role of the palace in them were not deemed clear enough at present.

Table 12a: Palace remuneration, by profession (part a)

Profession	List of professionals	*ḫargalû* allotment	barley as wages	*miksu* field	*mēreštu* supplies	NÍG.BA gift? of the king	other foodstuffs	other supplies
NAGAR	●	●	●	●				
KÙ.DIM	●			●	●	●		●
URUDU NAGAR, SIMUG	●	●						●
AD.KID		●		●				●
AŠGAB	●		●	●			●	
SIPA		●		●				

176 In some cases, it is in fact possible to trace the same individuals in the list of professionals and as recipients of various allocations. For instance: the carpenter Iddin-ilu who receives a *ḫargalû*-allotment in year K (CUSAS 9, 371: 34) is probably the same who was already registered as a carpenter in year I in the list CUSAS 9, 381: rev. 21′. But with an incomplete archive and fragmentary texts, establishing correlations at the individual level would be too stringent a method. Proceeding at the profession level allows for general principles to emerge. Admittedly, these results are obtained at the detriment of more specific rules: for instance, if some workers of a certain profession were entirely attached to the palace, while others of the same profession worked for it only in an *ad hoc* fashion, the present analysis does not discriminate between their (probably) differing types of remuneration.

Table 12a: Palace remuneration, by profession (part a) *(continued)*

Profession	List of professionals	*ḫargalû* allotment	barley as wages	*miksu* field	*mērēštu* supplies	NÍG.BA gift? of the king	other food-stuffs	other sup-plies
LÚ.TÚG (KAL.KAL.LA)	●	●					●	
A.ZU	●			●			●	
ša rēši		●		●				
NU.^{giš}KIRI$_6$	●	●		●				
Ì.DU$_8$, LÚ.KÁ.GAL		●		●	●			
MUḪALDIM				●			●	
MÁŠ.ŠU.GÍD.GÍD				●				●
ŠU.I				●				●
NAR							●	
SANGA				●				

Table 12b: Palace remuneration, by profession (part b)

Profession	ŠE.BA	ŠE.ŠUKU-*at/tum*
ENGAR, *ikkaru*	●	
BUR.GUL		●
GEŠTIN?.NA^{meš}		●
ÉRIN^{meš}		●

According to the available expenditure records, the types of remuneration which found the widest use in the Sealand I palace administration were the allotment of *miksu*-fields and the distribution of *ḫargalû*-grain, often in conjunction. Many of the professional groups receiving these emoluments were included in the list of professionals CUSAS 9, 381. This list may have been used by the palace administration as a register of the current palace personnel. There was probably a close economic relation between the administrative center of Tell Khaiber and the palace, because a few workers found in that list of professionals also show up in the Tell Khaiber records, in particular leather-workers and carpenters (see above and Section 3.1.3). In addition, we find that one individual is identified as an ÉRIN.TAḪ É.GAL "auxiliary worker of the palace" in what is possibly an allocation list at Tell Khaiber (TK1 3064.49: rev. 12); this probably corresponds to the LÚ *tillati* of the palace *ḫargalû*-list CUSAS 9, 371. It seems thus not unlikely that at least some of the grain allotments at Tell Khaiber were distributed on behalf of the palace for its workforce.

5.4.1 Grain allotments and other food allocations

A few texts document the handing out of cereals by the palace as allotments to a large number of individuals. We know from seven or eight texts from the palace (and perhaps a few from Tell Khaiber[177]) that ŠE *ḫargalû* "*ḫargalû*-grain" was handed out; no other term specifies what type of allocation this represented. The lists recording the distribution of *ḫargalû*-grain are fairly long, one of them containing well over sixty names. The occupation of the recipient is sometimes mentioned and Table 12a shows that members of many different professions were entitled to this remuneration. The texts are often undated but, based on the few that are, we find that *ḫargalû* distributions took place at different periods of the year (at least in the months ii, iii, and vii).[178] The period for which the grain was distributed is never specified and the quantities vary greatly. In two records, they are fixed at 1 *sūtu* per recipient (CUSAS 9, 368A; 371), in the other cases they vary from 1 *qû* to 9 *qû* or 1 *sūtu*, depending on the recipient.[179] The great variation between the quantities allotted is puzzling; apparently it did not follow the type of profession.[180] A very small quantity of one or very few *qû* could be for one day, but several *qû* must be for a longer period, unless the allocation covered the needs of family dependents of the recipient.

A few expenditure texts record the handing out of other, more familiar types of allocation, namely the ŠE.BA[181] and the ŠE.ŠUKU-*at/tum*.[182] The evidence is

177 TK1 1124.04; perhaps TK1 1124.01; *ḫargalû*-flour is recorded in TK1 1114.40 and 1114.48. The exact transaction recorded in these documents in not clear.

178 These dates correspond respectively to the texts CUSAS 9, 369; 368A; 371.

179 These numbers show that the regular *sūtu* containing 10 *qû* was used for *ḫargalû*-distributions.

180 We find for instance shepherds receiving 2 *qû*, 5 *qû* and 6 *qû* in the same document (CUSAS 9, 377: 3, 4, and 14).

181 In texts CUSAS 9, 386; 387; 388; 431. Text CUSAS 9, 389 is very similar and could also be a ŠE.BA record but it has no header specifying what was handed out.

fairly thin, with a mere four texts for each of them, but it appears that these grain allotments were distributed to people who did not receive *ḫargalû*-grain or a *miksu*-field. The ŠE.BA was handed out to agricultural workers in the months vi and vii,[183] also to groups of workers (*ešertu*) at an undetermined time of the year.[184] In such lists, the number of recipients varies from two to ten. Twice, the records specify that the quantities handed out were for the month.[185] On a given record, each recipient receives the same quantity but from record to record, there are great variations from 2 *sūtu* to over one *kurru*. Which type of *kurru* was used is unclear,[186] which makes a study of the quantities allotted impossible. The ŠE.ŠUKU was allotted to a few people,[187] including one seal cutter (BUR.GUL),[188] workers or troops (ÉRIN^{meš}),[189]and perhaps innkeepers(?)[190] The texts are fully dated and cover the months iv, v, and vi. The allocation could be given for a determined period of time (between 25 days and 3 months). The quantities varied greatly and these variations cannot be explained only with the differing periods of time for which the allocation was given.[191] Dalley (2009: text 380 notes) considers that ŠE.ŠUKU was used for specific tasks; this seems to agree with the fact that the seal cutter received it for a very specific period of 25 days in CUSAS 9, 127.

---

182 In texts CUSAS 9, 127; 379; 380; 383. The term ŠUKU may appear as well as an entry in CUSAS 9, 451: 8. We also find (ŠE.) ŠUKU-*tum/ti* at the bottom of the *šibšu*-ledgers CUSAS 9, 426; 432; 434. It could mean that this grain was intended for such allotments.

183 CUSAS 9, 386 & 431.

184 CUSAS 9, 387 & 388.

185 CUSAS 9, 387 & 431.

186 If the same standards were used for the ŠE.BA and the ŠE.ŠUKU, the *sūtu* contained at least 8 *qû* since such a quantity is recorded in CUSAS 9, 383. None of the quantities recorded give us a definite indication of the number of *pānu* per *kurru*. The fact that as much as 1,1,4,0 was recorded in CUSAS 9, 387 per individual for one month, seems to suggest that a small *kurru* was used (Powell 1987–90: 498) although even with a *kurru* as small as 120 *qû*, the allotment appears surprisingly large in comparison to the usual quantities for men, which are between 60 and 90, rarely going above 100 *qû* in the second millennium, and not higher in other periods (Stol 2006–08: 266 ff.).

187 Only one individual in texts CUSAS 9, 127 & 379 and six in CUSAS 9, 380 & 383.

188 CUSAS 9, 127

189 CUSAS 9, 380 & 383; in the former text, they are organized as a "group of ten" (*ešertu*), although only six individuals are listed.

190 CUSAS 9, 383: 1. The reading of the sign GEŠTIN is considered certain by Dalley (2009). Collation from the photograph is extremely difficult.

191 The quantity of ŠE.ŠUKU and of ŠE.BA allotted to workers organized in an *ešertu* could be the same, namely 2 *sūtu* as shown by CUSAS 9, 380 & 388.

The rest of the evidence is unspecific and no clear principles governing the frequency and the volume of the distribution can be adduced from it.[192]

5.4.2 The *mēreštu* : requested supplies(?)

The term *mēreštu* can mean "wish, request," also "supplies (for consignment)" (CAD M, s.v. *mēreštu*). The notion of request appears to correspond best to the Sealand I evidence, more specifically the request for foodstuffs addressed to the palace by beneficiaries.[193] In these documents, the term applies indeed to various foodstuffs, most often barley. These supplies could be handed out to deities but most recipients were individuals whose profession is specified in the records (jeweler,[194] singer,[195] cook,[196] gate-keeper,[197] scribe[198]). This strongly suggests that it is the profession exercised by these individuals which put them in a position to request and receive these goods from the palace. Table 12a shows that these professionals also received fields for which they had to pay the *miksu*,[199] some of them received also *ḫargalû*-grain[200]and other allotments;[201] whether the term applied to extra-ordinary allocations is unclear.

Exceptionally the goods were recorded as received by the beneficiary (CUSAS 9, 116; 128), otherwise there is no transaction keyword. A GÌR official is sometimes named.[202] The *mēreštu*-request was compatible with the *isiḫtu*-allotment:

---

192 Waetzoldt (1987: 119) posited that ŠE.BA applied to "allotments issued to all personnel who were permanently attached to or employed by the state or by temple establishments," regardless of their status. For the early Old Babylonian period, in northern Babylonia, ŠE.ŠUKU has been considered "more collective" than ŠE.BA (Goddeeris 2002: 206).

193 The term may indeed have had the specific meaning of a request put to the palace, as opposed to an acquisition request by the palace (the *erištu* attested in CUSAS 9, 91).

194 CUSAS 9, 105; in one case the *mēreštu*-supplies were probably given to the sons of a jeweler (CUSAS 9, 138: 8–9).

195 CUSAS 9, 87. This expenditure is very similar to the *aširtu*, discussed in 5.4.4.

196 CUSAS 9, 118; 437: 6.

197 CUSAS 9, 116.

198 CUSAS 9, 133.

199 CUSAS 9, 384: 10; 413: 58 and 62; 443: 9 and 31; 448: 21.

200 Gate-keepers: CUSAS 9, 371: 30; 374: rev. 22′; 377: 6; cooks: CUSAS 9, 374: rev. 3′.

201 Cooks: CUSAS 9, 393: 16; perhaps also 394: 2.

202 Interestingly, this official is present always and only in texts post-dating the middle of year L (CUSAS 9, 74; 118; 128; 133; 138). However, with only thirteen *mēreštu*- texts, the sample is too small to establish that a new procedure had been put in place. Dalley saw a GÌR in the record CUSAS 9, 87: 3, but this title at the end of a line would be very unusual. The sign is probably to be read *lum: ù i-bi-*DINGIR*-lum*.

they co-occur in two records (CUSAS 9, 99; 110).[203] It was also probably compatible with the *aširtu:* CUSAS 9, 87 records a *mēreštu*-expenditure for singers who sang at the palace gate and this record is very similar to the *aširtu*-expenditure records, even the quantity given to the musicians is the same (see Section 5.4.4); they may have been more of less interchangeable in that context.

5.4.3 The *isiḫtu*-allotment(?)

The term *isiḫtu*, derived from *esēḫum* "to allot, assign," applies to tasks, personnel, fields, also to wages (CAD I/J, s.v. *isiḫtu* 1). As observed by Stol (2001: 462), it usually means field allotment, task assignment, or the like. He concurs with Durand's comment based on evidence from Mari, that an agreement between the palace and a worker concerning a task is implied and he considers this explanation still valid when the term is applied to fields and barley, since "the beneficiaries have agreed to work the fields for the state" (*ibid.*). This notion of contract or agreement is not apparent in the Sealand I documents. In them, the *isiḫtu* appears to simply mean an allotment of supplies, always foodstuffs. The reasons underlying the handing out of an *isiḫtu* are varied: a journey of the king,[204] *mēreštu*-requested supplies(?) for individuals or deities,[205] and other types of offerings to deities.[206] The term *isiḫtu* is always in the bound form in this archive: *isiḫtu* of the night meal, of the sacrifice, of (a given day), of (a given) town. I would suggest that the meaning here is "allotment (of foodstuffs)."

5.4.4 The *aširtu* : pious gift(?)

This type of expenditure occurs only three times in the archive,[207] always with singers as the beneficiaries and apparently in direct relation to a specific performance.[208] The *aširtu*-expenditure consisted of barley, once with the addition of dates (CUSAS 9, 88). The quantity of barley is always one *kurru* per day of per-

---

203 See Section 5.4.3.
204 CUSAS 9, 101.
205 CUSAS 9, 99; 110.
206 CUSAS 9, 65; 73; 75; 109.
207 CUSAS 9, 88; 95; 96. (CUSAS 9, 87 records a *mēreštu* of the same quantity of barley to singers who performed at the gate of the palace. It shows that the *aširtu* and the *mēreštu* were compatible).
208 "At the palace gate" : *i-na* KÁ É.GAL in CUSAS 9, 88: 3 and 95: 3.

formance.[209] A GÌR was involved in all cases.[210] It is difficult to determine whether the barley given was intended as compensation for the pious performance or was partly used by the singers as offering during their performance. We do not know the number of singers involved, which makes it impossible to estimate individual quantities. Singers apparently received food allocations from the palace (CUSAS 9, 114; 115), although they do not appear in any text explicitly recording grain allotments.

5.4.5 The NÍG.BA of the king

The NÍG.BA[211] of the king, translated by Dalley as "gift of the king," appears several times in this archive. Very often, the NÍG.BA records are cast as receipts,[212] and the goods handed out by the palace are varied: barley and sesame are the most common ones but we find also other foodstuffs, wool, and perhaps bronze tables. The beneficiaries are almost always individuals, including a jeweler, also sons of a jeweler.[213] One record suggests that the NÍG.BA and the *mēreštu* may have been mutually exclusive: in CUSAS 9, 138, flour and beer are given to sons of a jeweler as a NÍG.BA of the king (lines 1–5) while barley is given to the same individuals as *mēreštu* (lines 6–10). Sesame was handed out as NÍG.BA to an individual who was probably an oil-presser; it could imply that the meaning of NÍG.BA, at least in this case, is rather "compensation" (see Section 5.3.5.1). With only one exception,[214] a GÌR was always involved in such an expenditure. It seems that the term could also be used in a ritual context, since we find the king giving offerings recorded as NÍG.BA for a ritual (CUSAS 9, 106: 1–5).

---

209 In CUSAS 9, 96 which records an expenditure for three successive days of performance, three *kurrū* are handed out. The barley is always measured by the BÁN 6 2/3, which shows that a *sūtu* divergent from the standard 10 *qû* was occasionally used. Powell (1987–90: 500) noted that more variations appeared after ~1600.
210 The records are all cast from the point of view of the administration with the key word *nadin* although one adds the reception by the beneficiary with the key word *maḫir* (CUSAS 9, 96).
211 Steinkeller (2013a: 384; 415–19) demonstrated that in the Ur III period, the níg.ba was an expenditure of the central state institutions that was directly authorized by the government. It could be credited to a province toward its bala obligation. He translates it as "king's allotment."
212 There are seven instances: five times with the key word *maḫir* (CUSAS 9, 119; 129; 134; 136; 139) and two with the key word ŠU.TI.A (CUSAS 9, 106; 123).
213 CUSAS 9, 457; 138: 1–5.
214 CUSAS 9, 123.

5.5 The palatial economy

The palatial archive presents the palace in a number of roles.[215] Mentions of the king himself[216] and of members of his family[217] associate it with the king's household, the presence of foreign envoys[218] makes it a locus of diplomatic relations. But what the texts illuminate best is that the palace was an active economic body that acquired, stored, and transformed goods on a scale much beyond its internal requirements; it certainly functioned as an important central provider for several cults taking place in at least a few temples.

The extant documents allow us to reconstruct certain elements of this economic body. A large sub-group of the tablets were issued by what we could call a "Beer bureau" or "Bureau of malt and beer," and another by a "Bureau of livestock and carcasses." That these two sub-groups of texts were produced by separate bureaus is not only visible in the resources that were recorded, their book-keeping practices differed. Incoming livestock and animal carcasses were recorded in standardized transaction notes (delivery records; see Boivin 2016c: 8 for the formulary of these texts), even when compiling several deliveries (e.g. CUSAS 9, 25). In contrast, incoming malt was recorded in short two-column[219] tables; the header is underlined and the keywords identifying the nature of the transaction (e.g. MU.DU, ŠU.TI.A) are part of that header. Incoming beer is usually recorded in transaction notes of the type also used for livestock and animal carcasses but, when sealed—and they are less often than for deliveries of animals—the seals used are not the same and the sealing habits differ. Delivery records for animals were sealed with the seals 1, 2, 3, and 4 (see Dalley 2009: 32), those for beer jars—when sealed—with the seals 5, 6, and 7 (Dalley 2009: 142). Also, the seal impression on delivery records of livestock and animal carcasses is usually on the obverse and the reverse of the tablet with the seal inscription running parallel to the text, and the emphasis seems to have been on imprinting the entire inscription, less so the iconographic portion; in contrast, beer records, when sealed, usually bear the seal impression on the top edge, and often only the iconographic part of it (see also Section 5.3.4).

215 For a discussion of the various roles of the Sealand I palace, see Boivin forthcoming.

216 For instance, the journey of the king in CUSAS 9, 101; or goods destined "for the hand of the king" in CUSAS 9, 50.

217 The queen is mentioned a few times, e.g. in CUSAS 9, 312; the daughter of the king figures once in CUSAS 9, 423: 8.

218 At least in CUSAS 9, 40: 3–4 and BC 435 cited in Dalley 2009: 47. See also the discussion in Sections 4.4.1 and 4.4.2.

219 Occasionally more, e.g. CUSAS 9, 269.

The *Egirmaḫ*—the kitchen—seems to have functioned as a palace-internal service responsible for processing carcasses and transforming foodstuffs (animal and non-animal). The *Egipar* may have served as a palatial brewery.[220] There may have been a "Bureau of grain and other agricultural products"—perhaps attached to the palace granary—, which administered the procurement, storage, and expenditure of agricultural produce. A *nupāru*-workshop probably milled flour for the palace, using was appears to be a captive labor force, and it was attached to it, but the records do not show explicitly whether it functioned completely inside its economy.

Other segments of the palatial economy are not well represented in the records and it is not always clear whether certain activities took place inside it or only within the palace's administrative purview.

Figure 5 summarizes the information adduced from the archive and schematizes the flow of goods entering and leaving the palace and between the services belonging to the palatial economic system.

The economic purview of the extant archive is too limited to venture on considerations on the role of the palace in the state economy.[221] The texts available to us show that the palace was very involved in the local economy, owning flocks, some fields, receiving agricultural produce, and employing a large and diverse staff. There are no signs of Old Babylonian *Palastgeschäfte* (Boivin forthcoming), on the contrary, as far as the extant documents show us, the palace used and transformed much of the primary resources it received itself.

This centralized management of local resources, to a large extent non-luxury resources,[222] by the palace clearly occurred partly, perhaps even largely, on behalf of temples; the palace seemed in fact to go beyond the mere sponsoring, it acted in their stead as an economic unit of production and transformation for their needs. In addition to providing for the cult, certainly on varied occasions and in many shrines and temples (see Chapter 6), the palace apparently transformed carcasses of animals belonging to the Šamaš temple (see Section 5.2.2.2), and provided for priests, for instance in giving them *miksu*-fields.[223]

This strongly suggests that the temples as economic institutions were largely absent or dysfunctional in that location when the Sealand I rulers established

220 See Section 5.3.4.2 on whether it functioned entirely inside the palace economy.
221 There is not enough evidence to warrant a parallel with the centralization effected by the palace at Larsa during Rīm-Sîn I's reign, as observed by Van de Mieroop (1993: 62–64).
222 In his review of palace archives, Sallaberger (2013: 225; 244) concluded that the management of luxury goods was the main characteristic of Babylonian palace economy. See also Boivin forthcoming.
223 See Table 12a and Boivin forthcoming.

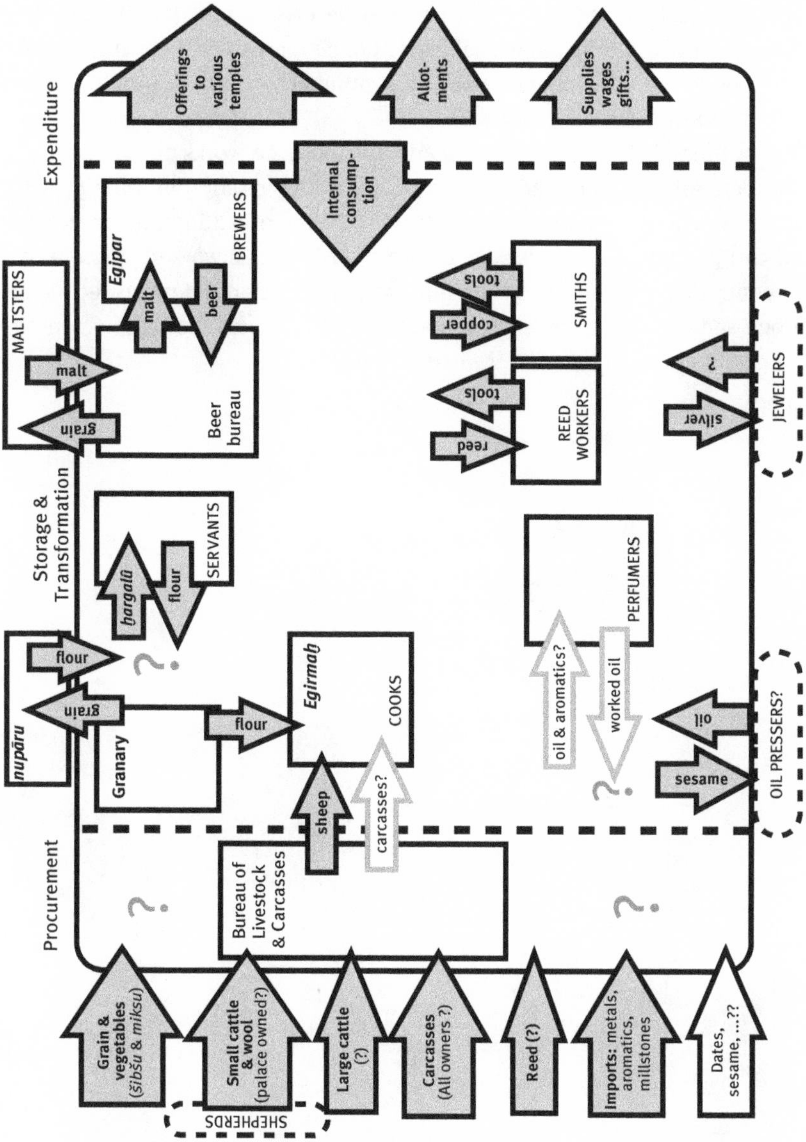

Figure 5: The Sealand I palace as an economic body

their palace administration. The town may have been a new foundation, or it may have been affected by the partial exodus of clergies having fled northwards, a phenomenon which probably affected a number of large southern centers when Babylon lost control over them.

Without functioning organizations and economic networks of their own, the temples were integrated by the Sealand I royal administration into the palace's economic system. It was probably an efficient means of getting the official cult up and running quickly. In this way, the output of various workers and of other palace-controlled institutions, or institutions partly tied to the palace economy, could be used not only to meet the palace's needs but also the requirements of the temples it chose to integrate in its economy.

6 The Sealand I panthea and religious history

6.1 Scribal and religious milieux in the Sealand kingdom

6.1.1 Tradition, innovation, and palatial agency

The rebellion against Babylon and the emergence of the Sealand kingdom during Samsu-iluna's reign changed the geo-political landscape of Babylonia, ushering a redesign of trading and diplomatic networks, but it also disrupted the religious and intellectual spheres. Scribes, intellectual and religious elites attached to centers which came under Sealand I control found themselves cut off to some degree from northern Babylonian influence. Many also probably found their immediate working environment greatly disturbed since at least some clergy members had fled north, into cities still under Babylon's control (Pientka 1998: 179–96), and they may have been followed by other intellectual elites whose last generation had been drawn close to the royal entourage. At any rate, those who remained —and some must have—certainly faced a dramatically changed situation.

They were heirs to ancient traditions, upon which the first dynasty of Babylon, the very power ousted by the southern rebels, had looked with respect. The memory of these traditions as being something independent from any recent sponsorship by the Babylonian crown was certainly still very much alive in southern scribal circles since Babylon's dominion in the area had been but a brief one. In such a position, the founders of the new dynasty and the local elites found themselves in theory in no immediate need to innovate in areas such as cult and literature: everything was there, and not only there, but ancient and legitimate. At the same time, the changed political and institutional environment as well as the reduced personnel, due to the partial exodus, probably led to a certain freedom in scribal milieux, for a time possibly to a real necessity to innovate, or even improvise, before large scriptoria could be (re-)established. The profoundly upset material and social circumstances of scribal and religious life offered conditions propitious for renewal. At the time there were probably close exchanges between Sealand and Susean scribal milieux. Indeed, based on small corpora of divinatory texts from Susa and the Sealand kingdom, George (2013: 139 ff.) identified a high level of similarity in scribal practices. He could even establish that a specific Susean tablet (MDP 57, 4) was based on works by the Sealand I scribe of CUSAS 18, 24; 27; and 29; or on "a tablet in linear de-

https://doi.org/10.1515/9781501507823-007

scent from one such" (*ibid.*: 140).[1] This cultural proximity is assuredly a reflection of friendly relations between the southern Babylonian polity and Elam.

The innovative atmosphere transpires in the creative use of logograms and in the new orthographies which characterize Sealand I texts (George 2013: 132 ff.).[2] Even in administrative records a rare logographic orthography is attested, UN.GAL for *šarratu*, a writing known from the lexical list LÚ = *ša*;[3] this entry (Tablet I, line 45 of the canonical list) was present in Old Babylonian forerunners (Civil et al. 1969: 28 ff.) which could have been used by the Sealand I scribes of the palace administration. This apparent use of learned texts as source material characterizes also the Sealand I hymn P431311 (Gabbay and Boivin forthcoming).

The emergence of a new political power, probably keen to leave its mark, in a religious and intellectual landscape where a number of institutions had been dismantled and partly abandoned, was also fertile ground for political influence in these realms. Gabbay (2014a: 153) is certainly right in warning about the fallacy of reducing the religious to a mere mirror of the political, but religious and cultic practices are partly exogenous and, in particular in a time of weakened religious institutions, political influence may certainly be surmised. The kings of a newly formed kingdom would certainly seek to influence the intellectual and religious landscape in carefully combining continuation and change in order to reflect the political reality of their rule. The Sealand I palace-sponsored religious practices and state pantheon are thus a certain type of reflections of the political and social entities in which they existed.

Perhaps we may ascribe to such state influence the enigmatic variations found in the Sealand I tablet of the Epic of Gilgameš, in particular the substitution of the usual Uruk by Ur, but also that of Gilgameš and Enkidu by Sîn and Ea, written respectively ^{d}30 and ^{d}40.[4] George (2007: 60) raised the possibility that

---

1 It seems that a number of orthographic innovations of the Sealand I scribes survived in Elam and were briefly reintroduced from there in Babylonia in the late second millennium, before being abandoned (George 2013: 141). A bilingual verbal paradigm, presumably written in a Sealand I scriptorium, also appears to reflect access to and knowledge of the Old Babylonian scribal tradition, with some unusual departures (Veldhuis 2017: 367–78).

2 George notes on p.132 that "The individual tablets exhibit a variety of orthographic styles, so that one gains the impression that they were written at a time of innovation and experimentation."

3 CUSAS 9, 312; 321; 333; 337; 345; 351. Dalley (2009: 163 note to text 312) comments on this.

4 Edited in George 2007. The attribution to a Sealand I origin is based on ductus and information to the effect that the tablet belonged to a group of Sealand I texts (George 2007: 62–63). Since the publication of other Sealand I texts, more aspects of the writing appear typical of the mid-dynastic Sealand I scribal practice: the ligature *a-na*; the position of the *Winkelhaken* in the sign RI and ḪU at the bottom of the last vertical. They are discussed in George 2013: 131 ff.

these writings were cryptic abbreviations; if they are, they certainly attest of a climate of creative experimentation (see also Section 2.1.1.1). If, however, they are to be taken at face value and the Sealand I rulers wanted to glorify Ur, these textual variants could be understood as being part of a programmatic undertaking that also puts Sîn in the role of the ancient ruler of his city. As for Ea, the southern deity seems to have been quite prominent for the Sealand I dynasty as evidenced in year names and cult. Therefore, one of the possible interpretations of the idiosyncrasies in the Sealand I Gilgameš manuscript, namely that the substitutions were indeed meaningful, would put them in close alignment with the royal ideals and the geographical reality of the kingdom.[5] Frazer (2016) suggested that the association of Gilgameš (and Uruk) with Ur indeed reflects the Sealand I political reality, an association also discernible in the so-called "Gilgameš Letter," which calls the main protagonist King of Ur, and which Frazer suggests to be the product of a Sealand I scriptorium (for an edition of the text, see Kraus 1980). The Old Babylonian literary corpus at Ur is in general more anchored locally than the Nippur corpus, including references to Nanna and early Old Babylonian Larsean rulers (Delnero 2016: 32ff.), and, indeed, some Sealand I scribes were very probably trained in that tradition and ultimately passed it down.

The Sealand I material shows that no religious revolution took place,[6] but clearly some adjustments to existing traditions were effected. A balag to Enlil, attributable to a Sealand I scriptorium on the basis of internal criteria (Gabbay 2014a: 148), shows an interesting combination of perpetuation of textual tradition (*ibid.*: 151) and innovation since it seems to introduce into it elements more typical of a Ninurta litany (*ibid.*: 152; 159 Table 1). This passage, which is unfortunately lacunary, pertains to a list of temples in a number of towns. Such changes may have reflected Sealand I state discourse, although not necessarily at the geographical level directly.[7] Indeed, Gabbay's (*ibid.*: 152) suggestion

5 Hallo (1975: 188), commenting on the adaptation of another composition, described such a process as a text being "creatively transformed to meet ideological requirements of a new age."

6 The Sealand I texts show the already well-attested (in the Old Babylonian period) conflation of the Akkadian and Sumerian panthea (Edzard 2004: 580–82). While the names of a number of deities, for instance the sun god, are systematically written with their Sumerian orthography, some are always written in Akkadian (e.g., ^{d}*na-zi*), and others alternate between both forms (e.g., ^{d}en-ki/^{d}*é-a*, the latter being used in personal names).

7 In other words, the towns listed in this passage need not necessarily have been under Sealand I political control for them to be included in the text. This would be all the more true if the list was copied from an existing source, which is not certain. All elements of the list of toponyms as Gabbay reconstructed it are also known from later versions of the text, but it is only partly the case for potential antecedents.

that the list of toponyms could reflect syncretism around the figure of Ninurta as warrior god is interesting; it could echo the prominent place which Ninurta enjoyed in the Sealand I palace-sponsored cult, at least during the reign of Ayadaragalama (see Section 6.4.2). Therefore, although it is impossible at present to decide whether the toponym sequence in that Sealand I text was the result of merging existing sources—at least two concerning two distinct deities (Enlil and Ninurta)—or whether it entailed original composition as a variant of only one ancient source, the result testifies to a combination of innovation and tradition in the Sealand I scribal milieu; and that innovation was apparently coherent with royal ideology and cult.

On the whole, the sources suggest that the Sealand I kings did leave their own imprint on the official cult and theology, probably to express the geo-political reality of their kingdom, and perhaps their ambitions for it, but this was made in careful respect of the received pan-Babylonian traditions. At least one king, Ayadaragalama, anchored the legitimacy of his kingship in the old *topos* of Enlil conferring on him the shepherding of the land. He also had a hymn to the main gods of Nippur composed (P431311, see Gabbay and Boivin forthcoming), reflecting the importance of the Nippur pantheon in the Sealand I state pantheon in that period.

The records show that the types of offerings to the gods and the marking of lunar phases were all very Babylonian. The major pan-Babylonian gods remained present and important in the Sealand kingdom, but one discerns also elements of deliberate design in the mosaic of cults sponsored by the palace: the new power at work. The state pantheon—I will explain in Section 6.1.2 what I call by that term—appears to be an amalgamation of imports from local panthea. We observe for instance that some importance was given to Nazi but that she was extracted from her local environment and integrated into the state pantheon alone, without her circle, which seems to indicate a positive but limited regional influence of the Lagaš area. Singular importance is also given to Ea, which, besides of course reflecting a possible importance of Eridu, probably reaches back to a Larsean tradition from before the Babylonian conquest. Other signs reminiscent of the Larsean kingdom include the presence of Enlil and Ea in year names (perhaps harking back to name formulae of Rīm-Sîn I), as well as the presence of the obscure Nin-é.NIM.ma, a deity apparently favored by the Kudur-Mabuk dynasty, in a number of gods lists.

As for the prominence of the Nippurite pantheon, visible mainly through the high rank occupied by Ninurta—who is usually presented in lists in a Nippurite context—, it suggests acknowledgement of the importance of this cultic center, perhaps nominal control over it (following the fall of Babylon).

6.1.2 Extracting the panthea from the documents

Religious life in the Sealand kingdom in the middle years of its existence presents itself to us mainly through a set of documents issued in the context of palatial economic activity, already discussed in the previous chapter. That most available sources reflect institutional cultic practice (as opposed to personal devotion) is very typical of Mesopotamia; what is less so is that the archive comes from a palace, not a temple. This certainly introduces a very strong bias in the documentation but it is also the occasion to witness the state at work in sponsoring the cult. It is prudently assumed that this palace archive comes from the main capital (see Section 1.3.2.1), and thus that the cult reflected in it is largely an official state cult. But even if we are dealing with a provincial palace, many conclusions reached in the present analysis remain valid because some of the information on the palace-sponsored cult can be corroborated by year names and religious texts, sources certainly reflecting more than a local cult. Therefore, it is surmised here that the cults which this palace integrated in its economy (see Section 5.5) reflect at least in part the Sealand I state pantheon.

Most texts are strongly anchored in daily material preoccupations and inform us essentially about the economic aspects of the cult, more precisely the sacrificial economy in which the palace was involved. The following relevant documents are available to us: offering lists, records of deliveries (to the palace) and of expenditures (by the palace) for animals and other foodstuffs destined for offerings—the latter could take place either at the palace or in temples. There may also be one short god list without cultic function (CUSAS 9, 81). In addition to these tablets issued from the palace administration, the following religious texts are known to come from Sealand I scriptoria: a balag to Enlil (Gabbay 2014a) and a hymn of Ayadaragalama (Gabbay and Boivin forthcoming). A temple list recently published (CUSAS 30, 451) could be a Sealand I text (van Soldt 2015: 529); it lists temples of Ištar in all of Babylonia.

Despite the fluidity and sometimes apparent contradictions which generally characterize the Babylonian divine realm, at any given time and place principles of organization are recognizable. The relative importance ascribed to deities can be described as a (partly hierarchical) pantheon, or in fact as superimposed panthea, since a number of concurrent traditions and principles were at work. Various typologies of panthea have been suggested by assyriologists (Sallaberger 2004: 294). Komoróczy (1976) puts much emphasis on fundamental differences between the distinct panthea that are reflected in different types of sources. He distinguishes between three main expressions of panthea: the local pantheon[8] in texts relating to cult, the theological pantheon of god lists (and secondarily the state pantheon in royal inscriptions), and the pantheon of mythological literature. A problem with this model is that it applies the same typology to sources on one hand and to the cultural constructs that are panthea on the other, another problem is that it compartmentalizes panthea in a rigid, more or less immutable manner. Sallaberger (2004) proceeds differently and stresses the complex interrelations between the various panthea, which he identifies as: the local pantheon, the state pantheon (which may in fact be split into state pantheon and *Reichspantheon*), and the mythological pantheon. His definition of the local pantheon concords with Komoróczy's, but Sallaberger considers that both god lists and literature, religious as well as mythological, express the mythological pantheon. As for the cult at the temple of the main god, he considers it to be modeled on the state pantheon. Rubio (2011) avoids the notions of local and state panthea and concentrates on the milieux from which panthea are issued. Basing himself on a quantitative analysis to determine the frequency of co-occurrences of god names in Early Dynastic texts and personal names, he concludes that there were three panthea: at one extremity of the spectrum, he sees the expression of popular religiosity in personal names (popular pantheon), at the other extremity he sees in god lists and literature the product of learned scribal circles (the scholarly pantheon);[9] in the middle he places the pantheon of the official cult as expressed in offering lists and cultic texts.[10] Despite their differences, all models agree on the co-existence of different panthea as conceptual constructs determined by social, political, and cultural factors.

If we consider the available Sealand I sources, we can extract the following data: theophoric elements in personal names, religious *topoi* in year name formulae, state-sponsored cultic activity favoring certain gods over others (offerings in administrative documents; dedication in year names), and, to a very limited extent, divinities and temples for which religious literature was composed. These concrete, observable phenomena are compound expressions of panthea and traditional patterns. In my analysis, I use the following hypotheses to reconcile the former with the latter: I consider (1) that the palace-sponsored cult is the compound expression of the (political-ideological) state pantheon and the local

8 According to Amiet (1976: 32) the iconography of the local pantheon suggests that it was not a complete pantheon but rather a divine family with a divine couple at its head that was venerated locally.

9 Lambert (1975: 194) defined this "Mesopotamian pantheon (as) a multitude of city cults, and thinkers who tried to reduce them to an ordered whole."

10 In addition, he considers that the official pantheon also has an influence on personal names (Rubio 2011: 107).

pantheon;[11] (2) that religious *topoi* in year names are the compound expression of the state pantheon and traditional patterns;[12] (3) that theophoric elements in PNs express the local pantheon[13] and traditional patterns; and (4) that hymnic literature reflects mainly the (political-ideological) state pantheon. The sources available to us certainly do not make it realistically possible to discriminate between more variants of panthea than two main ones, the local pantheon and the state pantheon;[14] in fact, it is not always possible to disentangle them clearly, a problem which is raised when assessing the position of each main deity in this chapter.

6.2 Religious *topoi* in year names

The state pantheon and the special relationship between kingship and the divine sphere in Mesopotamia are often expressed in royal epithets and other formulae well represented in royal inscriptions. For the Sealand I dynasty the only products of official royal communication that are available to us are a few year names.

Year names are, in comparison to long and elaborate building or other official inscriptions, much shorter and sometimes rather laconic, but they represent a form of official communication that was circulated among a fairly large audience throughout the kingdom. This made them an attractive vehicle for kings to establish cardinal facts of their rule, although their brevity, imposed by obvious

---

11 Indeed, a ruler establishing or taking over a palace and the administration of the cult certainly sought to conciliate between local practices and state or dynastic religious principles.

12 A dynasty has no need of tenets, such as are conveyed by the state pantheon, that it cannot communicate broadly. Royal inscriptions were certainly a good means of communication but they probably reached a limited audience. At any rate, we have no Sealand I building inscription. Year-names certainly penetrated larger segments of society but are, for obvious practical reasons, severely restricted in how much they can express. Therefore, the building of temples and the sponsoring of cultic activities, through conspicuous consumption, must have been another choice means for the ruler to display political-theological principles; again, because of the absence of building inscriptions we lack information on the pious building activities of the Sealand I kings.

13 However, in a context of population movements and partial abandonment of towns, a somewhat wider area may be expected in the personal names represented in the archive.

14 Other nuances which could have been conceptualized in mythological, ethnic, or other panthea (Sallaberger 2004), either entirely lack any evidential basis to define them for the Sealand kingdom or can only be glimpsed at through punctual attestation.

pragmatic considerations, compelled the royal administration to make yearly a very restrictive selection of what should be communicated.

Year names of four Sealand I kings have been discovered: Ilī-ma-ilu, Pešgal-darameš, Ayadaragalama, and Ea-gāmil; the year formula of Gulkišar used in the glass-making treatise BM 120960 is almost certainly a forgery.[15] The year names concerning pious deeds of the king and the divine favor that he enjoyed all date to Ayadaragalama.[16] Only two religious *topoi* are represented in these formulae: the expression of divine favor through the granting of ruling authority to the king and the expression of the king's devotion through the building of temples and the dedication of votive objects to the gods.

The relevant year names are grouped in Table 13.[17]

Enlil held a prominent place in these claims of divine patronage and royal piety. We find him in the long version of year name E alongside Ninurta as the co-beneficiary of a cultic place or device, in year name J he is the co-recipient with Ea of gilded wooden statues, and also perhaps most significantly, he is the god establishing the shepherding of Ayadaragalama over the totality in year name G.[18] Ea appears in two year names of Ayadaragalama: besides year name J just mentioned, he is the recipient of a ring of gold and lapis-lazuli in year name I. This choice of deities in year name formulae, which was undoubtedly influenced by the state pantheon and by tradition, deserves some attention. Enlil, Ea, and Ninurta, the gods represented in year names, all occupy prominent places in offering lists, although only for Ninurta do we have evidence that this high position coincided with, or translated into abundant offerings.

An investigation of the broader context is required to assess how tradition played a role in shaping the religious claims in Ayadaragalama's year names. The Larsean king Rīm-Sîn I began to include systematically Anu, Enlil, and Ea[19] in his year names from his twenty-second[20] until the introduction of the

15 The formula reads (line 43): mu.ús.sa gul-ki-šár lugal.e (Oppenheim 1970: 63). See also Section 4.7.

16 The year identifiers given in the first column refer to Dalley's (2009: 11 ff.) preliminary ordering of the year name formulae. See Appendix 2 for a complete inventory, and Section 1.3.2.2 for a discussion of the types and proposed sequence of year names.

17 Variants are listed in Dalley 2009: 11 f. See also Appendix 2.

18 In addition, Enlil may be the chief deity of the é.unú, whose reconstruction(?) is celebrated in year name H, since it is located in a town called Dūr-Enlilē. Also, the fragmentary year name P, attested only once, may refer to the Ekur (see Appendix 2).

19 This triad came to occupy the top of the pantheon as reflected in royal inscriptions and hymnic literature towards the end of the Ur III period (Espak 2015: 70).

20 Before that, between his seventeenth and his twenty-second year, we find reference to Enlil's patronage of military deeds, possibly a reflection of the control over Nippur (only year 19 does

Table 13: Year names with a religious *topos*

Year	Year name	Deity	*topos*
G	mu a.a-dàra-galam.ma lugal.e nam sipa ki.šár.ra.ta ^{d}en.líl.le mu.un.gar.ra.a.ba Year when Ayadaragalama (was?) king, after Enlil established (for him?) the shepherding of the totality.	Enlil	Divine favor
E	mu a.a-dàra-galam.ma lugal.e á.kal nigin lú.kúr.min.a.bi ì.zi.ga.eš.a ka?.⌜dù?⌝ gu.la ^{d}en.líl ^{d}nin.urta in.ne.[...] Year when king Ayadaragalama, when the massed might (of?) the two enemies rose (and) (...) the great beer-jar(?) of Enlil (and) Ninurta.	Enlil & Ni-nurta	Pious deed
H	mu a.a-dàra-galam.ma lugal.e é.unú libir.ra bàd-^{d}en.líl.le.ke$_{4}$ mu.un.dù? Year when king Ayadaragalama built(?) the ancient É.UNÚ in Dūr-Enlilē.	?	Pious deed
I	mu a.a-dàra-galam.ma lugal.e ḫar ^{na4}za.gìn.na kù.gi peš.peš sal.la gar.ra šu ^{d}en.ki lugal.a.ni gar.ra.a Year when king Ayadaragalama placed a circlet of lapis-lazuli and gold set with fine figs(?) (on) the hand of Ea, his king.	Ea	Pious deed
J	mu a.a-dàra-galam.ma lugal.e giš.alam didli kù.gi ḫuš.a gar.ra ^{d}en.líl ^{d}en.ki in.ne.en.ku$_{4}$.ra.a Year when king Ayadaragalama installed wooden statues overlaid with red gold for Enlil and Ea.	Enlil & Ea	Pious deed

era system in his thirty-first year,[21] thus placing it at the heart of his military and civil deeds. Rīm-Sîn's invoking of Anu, Enlil, and Ea probably stemmed from his expansionist politics: his ambitions and conquests encompassed all southern Babylonia; this had to be reflected in official communication, and the Larsean royal administration shaped the year names into powerful vehicles to that effect.[22] Most significantly, this divine triad appeared after Rīm-Sîn I's conquest

---

not cite a military event). Years 1 to 16, and year 19 make mention, when deities are referred to, to pious deeds (Fitzgerald 2002: Appendix 3).

21 For Rīm-Sîn's year names, see Sigrist 1990: 37ff. or Fitzgerald 2002: Appendix 3.

22 Already his distant predecessor Gungunum had claimed in his nineteenth year that his military actions took place "at the command of An, Enlil and Nanna," probably a reflection of the extent of his control over the important cities of Uruk, Nippur (briefly?), and Ur (Fitzgerald 2002: 42; Charpin 2004: 72, in particular n.229 for a summary of the evidence for the control over Nippur). But this claim of divine patronage and of a divine command in military action did not immediately become a *topos* in Larsean year names. Indeed, after this instance, Gungunum re-of Uruk, celebrated in his twenty-first year name; it figured also in building inscriptions, for instance "when the gods An, Enlil, (and) Enki, the great gods, entrusted Uruk, the ancient city, into my hands" (Frayne 1990: E4.2.14.12, lines 14–18).[23] The Larsean king proclaimed a divine patronage representative of his political realm, placing the supra-regional southern Babylonian pantheon in the foreground instead of the gods of Larsa.[24] The presence of Ea[25] in the triad is particularly significant because he later seems to vanish from year name formulae, to resurface only with the Sealand I kings.

The year names of the Urukean dynasty of Sîn-kāšid make no claim of divine patronage (Falkenstein 1963: 8 ff.; Sanati-Müller 2000a: 87 ff.).[26] Pious deeds for Urukean deities were recorded, in particular for An and Inanna, and the temple

turned to shorter, simpler formulae, in which deities were named only in the context of pious deeds. This changed only well into the reign of Rīm-Sîn I.

23 The same phrase is also found in another inscription (Frayne 1990: E4.2.14.13, lines 23–26). The 'Anu, Enlil, and Ea/Enki' triad is present in several inscriptions from the Larsean conquest of Uruk on (*ibid.*: 289 ff.). A cone inscription from Ur reflects the newly achieved supra-regional extent of Rīm-Sîn's kingdom: the king claims to have built a temple "by the word of the god An (…), by the supreme decree of the god Enlil, [follows Enlil's circle Ninlil, Ninurta, Nuska], by the wisdom that the god Enki gave to me [follow several other gods: Ninḫursag, Nanna, Utu, Iškur, Nergal, Inanna, Ninisina, Ninšenšena]" (Frayne 1990: E4.2.14.10, lines 20–25). This inscription makes clear that the king was invoking the main deities of the entire Babylonian pantheon. The several other inscriptions and year names in which he mentions only the triad Anu, Enlil, and Ea could be understood as a short version of this by naming only the most prominent deities.

24 These gods are not only representative of central, southern, and southernmost Babylonia, they are also the top of the pantheon as reflected in Babylonian tradition (sometimes with the addition of the mother-goddess), as a result of the "Systematisierung des sumerischen Pantheons," perhaps also symbolizing the elements heaven, earth, and *apsû* (Galter 1983: 144 ff.). It could also be interpreted as a genealogy of Enlil who had gained prominence by the Old Babylonian period, as reflected in god lists, and whose father is identified as Anu early in the Uruk tradition (VAB 1, 154, col.III 14–16; for the relationship between Anu, Enlil, and Ea in the Old Babylonian period, see also Edzard 2004: 578 ff.). The same structure is still visible in AN = ^{d}Anum (Lambert 1975: 195).

25 It must also be noted that Ea and Eridu appeared to be particularly important for the Larsean king who often used in his inscriptions the epithet "who perfectly executes the me's (and rites) of Eridu" (for instance Frayne 1990: E4.2.14.6, line 18; E4.2.14.7, line 4′; E4.2.14.8, line 14). He also rebuilt Ea's temple at Larsa and Ur (Galter 1983: 291).

26 In addition, Sanati-Müller (1990: texts no.120 and no.148) identified one year name of the type mu ús-sa + year no.31, the latter formula being as listed in Falkenstein 1963: 14. A few other fragmentary year names are unclear; they were so damaged that no reconstruction could be attempted (for instance in Sanati-Müller 2000a: texts no. 309, no.339, no.342).

of Nanna is mentioned; Ea is entirely absent from the year names[27] and Enlil only present in the context of the liberation of Nippurites by IRnene (Falkenstein 1963: 9 no.8; Charpin 2004: 112 and n.463).

Meanwhile, the Babylonian rulers used, until late into Hammurapi's reign, fairly short and simple year names, without mention of divine patronage, similar to the year names of the earlier Larsa kings. With the exception of one long formula in his fourteenth year, Hammurapi introduced long, elaborate year names claiming divine favor only from his thirtieth year on. In that year formula he called himself the "beloved of Marduk" and explained his military success by "the supreme power of the great gods" (Horsnell 1999: vol.II 139). In the following year formula he celebrated the conquest of Larsa, introducing the patronage of Anu and Enlil (*ibid.*:141):[28] in taking over Rīm-Sîn's kingdom, Hammurapi also claimed for himself the help of these great gods, yet leaving Ea aside. In fact, the kings of the first dynasty of Babylon never recorded pious deeds towards Ea nor did they claim his patronage in their year names.[29] Hammurapi, while clearly wishing to give importance to pan-Babylonian gods, also had a northern Babylonian focus, which was represented by the god of Babylon Marduk who becomes quite present in the year formulae of the last third of his reign.[30] It was observed that Hammurapi borrowed from Rīm-Sîn I his short-lived style of

27 But we know from a building inscription of Sîn-kāšid that he built a shrine(?) for him at Uruk (Frayne 1990: E4.4.1.10).

28 The same holds probably true for inscriptions. The few known inscriptions of Hammurapi dating from before his conquest of Larsa do not seem to refer to 'Anu and Enlil' (Frayne 1990: E4.3.6.1 – E4.3.6.3), while these two deities appear in the later inscriptions (*ibid.:* from E4.3.6.4 on; E4.3.6.4 probably commemorates the Babylonian victory over Larsa). In his early study of deities in year names from the first dynasty of Babylon, Ravn (1929: 85) considered Hammurapi to have remained within "the traditional Enlil-system" but his analysis ignored for the most part changes within the king's reign.

29 Mentions of Ea in royal inscriptions of the kings of the first dynasty of Babylon are rare. He appears for instance in a building inscription from the year 23 or 24 of Samsu-iluna within the enumeration An, Enlil, Marduk, Enki, and Inanna (Frayne 1990: E4.3.7.8, lines 78 ff.); at the time, southern Mesopotamia had already been lost to Babylonian control. Ea reappeared in inscriptions of Ammī-ditāna, as the god giving him wisdom (Frayne 1990: E4.3.9.2, lines 19′–21′ and, partly reconstructed: E4.3.9.1, col.II 6–8). See also Galter 1983: 188–89. Contrasting with the limited importance accorded to Ea in the royal inscriptions and year names is hymn TCL 16, 61 in which Ea endows Hammurapi with the dominion of the lands, this has been interpreted by van Dijk (1966–67: 63 ff.) as evidence that the king was crowned at Eridu. Ea stands also in prominent place in Hymn C of Hammurapi (Green 1975: 70 ff.; see also Galter 1983: 178).

30 Marduk appears in years 30, 32, 37, 38. In year 38 where Anu and Enlil are also named, they are given different roles: "at the command of Anu and Enlil" and "by the cleverness which Marduk gave him" (Horsnell 1999: vol.II 157).

long, elaborate year names (Fitzgerald 2002: 150),[31] but the Babylonian king clearly did not simply copy it.[32] He adapted the content to the reality of his own, larger kingdom. It is surely no coincidence that Hammurapi's successor, Samsu-iluna, reintroduced the pair Anu and Enlil in his eleventh year name to mark his (brief) reconquest of southern Babylonia and the destruction of the "(great) walls of Ur, (Larsa and) Uruk" (Horsnell 1999: vol.II 195). This *topos*, after being introduced by his father upon his defeating Rīm-Sîn I, had remained unused for fifteen years, and after this sole instance Samsu-iluna never again claimed patronage of the pair Anu and Enlil.[33] It is also probably significant that his thirteenth year name, coined after he had definitely lost the extreme south but was still desperately trying to maintain control over central Babylonia (from the area of Kisurra northwards), claimed the divine patronage of Enlil only[34] (Horsnell 1999: vol.II 198). Following his loss of central Babylonia between his twenty-eighth and thirtieth years Samsu-iluna dropped the patronage of Enlil in his year names altogether, as well as the style of long, complex formulae, reverting to the short ones of earlier times. The later kings of the dynasty invoked Anu and Enlil in year names only at the very beginning of their reigns:[35] the patronage of the pair Anu and Enlil had become an ancient, frozen formula, proper for justifying the status of the king and, by emulating an archaic style, inscribing it in a long-lived tradition. The claim of their protection had become by that time

31 The standard year names are discussed here, not the local year names used at Larsa in the style of "the xth year of the king" (Fitzgerald 2002: 149).

32 As mentioned above, Hammurapi introduced this style for his thirtieth and thirty-first year names, roughly three decades after Rīm-Sîn had replaced his long year names by the era-style dating following the conquest of Isin. The similarity between the year name style of Rīm-Sîn I and of Hammurapi, after Ha 30, has been noted before. See for instance Edzard 1957: 180 who considers that this phraseology derives from hymns, first introduced into royal inscriptions by early Larsean kings, then into year names by Rīm-Sîn I.

33 From Si 10 to Si 13, military action was recorded in year names invoking twice Marduk (Si 10 and 12), once Anu and Enlil (Si 11), once Enlil alone (Si 13).

34 He claimed the patronage of Enlil for military deeds in year names for the last time in Si 28, commemorating his campaign on the middle Euphrates (Horsnell 1999: vol.II 220–21), at a period when his control over central Babylonia was probably already menaced, just before it was definitively lost to him between Si 28 and Si 30 (Charpin 2004: 360).

35 For Abī-ešuḫ: Anu and Enlil figure only in his second and third year names (Horsnell 1999: Vol.II 244–45); for Ammī-ṣaduqa: they figure in his second year (*ibid.*: 327); for Samsu-ditāna: in his third year (*ibid.*: 361).

devoid of any actual territorial reality but carried with it the remembrance of a glorious past still near enough to be remembered in Babylonian royal circles.[36]

Of the other southern Babylonian kings who briefly ruled in the latter part of the Old Babylonian period, Rīm-Sîn II claimed to have been elevated to kingship by Ninmaḫ (year name b; Stol 1976: 54), while Rīm-Anum did not refer to divine favor at all (Seri 2013: 30).[37]

All extant Sealand I year formulae referring to an event are fairly short and simple although one of them has at least two clauses, as noted by Dalley (year name E; Dalley 2009: 11).[38] This may indicate that there were longer versions of some year names but the size of the sample is too modest to make any definitive statement. The limited evidence does not make it possible to determine whether Ayadaragalama reintroduced the *topos* of divine command and patronage in military deeds used by Larsean and Babylonian kings. However, a pious deed toward Enlil and Ninurta appears in the second clause of year name E, whose first clause celebrates a military victory; this may establish a relationship between the patronage of the two gods and the military success thus recorded.[39] The choice of Ninurta, who has a warrior aspect, certainly conveys this impression.

But Ayadaragalama's year names clearly echo the short-lived Larsean tradition from the early second millennium in one respect: the reintroduction of Ea. And not only do we find again Ea in two out of five such year names, but he appears once alongside Enlil. The two gods, part of the triad introduced by Rīm-Sîn I into year names represent here perhaps central and southern Babylonia; their association is certainly reminiscent of the Larsean tradition of naming the triad Anu, Enlil, and Ea in year formulae.

In one year name we have proof that the king also invoked divine patronage from Enlil for his kingship, that is for his "shepherding of the totality" (year name G; Dalley 2009: 11). The *topos* of Enlil conferring rulership was common among the late Old Babylonian kings; the king as a shepherd was a well established, very ancient, royal epithet, which is already attested for Early Dynastic

---

36 Admittedly, the evidence is limited and since Anu and Enlil are prominent deities of the pan-Babylonian pantheon, invoking them in year names may or may not be indicative of the control of a specific region.

37 In the periphery, Ešnunnean and Mari rulers occasionally recorded pious deeds to various deities in their year names but Ea is never mentioned (Wu 1994; cdli.ucla.edu/tools/yearnames/glossar.htm).

38 This year name is also attested in a longer but heavily damaged version in CUSAS 9, 452. There may be a third clause in this version.

39 Ninurta appears twice in the year names of kings of the First Dynasty of Babylon: Si 38 and Ad 31.

rulers (Seux 1967: 441 ff.), and the image of the ruler as a shepherd of Enlil or for Enlil goes back at least to Ur III times with Ur-Namma (*ibid.*: 442). Whether the choice of Enlil as the deity establishing the king's shepherding implies control over Nippur, or was simply used as a traditional *topos*, almost a frozen formula,[40] is unclear. At any rate, this reference to Enlil, in combination with the reference to the totality KI.ŠÁR(.RA), does suggest a claim over a fairly extensive kingdom.

All in all, except for the laconic Ilī-ma-ilu year names from Nippur, we have no data for the early Sealand I kings, and only a few informative formulae for the later ones. The gap in time in the available evidence and the fact that this evidence is very thin both render the analysis difficult and firm conclusions hazardous. But the presence of Ea and his association with Enlil certainly seem to hark back to earlier Larsean year names. While this acknowledgment of the importance of Enlil and Ea probably derives partly from tradition, as it was shown in this section, it may also reflect the status of these deities in the state pantheon, as is perhaps the case for Ninurta.

6.3 The palace-sponsored cult

The main source of information on the Sealand I panthea that is available to us at present is the large sub-set of archival texts pertaining to the palace-sponsored cult, that is, administrative records from the palatial administration keeping track of economic activity directed towards the offering of various goods, in particular foodstuffs, to the gods. The relevant texts comprise (1) a few offering lists in which commodities are attributed to several deities; (2) livestock delivery records to the palace in which the divine end beneficiary of the animals is indicated; (3) expenditure records of sacrificial animals and foodstuffs offered to a deity on a specific date or occasion.

Offering lists, a type of expenditure records, keep track of one or a few commodities allocated to several deities; they make it thus possible to compare directly the relative hierarchical rank of the deities and the quantities attributed to them. These lists are not always (fully) dated, which could point to regular offerings. Delivery records of (sacrificial) animals may register only one or several

40 The general association of Enlil and the kingship of the land in southern Mesopotamia is very ancient (Wang 2011: 237; 245).

deliveries in the same document and are always fully dated.[41] The exact date of sacrifice is not always clear since we do not know the time lapse between the delivery of the animals to the palace, the recording of the delivery, and the sacrifice. Expenditure records drawn up for specific sacrifices inform us on the composition of the full offering and sometimes on its location; they are also fully dated. The occasion of sacrifice, for instance the name of a festival, is rarely mentioned so that often only the date and the composition of the offerings give us a clue as to the nature of the event.

6.3.1 Hierarchy in offering lists

Offering lists[42] in this archive usually begin with great gods of the pan-Babylonian pantheon, reflecting a somewhat unstable hierarchy which very roughly agrees with the god list AN = ^{d}Anum[43] and its Old Babylonian precursor TCL 15, 10. The offering lists that present theses features[44] are CUSAS 9, 59; 64;[45]

---

41 Some delivery records bear only a date formula but others, which comprise several entries, are cast as cumulative records and add "day X" on some lines. The specific date indicated in such cases probably corresponds to the date of delivery of the animal(s) which may or may not be identical with the date of offering. This is the date which I included in the tables below.
42 Two documents may or may not be offering lists: CUSAS 9, 82 and 83. The latter bears neither header nor date and usually features only one vertical wedge at the beginning of each line. But since one line features three verticals instead of one, the most immediate explanation is that these are to be read as quantities of an unspecified commodity. Document CUSAS 9, 82 is similar but the top is broken off, so that it is unclear whether a commodity was specified; all preserved lines begin with one vertical. They will be considered offering lists in the discussion.
43 Lambert (1975: 195) considered that only tablets I to IV were organized according to a systematic hierarchy, following the "order of seniority": Anu > Enlil with Ninurta > Ninḫursag > Ea with Marduk > Sîn > Šamaš > Adad > Ištar. This corresponds also roughly to the order of gods invoked in several curse formulae on Kassite *kudurrū*, which often begin with Anu, Enlil, and Ea (see Paulus 2014a for examples). In general, Marduk and Ninḫursag are more prominent in them and in AN = ^{d}Anum than in the Sealand I lists.
44 The remaining lists are peculiar. CUSAS 9, 78 and 84 are split into two sections. In the former text, each section begins with a prominent deity (Enlil in section 1 and Ninurta in section 2). The latter text seems devoid of any hierarchical consideration: its first section begins with Nin-é.NIM.ma (with Enlil only in fifth position) and its second section begins with what is probably an aspect of Enlil (Enlil-of-the-akitu?). Text CUSAS 9, 83 presents an amalgam of god pairs and single deities in no clear order. Several major deities are absent, for instance Anu, Enlil, Ninurta, and also Ea although the list begins with three gods associated with him (Damgalnunna, Asalluḫi, and Usumû).

79;[46] 82. The great gods are usually followed by a large number of minor deities or minor aspects of deities in apparent disorder. The lists differ from one another, therefore no single hierarchy or grouping pattern can be extracted from them, but a number of general characteristics emerge: (1) Anu, when present, is at the top of the list, followed by Enlil; (2) Ninurta does not always appear as a member of Enlil's circle, he stands in prominent but variable position, sometimes without connection with Enlil;[47] (3) Sîn, Šamaš, and Adad are usually present, roughly in that hierarchical order; (4) both Marduk and the mother goddess are often absent or given a much lower rank than in AN = ^{d}Anum, and Marduk is not integrated in Ea's circle; (5) in the preserved portions of the lists, Ištar is always represented by her hypostases (or at least with her name followed by an epithet).

Keeping in mind that the hierarchy is unstable and based on very few documents, we can nonetheless crystallize the arrangement of most Sealand I offering lists as follows: in the top part (Anu), Enlil, Ea/Ninurta, (Sîn), and Šamaš; after these deities are usually present in varying order Adad, Marduk, Gula, Nergal/Lugal-irra, Nin-é.NIM.ma, and hypostases of Ištar, sometimes also Nusku, Ninmaḫ, and the Sibitti. The bottom part of the lists usually lacks any obvious grouping or ordering principle.

It is difficult to determine what exactly the structure of these lists tells us. There are important discrepancies between this hierarchical structure and other evidence about the palace-sponsored cult, for instance the complete absence of Nazi and of Ištar—at least under that name—from the lists, while other records show that they received larger numbers of sacrificial animals than many other deities. Some offering lists may have been drawn up for specific temples, perhaps also the animal delivery records show a very fragmentary, and biased picture of the palace-sponsored cult.

6.3.2 The god list CUSAS 9, 81

Among the lists from the Sealand I archive, only one undated and extremely short document could be a god list without any immediate administrative pur-

45 Offering list CUSAS 9, 64 presents a unique peculiarity: it features two successive enumerations beginning with Anu, namely: Anu, Enlil, Ninurta (lines 3–5) and Anu, Enlil, Ninlil, U_4.BI.A.NU.ÍL.LA, Ninurta (lines 6–10).

46 The obverse was probably mistaken for the reverse by Dalley (2009) in her edition. I assume that the obverse corresponds to lines 8–14 (Dalley's numbering).

47 See also Section 6.4.2 for more detail.

pose: CUSAS 9, 81.[48] It will therefore be examined in more detail. Fifteen deities are simply listed, one name per line, using both sides of the tablet and the lower edge (from line 1 through 15): Enlil, Ninlil, Ninurta, Nusku, Nin-Nibru, Usumû, Nin-é.NIM.ma, Marduk, Ṣarpanītu, Gula, Šamaš, Sukkal,[49] Bēlet-Akkade, Šarrat-Nina, Sibitti.

This document is shorter than most offering lists and it includes only divine names. Also, it never features two deities on the same line, which happens at least once in all offering lists but one.[50] The first five deities seem to reflect the top of the Nippurite pantheon, and they may correspond to the structure of the hymn P431311 of Ayadaragalama (Gabbay and Boivin forthcoming). It also presents some similarities with Babylonian canonical lists, with some departures: if we use the later AN = ^{d}Anum as a gauge, the overall hierarchy is comparable, but a number of major deities seem to be represented solely by a minor member of their retinue, and two were entirely left out.

The god Anu is absent from this list, which therefore begins directly with Enlil. Contrarily to the offering lists in the archive, CUSAS 9, 81 integrates Ninurta in Enlil's circle, as is also the case in AN = ^{d}Anum: the circle comprises Enlil's spouse Ninlil, his sons Ninurta and Nusku, and Ninurta's spouse Nin-Nibru.[51] Usumû, Ea's vizier, appears surprisingly on his own following Enlil's circle, apparently in lieu of Ea. Still using AN = ^{d}Anum as comparandum, one notes the absence of the mother goddess' circle. The deity Nin-é.NIM.ma[52] follows; her

---

48 A parallel comes to mind: a short Old Babylonian god list from Mari (ARM 24, 263) which has been shown to be a copy of another Mari god list dating to the Ur III period (T.142 edited by Dossin 1967: 99 ff.) with the difference that T.142 contained quantities of various items of food offerings. Durand (1985: 163) concluded that such lists not only reflected the "'ordre canonique' de préséance des divinités à Mari" but that at least the full version of the document was a "*mémento de rituel.*" This conclusion could probably extend to the shortest version of the document containing only the gods' names. Similarly, it is not impossible that CUSAS 9, 81 is a list reflecting a hierarchy to be followed within ritual actions, however, the extant offering records do not corroborate this suggestion.

49 See Section 6.4.4 for the reading of that sign and a discussion of the association of Šamaš, Sukkal, (Nin)-Šubur, and Lugal-namtarra.

50 CUSAS 9, 83.

51 Nin-Nibru is also a by-name of Ninlil but appears here separately from her, as spouse of Ninurta; given the importance of Ninurta in the Sealand I documents, it is no surprise to find his spouse in this god list. For a review of literature on Nin-Nibru, see Richter 2004: 71 n.320. For a discussion of Ištar's possible association with Nin-Nibru as Šarrat-Nippuri, see Section 6.4.2.

52 The name was formerly read ^{d}NIN-LÍL-ELAM-MA (Edzard 1957: 177 n.970; also Renger 1967: 159 who lists her among the deities of Ur), then corrected to ^{d}Nin-é.NIM.ma by Stol (1976: 19 n.8; followed by Cavigneaux and Krebernik 1998–2001: 349). Stol (1976: 20) pointed out that in the at-

(his?) presence and position in this list correspond to the relatively high importance given to her(him?) elsewhere in the Sealand I archive (see Section 6.4.12).[53]

After Nin-é.NIM.ma, come Marduk and his spouse Ṣarpanītu. Through syncretism with Asalluḫi, Marduk came to be viewed as Ea's son and this proximity is already reflected in Old Babylonian forerunners of AN = ᵈAnum in which Marduk's circle immediately follows Ea's.[54] However, CUSAS 9, 81 presents him and his spouse separately from any relationship to Ea. Gula comes in CUSAS 9, 81 quite unexpectedly just after Marduk and Ṣarpanītu, therefore certainly not as spouse of Ninurta since she is separated from his circle by several deities. She is not very prominent in this archive in general, but does appear in a number of lists (see Section 6.4.13). In the Weidner god list (KAV 46, l. 19 and KAV 63, II 1), she is equated with Šuziana. If we combine this equation with the fact that, in one tradition, Šuziana was probably assimilated with or considered a by-name of Ṣarpanītu (Richter 2004: 89), we could interpret Gula's position in CUSAS 9, 81 as the result of these associative processes, making her a member of Marduk's circle. But the association is very uncertain and cannot be considered as more than a tentative explanation for the deities' relative position in the Sealand I list.

The god Šamaš appears in CUSAS 9, 81 roughly in the hierarchical position which he occupies in AN = ᵈAnum, allowing for the differences in Sîn's circle. He is accompanied here by his vizier(?) SUKKAL, whose close association with the sun god is discussed in Section 6.4.4.[55] He is followed by a regional aspect of Ištar, Bēlet-Akkade. Since Adad is absent from CUSAS 9, 81, the goddess occupies the rank expected for Ištar, still using AN = ᵈAnum as comparandum.

The Queen-of-Nina follows, written *ᵈšar-ra-at-ni-na*. Dalley (2009: 7; text 81 notes) remained undecided concerning the reading of *ni-na* but suggested as one possibility that the name might refer to Ištar-of-Nineveh. However, Kutscher (1976: 197–98) reviewed the attested spellings of Nineveh and concluded that the spelling *ni-na-a* appeared only at the very end of the second millennium. A reference to the Lagašite town of Nina (Šurgul), or part of it (*ibid.:* 198), seems therefore more likely. Admittedly, Queen-of-Nina would be an unusual name for Nazi, as yet unattested elsewhere, and her relative position in the list would not cor-

---

testation on which the former reading was based, only the lower edge of the sign É is visible. He suggested the reading É instead of LÍL based on the GN ᵁᴿᵁé.NIM.ma.

53 This deity may have been associated with Ningal (see Section 6.4.12), and could thus be understood as a representative of the moon god's circle here, which is where one would expect him if we compare with the overall structure of AN = ᵈAnum.

54 Sommerfeld 1982: 13 ff.; Richter 2004: 15; Lambert 1975: 193–94.

55 The same section discusses the reading of the sign SUKKAL, interpreted differently by Dalley.

respond to her position in AN = ^{d}Anum.[56] But considering that Nazi, the chief goddess of Šurgul, is well represented in the archive, this interpretation appears the most consistent with the idiosyncrasies of the Sealand I state pantheon.

The list CUSAS 9, 81 ends with the Sibitti, which are quite present in this archive and are discussed in Section 6.4.9. In AN = ^{d}Anum, they appear only in the regional groupings on tablet VI.

6.3.3 The palace as a place of cult

Expenditure records for cultic offerings and delivery records for sacrificial animals often specify only the deity for whom they are intended, sometimes the place of offering, mostly a shrine or temple.[57] Exceptionally, the offering is recorded as taking place at the palace itself.[58] In one case the sacrifice, which was carried out on the roof, was for the goddess Ištar (CUSAS 9, 69). The other texts do not specify the deity to whom the offerings at the palace were dedicated (CUSAS 9, 65: 25–28; 86; 109; BC 240; BC 365; BC 370[59]).

The full moon was probably one of the occasions for such sacrifices since four of these records are dated to the fourteenth, fifteenth, or sixteenth day of the month. It seems that the offerings took place at night because they are twice called *akal mūši* (*ša* É.GAL) (CUSAS 9, 86; 109).

The roof and the gates were privileged places for ritual offering as evidenced respectively in CUSAS 9, 69 and BC 365 (roof), and BC 240[60] (gates). In addition, singers sometimes performed at the palace gates (CUSAS 9, 87; 88; 95; 96[61]).

---

56 In AN = ^{d}Anum Nazi comes between Sîn and Šamaš on the third tablet (Litke 1998: 124 f.).

57 These shrines and temples, and their possible associations, are discussed below in the subsections dedicated to specific deities.

58 For evidence of shrines in Mesopotamian palaces, see Postgate 2003–05: 198 and Miglus 2003–05: 238–39; for the Old Babylonian period, Edzard 2003–05: 207 and Miglus 2003–05: 245–47.

59 These texts are unpublished. They are cited in Dalley 2009: BC 240 on p.68; BC 365 on p.72; BC 370 on p.85.

60 This text is unpublished; it is cited in Dalley 2009: 68.

61 The text CUSAS 9, 96 does not mention the palace gates but the analogy with the other records, in particular with text 95 makes it almost certain that the singers performed there.

6.3.4 Some events of the cultic calendar

The occasion of sacrifice is rarely recorded in the administrative documents pertaining to cultic offerings sponsored by the palace. But we do find some direct and indirect evidence for the *kinūnu*-festival and the rituals marking the phases of the moon[62].

6.3.4.1 Rituals marking lunar phases

Several offerings appear to coincide with the main phases of the lunar cycle:[63] the new moon, the first quarter, and the full moon.[64] Some of these sacrifices took place at the palace.

New moon

Two texts mention a "sacrifice of the new moon" SÍZKUR *ša ar-ḫi* as the reason for the delivery of sheep to the palace at the beginning of the month,[65] and a few more texts record the delivery of sheep to the palace "for sacrifice" on the first day of the month (CUSAS 9, 25? and 29?;[66] 30;[67] 42). We have no indication as to the location of this offering. Several deities received animal sacrifices at the beginning of the month: Sîn (three times), Nazi (possibly four times), Ištar (once), Ninurta (once if we count New Year's Day but also possibly three times

---

62 One text may refer to a festival of the month of Abu (in Dalley's translation), CUSAS 9, 43: lines 5–6 (the numbering follows here that of the hand copy, not that of the transliteration). The passage reads simply 1 UDU.NITÁ / *a-na* ITI NE.NE.GAR and is thus fairly unspecific. Should it indeed refer to a festival, it would be the sole reference to it in the archive. Cohen (1993: 320) notes that Neo-Assyrian sources show that the month of Abu was the occasion of celebrating the dead.

63 The term *eššeššu* is never used to designate the occasion of offering but we find it in the personal name Arad-eššešši written ÌR-U_4.ÈŠ.ÈŠ (CUSAS 9, 74: 5).

64 There is no clear Sealand I evidence for a celebration of the last lunar quarter. Only for Ištar do we find a few occurrences of offerings that coincide with that period of the month (see Table 14).

65 The texts are CUSAS 9, 38: 3–4 and 39: 2–3. The former is dated to the first day, the latter to the second of month iii of year N. The latter text is a cumulative record indicating "day 1" a few lines below the entry concerning the new moon, therefore all lines above were probably indeed records of the first day.

66 Both texts are cumulative records dated to the fourth of a month but in both cases "day 1" stands on a line below the entry "(x animals) for sacrifice;" this sacrifice was therefore probably on the first day.

67 This text is dated to New Year's Day.

on the second day of the month), Enlil and Ea (once each), and Nin-Šubur (once on the second day).[68] These sacrifices are discussed in the relevant sub-sections on each deity.

First quarter

The first lunar quarter may have been marked in the cult of some deities. We find that Ninurta and Šamaš[69] received animal sacrifice on the seventh day, at least of month vii (see Tables 15 and 17). Also, offerings of flour, ghee, dates, and beer are recorded for the palace and Lugal-irra (see Sections 6.3.3 and 6.4.10).

Full moon

The full moon was certainly of importance in the cultic calendar. In particular, the full moon of the month viii may have been of special significance for the palace since on three occasions offerings of rams and other foodstuffs are recorded for the night meal *akal mūši* or simply the sacrifices of the palace on that day (on days 14 or 15 of month viii in CUSAS 9, 86; 109; unpublished BC 370 cited in Dalley 2009: 85). In addition, offerings of flour, dates, and ghee took place at the palace on the 16.x (year J in the unpublished BC 240 cited in Dalley 2009: 68).

The term *nindabû*-offering may have been associated with the celebration of the full moon since we find this type of offering attested three times in the middle of the month, namely for Nazi,[70] Lugal-irra, and the Sibitti (CUSAS 9, 75; 61). The *ninbadû*, usually understood as a cereal offering (CAD N, s.v. *nindabû*), appears to have been compatible with non-cereal offerings in the Sealand I cult because the foods given in CUSAS 9, 75 included not only flour and beer but also four rams and ghee.[71] The same text, which calls the occasion the "ŠUKU ^{d}INNIN (*nindabû*) of the fifteenth day" (lines 1–2), adds that the foods were given for the *tākultu*. Therefore, Dalley has interpreted the term as the "*tākultu*-festival" (line 9), for which there is no additional evidence, however. I would suggest that a special meal was simply offered to the goddess on the fifteenth day of the month.

---

68 Text BC 365 (Dalley 2009: 72). For the other deities, see Tables 14–16; 19; and Section 6.4.6.

69 The sacrifice to the Sibitti specified to be at night on the sixth day may also be related (CUSAS 9, 65).

70 Nazi receives animal offerings in the middle of the month on another occasion (CUSAS 9, 54).

71 However, the flour stands before the rams in the list of foods offered, which is unusual.

6.3.4.2 The festival of the braziers

The festival of the braziers (written *kinūnu* and plural *kinūnâtu)* is attested in two texts, once for Marduk alone in year L (CUSAS 9, 26: 5–6) and once for various deities, including Marduk, in year I (CUSAS 9, 66). Both texts show that it was celebrated in the month ix; offerings on that occasion could include animals, flour, and dates.

The only Old Babylonian evidence of the festival of the braziers that does not come from northern Babylonia or further north is from Larsa and remains as yet unpublished, the month of the festival is thus unknown (L 74.126 mentioned in Arnaud 2001: 28 n.51; see also Arnaud 1976: 68–69).[72] But later evidence points toward the month ix for the observance of this festival at Uruk and perhaps at Babylon[73] (Cohen 1993: 393–94; for Uruk, see *LKU* 51, rev.13′–18′ in Beaulieu 2003: 373 ff.) In this light, there is at present no reason to assume that the date of the festival of the braziers in the Sealand kingdom was much different from other Babylonian instances of it.[74]

6.4 Deities in the palace-sponsored cult

The delivery records of animals identified for sacrifice to a specific deity or temple and the expenditure records for cultic offerings do not present the hierarchical structure found in offering or god lists. However, taken together, the over sixty records make it possible to infer the relative importance of some deities in the palace-sponsored cult because the number of sacrificial animals tends to remain constant for some of them. Of course, the representativity of the information retrieved depends heavily on the accident of discovery as well as on archival operations which the group of texts underwent in antiquity. Therefore, although we can infer some principles of palace-sponsored cultic practice from this corpus, other aspects of it certainly remain hidden to us. In particular, deities with temples whose economy was fairly independent from the palace may falsely appear of lesser importance in the palatial archive, in particular this may have been the case for Šamaš (see Section 6.4.4).

72 The ritual of the *kinūnu* is also attested as part of other ceremonies at Larsa, for instance as part of a seven day ritual (Kingsbury 1963: 21).

73 At Babylon, the festival may have lasted from the middle of month viii until the middle of month x, but most of the evidence is for month ix (Linssen 2004: 87–88).

74 Dalley noted that month ix was the date of the festival at Nuzi in the Old Babylonian period (Dalley 2009: 16 and n.1 to text 66; see also Cohen 1993: 392), but, given the Babylonian evidence, there is no need to look for northern influence on the Sealand I calendar.

The apparent hierarchical importance of the gods and goddesses as well as the cultic activities surrounding them are discussed in detail below. The deities are presented in order of their importance in the archive, namely, in terms of frequency and importance of the offerings. Ištar, Ninurta, and Nazi stand out, followed by Šamaš and Sîn; cults of lesser importance but presenting specific features of interest are also outlined in the following sub-sections.

6.4.1 The cult of Ištar and her hypostases

The goddess Ištar appears to occupy the foremost position in the offering texts, both in terms of frequency and quantities of offerings, especially of animals, all the more so if we take a holistic view and add up the numerous aspects[75] under which she appears in the documents. No temple of the goddess is ever mentioned[76] so that we do not know whether she possessed one in the town where the archive came from, or whether she was mainly venerated in shrines within other temples and at the palace.

She seems to have been indeed of special importance to the dynasty since she is given the pivotal role as the king's war companion in the unpublished royal epic of Gulkišar (HS 1885+), a text in which she also bears the epithet *narāmti* A.AB.BA, beloved of the Sea(-land?) (Zomer 2016; forthcoming); and we have proof in one document that sacrifices were offered to Ištar on the roof of the palace (CUSAS 9, 69).[77] Also of significance is that her hypostasis Nin-Eanna appears as patroness, alongside Enlil, in the seal inscription of a servant of the Sealand I king Ea-gāmil (Moorey and Gurney 1973: seal no.23). In addition, a list of temples, which may be the product of Sealand I scriptoria, enumerates several Ištar temples in various Babylonian locations (CUSAS 30, 451).

This prominence of the goddess in Sealand I sources seems confirmed by the entry ^{d}INANNA-A.AB.BA^{ki} among other local aspects of Ištar in the list AN =

75 This multiplication of aspects of Ištar, including astral aspects, is typical of her cult in all of Babylonia during the second millennium (Westenholz 2007: 339; 342).

76 With one possible exception; see Section 6.4.1.1.

77 For the roof as a place of sacrifice in the Sealand kingdom, see also the unpublished text BC 365, cited by Dalley (2009: text 69 n.1), in which "sacrifices of the roof(s)" are mentioned: siz-kúr.re *ú-re-e*. The roof as a place of sacrifice is attested elsewhere (CAD U, s.v. *ūru* A e, under 'sacrifices and offerings' p.263). That Ištar receives offerings on the roof appears cogent with her astral aspect as Venus, or perhaps other astral aspects discussed hereafter. However, Kingsbury (1963: 5 n.18) interpreted *ú-ri-im* as "evening" in a privately owned text from Old Babylonian Larsa, col.I, line 10.

^{d}Anum (tablet IV, line 129 in Litke 1998); the corresponding entry in the second column is *ia-bi-i-⌜tu⌝*, apparently meaning "the Sealander." The later theological tradition therefore retained an aspect of Ištar which specifically derived from her Sealand origin, and the Sealand I evidence suggests that the time of this close association is that of its first dynasty (see also Boivin 2016a).[78]

As Ištar, written ^{d}*iš*$_{8}$*-tár*, she received on five occasions the largest quantity of animals attested in this archive for a single sacrifice, namely seven;[79] four of these five documented occasions took place in the same year (see Table 14). Under the aspect "She-who-dwells-in-Uruk" she also received animal sacrifice; the matter is discussed further in Section 6.4.1.1. If we group the animal offerings by months, we obtain the pattern presented in Table 14.[80]

Besides the ancient rites of Uruk mentioned in CUSAS 9, 68 (see Section 6.4.1.1), no special occasion is ever identified except *ana* (SÍZKUR *ša*) Ištar.[81] As can be observed in Table 14, the month ix may have been of special importance for the cult of the goddess in the Sealand kingdom. This month is known neither as the occasion of a festival of Ištar nor of any major festival at Uruk, as far as its cultic calendar can be reconstructed (for Ur III, Cohen 1993: 215; for the Old Babylonian period, Richter 2004: 331). Curiously, Ištar does not figure in prominent position in Sealand I offering lists, and then, never under the name ^{d}*iš*$_{8}$*-tár*, which largely predominates in animal offering records; there, we find her represented only by other aspects,[82] always in the bottom part of the lists.[83]

---

78 Also, it has been suggested that the Sealand kingdom entered the Babylonian theological-mythological tradition in association with the primordial goddess Tiamat: Jacobsen (1975: 76) saw in the battle between Tiamat and Marduk a "political-historical" reflection of the Babylonian situation in the first half of the second millennium in which (Kassite) Babylon, represented by Marduk, vanquishes the Sealand kingdom, *māt tâmti*, embodied by Tiamat.

79 The goddess may have received more animals in CUSAS 9, 26A: 1 but the beginning of the line is slightly damaged and the quantity is uncertain. Dalley suggests "10?" On the photograph, it looks indeed like 10. Note that Kurigalzu I endows her with daily offerings of three rams as well as other foodstuffs in a *kudurru* (AOAT 51, Ku I 2, col. II, lines 5–10).

80 Remarkable is also the fact that the goddess received mostly the more valuable female animals (this is also the case for Nazi).

81 One date coincides with the beginning of the month, so that the occasion may have been the new moon, but the evidence is far too thin to conclude.

82 In addition to the aspects of Ištar represented in offering lists and detailed forthwith, *Bēlet-Akkade* figures in the short god list CUSAS 9, 81. In the same text, we also find ^{d}Nin-Nibru who has been considered to have become associated with Ištar during the Old Babylonian period (Richter 2004: 124), but nothing in the Sealand I material points toward a proximity between Ninurta and Ištar.

83 However, as Inana-Daughter-of-Sîn the goddess does receive more grain than the other deities in the first section of CUSAS 9, 84 (line 9: 2 SILÀ instead of 1). Also, as Lady-of-Zabalam she

Table 14: Animal offerings to Ištar

Month	Year	Day	Animals	Combined with other offerings	Type of offering/occasion	Name/aspect of deity	Text CUSAS 9,
iii	N	1?	7 ewe-lambs	–	SÍZKUR	Ištar	39
	L	4	2(?) rams	–	–	Ištar	25
	J	10	1 cow & 1 ram	flour, cedar, oil, *mersu*, ghee	SÍZKUR	She-who-dwells-in-Uruk	68
ix	N	22	7? ewe-lambs	–	–	Ištar	(BC 263 in Dalley 2009: 55)
	L	18 (?)	10(?) ewe-lambs	–	–	Ištar	26A
	N	?	7 ewe-lambs	–	SÍZKUR	Ištar	53
xi	J	20	6 kids & 1 ram	breads, beer, oil	SÍZKUR (roof of palace)	Ištar	69
xii (interc.)	L	25	6 ewe-lambs	–	SÍZKUR	Ištar	28
?	N	22	7 ewe-lambs	–	–	Ištar	57

The aspects of the goddess attested besides ^{d}*iš*$_{8}$-*tár* in the Sealand I archive can be grouped in two categories: the astral aspects and the local-geographical incarnations. The astral aspects of the goddess include ^{d}(INANA)-LUGAL(-*at*)-AN (-*e*) "Inana-queen-of-the-sky" (CUSAS 9, 66: 4; 70: 7?; 76: 20; 78: 14–15; 80: 5; 82: 21′; 83: 24′; 84: 10), ^{d}INANA-MUL "Inana-the-star" (CUSAS 9, 83: 41′), ^{d}KA.NI.SUR.RA Kanisura (CUSAS 9, 64: 26),[84] and ^{d}*na-na*(-*a*) Nanaya (CUSAS 9,

seems to be allocated more of an unidentified commodity in CUSAS 9, 83, where she is the only deity to be associated with a quantity of 3 (line 36′) instead of 1.

84 Steinkeller (2013b: 468) has proposed that since Kanisura's pre-Old Babylonian name Gansura(k) probably reflects etymologically her nature as a netherworld deity and since she is associated with Uruk—and therefore with Inana and Venus—she probably represents the period of invisibility of Venus as an astral hypostasis of Inana.

64: 28; 76: 21; 83: 32′).[85] Finally, her incarnation as ^{d}(INANA-)DUMU(.MÍ)-$^{(d)}$30 (-NA)/^{d}EN.ZU "Inana-Daughter-of-Sîn" (CUSAS 9, 59: 21; 76: 24; 78: 7; 83: 31′; 84: 9) could be considered predominantly astral as well;[86] it figures in more prominent position than other aspects of the goddess. Besides these mainly astral aspects, the Sealand I archive features a number of specifically local-geographical incarnations of Ištar: ^{d}INANA-*ša*/*šá*-UD.UNUG^{ki} "Inana-of-Larsa" (CUSAS 9, 59: 15; 64: 28; 82: 24′), ^{d}INANA-*ša*-UNUG^{ki} "Inana-of-Uruk" (CUSAS 9, 64: 25?), ^{d}NIN-*ak-kade* "Lady-of-Akkade" (CUSAS 9, 81: 13), ^{d}(INANA-)NIN-SU.GAL "Inana-lady-of-Zabalam" (CUSAS 9, 66: 6; 83: 36′),[87] also $^{(d)}$*a-ši-ib-ti*-UNUG^{ki} "She-who-dwells-in-Uruk" (CUSAS 9, 59: 17; 68: 2; 82: 30′), as well as ^{d}NIN-É.AN.NA "Lady-of-the-Eanna"[88] (CUSAS 9, 66: 9; 74: 5;[89] 82: 23′),[90] and ^{d}É.GI$_4$.A BÀD!.URUDU!.NAGAR^{ki} "Bride?(-of Dumuzi)-of-Bad-Tibira" (CUSAS 9, 83: 39′).[91] Three hypostases of Ištar received of-

---

85 Steinkeller (2013b: 468–69; 2013c) summarizes the evidence that presents Nanaya since the Ur III period as an astral incarnation of Inana; see also Beaulieu 2003: 183; 186–87.

86 Ištar's filiation from the moon god is well established (Wilcke 1976–80: 80 f.), although other, less prominent traditions coexisted; she is for instance called daughter of Sîn in an hymn to the Queen-of-Nippur (Lambert 1982: col.IV 26 and 71), besides claims of her being the daughter of Anu and of Enlil. Beaulieu (2003: 111 n.63) summarizes attestations of passages calling Ištar the daughter of Sîn in the literature, a survey which shows that the astral aspect of the goddess was sometimes put in the foreground in that context.

87 Dalley (2009: 68 n.6) discusses the reading of SU.GAL. See also Krebernik 2012. A goddess Inana-of-Zabalam is attested in the Old Babylonian period at Nippur, Isin, Uruk, and Larsa (Richter 2004: 128; 235; 291; 365).

88 Quite early on, perhaps in third millennium forerunners of the Enmerkar epic cycle, Ištar is associated with the Eanna. In "Enmerkar and the Lord of Aratta," the term ^{d}NIN-É-AN-NA-KA appears alone, in most manuscripts with the divine determinative (line 233 in the reconstructed text; for a recent edition, see Mittermayer 2009); this means that the epithet had (already?) a certain level of autonomy as a separate divine embodiment of the goddess. Further evidence of an early association of Ištar and the Eanna, including in the Basetki inscription, is presented in detail by Beaulieu (2002a; 2003: 106 ff.). He also discussed her cult at Udannu in the first millennium (2003: 289 ff.) At Udannu, Nin-Eanna was revered with ^{d}IGI.DU (Beaulieu 1992b: 401–03; 2003: 289), probably read Palil (Zadok 2014: 226, contra Dalley 2009: *passim*). While we have no evidence for a cult of ^{d}IGI.DU in the Sealand I archive, he appears in several personal names. Moreover, one text shows that the king journeyed to Udannu (CUSAS 9, 101). In addition, the presence of Lugal-irra in the texts seems to confirm the importance of the cults of Dūrum and Udannu which were apparently linked (Beaulieu 2003: 290); see Section 6.4.10 for a discussion.

89 Here, the line numbers correspond to each inscribed line counted separately (Dalley's method for numbering lines sometimes differ in the indices, editions, and copies).

90 See also Section 6.4.2 for a discussion of the possible association of Nin-Nibru with Ištar.

91 Dumuzi and Inana were revered together in the É.MÙŠ temple in Bad-Tibira (George 1993: no.829).

ferings, grain, and dates for the feast of the braziers:[92] ^{d}Queen-of-the-sky, ^{d}Lady-of-the-Eanna, and ^{d}Lady-of-Zabalam (CUSAS 9, 66).

The plurality of aspects, including a number of them referring directly to the city of origin (Larsa, Zabalam, Akkade, and of course Uruk), is in continuity with the nature and geographical extent of the Ištar cult in the Old Babylonian period, when the goddess was revered in all important Babylonian cities (Renger 1967).[93] Besides the obvious Urukean references, in particular to the ancient rites of Uruk (CUSAS 9, 68), the Sealand I cult cannot be placed within a clear local tradition; rather, it amalgamates several pan-Babylonian and regional aspects of the goddess. This probably bespeaks a prominence of the goddess in the state pantheon; it would agree with the fact that sacrifice was also offered to her at the palace, that she entered the theological tradition reflected in AN = ^{d}Anum as Ištar-of-the-Sealand, and that she is Gulkišar's companion in arms in his epic.

6.4.1.1 A displaced Urukean cult of Ištar (and other Urukean cults)?

Ištar received animal sacrifice as $^{(d)}$*a-ši-ib-ti*-UNUG^{ki} "She-who-dwells-in-Uruk" in a context described as, or including, GARZA UNUG^{ki} *la-bi-ri*, the "ancient rites of Uruk" (CUSAS 9, 68: 14).[94] This unusual formula refers directly to the Urukean cult itself, not only to the origin of the goddess (as presumably in the case of the hypostasis Lady-of-the-Eanna discussed above, and perhaps also Inana-of-Uruk).[95]

Considering that the official cult of Uruk had been in part transferred to Kiš at the time of the southern rebellion against Samsu-iluna, as attested by the presence there of cult personnel of Ištar-of-Uruk and other Urukean deities (Charpin 1986: 403–14; Pientka 1998: 179 ff.; 375 ff.), it appears that the Sealand I kings either revived in parallel or (re-)appropriated, after the fall of Babylon, ancient Urukean practices in their palace-sponsored cult. This impression is reinforced by the presence of other deities and aspects of Ištar that are strongly

92 For a discussion on the date of the feast of the braziers, see Section 6.3.4.2.

93 She received for instance regular offerings at least in the Ninurta and in the Enlil temples at Nippur (Richter 2004: 69; 50); her own temple may have been abandoned for a long period in the Old Babylonian period (Richter 2004: 123). She also received offerings in her own temple at Larsa, and also alongside Šamaš for the festival EZEN MÁ.AN.NA (*ibid.*: 364; 405).

94 We also find a reference to the ancient character of the Urukean rites (*pel-lu-de-e qú-ud-mu-ú-ti*) in the inscription of Nebuchadnezzar II in which he claims to have restored Ištar-of-Uruk to the Eanna (VAB 4, Nbk 9: Col. II 51); see Beaulieu 2003: 129.

95 In addition, there is a slight possibility that the Eanna appears in ledger CUSAS 9, 428: 2 (header of col. ii); I raised that possibility also in Boivin 2016b: 53 n.58.

associated with Uruk. We find Nanaya in a number of offering records (CUSAS 9, 64: 28; 76: 21; 83: 32′), and once her daughter Kanisura (CUSAS 9, 64: 26). While there is evidence that they were revered outside Uruk (and Kiš) in the Old Babylonian period (Richter 2004: 69; 115; 255; and *passim*), they appear in the Sealand I records partly in an explicitly Urukean context:[96] in CUSAS 9, 64 Kanisura follows Inana-of-Uruk on the next line (lines 25–26), while Nanaya receives offerings alongside the Queen-of-the-sky in CUSAS 9, 76: 20–21, and appears immediately after Inana-daughter-of-Sîn in CUSAS 9, 83: 31′–32′. In addition, a Urukean incarnation of Ninurta, Ninurta-of-Uruk, receives offerings (CUSAS 9, 65: 14). Incidentally, this also adds to the very slight evidence of a cult of Ninurta at Uruk in the preceding Old Babylonian period (Richter 2004: 328–29). The presumed displacement of his cult outside Uruk may be the reason why this local aspect of Ninurta was attributed that specific name, which is still attested in the later periods (Beaulieu 2003: 298).[97]

Since the city of Uruk does not appear in the archive, neither as a place of offering, nor as a place of delivery, also since the "ancient rites of Uruk" are simply described as taking place on the (opposite) river bank (CUSAS 9, 68: 15), it seems likely that these rites were not taking place at Uruk,[98] but were indeed part of a displaced cult.

6.4.2 The cult of Ninurta

The cult of Ninurta appears to have been quite prominent since he repeatedly received the second largest quantity of sacrificial animals recorded in this archive,

---

96 Nanaya may also appear once in the context of a Larsean cult: in the offering list CUSAS 9, 64: 28, she features on the same line as "Inana-of-Larsa" (^{d}INANA-*šá*-UD.UNUG^{ki} *ù* ^{d}*na-na-a*). Besides the explicit reference to Larsa, the association with this aspect of Ištar parallels Old Babylonian evidence of offerings to "Inana and Nanaya of Larsa" at Larsa in a few records (Richter 2004: 372). Also, Inana-of-Larsa, without being associated with Nanaya, is present in two other Sealand I offering lists (CUSAS 9, 59: 15; 82: 24′); in the latter, she immediately precedes Manzât, whose cult is attested at Larsa in the Old Babylonian period (Arnaud 2001: 25). This may indicate that a displaced Larsean cult was taking place in the Sealand I palace town. No evidence of Inana-of-Larsa has been found, as far as I know, in the context of the possible transfer of Larsean cults to Babylon during Samsu-iluna's reign (Charpin 1992: 211; Pientka 1998: 189).

97 Ninurta-of-the-Courtyard, an aspect of Ninurta revered at Uruk in later periods (Beaulieu 2003: 345 f.), is also attested in three Sealand I offering lists (CUSAS 9, 59: 9; 82: 16′; 84: 17), although he does not appear in a Urukean context in them.

98 This would agree with the absence of material evidence found in the Eanna, and in general at Uruk for that period (van Ess 1991b: 204; Boehmer 1991b: 207).

namely six. The records also bear twice the special mention that the offerings were sent or given by the king (CUSAS 9, 76; BC 365 in Dalley 2009: 72), which probably reflects the special significance of his cult for the rulers.

A temple was dedicated to him in the palace town where the archive was found, called by the unspecific name É ^{d}NIN.URTA, and a SANGA of Ninurta is attested once (in the *miksu*-tax remission list CUSAS 9, 384: 21). On a number of occasions, offerings for the temple of Ninurta and for other deities are recorded together; the offerings to the latter are often specifically destined to their dais (BARAG) or temple/shrine (É), and are usually markedly less plentiful.[99] We find that such offerings were made to: the dais of Šamaš (CUSAS 9, 65; 73), the dais of Enlil, the dais of Ea, and the dais of Nin-Šubur (all three in BC 365),[100] the shrine(?) of the Sibitti and the shrine(?) of Lugal-irra (both in CUSAS 9, 65), finally the shrine(?) of Marduk and of one Nin-[...] (both in CUSAS 9, 76). Some or all of these daises and shrines may have been housed in the temple of Ninurta, because they are not attested independently of it. However, the same deities, without reference to a specific place of cult, also received offerings with no apparent relation with the cult of Ninurta. If the daises and shrines mentioned above were not located in the temple of Ninurta, the co-occurrence and the relative importance of the offerings suggest at least that Ninurta was the central deity of these cultic events.

The evidence also may suggest a cultic relationship (and perhaps geographic proximity) between the temple of Ninurta and the palace, because in two documents modest offerings apparently for ritual activity at the palace were recorded alongside larger offerings for the temple of Ninurta and sometimes other offerings (CUSAS 9, 65; BC 365).[101]

Compiled by month, the animal offerings to Ninurta present the pattern shown in Table 15.

---

99 Also recorded together with offerings to the temple of Ninurta were offerings to the following Urukean deities, without any mention of a dais or shrine: Ninurta-of-Uruk (CUSAS 9, 65), Queen-of-the-sky, Nana(ya), and Daughter-of-Sîn (all in CUSAS 9, 76).

100 The text is unpublished; it is cited in Dalley 2009: 72.

101 In addition, if we posit that the shrines of the Sibitti and Lugal-irra were located in the temple of Ninurta, or that their cults were related, we may add to the relevant evidence the text BC 240 which records offerings to both deities and to the palace; it is cited in Dalley 2009: 68.

Table 15: Animal offerings to Ninurta

Month	Year	Day	Animals	Combined with other offerings	Type of offering/ occasion	Name/ aspect of deity	Text CUSAS 9,
i	N	1	6 rams	flour, beers, birds, fins	(given by the king)	Ninurta	76
	N	24	6 ewes	–	–	Ninurta	35 & 36
vi	K	2	6 rams	flour, dates, ghee	(sent by the king); on the roof?	Ninurta	(BC 365 in Dalley 2009: 72)
vii	I	7	6 rams	beer, flours, oil, ghee	(*isiḫtu*)	Ninurta	65
	K	7	6 rams	beer, flours, ghee	(*isiḫtu*) SÍZKUR	Ninurta	73
ix	L	2	4 ewes	–	–	Ninurta	26
	L	2?	1 lamb	–	–	Ninurta	25
–	–	–	1 ram	–	–	Ninurta	79

Table 15 shows that Ninurta received offerings on the first day of the year. Offerings on the seventh day of the month are attested twice, they may correspond to the Old Babylonian ÈŠ.ÈŠ-festival of the seventh day, during which Ninurta received offerings at Nippur (Richter 2004: 64).[102] Noteworthy is also the offering of six ewes on the twenty-fourth day of month ii; it coincides with the main feast of Ninurta at Nippur, the GU_4.SÍ.SU, which is well attested in Ur III times, less so in the Old Babylonian period (Richter 2004: 62–63; Sallaberger 1993: 114 ff.; Annus 2002: 61 ff.); however, with only one occurrence, the evidence is too limited to conclude to the observance of the festival.

Ninurta's deified cultic implement ᵈUD.BI.A.NU.ÍL.LA, which was set up in judicial proceedings, also received offerings (CUSAS 9, 64: 9). In cultic context, this

102 At Old Babylonian Nippur, Ninurta also probably received offerings on the other ÈŠ.ÈŠ days, namely the new moon, the full moon, and the last quarter, alongside other deities (Sigrist 1976: 299–301; see also Richter 2004: 164; 150). In the Ur III period, the celebration of the ÈŠ.ÈŠ appears to have been observed in several towns and have included several deities (Sallaberger 1993: 39 ff; 45; 56–57). The Sealand I evidence is not only for the 7th day but for the 7th day of the 7th month (both texts). The 7th day of the 7th month had special significance and was considered unfavorable in various Ancient Near Eastern traditions (Cohen 1993: 391), but there is no evidence that it was a special occasion of offerings to any gods. The fact that both relevant Sealand I texts are dated to month vii is probably an accident of discovery.

object is attested only at Old Babylonian Nippur (Richter 2004: 74). But it also appears in one of the later year names of Samsu-iluna (year 38), a period in which control over Nippur is unclear; this leaves unanswered the question as to whether the fashioning and consecrating of such an implement outside the Ešumeša was theologically admissible.[103] Therefore, the presence of ^{d}UD.BI.A.NU.ÍL.LA in the Sealand I material does not necessarily imply control (past or present) of Nippur, but it could point toward a cult of Ninurta that is modeled on the Nippur cult.[104]

Also, one cumulative delivery record lists that four ewes had been delivered to the palace "for the temple of Ninurta," and on the following line "two ewes, (for) the men of Nippur"[105] (CUSAS 9, 26: 1–3). Besides the fact that the city is referred to—the only time in the archive—as the origin of these persons, if the textual proximity of this reference with the entry for the temple of Ninurta is of significance, this would put the cult of Ninurta at this temple in a Nippurite context, perhaps with Nippurites on the temple staff: this could suggest a displaced Nippur cult. However the cumulative records in the archive sometimes compile together animal deliveries for entirely unrelated purposes, therefore the meaning that can be adduced from this text remains uncertain.

Ninurta figures in prominent position in offering lists. In CUSAS 9, 64,[106] he appears twice in the top part of the list: once in the triad Anu, Enlil, Ninurta (lines 3–5), a second time in the group Anu, Enlil, Ninlil, ^{d}UD.BI.A.NU.ÍL.LA, Ninurta (lines 6–10). In the god list CUSAS 9, 81, he comes in third position after Enlil and Ninlil and is followed by his brother Nusku and his spouse Nin-Nibru (lines 1–5). The presence of Ninurta's deified cultic implement in the former list and of his spouse in the latter suggests that these enumerations of deities are centered on Ninurta rather than Enlil, and that (Anu), Enlil, (Ninlil) represent his genealogy and family. In other offering lists, Ninurta stands in less prominent position[107] and also receives various commodities under other aspects.[108] He was probably the object of hymnic literature, presumably in the gen-

103 Richter (2004: 74 n.335) considered that this cultic weapon was outside Nippur. See also Dalley 2009: text 64 n.9.

104 Also, the associated Sumerian deity Ningirsu is mentioned only once (CUSAS 9, 83: 35′).

105 LÚ NIBRU^{ki}.MEŠ

106 This text dates probably to New Year's Day (of year I).

107 In CUSAS 9, 59, dated to New Year's Day of year D, Ninurta appears probably in the triad Enlil, Ea, Ninurta (on lines 1–3). In other lists, he is given somewhat less importance, for instance in CUSAS 9, 82 where he comes after Enlil, Ea, Sîn, and "The-one-who-dwells-in-the-sky", or in CUSAS 9, 78 where he stands at the top of the second section.

108 He appears as "Ninurta-of-the-Courtyard" and "Ninurta-of-the-town-of-the-Lioness?" in CUSAS 9, 59: 9; 64: 30; 84: 17.

eral context of the Nippur pantheon: elements of a Ninurta litany seem to have been introduced in a balag to Enlil, which can be attributed with some confidence to Sealand I scribes (Gabbay 2014a: 152; 159 Table 1); also, a section of the fragmentary hymn of Ayadaragalama P431311 to gods of Nippur was almost certainly dedicated to Ninurta (Gabbay and Boivin forthcoming).

There is no evidence of an active cult of Ninurta's spouse Nin-Nibru. Besides her presence in the hymn P431311 just mentioned, she appears only in god list CUSAS 9, 81: 5. But since her cult in the Old Babylonian period had been very modest even at Nippur (Richter 2004: 71), this does not necessarily undermine Ninurta's importance in the Sealand I palace-sponsored cult. Whether Nin-Nibru should be considered an aspect of Ištar is unclear. In the latter's incarnation as Šarrat-Nippuri, sometimes written ᵈUN.GAL-NIBRU, Ištar may have become associated with Nin-Nibru and the latter's cult place at Nippur, the Ešumeša (Krebernik 2009c: 77; Richter 2004: 124), but this identification of both deities is considered unresolved (Lambert 1982: 179–80), or at best of very limited scope; Krebernik (2009c: 77) merely admits one "nicht zu verallgemeinernden Beleg" in the Gula Hymn of Bulluṭsa-rabi, which associates ᵈUN.GAL-NIBRU with the Ešumeša (Lambert 1967: 124, line 129). In the Sealand I material, only one text could possibly point towards a relation between the cult of Ninurta and the cult of (aspects of) Ištar: CUSAS 9, 76. It records large offerings for the temple of Ninurta and modest ones for Marduk but also for a number of goddesses: Queen-of-the-sky, Nana(ya), Daughter-of-Sîn, and one Nin-[...].

As for the cult of Gula, who was sometimes considered Ninurta's wife in the second millennium, it is fairly marginal in the Sealand I archive, and the goddess is never presented in conjunction with Ninurta (see Section 6.4.13).

Finally, Ninurta is barely present in the Sealand I onomasticon.[109] On the whole, Ninurta's prominence in the Sealand I records, including religious compositions, appears to derive from his high rank in the state pantheon, not in the local pantheon of the palace town where the archive was retrieved.

6.4.3 The cult of Nazi

In this archive, the name of the Lagašite goddess is always written syllabically ᵈ*na-zi*. While she did not receive as many sacrificial animals as Ištar or Ninurta on any occasion (she almost always received four), animal sacrifices to her are well represented in the extant archive and seem to have taken place on several

109 The same holds true for Enlil; see also Section 3.1.3 on this topic.

distinct days in the month. Like Ištar, she appears to have received mainly ewes, very valuable animals in a flock.[110] We have no information on the place(s) of cult where she was revered but a SANGA of Nazi is attested (in the undated expenditure record CUSAS 9, 147).

Table 16 shows that there was a *nindabû*-offering of the fifteenth day for this goddess, at least in month v. The tenth day of the month may also have been important in her cult since we have up to four texts recording offerings to her on that day for various months. Nazi is not present, at least not under that name, in offering lists.[111]

Nazi, then written ^{d}NANŠE, was central in the old city-state of Lagaš (Falkenstein 1966: 84 ff.; Selz 1990: 118 ff.; Heimpel 1998–2001), where in Ur III times her cult included a festival in month v and offerings related to the moon phases (Sallaberger 1993: 95; 285–87). She probably never gained real prominence in other Babylonian local panthea. During the Ur III period her cult is attested on a limited basis at Uruk, Ur (Richter 2004: 282; 414), and Umma (Sallaberger 1993: 232). In the Old Babylonian period, she is mentioned a few times in texts from Nippur, and she was apparently assimilated into the retinue of Ningal at Ur where there is some slight evidence for her cult (Richter 2004: 162; 452; 498; Wasserman 1995). It follows that, at the time of the creation of the Sealand kingdom, Nazi cannot be strongly associated with any major Babylonian cities outside the ancient city-state of Lagaš.

The prominence of Nazi in the Sealand I material is contrasted by the remarkable absence of her spouse[112] and children and by the extremely modest presence of Ningirsu.[113] The evidence speaks therefore against a strongly Lagaš-influenced local pantheon. And indeed there is only one personal name

---

110 The sign U_8 is of peculiar shape in this archive. Its identification is considered certain by Dalley in her edition (2009). While the shape is somewhat more elongated than the typical U_8, it does seem different from the sign $SILA_4$ which is also well represented in the archive. $SILA_4$ usually ends with a vertical and is almost always accompanied by a specification of the type of lamb, either preceded by MÍ (female lamb), or followed by GA (unweaned) or GUB (half-weaned). The sign read U_8 always stands alone and ends with *Winkelhaken*.

111 She appears in an unpublished record of expenditure for flour, barley, and ghee given to her (BC 233, cited in Dalley 2009: 67). Also, barley, beer, and offering bowls were given to the SANGA of Nazi (CUSAS 9, 147).

112 Nazi does not seem to be closely associated with Sîn in the archive, therefore there is no immediate reason to assume that Nindara was represented by the moon god, although the former is equated with the latter in AN = ^{d}Anum (tablet III, line 65). Also, Ningal is present in the archive, even if merely once (CUSAS 9, 83: 9′). Therefore, Nazi's presence and role in the Sealand I panthea seem to be largely independent from Sîn's.

113 Ningirsu is mentioned only once near the end of an offering list (CUSAS 9, 83: 35′).

Table 16: Animal offerings to Nazi

Month	Year	Day	Animals	Combined with other offerings	Type of offering/ occasion	Name/ aspect of deity	Text CUSAS 9,
i	N	5	4 ewes	–	–	Nazi	31 & 32
iii	N	1 or 2	4 ewes	–	–	Nazi	39
	N	10	4 ewes	–	–	Nazi	40
iv	N	10?	4 ewes	–	–	Nazi	(BC 238 in Dalley 2009: 48)
v	N	1	2? (small cattle)	–	–	Nazi	42
	M	15	4 rams	flour, beer, ghee	*nindabû of the 15th day; tākultu*	Nazi	75
vi	N	12?	4 ewes?	–	–	Nazi	46
vii	L or N	10	4 ewes	–	–	Nazi	56
ix	L	1?	4 ewes	–	–	Nazi	25
xi	L	10	4 ewes	–	–	Nazi	27
	L	15	2 ewes	–	–	Nazi	54
xii (interc.)	L	1?	4 ewes & 1 lamb	–		Nazi	29
?	N	22?	2 lambs?	–	–	Nazi	57

with Nazi as theophoric element (discussed by Zadok 2014: 226), none with Ningirsu, and only two with Ba'u.

Nazi's cult, in which she is revered in isolation from her traditional retinue, appears to be an import, not a cult which grew organically for centuries. I would contend that her relative prominence in the palace-sponsored cult was probably the product of a political-theological decision and reflects a high rank given to her in the state pantheon.[114]

114 This in turn seems to suggest that the Sealand kingdom of that period included at least part

6.4.4 The cult of Šamaš

Attestations of a Sealand I cult of the sun god are not very numerous in the archive but they present interesting, and somewhat contradictory, characteristics. There is only fairly modest evidence of cultic activity, but at the same time Šamaš is associated with the cult of the royal ancestor Gulkišar, and also, the sun god offers the archive's most solid, even if still very limited, indication of the existence of a temple household of some importance.

Probably for the ancestor's cult of Gulkišar, we find that an aspect of Šamaš, dUTU-*a-na-gul-ki-šâr-ku-ru-ub* "Šamaš-bless-Gulkišar," receives offerings in the offering list CUSAS 9, 83: 15′. This association of the sun god with the cult of the deceased Sealand I king certainly indicates that the god was of great importance to the dynasty. As for his temple, a SANGA of Šamaš is mentioned in CUSAS 9, 97: 7–8 and perhaps in CUSAS 9, 384: 25. Also, it must have had control of cattle, because two carcass delivery records identify Šamaš as the owner of the dead cattle (CUSAS 9, 349; 363). It seems thus that this temple had some economic weight in the palace town,[115] and it is likely that many of the cultic activities related to Šamaš were recorded in a separate archive located in his temple—an archive that was apparently not found by the looters.[116] The fact that the temple is called by the generic "temple of Šamaš" instead of a proper temple name, reinforces the impression that the town was a new foundation, or at least some of its institutions were.

The palace records show that Šamaš was revered in at least two cultic locations: besides the temple of Šamaš, he received palace-sponsored offerings at the "dais of Šamaš."[117] The dais is attested in combination with Ninurta so that it may have been a small shrine in the latter's temple.[118]

---

of the ancient city-state of Lagaš but that this region was neither the origin of the dynasty nor the most influential element of the kingdom. Nazi was perhaps already of some importance during the reign of Gulkišar, which pre-dates most texts of the CUSAS 9 archive by two generations, since the later *kudurru* (BE I/1 83 = AOAT 51, ENAp 1) refers to an ancient land grant puportedly effected by Gulkišar for the benefit of Nazi, his lady (lines 3 ff.); see also Section 3.1.2.2.

115 If this town, or part of it, was indeed Kār-Šamaš (see Section 3.1.3), its name could have derived from the cult of the sun god and tally with the presence of an important(?) temple dedicated to him.

116 The fact that we find no trace of cattle being offered to Šamaš although he possessed some could speak for a separate, undiscovered temple archive.

117 The phrase "dais of Šamaš" is plainly legible in CUSAS 9, 73 in the passage *a-na* BARAG *ša* dUTU (line 19). A similar text, CUSAS 9, 65, is clearly to be read in parallel since the date of the offering is the same (for different years) and the offerings are almost exactly the same. It is therefore justified to expect the presence of the word BARAG in the corresponding passage (line 20).

Table 17: Animal offerings to Šamaš

Month	Year	Day	Animals	Combined with other offerings	Type of offering/ occasion	Name/aspect of deity	Text CUSAS 9,
vii	I	7	1 ram	beer, flours, ghee, dates	–	Šamaš	65
	K	7	1 ram	beer, flours, ghee, dates	–	Šamaš	73
viii	N	24?	4 rams		–	Šamaš	50
–	–	–	1 sheep	–	–	Šamaš	79

The offerings that include animal sacrifice are listed in Table 17.

The most important animal sacrifice to Šamaš is also the only offering recorded specifically for his temple: it comprised four rams (CUSAS 9, 50). The month of this offering is viii but the day is of uncertain reading so that we cannot associate it with well established practices.[119] The offerings on the seventh day of month vii (CUSAS 9, 65; 73), both for the dais of Šamaš, may have taken place in the context of the cult of Ninurta because they were recorded with the latter's offerings. The sun god also received various other commodities in offering

This slightly damaged line has been reconstructed by Dalley as: *a-na* UNUG^{ki} ⸢BARAG⸣? ^{d}UTU. But the sign which Dalley reads UNUG is partly damaged and should probably be read BARAG; indeed, the sign appears to have a somewhat more regular outer shape than the sign UNUG as it is written elsewhere in this archive. The traces that she reads BARAG could be interpreted as ŠA. Therefore, I suggest the following reading for this line: *ana* ⸢BARAG⸣-*ki* ⸢*ša*⸣ ^{d}UTU. This would not be a very common orthography of *parakku*, especially for that period (CAD P, s.v. *parakku* A), but the use of a phonetic ending after a logogram is attested, if not common, in this archive: it is attested for BÁN-*tum*, which Dalley discusses in 2009: 14. (If we include the Sealand I divinatory texts, the use of phonetic complements is better attested. See George 2013: 136 f.) The reading suggested here appears also sounder grammatically. A deity Šamaš-of-the-dais may also be attested in CUSAS 9, 82: line 27′.

118 See also Section 6.4.2.

119 The day is probably 14 or 24. It was copied as 14 and read as 24? by Dalley; the photograph does not make it possible to decide. Important days of the month in the cult of Šamaš were the 1st(?), the 8th, the 15th, and the 20th according to Krebernik 2011: 606. Arnaud (2001: 28 n.51) identified the 1st, the 19th, the 20th, the 29th, and the 30th for the Old Babylonian Ebabbar at Larsa.

lists,[120] in which he usually figures in fairly prominent position. In CUSAS 9, 59: 6; 64: 11 and 82: 6′, he comes after Enlil, Ninurta, Ea (and Sîn), which roughly concords with the hierarchy of AN = ^{d}Anum. In these lists, Šamaš also often appears in combination with another deity, either his spouse or (probably) a vizier.

Excursus: Viziers(?) of Šamaš

The sun god sometimes appears alongside his spouse Aya (^{d}*a-a*), either on the same line or on successive lines (e. g. CUSAS 9, 59: 8; 82: 6′; 83: 12′–13′). But, surprisingly, he seems to be more often associated with an aspect of Nin-Šubur(?) and also indirectly with Lugal-namtarra, since a name of the former (Šubur or Sukkal) followed by (Lugal-)namtarra is often repeated on the following line. The relevant occurrences are grouped in Table 18, showing how the deities are associated in the Sealand I material. The table also presents corrected readings following a collation based on photographs.[121] Because of the uncertain attestation of Nin-Šubur, this excursus is merely a tentative explanation of the pattern in which these deities occur.

Table 18: Occurrences of (Nin-)Šubur/Sukkal and (Lugal-)namtarra

Text Nr.	line	Suggested reading
CUSAS 9, 59	6	^{d}UTU *ù* ^{d}ŠUBUR
	7	^{d}ŠUBUR *ù* ^{d}LUGAL.NAM.TAR.RA
CUSAS 9, 78	4	^{d}UTU *ù* ^{d}SUKKAL
	5	^{d}SUKKAL *ù* ^{d}LUGAL.NAM.TAR.RA
CUSAS 9, 79	2	^{d}UTU *ù* ^{d}NIN-? x
	3	^{d}LUGAL.NAM?.DARÀ? x
CUSAS 9, 81	11	^{d}UTU
	12	^{d}SUKKAL
CUSAS 9, 82	8′	^{d}UTU ^{d}⌜SUKKAL⌝
	9′	^{d}SUKKAL(?) ^{d}⌜LUGAL⌝–<break>

120 He receives commodities in CUSAS 9, 59; 64; 78; 82; 83; 84. In these lists, he appears also as Šamaš-of-the-dais, Šamaš-of-Ur, and Šamaš-bless-Gulkišar. The SANGA of Šamaš also received flour, dates, ghee, and beer in CUSAS 9, 97.

121 The revised readings concern mainly the sign SUKKAL, which is of unusual shape in the Sealand I material and had been read in various ways by Dalley (2009): ^{d}*é-a!*, ^{d}EN?.LÍL?, and ^{d}IŠKUR. My identification of the sign is confirmed by its occurrence with the same shape in the bilingual hymn of Ayadaragalama (P431311) in which its reading is certain because it is applied to Nusku as an epithet in the Akkadian version and is equated with SAL.ḪÚB in the Sumerian version (rev. 14′; 24′). For an edition of the hymn, see Gabbay and Boivin forthcoming.

Table 18: Occurrences of (Nin-)Šubur/Sukkal and (Lugal-)namtarra *(continued)*

Text Nr.	line	Suggested reading
CUSAS 9, 83	19′	^{d}ŠUBUR
	20′	^{d}NAM.TAR.RA
CUSAS 9, 84	8	^{d}UTU *ù* ^{d}SUKKAL
	18	^{d}SUKKAL

Table 18 shows that there is a regular pattern in the occurrences of ^{d}ŠUBUR,[122] possibly once ^{d}NIN-ŠUBUR,[123] and ^{d}SUKKAL.[124] Considering that NIN-SUKKAL is given as a variant writing of NIN-ŠUBUR in an Old Babylonian copy of the *Silbenvokabular A* (line 72; Sollberger 1965: 23) and that ^{d}NIN-ŠUBUR can be written ^{d}ŠUBUR (Wiggermann 1998–2001b: 490), the following equivalence in the Sealand I texts appears acceptable: ^{d}NIN-ŠUBUR = ^{d}ŠUBUR = ^{d}SUKKAL. Indeed, this would account for the regular pattern displayed in Table 18. The apparent equivalence of these names in the Sealand I material could reflect the on-going syncretism between vizier deities, *sukkallū*, which resulted in Nin-Šubur being later absorbed by Pap-sukkal during the Kassite period (Wiggermann 1998–2001b: 492; Beaulieu 1992a: 64).[125] His close association with Šamaš in the Sealand I material may indicate that (Nin)-Šubur/Sukkal had become a vizier of the sun god in the local tradition.[126] This association of (Nin-)Šubur and Šamaš may have been initiated during Rīm-Sîn I's reign. Indeed, after his conquest of Uruk, the king of Larsa, Šamaš's hometown, seems to have begun referring to Nin-Šubur as male and sponsored his cult and hymnic literature dedicated to him (Wiggermann 1998–2001b: 491; Frayne 1990: E4.2.14.12; perhaps also the Letter-Prayer edited in Peterson 2016).

The association between (Nin)-Šubur/Sukkal and (Lugal-)namtarra is difficult to explain. They are named together in the blessing formula of an Old Babylonian letter (AbB 9, 230 line 4). Lugal-namtarra remains poorly attested but his identification with Namtar(ra) as suggested by Lambert (1987–90b) now seems confirmed by the Sealand I evidence because in that corpus they appear in the same context. Namtar(ra) is also a vizier in the netherworld (Klein 1998–2001: 142 ff.) He might fulfill here the function of vizier of Šamaš during his transit in the nether-

122 CUSAS 9, 59: lines 6–7; 83: line 19′.

123 CUSAS 9, 79: line 2 (fragmentary); Nin-Šubur is also attested in the unpublished BC 365 (discussed forthwith).

124 CUSAS 9, 78: lines 4–5; CUSAS 9, 81: line 12; CUSAS 9, 82: lines 8′–9′; CUSAS 9, 84: line 8 (and also on line 18).

125 This is cogent with the fact that, at least in the first millennium, SUKKAL could stand for Pap-sukkal (Gabbay 2014b: 242).

126 Incidentally, none of the viziers of Šamaš known from AN = ^{d}Anum are present in the Sealand I archive. Šamaš and Nin-Šubur were sometimes named together in blessing formulae in Old Babylonian letters. However the deities in these formulae are usually considered to have been selected separately from one another (see Albertz 1978: 135–36 for a discussion; in particular p.136 for the combination Šamaš and Nin-Šubur).

world[127] while (Nin)-Šubur/Sukkal, originally associated with the sky, acts as vizier of the sun god while he is in the sky.[128]

A dais of Nin-Šubur is attested in an unpublished Sealand I document (BC 365 cited in Dalley 2009: 72)[129] confirming an active cult of this deity. It is likely that both the male and female aspects of the deity were revered at Nippur throughout the Ur III and the Old Babylonian periods (Richter 2004: 134–36). We also find traces of an Old Babylonian cult of Nin-Šubur at Isin, where the deity was absorbed by the circle of Nin-Isina (*ibid.*: 214). Also, Rīm-Sîn I built temples to both aspects of the deity at Ur (George 2011: 125). The cult of Nin-Šubur was thus present in various centers. In the Sealand I tradition, Šubur may have partly retained his original association with the Urukean pantheon since in CUSAS 9, 83 (lines 19′–21′) we find him (again alongside Lugal-namtarra) listed before ᵈAMA.SÁG.NU.DI, an obscure Urukean deity identified as his female consort in AN = ᵈAnum and, remarkably enough, still so in documents from Seleucid Uruk,[130] when she had apparently gained in cultic prominence in that city (Litke 1998 Tablet I: 46; Beaulieu 1992a: 49 ff.). The Sealand I attestations add significantly to the small amount of evidence on this deity and on the long-term transmission of cultic traditions in the Babylonian south.

While the cult of the sun god is not yet clearly attested in every important Old Babylonian city (besides Sippar and Larsa), for instance at Uruk (Richter 2004: 325 ff.), it seems to have been fairly widespread, at least as part of the activities of temples of other deities. When absent from the cultic record of a city, Šamaš is often in some other manner present, for instance in year names (Renger 1967; Richter 2004: 69; 154 f.; 246 f.; 338 ff.; 493 ff.). The Sealand I archive now adds, indirectly, to the evidence for the cult of Šamaš at Ur in the Old Babylonian period[131] because a deity Šamaš-of-Ur (ᵈUTU-*šá*-ŠEŠ.UNUG^{ki}) appears in the offering list CUSAS 9, 83: 4′.

It shows also that in the period of demographic and institutional disturbances that followed, Šamaš had a temple of some importance in what was probably the Sealand capital in the south-western Euphrates area. Therefore, Šamaš certainly enjoyed a relatively prominent position locally,[132] he probably also held

127 Heimpel (1986) has shown that the sojourn of the sun god in the netherworld at night was very present in Babylonian mythology.

128 However, the association of the female Nin-Šubur with the netherworld deity Meslamtaea in the Old Babylonian god list TCL 15, 10 could speak against my suggested interpretation (Lambert 1987–90a: 144).

129 The dais is briefly discussed in Section 6.4.2.

130 He appears in these documents under the name Papsukkal.

131 That the sun god was revered at Ur at the time is already fairly well attested (Richter 2004: 493–96).

132 Attestations in personal names offer no additional insight since Šamaš was a very popular theophoric element in all of Babylonia in the Old and Middle Babylonian periods (Stol 1991: 202; Stamm 1968: 68–69; Hölscher 1996: 270). The Sealand I archive is no exception since Šamaš appears as the second favorite choice.

a high position in the state pantheon because he was associated with the cult of the dead king Gulkišar.

6.4.5 The cult of Sîn

The Sealand I documents show that the cult of the moon god was sponsored by the palace. Written in turn ^{d}30 and ^{d}EN.ZU, we find him in a few texts recording offerings without mention of the cultic location. The evidence speaks for a rather modest cult. If the term Eurukug—whether it is the name of the capital or the city of origin of the dynasty—indeed refers to the city of the moon-god Ur (Section 2.1.1.1), one would expect Sîn to be in much more prominent position. He may have been revered in a temple whose institutional and economic ties with the palace were loose or are not reflected in the extant corpus.

The evidence for offerings of animals is compiled in Table 19.

Table 19: Animal offerings to Sîn

Month	Year	Day	Animals	Combined with other offerings	Type of offering/ occasion	Name/aspect of deity	Text CUSAS 9,
iii	N	1?	1 ram	–	SÍZKUR	Sîn	39
v	N	1	1 lamb	–	–	Sîn	42
vii	N	1	1? (sheep?)	–	–	Sîn	56
–	–	–	1 ram	–	–	Sîn	79

Table 19 shows that the moon god received offerings for the new moon. He also received various commodities, including once alongside his spouse Ningal and once as the "Fruit," *inbu*[133] in CUSAS 9, 59: 5;[134] 82: 3′;[135] 83: 8′–9′ and 26′. In

133 It is written ^{d}GU.RU.UN (CUSAS 9, 83: 26′).

134 Dalley suggested to read ^{d}EN.ZU *a-ši-ib*-AN as Sîn-who-dwells-in-the-sky (CUSAS 9, 59: 5). However, we find in CUSAS 9, 82: 3′–4′ ^{d}EN.ZU on one line and DINGIR-*a-ši-ib*-AN on the next one; it would appear that these entries were counted as separate since there is a vertical wedge at the beginning of line 4′, as was apparently the case for each line of the list. Whether line 4′ should be understood and read as *ilu-a-ši-ib*-AN or ^{d}*a-ši-ib*-AN is unclear. That the moon god was strongly associated with the sky in the attributes given to him is well attested, also that these attributes could become separate deities (Krebernik 1993–97: 363), for instance as ^{d}Sîn-*ša-šamê* in the Tell Leilan treaties (Eidem 2011: Part II, texts L.T.–1: i 2; L.T.–2: i 2; L.T.–3: i 3); evi-

the two former lists, he stands in relatively prominent position, after Enlil and Ea, and before Šamaš, which concords with the hierarchy later found in AN = ^{d}Anum. He is curiously absent from the god list CUSAS 9, 81 (see Section 6.3.2), probably also from the offering list CUSAS 9, 64.

The cult of the moon god was not limited to Ur; in Babylonia it was omnipresent in the Old Babylonian period (Renger 1967; Krebernik 1993–97: 368–69; Richter 2004: 148 ff; 238 ff.; 316 f.; 388 ff.). Sîn was also a very popular theophoric element in the Old and Middle Babylonian onomastica in general (Stol 1991: 202; Stamm 1968: 68–69), and the Sealand I evidence is not at odds because the moon god is the most frequent theophoric element in the personal names in the archive.

On the whole, the cultic evidence available and the onomasticon do not make it possible to differentiate state from local influence in determining the relative importance of Sîn in Sealand I panthea. But the probable reference to Ur in the capital(?)'s name Eurukug, and the fact that Sîn replaces Gilgameš in a Sealand I version of the epic (George 2007; Section 6.1.1) point toward a fairly high rank of the moon god in the state pantheon. This could find confirmation in the fact that the moon god appears after Enlil and Ea with their spouses in the inscription on the cylinder seal P455982 of Akurduana.

6.4.6 The cult of Enlil and Ea

These two important deities are not widely attested in the Sealand I texts pertaining to the cult. But the available evidence presents two features of interest: the very fact that a cult of Ea is attested at all in post-Old Babylonian texts and the

---

dence from the Neo-Babylonian and also earlier periods is discussed by Beaulieu (2003: 346–47). The evidence of the Sealand I archive is somewhat contradictory; we may be witnessing *Götterspaltung* in the making. Dalley reconstructs *a-ši-ib*-[AN] on line 1 of CUSAS 9, 79; if her reconstruction is correct, this would put this attribute or divinity in a list in which Sîn is also represented in another section of the document (the reverse and the obverse of this tablet have very probably been wrongly identified). However, the photograph shows no residual trace of the missing sign(s) on the edge of the tablet, only that the space remaining was indeed limited, but that is too thin a basis to conclude to the suggested reconstruction. Moreover, the terms *a-ši-ib* and *a-ši-ib-ti* appear in association with other deities in this archive. The evidence of CUSAS 9, 79 seems thus inconclusive.

135 Dalley suggested to read the very fragmentary line CUSAS 9, 82: 13′ as ^{d}⸢ŠEŠ?.KI?⸣ but the traces do not appear sufficient to sustain this suggestion.

fact that Enlil and Ea usually appear together in the archive.[136] To the former point, a cult of Ea outside Eridu is barely attested in Babylonia after the Old Babylonian period (Galter 1983: 295), which means that the Sealand I material represents fairly late and probably exceptional evidence for his cult in Babylonia. If we add that he is mentioned in two of the few Sealand I year name formulae known to us (Section 6.2), it appears that Ea enjoyed a special position in the Sealand I state pantheon. Ea, written ^{d}40, also replaces Enkidu in the fragment of the Sealand I Gilgameš epic (George 2007) discussed in Section 6.1.1, which appears cogent with a high position in the state pantheon. He was also probably important locally as suggested by a fairly high proportion of PNs with Ea as a theophoric element in the palatial archive, a much higher proportion than in the near-contemporary archive of Dūr-Abī-ešuḫ for instance (see Section 3.1.3 for more detail).[137]

As for the association of Enlil and Ea in the Sealand I material, we observe that they were co-beneficiaries of statues in year name J, and that they received twice offerings on the same day, offerings that were recorded together: once they were given one lamb each (on 1.v.N in CUSAS 9, 42),[138] on another occasion they received each one ram at their daises (on 2.vi.K in unpublished BC 365, cited in Dalley 2009: 72). Enlil and Ea also appear in succession at the top or near the top of offering lists CUSAS 9, 59; 79; and 82. They also appear, with their respective spouse, in foremost position in the inscription on the cylinder seal of Akurduana P455982.

The association of Enlil and Ea in the cult does not seem to have been very common in Babylonia: a rare "Temple of Enlil and Ea" appears in an Old Babylonian letter from Larsa (HMA 9–01849 edited in Veldhuis 2008: text 10, rev. 2′), while no such temple is listed in George's *House Most High* (1993). Therefore, the association of Enlil and Ea in the Sealand I cult could certainly have a south-western, Larsean origin.

A cult of Enlil, without apparent association with Ea, is also attested: he received once one ram (on 8.viii.N in CUSAS 9, 49) and we know that a ritual installation was set up for him in month xi (CUSAS 9, 106). Enlil stands in very prominent position in most lists, either in foremost (CUSAS 9, 59; 81; 82) or sec-

136 In the Sealand I material, Enlil also appears once with Ninurta in year name E, apparently in the context of the royal bestowing(?) of a cultic installation for them. See Section 6.2.

137 Ea's overall popularity in the onomasticon seems to plummet after the Old Babylonian period (Galter 1983: 282; Stamm 1968: 68–69). Unsurprisingly, the Sealand I evidence suggests that this process may have been slower in the south-western Euphrates area, close to Ea's main cultic center at Eridu.

138 On that occasion, Sîn and Nazi also received offerings.

ond position, immediately after Anu (CUSAS 9, 64; 79). He is also the god bestowing the shepherding of the totality to king Ayadaragalama in year name G.[139] Also, one fragmentary year name, attested only once (in CUSAS 9, 243), may refer to the Ekur (year name P in Dalley 2009: 12).[140] A few other sources also suggest the prominence of Enlil in the Sealand kingdom. A newly published Sealand I balag hymn to Enlil attests to a continued interest for this deity in Sealand I scribal circles (Gabbay 2014a); also, a section of an hymn of Ayadaragalama was probably dedicated to him, preceding other sections on other deities of the Nippur pantheon (P431311; Gabbay and Boivin forthcoming). Finally, a servant of Sealand I king Ea-gāmil calls himself on his cylinder seal a servant of Enlil and Nin-Eanna (Moorey and Gurney 1973: seal no.23).

As in the case of Ninurta, Enlil is barely present in the onomasticon. Therefore, the overall evidence suggests that Enlil's importance in the archive results mainly from his prominence in the Sealand I state pantheon, not in the local pantheon. The local aspect of Enlil's cult was apparently his association with Ea.

6.4.7 The cult of Marduk

The patron god of Babylon is modestly represented in the Sealand I texts. He had a cult place in (or near) the palace town where the archive was unearthed; it may have been a shrine in Ninurta's temple because the palace offered fish fins and beer to the É-^{d}AMAR.UTU on New Year's day and recorded this together with a number of rams, birds, and large quantities of various other foodstuffs for the temple of Ninurta (CUSAS 9, 76); modest offerings similar to what was given to Marduk were recorded for a number of other deities on the same document. Marduk was also presented offerings during the feast of the braziers; we have evidence of this for two different years, year I (CUSAS 9, 66) and year L (CUSAS 9, 26). In offering lists, Marduk appears in middle position (CUSAS 9, 59: 14; 82:

139 The presence of Enlil in year name formulae is discussed in Section 6.2. Ea is curiously absent from god list CUSAS 9, 81 (this absence is based on my suggested reading of line 12 as ^{d}SUKKAL which differs from Dalley's who proposed ^{d}*é-a?* See Section 6.4.4 on this). He is also probably absent from offering list CUSAS 9, 64. His circle, represented by Damgalnunna, Asalluḫi, and Usumû, stands in foremost position in offering list CUSAS 9, 83; since the top of the tablet is missing, he may have featured in the portion that is broken off.

140 In addition, an aspect of Nusku apparently referring to a temple figures in the offering list CUSAS 9, 82, line 29′: ^{d}NUSKA-*ša*-É.[...]. It has been suggested that the name of the temple could be the É.KUR (U. Gabbay, personal communication). The traces of the sign immediately following É would be compatible but there is not much to go on. If this interpretation is correct, it could be evidence for a displaced Nippur cult.

10′),[141] confirming that he had gained some importance outside northern Babylonia; however, the date and the manner of this expansion are difficult to pin down (for opposite opinions see George 1992: 248–49; Richter 2004: 15). But clearly, his position was not as prestigious in the Sealand kingdom as it was in the area still controlled by Babylon in the late Old Babylonian period, where his cult is well attested and where Marduk had become extremely popular as theophoric element in personal names (Sommerfeld 1982: 88 ff.);[142] this stands in marked contrast with the onomasticon of the CUSAS 9 archive.[143] In southern and central Babylonia personal names with Marduk seem to have enjoyed a greater popularity only beginning in the Middle Babylonian period, as far as can be seen from the limited number of texts available (Sommerfeld 1982: 154). Given the Sealand I evidence, this increase in popularity probably took place after the Kassite conquest, in the reunified Babylonia. On the whole, the limited importance of Marduk in the Sealand I palace-sponsored cult as well as in the onomasticon seems to indicate that in both the local and the state pantheon he occupied a modest rank.[144]

6.4.8 The cult of the Holy Mound

We learn from two documents that sheep were offered to the Holy Mound, written DU_6.(KÙ). In one case, the month name is broken off (CUSAS 9, 57) but the other document shows that the Holy Mound received one ewe in month vii[145] (on the 11th day; CUSAS 9, 56). As of yet, there is no evidence of this cult in the Old Babylonian period (Renger 1967; Richter 2004) but we know that in the Ur III period the Holy Mound was revered at Nippur and that it received sheep also in month vii (Sallaberger 1993: 129–30). However, the term DU_6.KÙ

141 He is included in the list CUSAS 9, 79, probably as the last entry, but there is no corresponding offering. The reverse and the obverse were apparently wrongly identified in the edition.
142 Also at Late Old Babylonian Dūr-Abī-ešuḫ(canal), Marduk is fairly well represented in PNs (Van Lerberghe and Voet 2009: Index of personal names).
143 Sommerfeld (1982: 88) estimates that Marduk came in second or third position in the late Old Babylonian onomasticon of northern Babylonia. In the Sealand I archive, merely two personal names feature him (Dalley 2009: 307).
144 This could be an indication that the Sealand I kings, even after the fall of the Amorite dynasty at Babylon, did not control it and thus Marduk's main cultic center; or if they did, that it was not given much importance. However, the extant corpus may not reflect supra-regional matters faithfully, making it difficult to draw such conclusions.
145 This month may indeed have been of special significance in the cult of the Holy Mound; both are written DU_6.(KÙ).

is also attested outside Nippur as the name of various shrines (George 1993: 77), which makes it difficult to associate the Sealand I evidence with a specific tradition.

6.4.9 The cult of the Sibitti

The Sibitti, written ^{d}IMIN.BI, are fairly well represented in the Sealand I administrative texts, adding significantly to the extremely scarce evidence for their cult in second millennium Babylonia. One Sealand I text shows that they had a temple in which they received one ram, beer, flour, ghee, and dates probably at night (on 6.vii in CUSAS 9, 65: 29–35).[146] There were also sacrifices of lambs twice in month iii.[147] In addition, they received twice minor offerings of flour, dates, and ghee on the 16.x.[148] The Sibitti are also represented in offering lists CUSAS 9, 64: 16; 82: 18′ and appear at the end of god list CUSAS 9, 81. Additional textual evidence from Tell Khaiber, between Ur and Larsa, reinforces the case for a local cult of the Sibitti: one letter mentions that "(something) of the Sibitti (^{d}IMIN.BI)" was brought back by the mayor (TK1 1114.45), suggesting geographical proximity between their temple and Tell Khaiber (see also Section 3.1.3). One personal name with the theophoric element, ^{d}IMIN.BI-*na-da*, possibly always the same individual, is also widely attested in the Tell Khaiber corpus (e.g. TK1 3064.53: rev. 6; 3064.83: 6).

This clearly shows that the Sibitti were revered outside Nippur. Their cult is barely attested in second millennium Babylonia, and, until the Sealand I evidence surfaced, this evidence had centered on Nippur, namely on indications for a cult at Nippur during the Old Babylonian period and for a Middle Babylonian temple, probably also at Nippur (Wiggermann 2010: 464; Richter 2004: 158).

Finally, while the Sealand I sources show that a palace-sponsored cult of the Sibitti certainly took place locally, in the south-western Euphrates area, the evidence is not sufficient to decide whether this derived mainly from their presence in the local or in the state pantheon.

146 See line 33 of the text (and corresponding note by Dalley) for the reference to a night ritual.

147 In CUSAS 9, 39 the relevant passage is fragmentary; the quantity of animals is broken off but IMIN.BI is fairly legible on line 13. In addition, the unpublished text BC 435 records that they received two lambs (Dalley 2009: 47).

148 In years G and J, respectively in CUSAS 9, 61 and in the unpublished text BC 240 (Dalley 2009: 68). On the same day, Lugal-irra received offerings.

6.4.10 The cult of Lugal-irra

The Sealand I texts show evidence of a cult of the netherworld deity[149] Lugal-irra, written ^{d}LUGAL-GÌR-RA, who uncharacteristically appears alone, whereas he is usually attested in the company of his twin Meslamtaea or his spouse ^{d}KÙ$^{ka\text{-}a\text{-}nu}$-AN-NÉ-SI (Lambert 1987–90a: 144). One Sealand I text may mention a temple dedicated to him; the evidence is based on a fragmentary passage (CUSAS 9, 65: 24) but the reconstruction "to the temple of Lugal-irra" appears probable.[150] In that text beer, flour, and ghee were probably offered there on the seventh day of month vii, which was a day of offerings to Ninurta and other gods. The records show that two rams were offered twice to Lugal-irra, as well as beer (and flours, dates, and ghee) on the sixteenth day of month x.[151] Lugal-irra was also allotted flour on the thirtieth day of month iii (CUSAS 9, 60) and received various other commodities (CUSAS 9, 59: 20; 78: 11; 82: 11′; 83: 28′; 84: 7). The presence of Lugal-irra alone, without Meslamtaea, is peculiar and so is his relative importance in the cult. As a netherworld deity, he may in fact have been given more importance than Nergal (written ^{d}GÌR.UNUG.GAL).[152] Indeed, the latter is not well represented in the Sealand I texts: one record shows that he received one lamb on one occasion (CUSAS 9, 44); in CUSAS 9, 59 both Lugal-irra and Nergal received the same quantity of (illegible) items.

For all periods, there is only limited evidence for the Babylonian worship of Lugal-irra. In the Old Babylonian period, he and his twin Meslamtaea were probably mainly revered at Dūrum (BÀD^{ki}), where they possessed temples (Lambert 1987–90a: 144; George 1993: 127 no.804; 132 n.869; Hallo 1991: 379). Lugal-irra and Meslamtaea also received offerings at Nippur as part of the cult of Nusku, in whose temple they guarded doors (Richter 2004: 81). One text from the reign of Rīm-Anum shows that the pair was probably revered at Uruk since slaves dedicated to them were sent there (Nisaba 4 II.25; Seri 2013: 233).

---

149 In two cases he stands immediately before (CUSAS 9, 82: 11′–12′) or after (CUSAS 9, 83: 27′–28′) Nergal but this is not always the case (for instance CUSAS 9, 59: 11 and 20).

150 The traces point towards it: *a-na* É ^{d}LUGAL is well preserved; follow traces which could be cogent with GÌR. The remainder is lost.

151 In years G and J, respectively in CUSAS 9, 61 and the unpublished text BC 240 (Dalley 2009: 68). On that day, the Sibitti also received offerings.

152 In the Sealand I archive, the first sign used to write Nergal's name is identical with the sign GÌR attested in other contexts, an orthography probably resulting from the coalescence of KIŠ and GÌR in the Old Babylonian period (Steinkeller 1987: 162 ff.; Wiggermann 1998–2001a: 216); for another opinion based on a phonetic use of the sign with the value NÈ, see Lambert 1990a: 52.

The evidence is limited but the presence of Lugal-irra in the Sealand I texts, taken together with the mention of the town of Udannu and of its deities ^{d}NIN-É.AN.NA and ^{d}IGI.DU (see section 6.4.1), could give some weight to Beaulieu's (1992b: 419) suggestion that the Old Babylonian Dūrum and the later Udannu are one and the same, or that the cults of Dūrum were transferred to Udannu. This seems also to speak for a local importance of these deities; admittedly, the absence of Meslamtaea alongside his twin remains puzzling.

6.4.11 The cult of Manzât

A cult of the rainbow goddess Manzât, written ^{d}TIR.AN.NA, possibly of Elamite origin,[153] is attested in three Sealand I documents. She received commodities at least twice for New Year's Day (CUSAS 9, 59: 19; 64: 27; 82: 25′[154]). The god Šimut, probably her husband (Lambert 1987–90c: 345), is represented in several personal names,[155] Manzât only in one (Dalley 2009: Index of Personal Names). The evidence for a cult of Manzât in Babylonia is extremely scarce but we know that she was revered at Nippur (Richter 2004: 161) and at Larsa (Arnaud 2001: 25) in the Old Babylonian period; we also know that there was a shrine of Manzât in Middle Babylonian Nippur (George 1993: 166, no. 1354).

The Sealand I attestations of Manzât are in themselves exceptional. Because of the prevalence of Šimut in the onomasticon, we may infer that he and his spouse Manzât were of some importance in the local pantheon. This importance may have derived from Manzât's Larsean cult in the Old Babylonian period because in the Sealand I records she seems to appear in a Larsean context: in both CUSAS 9, 64: 27–28 and 82: 24′–25′, she appears immediately before or after Inana-of-Larsa.

153 Manzât is attested as early as in the Ur III period at Girsu in an Akkadian personal name (ITT 2 3782; ITT 5 9965; and probably ITT 5 9879). The texts, although listed as Ur III in ITT 2 and 5, were labelled as Old Akkadian in CAD M, s.v. *Manzât* 1c1′ and in AHw II, s.v. *Manziat, Manzât*. Lambert (1987–90c: 345) labelled them as Ur III, and indeed, the only copy available, that of ITT 2 3782, presents an Ur III script. We can therefore consider the Old Akkadian date indicated in CAD and AHw as erroneous, therefore, there is at present no evidence for this deity in Babylonia before the Ur III period. And since the goddess is attested as one of the Elamite state gods in a treaty of Old Akkadian date, one may prudently surmise that she is of Elamite origin (Lambert 1987–90c: 344; Hinz 1967: 91, line i 20).

154 The date of the latter text (CUSAS 9, 82) is lost.

155 Probably in six. Some of these names are discussed in Zadok 2014: 225–26.

6.4.12 The cult of Nin-é.NIM.ma

This god(dess) seems to be much more present in Sealand I texts than in Babylonian written evidence in general. Indeed, (s)he appears in all Sealand I offering lists, and in CUSAS 9, 81 (s)he occupies a fairly prominent position (seventh name, following Enlil's circle and Usumû).

On the basis of a personal name featuring a predicate with masculine agreement, it was suggested that Nin-é.NIM.ma is a male deity (Cavigneaux and Krebernik 1998–2001: 349), however, other evidence points towards a feminine aspect to the divinity. This could find expression in an inscription found in the Ur *giparu*, which celebrates the installation of Kubur-Mabuk's daughter and Warad-Sîn's sister Enanedu as en-priestess of Nanna. The lacunary passage may simply mention a shrine called é.NIM.ma (Frayne 1990: E4.2.13.15, fragm.16, 10′), in which jewelry is offered to a deity whose name is lost; but it has been restored differently by George (1993: 133 n.888) who views ^{d}Nin-é.NIM.ma as the recipient of the ornament. Moreover, since the rest of the inscription makes frequent and sole mention of "my lady Ningal," Nin-é.NIM.ma appears to be either a by-name of Ningal or a member of her entourage.[156]

That the deity was important to the Larsean kings of the Kudur-Mabuk dynasty appears certain because the long version of year name 8 of Rīm-Sîn I informs us that the king built a shrine to her(him?) in a temple of Ninmar; this temple may have been at Ur because the first part of the year name commemorates the building of another temple in that city.[157] Nin-é.NIM.ma also appears along Šamaš in the blessing formula of an Old Babylonian letter from Larsa, reinforcing the association with the Larsean dynasty (*AbB* 11, 184).

---

156 Since Nin-é.NIM.ma appears to have been of some importance for early Old Babylonian kings of Larsa, she may have been a deity from Larsa whom Enanedu continued to venerate in her new position at the *giparu* at Ur, therefore establishing a new relationship between two previously unconnected deities. Alternatively, the kings of the Kudur-Mabuk dynasty could have embraced her cult when establishing their rule over Ur.

157 MU (...) É ^{d}EN.KI ŠÀ ŠEŠ.UNUG^{ki}-*ma* *ù* É ^{d}NIN-É.NIM.MA *ša* É ^{d}NIN-MAR-KI MU-UN-DÙ.A (Sigrist 1990: 40). Cavigneaux and Krebernik (1998–2001: 349) consider the Ninmar(ki) temple to be located at Ur; I could not find other evidence for the construction of this temple there. The main alternative is that the temple was built at Gu'abba, the main cultic center of Ninmar (see most recently on this Laursen and Steinkeller 2017: 71).

6.4.13 The cult of Gula

Gula's cult is fairly marginal in the Sealand I archive. She receives barley and grain-based offerings on at least three occasions (CUSAS 9, 62; 63; 74). She appears also in a number of offering lists (CUSAS 9, 59: 12; 64: 14; 78: 10; 82: 20′). The goddess is sometimes considered Ninurta's wife during the second millennium (Biggs 1998–2001: 477), but she is never associated with him in the Sealand I palace archive.

The goddess, strongly associated with Nin-Isina[158] and Ninkarak (Kraus 1951: 64 ff.), entered several local Babylonian panthea and was incorporated in various genealogies (Lambert 1967: 109 ff.) Mainly a healing goddess, she also acquired through her convergence with Ba'u traits of a mother goddess (Frankena 1957–71: 695; Richter 2004: 89).

She also appears in the god list CUSAS 9, 81, after Marduk and Ṣarpanītu; see on this Section 6.3.2.

6.5 Panthea in the Sealand I kingdom

Evidence for the reconstruction of Sealand I panthea was extracted mainly from archival tablets, but also from two religious compositions,[159] and one cylinder seal belonging to a servant(?) of Ea-gāmil. These sources yielded a limited number of year names, as well as information on the onomasticon, on the palace-sponsored cult, and on the deities to whom hymnic literature was dedicated. This makes it possible to reconstruct part of the Sealand I state pantheon, to identify a number of deities with particularly close ties with the dynasty, to discern a probable influence of early Old Babylonian Larsean tradition—with which the Sealand I kings may have identified—, as well as the prominence of the Nippur pantheon. In addition, a few elements of the local, or perhaps rather the regional pantheon of the area where the archive was retrieved could be identified.

---

158 Römer (2001: 107–08) considers Gula to be at home in Isin, alongside Ninisina, an opinion not shared by Richter (2004: 181 n.798) who considers that while she was a southern Babylonian goddess, we have no evidence for her exact place of origin. See also Kraus 1951: 64 ff. and Richter 2004: 524 n.2234 concerning the etymology of her name, which may reflect her origin.

159 Gabbay 2014a; Gabbay and Boivin forthcoming. The principal other sources discussed were: the unpublished epic of Gulkišar (Zomer forthcoming) and a passage of a Sealand I Epic of Gilgameš (George 2007).

6.5.1 The Sealand I state pantheon

The review of the evidence suggests that many major pan-Babylonian gods are present in the Sealand I palace-sponsored cult, and presumably in the state pantheon. It was shown that most palatial offering lists begin with a structure roughly corresponding to that of AN=^{d}Anum and its Old Babylonian forerunners; the top deities in these lists, (Anu), Enlil, Ea, Ninurta, (Sîn), and Šamaš,[160] were almost certainly of importance in the Sealand I state pantheon. Other textual evidence makes clear that Ištar, despite her absence from (or lower rank in) such lists, enjoyed great prominence in that state pantheon; to a lesser extent, this was presumably also the case for the Lagašite goddess Nazi. Also, year names confirm that Enlil and Ea, as well as Ninurta were of some importance in Sealand I royal ideology.

On the whole the Sealand I state pantheon presents itself as an amalgamation of imports from local panthea, or individual deities. This amalgamation is also visible in the fact that one deity can be represented by several—including regional—aspects, for instance Ninurta-of-Uruk. The deity with most hypostases is Ištar with at least thirteen separate incarnations of herself, giving her a decidedly supra-regional persona.

The relative importance of each deity is difficult to determine because the representativity of the extant corpus itself cannot be assessed with certainty. In terms of number of sacrificial animals offered by the palace, Ištar received repeatedly and consistently the largest number (seven), followed by Ninurta (six), and Nazi (four), but activities taking place in temples whose economy was less integrated with that of the palace would be underrepresented or entirely absent in the retrieved archive. We know for instance that the temple of Šamaš possessed cattle but we never see, in the palace records, these animals being offered to the sun god; therefore, the chances are that his overall importance is misrepresented in the documents available to us.

The evidence suggests also that Ištar and Šamaš, and perhaps Ninurta, were important deities not only in the state pantheon but also for the Sealand I kings. Ištar received sacrifice at the palace, and she is the deity who appears at the side of Gulkišar in the epic exalting the king as a warrior. An aspect of Šamaš, Šamaš-bless-Gulkišar, is involved in the ancestor's cult of the king Gulkišar, establishing a very close tie between the sun god and the dynasty. As for Ninurta, he is invoked in one year name, and he received offerings that were sometimes specified

160 Deities whose presence in these lists is less stable are in brackets.

as being given by the king. Also, he was almost certainly the object of a segment in a hymn of Ayadaragalama to gods of Nippur.

Other major Babylonian deities appear of lesser importance in the extant documents. For instance, the cult of Marduk, who if also characterized by a somewhat low rank in lists, appears to have been rather modest, showing that Marduk had entered southern panthea but had not achieved high recognition there yet. As for the mother goddess, she is almost absent. Adad's position is difficult to assess; he is not very well attested in the archive, but he did receive some offerings from the palace. His presence in the onomasticon may not signify much since he seems to have been a popular theophoric element supra-regionally in the Old Babylonian period. Therefore, with the limited evidence we have, it appears impossible to decide whether he was moderately important in the state pantheon and/or in the local pantheon.

6.5.2 A Larsean influence

There are a number of signs of a Larsean influence in the Sealand I panthea. Some evidence speaks for an influence on royal ideology, perhaps indicative of the origin of the dynasty, or at least of an ideological identification of the kings with Larsean traditions. Other signs of Larsean influence could be merely local, due to the provenance of the archive in the south-western Euphrates area. In fact, it is likely that both fall together.

Enlil and Ea both appear in year formulae, once together; this is unlike other near-contemporary year name traditions and appears to hark back to formulae of Rīm-Sîn I. Enlil and Ea were sometimes associated also in the cult, and this association could have its roots in Larsa; indeed, the sole joint temple of both deities to be attested as yet appears in an Old Babylonian letter from Larsa.

The fact that Šamaš is strongly associated with the cult of the deified ancestor Gulkišar certainly conveys the impression that the Larsean pantheon was very important for the dynasty. Also, the relative importance of (the male) Nin-Šubur and his unusual association with Šamaš in this archive could go back to Rīm-Sîn I's sponsorship of Nin-Šubur's cult, following his conquest of Uruk.

The presence of the obscure Nin-é.NIM.ma, a deity favored by the Kudur-Mabuk dynasty, in a number of Sealand I offering and god lists suggests the same Larsean influence. Also, all these deities are included in the seal inscription of Akurduana (P455982), reinforcing this impression. Finally, the presence of the Elamite(?) goddess Manzât in the palace-sponsored cult probably derives from an Old Babylonian Larsean tradition, Larsa being one of the rare locations where her cult is attested; indeed, she appears in a Larsean context, alongside Inana-of-Larsa, in a Sealand I offering list.

6.5.3 The Nippurite pantheon and cults in the Sealand kingdom

It was already expounded that, because Enlil and Ninurta are barely represented as theophoric elements in the Sealand I onomasticon (Section 3.1.3),[161] we can exclude that these deities were prominent in the local pantheon of the town where the archive was retrieved. But they were certainly prominent in the Sealand I state pantheon, since they are well-represented in year names, in hymnic literature, and in the palace-sponsored cult.

There might be amalgamation of two causes for this relative prominence of Nippur deities in the state pantheon. Indeed, Enlil appears most often—in year names and partly in the cult—in conjunction with Ea, a pairing that does not reflect Nippurite theology, as discussed above. However, the hymn of Ayadaragalama P431311 does refer directly to Nippur, and Nippurite deities seem to appear in it indeed in the context of their belonging to its pantheon (Gabbay and Boivin forthcoming). Enlil and Ninurta also feature together in one year name. This more direct Nippurite influence could derive from an actual control over the city of Nippur, which may have ensued from the collapse of the Old Babylonian state and resulted in the Sealand I kings taking over its major cults.

If such was the case, it is not clear whether Nippur cults were still partly performed at Nippur at the time or in another location. Indeed, the archive of the fortress Dūr-Abī-ešuḫ$^{\text{(canal)}}$ suggests that cultic activities of the Ekur had been partially relocated there in the late Old Babylonian period (Van Lerberghe and Voet 2009: 2–4; and Section 4.3.1), an operation which probably followed an earlier partial relocation toward Babylon and Sippar (Pientka 1998: 190–95; Charpin 1999–2000: 324). We know that at least some offerings were presented at Nippur itself until Aṣ 8 or 9, perhaps as late as Sd 15; they were sent from Dūr-Abī-ešuḫ while both locations were under Babylon's control (see Table 7). But the situation at the time of the fall of the Amorite dynasty of Babylon is unknown.

The Sealand I evidence of the time of Ayadaragalama, shortly after these events, suggests that the southern kings took over the responsibility for that cult, in whatever constellation they found it (see also Gabbay and Boivin forthcoming). Also, there are some slight indications that a displaced Nippur cult to

161 Other Nippur deities, such as Nin-Nibru or Nusku are not attested at all in PNs.

Ninurta, Enlil, and Nusku may have taken place locally; the evidence is presented in Sections 6.4.2 and 6.4.6.

6.5.4 The local pantheon

Gods whose presence in the archival documents is clearly founded on their importance in the local pantheon are difficult to identify. While sacrificial animals and foodstuffs were given by the palace for offerings in temples, the latter are never identified by their specific names, always by the generic "temple (or dais) of DN," leaving the records without any specific geographical reference to which we could associate a traditional local pantheon.

Also, because of the demographic and cultic disruptions that marked the period of emergence of the Sealand kingdom, the onomasticon is probably less an indication of a town, and more of a region, as well in terms of the origin of persons and corresponding local panthea, as in terms of local cults which may have been partly displaced. Accordingly, the local pantheon discussed here should perhaps rather be understood as regional. The nature of the extant documentation does not allow for more precision at present.

Based on the occurrence of theophoric elements in the onomasticon, we find at the top: Sîn, Šamaš and Ea, Adad, then Ištar and Amurru.[162] However, most of these theophoric elements were popular in many areas in the Old Babylonian period, making them fairly unspecific. Nonetheless, based on a comparison with the near-contemporary archive of Dūr-Abī-ešuḫ, it could be shown that Ea was significantly less popular in central Babylonia than he was in the Sealand I archive, therefore one can conclude to his prominence in the local pantheon.

The near absence of Enlil and Ninurta in the onomasticon, and hence in the local pantheon, is remarkable and stands in stark contrast to their rank in the state pantheon. They are the sole deities of importance in the state pantheon for whom we can say with some confidence that they were not very prominent

162 In order of prevalence, the most popular theophoric elements in the CUSAS 9 archive are: Sîn (with over 50 different PNs), followed by Šamaš and Ea who are equally well represented (with over 30 PNs each), then Adad (over 20 PNs), followed by Amurru and Ištar (between 10 and 15 PNs each). Other theophoric elements occur in less than ten personal names each. Cases of probable or certain homonymy were not taken into account. As previously discussed in the specific sub-sections on the main deities, the most popular theophoric elements were attested throughout Babylonia in the Old Babylonian period, making it difficult to base the identification of the local pantheon mainly on them.

also in the local pantheon. In fact, Enlil may have been, when associated with Ea, as seen above.

In addition, although he is not attested in personal names, Lugal-irra could be part of the local pantheon. He seems more important than Nergal in the administrative records, which is peculiar. It may derive from the proximity of the town Udannu, probably Lugal-irra's place of cult and presumably between Larsa and Uruk. Indeed, it was a destination of travel for the Sealand I king, and other deities revered there are well attested in the archive, IGI.DU in the onomasticon and Nin-Eanna in the palace-sponsored cult. A number of other, uncommon, cults, for instance that of Nin-é.NIM.ma and of Manzât, could also be traced back to Old Babylonian cults in the south-western area, at Ur and Larsa.

7 Conclusion

The aim of this study was to write a history of the first Sealand dynasty and kingdom by exploiting the contemporary textual evidence that has become available in the last few years, in particular the publication of a large, unprovenanced, palatial archive in 2009 (CUSAS 9). The study was also the occasion to revisit the interpretation and significance of other sources pertaining to the Sealand I dynasty, mainly secondary sources—later king lists and chronicles—that have been known to assyriologists for several decades. From king lists we know that at least eleven kings belonged to the Sealand I dynasty, but there may have been one or two more. At present, six of them are attested in other sources.

The palatial archive, the evidential cornerstone of this study, dates to the reigns of two kings of the beginning of the second half of the Sealand I dynasty, Pešgaldarameš and Ayadaragalama, a few decades after the fall of Babylon. It comes in all likelihood from the south-western Euphrates area, presumably in the triangle Ur-Larsa-Eridu. It could be the product of administrative services of the main palace in the kingdom at the time, although this remains uncertain. Several mentions of the toponym Kār-Šamaš in the archive show that it comes from (or very near) that town, or else a district in it was called by that name.

The dynasty is associated in later sources with two name traditions, which probably both find their origin in the southern Euphrates area where the Sealand capital was presumably located. In king lists, it is called the dynasty of Eurukug, a toponym that may be the origin of the dynasty, or its capital, and which appears to be based on the name of the city of Ur, partly abandoned at the time. In chronicles, it is associated with the toponym Sealand, which apparently began as the local name for an area in the south-western Euphrates region and came to be applied to the Sealand kingdom in a *pars pro toto* fashion.

The Sealand kingdom emerged in southern Mesopotamia when the Babylonian Amorite kingdom started to wither in the second half of the eighteenth century, during the reign of Samsu-iluna. While it is not possible to find positive evidence for its existence during the southern rebellion, it certainly rapidly took over stretches of southern Babylonia left in disarray following Babylon's destructive interventions to quell the rebellion. Under the lead of its first king Ilī-ma-ilu, the newly formed kingdom controlled Nippur briefly late in Samsu-iluna's reign, an episode which may have been part of a larger operation in central Babylonia aimed at securing a stable water supply downstream. But Babylon cut these ambitions short by militarizing the area as well as stretches along the Tigris and the Euphrates. The Sealand kingdom appears to have depended on both river systems, and both areas were the theater of belligerent action between Babylon

https://doi.org/10.1515/9781501507823-008

and its southern neighbor, the damming of the Tigris by Abī-ešuḫ and the struggle over Udannu a little later. The Sealand kingdom entertained friendly relations with Elam—which is partly visible in common scribal practices—and some Kassite groups, and it was politically involved in the Gulf trade, eventually taking control over Dilmun. It may also have had episodes of relative peace with Babylon but the evidence is thin. At the latest shortly before the fall of Babylon the Sealand kingdom was again at war with its northern neighbor, but wether it contributed directly to its final demise is not known. However, texts from the reign of Ayadaragalama, who reigned shortly later, suggest that he controlled the Nippurite cults and, thus, very possibly Nippur; this could be a result of Sealand involvement in the final blow against Babylon.

The geography of the kingdom cannot be best defined in terms of the control over ancient cities and their hinterland, indeed there are clear signs of abandonment, or at least severe neglect of these centers. This corresponds also to an apparent hiatus in text production, and, if there are material remains of Sealand occupation in parts of these sites, we have no solid basis to recognize them, because, as yet, we have no continuous pottery sequence in southern Mesopotamia. The period is also characterized by hydrographic changes, a general western shift of Euphrates branches, and probably reduced and unpredictable precipitations. Therefore, the Sealand kingdom existed in a changed geodemographic landscape, and, until now, we may not have looked in the right places for the Sealand I living and built environment. This probably explains why we have until now found so few texts, and even fewer in controlled excavations, which have mainly concentrated on the large, ancient cities. The recent discovery at Tell Khaiber, between Ur and Larsa, of Sealand I texts contemporary with the palatial archive marks a turning point in scholarship on the Sealand I dynasty and will, hopefully, allow for the characterization of a material assemblage diagnostic of that period in the southern Mesopotamian plain.

The palatial archive depicts the Sealand I palace as an active economic body in the local economy, procuring agricultural and animal resources beyond its own needs, transforming them, and supplying temples with sacrificial animals and various cultic requisites, as well as providing for its own varied workforce and dependents, and also temple personnel. Cereals dominate in texts about agricultural produce and, although barley is the most common crop, wheat was grown in no insignificant quantities, showing that the conditions were not too saline for this sensitive plant. Sheep are very well represented in the records, to a lesser extent large cattle and goats. The palace appears to have owned fields, flocks of sheep, and some cattle. Some of the fields were given as subsistence fields to various craftsmen and other professionals attached either to the palace or probably also temples. Several received also various forms of emoluments, including allotments of grain.

The palace had grain milled by palace servants as well as by a captive workforce in a guarded *nupāru*-workhouse. The palace also brew beer, presumably in an internal service called the *Egipar*, or else it had close economic ties with this institution. Some workmen attached to the administrative center unearthed at the site of Tell Khaiber were apparently employees of the palace, and the "palace" named in several Tell Khaiber texts is probably the same that produced the archive published in CUSAS 9. The archive's purview is mainly limited to local affairs but there are some slight indications that Kassites may have been involved in state-controlled trade, receiving copper and textiles from the palace.

Offering lists, other administrative texts pertaining to sacrifice, and one god list show that the Sealand I state pantheon was an amalgamation of several southern Mesopotamian panthea, probably roughly a reflection of the territorial extent of the kingdom. Ištar, Šamaš, and perhaps Ninurta appear to have been particularly important to the dynasty. There are some signs of displaced cults modeled on their place of origin, in particular for Uruk, perhaps also for Larsa and Nippur; this was presumably a result of the derelict state in which a number of ancient temples found themselves at the time, perhaps allowing only for limited cultic activity. A Larsean influence is discernible in year names featuring Enlil and Ea, as well as in the cult, although it is not always clear whether that influence is mainly on the local-regional pantheon or on the state pantheon. Also, Nippurite gods are very prominent in the Sealand I state pantheon.

The Sealand kingdom did not resist long the expansionist velleities of the Kassite dynasty which eventually installed itself at Babylon. It was annexed starting in the reign of Burna-buriaš, and the conquest was completed in the reign of Agum (III). Dilmun, which had apparently been a Sealand dependency, also fell under their sway. The Kassite rulers embarked on a large program aimed at reviving the ancient central and southern Babylonian urban centers and their temples, perhaps wiping off some traces of modest Sealand I occupation and repairs at these sites.

With the Kassite conquest, Babylonia was united again, after several generations. Despite the fact that, throughout its history, it stood mostly or entirely against the Babylonian power, the Sealand I dynasty entered the main Babylonian historiographic tradition. It had certainly done so by the early first millennium, using sources that had probably been produced in more than one scriptorial environments. One of them may have created and passed down a continuous Sealand royal chronography presenting the Sealand I and the later Sealand II kings in a sequence. The unification of Sumer and Akkad under Hammurapi, the secession of the southern portion of it, and the reunification under the Kassite kings appear to have been of interest to sixth and seventh century chroniclers, certainly to the compiler of the chronicle *ABC* 20B who presents in this text the Sealand I dynasty on a par with dynasties who reigned at Babylon, and its kings as legitimate stakeholders in second millennium Babylonian history.

Appendix 1: BKL A and Babylon I—Sealand I synchronism

In order to assess the trustworthiness of the figures given in BKL A, we need to determine whether they are compatible with known synchronisms involving the Sealand I rulers. Starting from the first incontrovertible attestation of the rule of Ilī-ma-ilu, namely documents from Nippur dated to what appears to be his first year, we can examine the relative chronology of the Sealand I and the Babylon I dynasties.

Ilī 1 = Si 29?

The first synchronism is putative and cannot be established with exactitude; the first uncertainty arises from the exact position of the Ilī-ma-ilu texts (BE 6/2 68; ARN 123; SAOC 44 12; PBS 8/1 89; TMH 10 54) in the documentary sequence at Nippur, and the second from the position of the year 1 of Ilī-ma-ilu at Nippur within the reckoning of BKL A. To the former point, given the overall distribution of textual evidence from that city, the year Ilī 1 can be equated at the earliest with Si 29, the year in which the last document bearing a date formula of Samsu-iluna whose identification is certain is attested (TMH 10 185 dated to 2.iii.Si 29). Indeed, an examination of the Nippur texts dating to Samsu-iluna shows that, before Si 29, there is only one long interruption from vi.Si 8 to xii.Si 9, but since a few texts show that Rīm-Sîn II controlled Nippur at least from month iv until month x during his second year,[1] which corresponds to Si 9, this interval in the textual record is too narrow to fit in the minimal period of control by Ilī-ma-ilu.[2] The only possible scenario remaining for Ilī-ma-ilu's rule over the city is therefore after the latest texts dating to Samsu-iluna.

It was long thought that texts dating to Si 30 had been found at Nippur, following a comment by Oelsner (1974: 261). Although he referred to five texts in the

1 There are four texts dated to Rīm-Sîn II, all with the year name b (Stol 1976: 57), respectively in the months iv, vii, viii, and x: OECT 8, 14; ARN 124; ARN 125; OECT 8, 19.

2 Jacobsen (1939: 195 n.15), working with fewer texts than we have at our disposal today, had surmised that Ilī-ma-ilu controlled Nippur during the year Si 9. Thureau-Dangin (1951: 242) then prudently suggested that Ilī-ma-ilu may have joined Rīm-Sîn II's rebellion. Shortly after, Landsberger (1954: 68 n.174) introduced the idea that Ilī-ma-ilu's presence at Nippur probably occurred after the last texts dated to Samsu-iluna; he suggested his presence in the years Si 30 and 31.

https://doi.org/10.1515/9781501507823-009

Hilprecht-Sammlung, there are in fact eight documents with the year formula mu gibil 2–kam-ma which he assumed to correspond to Si 30: one barley delivery TMH 10 141 (=HS 2236), three perforated tags TMH 10 178–80 (=HS 2163; 2370; 2223), two barley expenditures records TMH 10 186–87 (=HS 2359; 2178), one date expenditure TMH 10 196 (=HS 2164), and one text concerning oil TMH 10 208 (=HS 2358). In her edition, Goddeeris (2016; in note to line 7 of TMH 10 186) remains careful and does not equate this year name with another formula, merely raising the possibility that it could be an abbreviated form of Si 29, attested in TMH 10 185. This appears questionable because the year name Si 29 has the morphology "mu RN lugal.e gibil[3] (egir) + Si 28" or a shorter form thereof (Horsnell 1999: vol.II 222), the egir being optional and certainly not cumulative with gibil. If the unspecific mu gibil 2–kam-ma is from the reign of Samsu-iluna, a better candidate for its equivalent appears indeed to be the formula Si 30,[4] which has a variant "mu RN lugal.e gibil 2–kam-ma[5] (*ša* egir) + Si 28" (Horsnell 1999: vol.II 223). In fact, when discussing texts (mainly) from Lagaba, Leemans (1960c: 81 n.21) considered that the formula mu gibil 2–kam-ma, even without the king's name, was an abbreviated form of it.[6]

However, the term gibil was also used in Ilī-ma-ilu's second year name at Nippur (mu gibil mu RN lugal.e). Therefore, the Nippur texts dated to the unspecific mu gibil 2–kam-ma could be from Ilī-ma-ilu's third year name, of which we have otherwise no attestation. Also, considering that the use of gibil increased in year names of the latter part of the first dynasty of Babylon (Horsnell 1999: vol.II 222 n.153), and that Nippur was at some point under Babylon's control again (see Section 4.3.1), we cannot exclude that a date formula of one of the later kings was implied. The possibilities are many and the matter remains at present unresolved. Therefore, in order to consider here only evidence that is certain, Si 29 is a *terminus post quem* for the reign of Ilī-ma-ilu.

Prosopography makes clear that the date of the Ilī-ma-ilu documents cannot be much later than Si 29. Indeed, examination of the Nippur texts shows that scribes and *burgul*s remained in place when control over the city went from

3 Or ús-sa.

4 A dating of these texts as Si 30 would be compatible with the presence of the Ilī-ma-ilu's texts at Nippur in the same year because the former were all written in the first four months of the year, while the latter are attested from month vii.

5 As a variant of ús-sa (mu) ús-sa.

6 Horsnell (1999: vol.II 222 n.152) follows Leemans, although he does not list this variant separately; he also discusses further evidence from Lagaba, referring to works by Tammuz.

Samsu-iluna to the Sealand I king[7]. We find an additional indication of this in a family archive, which is also less liable to homonymy since it concerns two documents from the same family found in the same archaeological locus: SAOC 44 11 and 12. The former is dated to the 54th year of Rīm-Sîn I and records a division of temple offices between one Ubar-Ba'u and other individuals, the latter dates to Ilī 1 and records an exchange of house plots between two brothers, the sons of Ubar-Ba'u. Since we have two generations involved, this evidence does not allow for a precise dating but it certainly excludes a long hiatus between Si 29 and Ilī 1.[8]

Additional uncertainty for that synchronism comes from the fact that we do not know beyond doubt whether the year mu *ì-lí-ma*-DINGIR lugal.e at Nippur indeed reflects the beginning of Ilī-ma-ilu's reign in the reckoning of king lists, in particular of BKL A. The moment of accession to kingship over a new political entity can be difficult to define and we cannot exclude that the compilers had access to sources from an earlier phase of leadership further south, which they deemed acceptable for their purpose, while the scribes at Nippur simply considered the new comer to be in his first year from their point of view, and used accordingly a local form of year names.

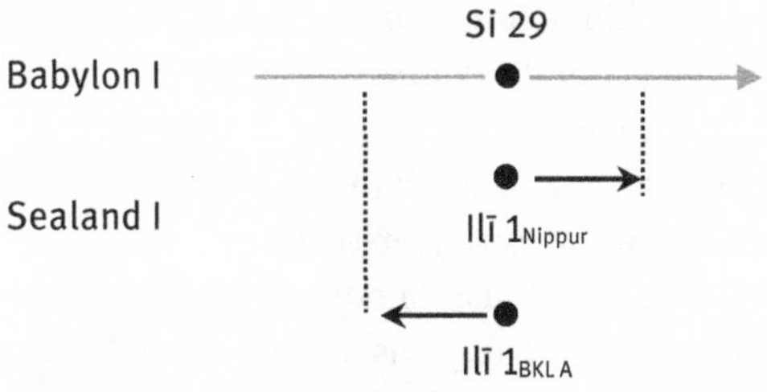

Figure 6: Synchronism Si 29 and Ilī 1

7 Chiera (1914: 66) noted that the *burgul* Awīlīja named in a text dated to Ilī-ma-ilu was also present in texts dated from Ha 33 until well into Samsu-iluna's reign. Landsberger (1954: 68 n.174) pointed out that Idišum is attested for the years Si 6, 12, 13, and 29 as well as in a text dated to Ilī-ma-ilu. Stone (1977: 281 n.21) simply noted agreement between several personal names in the texts dated to Ilī-ma-ilu and the latest texts dated to Samsu-iluna at Nippur. We may now add that the scribe Ninurta-muballiṭ of text TMH 10 54a (and envelope 54b), dated Ilī 1, was already in function in Si 23 (TMH 10 9).

8 Indeed, Ubar-Ba'u must have been at least a young adult in the 54th year of Rīm-Sîn I when he received his temple office and sealed the document with a *burgul*-seal cut out in his name. If we put tentatively the first year of Ilī-ma-ilu as concurrent with the 29th of Samsu-iluna, we have a time span of 49 years between the two documents.

Keeping these uncertainties in mind, we may nonetheless posit Si 29 = Ilī 1 as a starting point for further computations, with Ilī 1 being the first date formula known at Nippur and taken as the beginning of the dynasty.

Gu x = Sd y

Since we now know that Samsu-ditāna and Sealand I's sixth king Gulkišar were contemporary, if we consider the literary relation of their battle as admissible evidence, we have a late synchronism between both dynasties; we can thus use the reign lengths of the Babylon I kings, which are fairly well established, to determine how much time elapsed between Ilī-ma-ilu and Gulkišar. In order for Samsu-ditāna and Gulkišar to have fought one another, they must have had at least one concurrent year of reign: at the latest, Gulkišar ascended the Sealand I throne in the last year of the king of Babylon, at the earliest Gulkišar's reign ended in the first year of Samsu-ditāna. Of the two, the computation of the *terminus ante quem* of Gulkišar's accession rests on more solid ground since it is based solely on the chronology of the Babylon I kings. The only uncertainty there concerns the reign lengths of the last two kings Ammī-ṣaduqa and Samsu-ditāna. These are given in BKL B as twenty-one and thirty-one years, respectively; in both cases what would be their few final years are not attested in date lists. For Ammī-ṣaduqa, a number of additional year names are known so that it is considered fairly certain that he did rule for twenty-one years (Horsnell 1999: vol.I 86–91). The case of Samsu-ditāna is more nebulous; date-list N seems to have kept four additional lines after what was probably his twenty-seventh year name, however these lines have remained uninscribed but for an initial mu (Horsnell 1999: vol.I 274–75). The main argument for a reign length of thirty-one years is that in this case the entry in BKL B could be trusted because it is not a "round number" in 0 or 5; this argument is based on initial work by Poebel (1947) and well summarized in Horsnell 1999: vol.I 87. I will therefore use reign lengths of twenty-one and thirty-one years for the last two Babylon I kings; the residual uncertainty cannot exceed a few years. Using these numbers, we find that a maximum of 126 years (10 + 28 + 37 + 21 + 30) could have elapsed *before* the beginning of the reign of Gulkišar in order for him to ascend the throne in the last year of Samsu-ditāna (that is if Gu 1 = Sd 31). This scenario represents an extreme upper limit and would imply that king Gulkišar was able to campaign against the Old Babylonian king in the year in which he assumed kingship.

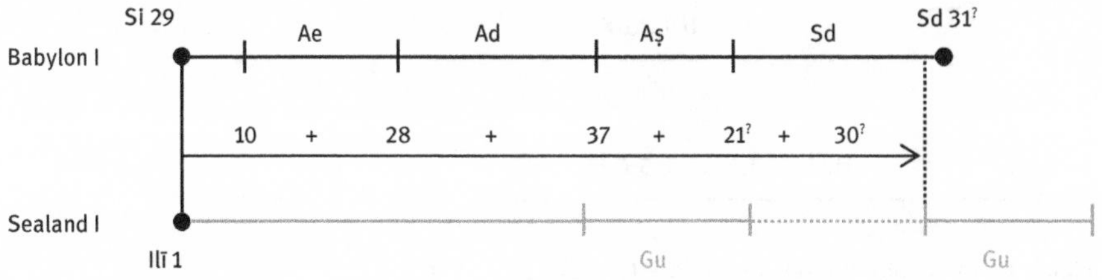

Figure 7: Maximal time elapsed before Gulkišar's accession

Putting BKL A to the test for the time lapse between Ilī-ma-ilu and Gulkišar

We can use the maximal time lapse established above to put the BKL A figures to the test since the sum of the reign lengths of the Sealand I kings before Gulkišar need to be equal to or lower than 126 years. The case of Ilī-ma-ilu's reign length requires a little more analysis than the others (see Table 6). It almost certainly ends with the digit one; moreover, we know that the reign of the first Sealand I king spread over two reigns of Babylon I kings, from Si 29 (according to the starting point of our analysis) at least until the damming of the Tigris in Ae o. The chronology of Abī-ešuḫ's reign is not definitively established but it seems fairly certain that this year name would belong, using Horsnell's classification, if not to the later range of the middle years Ae 19–23 (more probable), then to the middle range of the middle years Ae 13–18 (less probable but possible) (Horsnell 1999: vol.I 74–76). In other words, Ilī-ma-ilu must have reigned at the very least twenty-three years (Si 29 – Ae 13). It follows that the reign length given for Ilī-ma-ilu in BKL A has to be thirty-one or a higher numeral finishing with one (or indeed 60, depending on how one understands the sign DIŠ). Now using the most conservative reading for each reign length (Table 6), that is the lowest possible numeral for each of them, we obtain as the lowest possible total of regnal years from the accession of Ilī-ma-ilu until the end of the reign of Šušši 31 + 45 + 16 + 15 + 24 = 131 years. This is greater than the maximum of 126 years established using the Babylon I reign lengths and suggests that the reign lengths in BKL A are too high. The only possibility for the reign lengths of BKL A to be tenable would be to posit that its compilers considered that Ilī-ma-ilu began his reign before his first year at Nippur.

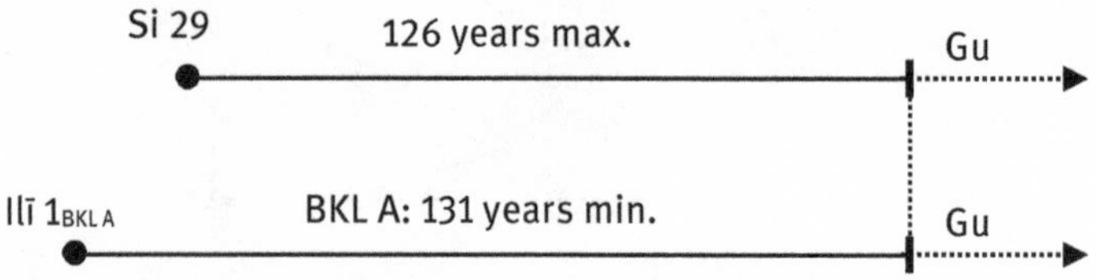

Figure 8: Minimal time elapsed before Gulkišar according to BKL A

Di ≤ Ad 36

Another anchor for the relative chronology is given in the last year name of Ammī-ditāna, the 37th. It refers to an event which probably took place in his 36th regnal year: "The year Ammiditāna, the king, destroyed the wall of Udannu(?) which (the troops of) Dam(i)q-ilišu had built."[9] This informs us that the third Sealand I king preceded or was contemporary with Ammī-ditāna; his reign must have begun at the very latest in Ad 36, giving us the *terminus ante quem* for it: Di 1 ≤ Ad 36. This represents an extreme limit since if Di 1 = Ad 36, Dam(i)q-ilišu would have built or completed the wall in his accession year, and the king of Babylon destroyed it immediately thereafter.

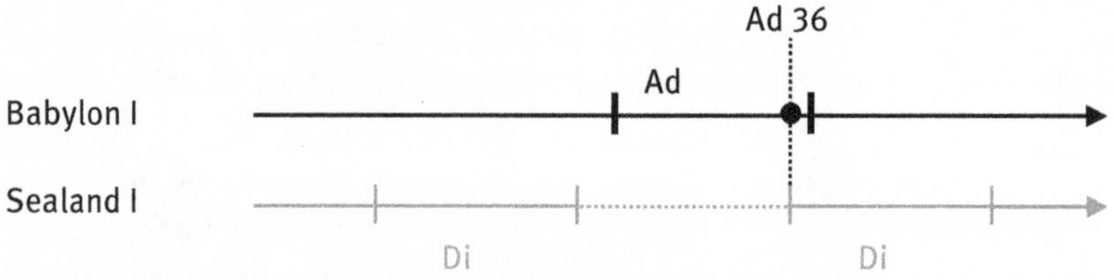

Figure 9: *Terminus ante quem* for Dam(i)q-ilišu's accession year

Putting BKL A to the test for the time elapsed before and after Dam(i)q-ilišu

If we compute the time which elapsed from the accession of Ilī-ma-ilu (using the putative synchronism Ilī 1 = Si 29) until the accession of Dam(i)q-ilišu, the reign lengths in BKL A cannot be correct since we obtain an earliest possible begin-

9 Horsnell (1999: vol.II 320) reads the city name Udinim; I follow Beaulieu (1992b: 419) who suggested that the town may correspond to Udannu.

ning of the reign of Dam(i)q-ilišu past the end of Ammī-ditāna's reign (31 + 45 = 76 years from Si 29; this would put the accession year of Dam(i)q-ilišu in Aṣ 2). In order for the BKL A figures to be tenable, we would have to assume that the king list reckoned a reign for Ilī-ma-ilu which started before his first year at Nippur.

To circumvent the uncertainties surrounding Ilī-ma-ilu's accession year, we can work instead from the earliest possible time for the end of his reign. For this, we have a *terminus post quem* in the damming of the Tigris undertaken by Abī-ešuḫ and commemorated in his year name o, which, as expounded above, is almost certainly after, or at the earliest in year Ae 13. We can therefore posit that Ilī-ma-ilu died at the earliest in the year of the failed damming of the Tigris, in or after Ae 13. Consequently, if we put Itti-ili-nībī's accession in Ae 14, still using the lowest possible reading for his reign length in BKL A, we arrive at the earliest possible accession of Dam(i)q-ilišu in year Ad 31, six years before Ammī-ditāna's claim to have destroyed a wall build by him. This scenario is certainly tenable, mathematically. It would also be compatible, even if barely so, with the lowest possible interval reckoned in BKL A for the time from Dam(i)q-ilišu's accession until Gulkišar's accession, which would then fall at the earliest in year Sd 28 (16 + 15 + 24 = 55 years from Ad 31).

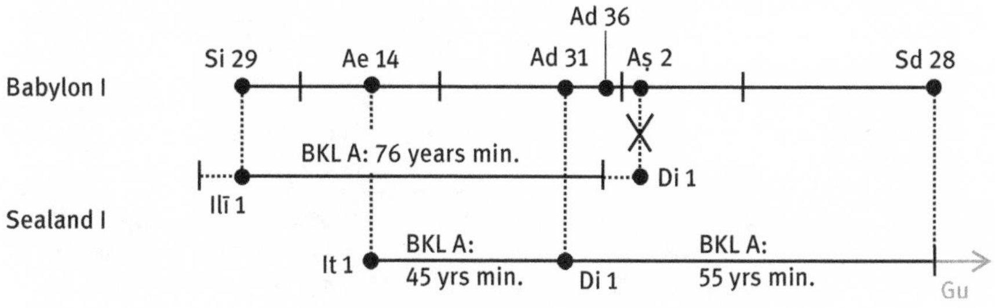

Figure 10: Time elapsed before and after Di 1 according to BKL A

Historically, the balance of probabilities is against the reign lengths of BKL A to be correct. The findings are summarized in 3.2.1.2 and 3.2.1.3.

Appendix 2: Sealand I year names

Table 20: Sealand I year formulae

King	Year	Year formula (partly reconstructed)	Source
Ilī-ma-ilu	Ilī 1	mu *ì-lí-ma*-DINGIR lugal.e	ARN 123=Ni9271; UM 55-21-239=3N-T87=SAOC 44 12; TMH 10 54a & b
	Ilī 2	mu gibil *ì-lí-ma*-DINGIR lugal.e	BE 6/2 68
		mu ús-sa *ì-lí-ma*-DINGIR [lugal.e]	PBS 8/1 89
Pešgaldarameš	Pe 1	mu peš$_{11}$.gal-dàra.meš lugal.e	CUSAS 18, 28
	Pe 24?	mu pe[š.gal-dàra.meš lugal.e] ki 24(25?) k[am]	CUSAS 18, 32
	Pe 27 = A	mu peš.gal-dàra.meš lugal.e ki 27	CUSAS 9, 85
	Pe 29 = C	mu peš.gal-dàra.meš lugal.e ki 29 kam	CUSAS 9, 16; 407
		mu peš.gal-dàra.meš ki 29 lugal.e	BC 363
Ayadaragalama	Aa 1 = D	mu a.a-dàra-galam.ma lugal.(e)	CUSAS 9, 59; 86; 151; 247; 408; BC 252
	Aa E	mu a.a-dàra-galam.ma lugal.e á.kal nigin lú.kúr.min.a.bi ì.zi.ga.eš.a (ka?.⌈dù?⌉ gu.la ^{d}en.líl ^{d}nin.urta in.ne.[...])	CUSAS 9, 17–20; 60; 87–88; 152–155; 248–249; 368; 368A?; 452; BC 370
	Aa F	mu a.a-dàra-galam.ma lugal.e bàd zag.(gar) ((íd) ḫar gu.la$^{(ki)}$) (lú.kúr kal-*šu-ú*(?) mu.un.na.an.dù.a)	CUSAS 9, 21–22; 89; 156–159; 378; 409–410; 411?; 412–413; 413A
	Aa G	mu a.a-dàra-galam.ma lugal.e nam sipa ki.šár(.ra.ta ^{d}en.líl.le mu.un.gar.ra.a.ba)	CUSAS 9, 61; 160–162; BC 310
	Aa H	mu a.a-dàra-galam.ma lugal.e é.unú$^{(ki)}$ libir.ra (bàd.^{d}en.líl.le.ke$_4$ mu.un.dù?)	CUSAS 9, 23?; 62; 162A; 163; 165A; 165–171; 309–310; 369–370; 414
	Aa I	mu a.a-dàra-galam.ma lugal.e ḫar ($^{(na4)}$za.gìn(.na)) (kù.gi) (na$_4$?)	CUSAS 9, 1; 63–66; 90–93; 94?; 95–99; 172–177; 250–251;

https://doi.org/10.1515/9781501507823-010

Table 20: Sealand I year formulae *(continued)*

King	Year	Year formula (partly reconstructed)	Source
		(peš.peš sal.la gar.ra šu ^{d}en.ki lugal.a.ni gar.ra(.a))	379–381; 415; 453–457; BC 165; 233
Ayadaragalama	Aa J	mu a.a-dàra-galam.ma lugal.e giš.alam didli (kù.gi ḫuš.a (ŠI) gar.ra ^{d}en.líl ^{d}en.ki(.ra) in.ne.en.-ku_4.ra(.a))	CUSAS 9, 67–72; 100–107; 108?; 178–180; 252; 382; 416–417; 459–461; BC 166; 210; 231; 240; 424; TK1 3064.135
	Aa K (=L=7?)	(mu a.a-dàra-galam.ma lugal.e) mu gibil * As per Robson's transliteration the Tell Khaiber texts have the formula mu a.a-dàra-galam.ma lugal.e mu sar(?) (oracc.upenn.museum.edu/urap/corpus accessed on 7 Oct. 2016). Given the fact that both the sign GIBIL and SAR are attested with varying, and sometimes very similar, shapes in the CUSAS 9 archive (e. g. SAR in text 443: 10 and text 426: 18; GIBIL in text 420: 25 and text 188A: 7) it seems possible that SAR could be read GIBIL in these texts. Without access to photographs, it remains merely a suggestion.	CUSAS 9, 2; 24; 73; 109–110; 164; 181–188; 188A; 253; 371–372; 418–424; BC 365; TK1 3064.67(?)*; TK1 3006.17(?)*
	Aa 7 = L	mu (a.a-dàra-galam.ma) (ki) 7	CUSAS 9, 25–29; 26A; 54; 56?; 111–122; 123–125?; 189–190; 191–193?; 303–304?; 311; 312–315?; 425–426; 434?; 462; BC 215
	Aa M (=N=8?)	mu gibil egir	CUSAS 9, 29A; 74–75; 126–127; 194–200; 427–431; BC 259
	Aa 8 = N	mu (ki) 8 (kam)	CUSAS 9, 30–53; 55; 57–58; 76; 123–125?; 128–141; 191–193?; 201–241; 242?; 254–287; 288?; 289–301; 302?–304?; 312–315?; 316–336; 337?; 338–365; 342A; 350A; 353A; 355A; 365A; 373; 383–385; 431A; 432–433;

Table 20: Sealand I year formulae *(continued)*

King	Year	Year formula (partly reconstructed)	Source
			434?; 463; BC 211–212; 238–239; 244; 255; 263; 425; 435
	Aa O	mu a.a-dàra-galam.ma lugal.e kalam.ma.a.ni mu.un.bal.e	CUSAS 9, 435; another unidentified text (Dalley 2009: 12)
	Aa P	mu a.a-dàra-galam.ma lugal.e [...] MU NI é.kur? ba.dù?	CUSAS 9, 243
Ea-gāmil	Eg 4	mu ^{d}*é-a-ga-mil* lugal.[x] mu ki 4	QA 94.46

The years designated by a capital letter refer to Dalley's (2009: 10–12) analysis of the formulae attested in the archive published in CUSAS 9. Dalley (2009: 12) mentions another possible year name (Q) too damaged for reconstruction in CUSAS 9, 137, but that text features in fact the year N and I could not find another corresponding text. I concur with Dalley (*ibid*) that the year name R was probably a scribal mistake for N; it is included as such in the table.

The unpublished text BC 218 apparently features an unidentified year formula of Ayadaragalama (Dalley 2009: 282). With the exception of the year formula of text BC 363, the year names of the tablets in the Belgian Collection have not been published yet; their attribution to a specific year in Table 19 is based on the information provided in Dalley 2009: *passim*. The dating of the texts from Tell Khaiber is based on the transliterations available on oracc.museum.upenn.edu/urap/corpus.

The year formula featuring Gulkišar in a glass-making treatise (BM 120960) is not included because it is almost certainly a forgery (see Section 4.7).

Appendix 3: Text numbers corresponding to Table 8

Table 21: Texts numbers corresponding to Table 8

Function	Aspect of the transaction	Main key word	Texts CUSAS 9,...
Incoming goods	Delivery (to the palace)	MU.DU	16–26; 26A; 27–58; 78; 91; 107; 155; 157; 162A; 168; 172–173; 175–180; 183; 189–192; 195; 197–199; 203–204; 211; 213; 216–217; 220; 222; 225–231; 234; 237–238; 240–241; 243; 246–259; (260); 261–268; 270–295; (296); 297–342; 342A; 343–350; 350A; 352–353; 353A; 354–355; 355A; 356–365; 365A; 366–367; 413; 413A; 415; 419–420; 425–426; 428; 431A; 432; 434; (442); 443; (445); 446; 458; 461
		wabālu	113
		ana	94; 120; 370
	Purchase	*šâmu*	421
Incoming goods & material outgoing/ transferred for transformation	Delivery (to the palace) & reception	MU.DU & ŠU.TI.A	151; 161; 232; 409; (419); 422; 424; 436
		MU.DU & *maḫāru*	368
	(Delivery) to the palace & expenditure	*ana* É.GAL & exp.	121
Material outgoing /transferred for transformation	Reception	ŠU.TI.A	85; 131; 152–154; 156; 158–160; 162–165; 165A; 166–167; 169; 171; 174; 181–182; 184–187; 188A; 196; 201–202; 205–210; 212; 214; 218–219; 221; 223–224; 233; 235–236; 239; 242; 244; (245); 416; 418;
		maḫāru	372
	–	–	143
	Expenditure & reception	*nadānu* & ŠU.TI.A	452; 459

https://doi.org/10.1515/9781501507823-011

Table 21: Texts numbers corresponding to Table 8 *(continued)*

Function	Aspect of the transaction	Main key word	Texts CUSAS 9,...
Outgoing goods (...)	Reception	ŠU.TI.A	29A; 93; 97; (102); 103; 108; 111; 123; 125; 128; 135; 140; (142); 145; (245); 371; 412; 437; 439; 448; 455; 462
		maḫāru	64; 98; 114–116; 119; 122; 127; 129–130; 134; 136; 137; 139; 188; 200; 373; 379
	Expenditure & reception	*nadānu* & ŠU.TI.A	106; 132
		nadānu & *maḫāru*	96
	Expenditure	ZI.GA	77; 414; 417
		nadānu	(59); 63; 65–66; 73; 75; 88; 95; 99–101; 104–105; 109–110; 112; 124; 138; 147; 378; 423; 433
		SUM	76
		ZI.GA & *nadānu?*	269
		naqû	68–69
		ana	60; 62; 79; 87; 89; 133; 144; 456–457; 460
		–	61; 67; (70); 71–72; 74; 84; 86; 90; 117–118; 126; 148; 150; 368A; 369; 374–377; 380; 383; 385–395; 407–408; 431; 440; 451
Other or unclear			141; 146; 429; 444; 449; 450; 453

Bibliography

Abraham, Kathleen, and Uri Gabbay. 2013. Kaštiliašu and the Sumundar Canal: A New Middle Babylonian Royal Inscription. *ZA* 103 (2): 183–95.

Abraham, Kathleen, Karel Van Lerberghe, and Gabriella Voet. 2017. *A Late Old Babylonian military archive from Dur-Abieshuh.* CUSAS 29. Bethesda: CDL Press.

Adams, Robert McC. 1981. *Heartland of Cities.: Surveys of Ancient Settlement and Land Use on the Central Floodplain of the Euphrates.* Chicago, London: The University of Chicago Press.

Adams, Robert McC., and Hans J. Nissen. 1972. *The Uruk Countryside: The Natural Setting of Urban Societies.* Chicago, London: The University of Chicago Press.

Albertz, Rainer. 1978. *Persönliche Frömmigkeit und offizielle Religion.* Calwer Theologische Monographien 9. Stuttgart: Calwer Verlag.

al-Hamdani, Abdulamir. 2008. Protecting and Recording our Archaeological Heritage in Southern Iraq. *Near Eastern Archaeology* 71: 221–30.

al-Hamdani, Abdulamir. 2015. *Shadow States: The Archaeology of Power in the Marshes of Southern Mesopotamia.* Doctoral Dissertation submitted at Stony Brook University [under the name al-Dafar].

Alhawi, Nagham A., Badir N. Albadran, and Jennifer R. Pournelle. 2017. The Archaeological Sites along the Ancient Course of Euphrates River. *American Scientific Research Journal for Engineering, Technology, and Sciences* 29: 1–20.

al-Ubaid, Iman Jamil. 1983. *Unpublished Cuneiform Texts from Old Babylonian Period—Diyala Region, Tell Muhammad.* Master Thesis submitted to the University of Baghdad [in Arabic].

Amiet, Pierre. 1976. Introduction à l'étude archéologique du Panthéon systématique et des Panthéons locaux dans l'Ancien Orient. *Or.* 45: 15–32.

André-Salvini, Béatrice, and Pierre Lombard. 1997. La découverte épigraphique de 1995 à Qalʿat al-Bahrein: un jalon pour la chronologie de la phase Dilmoun Moyen dans le Golfe arabe. *Proceedings of the Seminar for Arabian Studies* 27: 165–70.

Annus, Amar. 2002. *The God Ninurta in the Mythology and Royal Ideology of Ancient Mesopotamia.* SAAS 14. Helsinki: The Neo-Assyrian Text Corpus Project.

Armstrong, James A., and Hermann Gasche. 2014. *Mesopotamian Pottery. A Guide to the Babylonian Tradition in the Second Millennium B.C.* MHE II/4. Ghent, Chicago: University of Ghent and The Oriental Institute of the University of Chicago.

Arnaud, Daniel. 1976. Larsa. Catalogue des textes et des objets inscrits trouvés au cours de la sixième campagne. *Syria* 53: 47–81.

Arnaud, Daniel. 2001. Le panthéon de l'Ebabbar de Larsa à l'époque paléo-babylonienne. Pp. 21–32 in *Études mésopotamiennes: Recueil de textes offert à Jean-Louis Huot*, ed. Catherine Breniquet, and Christine Kepinski. Paris: Éditions Recherche sur les Civilisations.

Arnaud, Daniel. 2007. Documents à contenu 'historique', de l'époque présargonique au VIe siècle. *AulaOr.* 25: 5–84.

Baker, Heather D. 2011. Babylonian Land Survey in Socio-political Context. Pp. 293–323 in *The Empirical Dimension of Ancient Near Eastern Studies*, ed. Gebhard J. Selz. WOO 6. Vienna: Lit Verlag.

https://doi.org/10.1515/9781501507823-012

Balkan, Kemal. 1954. *Kassitenstudien. 1. Die Sprache der Kassiten.* AOS 37. New Haven: American Oriental Society.

Bartelmus, Alexa. 2010. Restoring the Past. A Historical Analysis of the Royal Temple Building Inscriptions from the Kassite Period. *Kaskal* 7: 143–71.

Bartelmus, Alexa. 2016. *Fragmente einer großen Sprache: Sumerisch im Kontext der Schreiberausbildung des kassitenzeitlichen Babyloniens.* Boston, Berlin: Walter de Gruyter.

Bauer, Josef. 1989–90. Altsumerische Wirtschaftsurkunden in Leningrad. *AfO* 36/37: 76–91.

Beaulieu, Paul-Alain. 1991. UBARA (EZENxKASKAL)^ki^ = Udannu. *ASJ* 13: 97–109.

Beaulieu, Paul-Alain. 1992a. Antiquarian Theology in Seleucid Uruk. *ASJ* 14: 47–75.

Beaulieu, Paul-Alain. 1992b. Kissik, Dūru and Udannu. *Or.* 61: 400–424.

Beaulieu, Paul-Alain. 1995. The Brewers of Nippur. *JCS* 47: 85–96.

Beaulieu, Paul-Alain. 2002a. Eanna = *Ayakkum* in the Basetki Inscription of Narām-Sîn. *NABU* 2002/2: no. 36.

Beaulieu, Paul-Alain. 2002b. Ea-dayān, Governor of the Sealand, and Other Dignitaries of the Neo- Babylonian Empire. *JCS* 54: 99–123.

Beaulieu, Paul-Alain. 2003. *The Pantheon of Uruk During the Neo-Babylonian Period.* CM23. Leiden, Boston: Brill, Styx.

Bedigian, Dorothea. 1985. Is še-giš-ì Sesame or Flax? Pp. 159–78 in *BSA* 2. Cambridge: University Press.

Biggs, Robert D. 1998–2001. Nin-Nibru. Pp. 476–77 in *RlA* 9. Berlin, New York: Walter de Gruyter.

Boehmer, Rainer M. 1991a. Die Keramik: Die Typen und ihre Verbreitung nach Zeitstufen. Mittelbabylonische Zeit. Pp. 100–02 in *Uruk. Kampagne 35–37. 1982–1984. Die archäologische Oberflächenuntersuchung (Survey),* ed. Uwe Finkbeiner. AUWE 4 Text. Mainz: Philipp von Zabern.

Boehmer, Rainer M. 1991b. Die historische Topographie von Uruk-Warka. Mittelbabylonische Zeit. Pp. 207–08 in *Uruk. Kampagne 35–37. 1982–1984. Die archäologische Oberflächenuntersuchung (Survey),* ed. Uwe Finkbeiner. AUWE 4 Text. Mainz: Philipp von Zabern.

Boese, Johannes. 2008. 'Ḫarbašipak', 'Tiptakzi' und die Chronologie der älteren Kassitenzeit. *ZA* 98: 201–10.

Boivin, Odette. 2015. Kār-Šamaš as a south-western palace town of the Sealand I kingdom. *NABU* 2008/4: no. 97.

Boivin, Odette. 2016a. On the origin of the goddess Ištar-of-the-Sealand, Ayabbītu. *NABU* 2016/1: no. 15.

Boivin, Odette. 2016b. Agricultural Economy and Taxation in the Sealand I Kingdom. *JCS* 68: 45–65.

Boivin, Odette. 2016c. Accounting for Livestock: Principles of Palatial Administration in Sealand I Babylonia. *Iraq* 78: 3–23.

Boivin, Odette. forthcoming. The Palace as Economic Production Unit in the Sealand I Kingdom. In *Studies on the Sealand and Babylonia under the Kassites—Proceedings of Workshop Held at the 62nd RAI* [provisory title], ed. Susanne Paulus and Tim Clayden. SANER. Berlin, Boston: Walter de Gruyter.

Bottéro, Jean. 1958. Lettres de la salle 110 du Palais de Mari. *RA* 52: 163–76.

Bottéro, Jean. 1995. *Textes culinaires mésopotamiens.* MC 6. Winona Lake: Eisenbrauns.

Breniquet, Catherine. 2009. Boire de la bière en Mésopotamie… Pp. 183–96 in *Et il y eut un esprit dans l'homme. Jean Bottéro et la Mésopotamie,* ed. Xavier Faivre, Brigitte Lion, and Cécile Michel. Travaux de la Maison René-Ginouvès 6. Paris: de Boccard.

Bridges, Susan J. 1981. *The Mesag Archive : A Study of Sargonic Society and Economy.* Doctoral dissertation submitted at Yale University.

Brinkman, John A. 1963. Provincial Administration in Babylonia under the Second Dynasty of Isin. *JESHO* 6: 233–42.

Brinkman, John A. 1964. Merodach-Baladan II. Pp. 6–53 in *Studies Presented to A. Leo Oppenheim*, ed. Robert D. Biggs and John A. Brinkman. Chicago: The Oriental Institute of the University of Chicago.

Brinkman, John A. 1968. *A Political History of Post-Kassite Babylonia 1158–722 B.C.* AnOr 43. Rome: Pontificium Institutum Biblicum.

Brinkman, John A. 1976. *Materials and Studies for Kassite History I. A Catalogue of Cuneiform Sources Pertaining to Specific Monarchs of the Kassite Dynasty.* Chicago: The Oriental Institute of the University of Chicago.

Brinkman, John A. 1977. Mesopotamian Chronology of the Historical Period. Pp. 335–48 in A. Leo Oppenheim, *Ancient Mesopotamia, Portrait of a Dead Civilization.* Revised Edition. Chicago: University of Chicago Press.

Brinkman, John A. 1990. The Babylonian Chronicle Revisited. Pp. 73–104 in *Lingering over Words. Studies in Ancient Near Eastern Literature in Honor of William L. Moran,* ed. Tzvi Abusch et al. HSS 37. Atlanta: Scholars Press.

Brinkman, John A. 1993–97. Meerland. Pp. 6–10 in *RlA* 8. Berlin, New York: Walter de Gruyter.

Brinkman, John A. 2003–05. Pešgaldarameš (Pešgaldaramaš). P. 436 in *RlA* 10. Berlin, New York: Walter de Gruyter.

Brinkman, John A. 2015. Dating YBC 2242, the Kadašman-Ḫarbe I stone. *NABU* 2015/1: no. 18.

Brunke, Hagan. 2011. *Essen in Sumer: Metrologie, Herstellung und Terminologie nach Zeugnis der Ur III-zeitlichen Wirtschaftsurkunden.* Geschichtswissenschaften 26. Munich: Herbert Utz Verlag.

Brunke, Hagan, and Walther Sallaberger. 2010. Aromata für Duftöle. Pp. 41–74 in *Why Should Someone Who Knows Something Conceal It?, Cuneiform Studies in Honor of David I. Owen on His 70th Birthday,* ed. Alexandra Kleinerman and Jack M. Sasson. Bethesda: CDL Press.

Buccellati, Giorgio. 1996. *A Structural Grammar of Babylonian.* Wiesbaden: Harrassowitz Verlag.

Campbell, Stuart, Jane Moon, Robert Killick, Daniel Calderbank, Eleonor Robson, Mary Shepperdson, and Fay Slater. 2017. Tell Khaiber: an administrative centre of the Sealand period. *Iraq* 79: 21–46.

Cavigneaux, Antoine, and Béatrice André-Salvini. forthcoming. Cuneiform Tablets from Qal'a. Dilmun and the Sealand at the dawn of the Kassite era. In *Twenty Years of Bahrain Archaeology,* 1986–2006. Actes du colloque international de Manama, 9–12 décembre 2007, ed. Pierre Lombard and Khalid M. al-Sindi. Ministry of Culture, Bahrain.

Cavigneaux, Antoine, and Manfred Krebernik. 1998–2001. ^{d}Nin-é-NIM-ma. P. 349 in *RlA* 9. Berlin, New York: Walter de Gruyter.

Charles, Michael P. 1984. Introductory Remarks on the Cereals. Pp. 17–31 in *BSA* 1. Cambridge: University Press.

Charles, Michael P. 1985. An Introduction to the Legumes and Oil Plants of Mesopotamia. Pp. 39–61 in *BSA* 2. Cambridge: University Press.

Charles, Michael P. 1987. Onions, Cucumbers and the Date Palm. Pp. 1–21 in *BSA* 3. Cambridge: University Press.

Charpin, Dominique. 1981. La Babylonie de Samsu-iluna à la lumière de nouveaux documents. *BiOr* 38: 518–47.

Charpin, Dominique. 1986. *Le clergé d'Ur au siècle d'Hammurabi (XIXe-XVIIIe siècles av. J.-C.).* Hautes études orientales 22. Paris: Librairie Droz.

Charpin, Dominique. 1992. Immigrés, réfugiés et déportés en Babylonie sous Hammu-rabi et ses successeurs. Pp. 207–18 in *La circulation des biens, des personnes et des idées dans le Proche-Orient ancien*, ed. Dominique Charpin and Francis Joannès. CRRAI 38. Paris: Éditions Recherche sur les Civilisations.

Charpin, Dominique. 1995. La fin des archives dans le Palais de Mari. *RA* 89: 29–40.

Charpin, Dominique. 1997. D.J.Wiseman et J.A. Black, *Literary Texts from the Temple of Nabû, Cuneiform Texts from Nimrud* IV, Londres, 1996. *RA* 91: 188–90.

Charpin, Dominique. 1998. Iluni, roi d'Ešnunna. *NABU* 1998/1: no. 29.

Charpin, Dominique. 1999–2000. R. Pientka, Die spätaltbabylonische Zeit: Abiešuḫ bis Samsuditana. Quellen, Jahresdaten, Geschiche. xiv+696 pp. en 2 vol. Münster, Rhema, 1998 (= *Imgula* 2). DM 100,–. *AfO* 46/47: 322–24.

Charpin, Dominique. 2000. Les prêteurs et le palais: les édits de *mîšarum* des rois de Babylone et leurs traces dans les archives privées. Pp.185–211 in *Interdependency of Institutions and Private Entrepreneurs*, ed. A.C.V.M. Bongenaar. MOS 2 = PIHANS 87. Leiden: Nederlands Historisch-archaeologisch Instituut te Istanbul.

Charpin, Dominique. 2002. La politique hydraulique des rois paléo-babyloniens. *Annales. Histoire, Sciences sociales* 57/3: 545–59.

Charpin, Dominique. 2004. Histoire politique du Proche-Orient amorrite (2002–1595). Pp. 23–482 in *Mesopotamien. Die altbabylonische Zeit.* OBO 160/4. Fribourg, Göttingen: Academic Press, Vandenhoeck & Ruprecht Verlag.

Charpin, Dominique. 2014. Chroniques bibliographiques 15. Le royaume d'Uruk et le pays d'Apum, deux voisins de Babylone vaincus par Samsu-iluna. *RA* 108: 121–60.

Charpin, Dominique. 2015a. En marge d'Archibab, 21: noms d'années du roi Damiq-ilishu d'Isin. *NABU* 2015/2: no. 35.

Charpin, Dominique. 2015b. Chroniques bibliographiques 17. Six nouveaux recueils de documents paléo-babyloniens. *RA* 109: 143–96.

Charpin, Dominique, Francis Joannès, Sylvie Lackenbacher, and Bertrand Lafont. 1988. *Archives épistolaires de Mari I/2.* ARM 26. Paris: Éditions Recherche sur les Civilisations.

Chiera, Edward. 1914. *Legal and Administrative Documents from Nippur Chiefly from the Dynasties of Isin and Larsa.* PBS 8/1. Philadelphia: University of Pennsylvania.

Civil, Miguel. 1987. Ur III Bureaucracy: Quantitative Aspects. Pp. 43–53 in *The Organization of Power. Aspects of Bureaucracy in the Ancient Near East*, ed. McGuire Gibson and Robert D. Biggs. SAOC 46. Chicago: The University of Chicago.

Civil, Miguel, et al. 1969. *The Series* lú = *ša and Related Texts.* MSL XII. Rome: Pontificium Institutum Biblicum.

Civil, Miguel, et al. 1979. Ea A = *nâqu,* Aa A = *nâqu, with their Forerunners and Related Texts.* MSL XIV. Rome: Pontificium Institutum Biblicum.

Clayden, Tim. 2014. Kassite Housing at Ur: The Dates of the EM, YC, XNCF, AH and KPS Houses. *Iraq* 76: 19–64.

Cohen, Mark E. 1993. *The Cultic Calendars of the Ancient Near East.* Bethesda: CDL Press.

Cole, Steven W. 1994. Marsh Formation in the Borsippa Region and the Course of the Lower Euphrates. *JNES* 53: 81–109.

Cole, Steven W., and Hermann Gasche. 1998. Second- and First-Millennium BC Rivers in Northern Babylonia. Pp. 1–64 in *Changing Watercourses in Babylonia. Towards a Reconstruction of the Ancient Environment in Lower Mesopotamia.* Vol.I, ed. Hermann Gasche and Michel Tanret. MHE II/V. Ghent: University of Ghent and the Oriental Institute of the University of Chicago.

Cooley, Jeffrey. 2016. A Scribalized Past: VR44's Onomastic Reflections on the History of the Land. Paper presented at the 62nd Rencontre assyriologique internationale, Philadelphia, July 10–15, 2016.

Cooper, Jerrold S. 1972. Bilinguals from Boghazköi.II. *ZA* 62: 62–81.

Cooper, Jerrold S. 1980. Apodotic Death and the Historicity of 'Historical' Omens. Pp. 99–105 in *Death in Mesopotamia,* ed. Bendt Alster. CRRAI 26. Mesopotamia 8. Copenhagen: Akademisk forlag.

Crawford, Harriet. 2001. *Early Dilmun Seals from Saar. Art and Commerce in Bronze Age Bahrain.* Ludlow: Archaeology International.

Crawford, Vaughn E. 1974. Lagash. *Iraq* 36: 29–35.

Dalley, Stephanie. 2005. *Old Babylonian Texts in the Ashmolean Museum, mainly from Larsa, Sippir, Kish and Lagaba.* OECT 15. Oxford: Oxford University Press.

Dalley, Stephanie. 2009. *Babylonian Tablets from The First Sealand Dynasty in the Schøyen Collection.* CUSAS 9. Bethesda: CDL Press.

Dalley, Stephanie. 2013. Gods from north-eastern and north-western Arabia in cuneiform texts from the First Sealand Dynasty, and a cuneiform inscription from Tell en-Naṣbeh, *c.* 1500 BC. *Arabian archaeology and epigraphy* 24(2): 177–85.

de Genouillac, Henri. 1923. Grande liste de noms divins sumériens. *RA* 20: 89–106.

Deheselle, Danielle. 2004. Meuniers et brasseurs kassites, travailleurs itinérants. Pp. 273–85 in *Nomades et sédentaires dans le Proche-Orient ancien,* ed. Christophe Nicolle. CRRAI 46=Amurru 3. Paris: Éditions Recherche sur les Civilisations.

Delnero, Paul A. 2016. Literature and Identity in Mesopotamia during the Old Babylonian Period. Pp. 19–50 in *Problems of Canonicity and Identity Formation in Ancient Egypt and Mesopotamia.* K. Ryholt and G. Barjamovic, ed. CNI Publications 43. Copenhagen: Museum Tusculanum Press.

Devecchi, Elena. forthcoming. *Middle Babylonian Texts in the Cornell University Collections. II. The Early Kings.* CUSAS. Bethesda: CDL Press.

Dietrich, Manfried. 2003. *The Babylonian Correspondence of Sargon and Sennacherib.* SAA 17. Helsinki: Helsinki University Press.

Dossin, Georges. 1950. Le panthéon de Mari. Pp. 41–50 in *Studia Mariana,* ed. André Parrot. Documenta et Monumenta Orientis Antiquis 4. Leiden: Brill.

Dossin, Georges. 1967. Un 'panthéon' d'Ur III à Mari. *RA* 61: 97–104.

Dougherty, Raymond P. 1932. *The Sealand of Ancient Arabia.* YOSR 19. New Haven: Yale University Press.

Durand, Jean-Marie. 1985. La situation historique des šakkanakku: nouvelle approche. Pp. 147–72 in *MARI* 4. Paris: Éditions Recherche sur les civilisations.

Durand, Jean-Marie. 2013. La 'suprématie élamite' sur les Amorrites. Réexamen, vingt ans après la XXXVIe RAI (1989). Pp. 329–39. in *Susa and Elam. Archaeological, Philological, Historical and Geographical Perspectives.* Proceedings of the International Congress held at Ghent University, Dec. 14–17, 2009, ed. Katrien De Graef and Jan Tavernier. MDP 58. Leiden, Boston: Brill.

Eastlake, F.W. 1881–82. URUKU *versus* ŠIŠKU. *PSBA* 4: 36–40.

Ebeling, Erich. 1939. *Die Eigennamen der mittelassyrischen Rechts- und Geschäftsurkunden.* MAOG 13(1). Leipzig: Verlag von Otto Harrassowitz.

Edzard, Dietz-Otto. 1957. *Die "zweite Zwischenzeit" Babyloniens.* Wiesbaden: Otto Harrassowitz Verlag.

Edzard, Dietz-Otto. 2003–05. Palast. A. III. Altbabylonisch. Pp. 205–08 in *RlA* 10. Berlin, New York: Walter de Gruyter.

Edzard, Dietz-Otto. 2004. Altbabylonische Literatur und Religion. Pp. 481–640 in *Mesopotamien. Die altbabylonische Zeit.* OBO 160/4. Fribourg, Göttingen: Academic Press, Vandenhoeck & Ruprecht Verlag.

Eidem, Jesper. 2011. *The Royal Archives from Tell Leilan. Old Babylonian Letters and Treaties from the Lower Town Palace East.* PIHANS 117. Leiden: Nederlands Instituut voor het Nabije Oosten.

Elayi, Josette. 1984. Terminologie de la Mer Méditerranée dans les annales assyriennes. *OrAnt* 23: 75–92.

Englund, Robert K. 1990. *Organisation und Verwaltung der Ur III-Fischerei.* BBVO 10. Berlin: Dietrich Reimer Verlag.

Espak, Peeter. 2015. *The God Enki in Sumerian Royal Ideology and Mythology.* Philippika Altertumswissenschaftliche Abhandlungen—Contributions to the Study of Ancient World Cultures 87. Wiesbaden: Otto Harrassowitz Verlag.

Falkenstein, Adam. 1963. Zu den Inschriftenfunden der Grabung in Uruk-Warka 1960–1961. *BagM* 2: 1–82.

Falkenstein, Adam. 1966. *Die Inschriften Gudeas von Lagaš. I. Einleitung.* AnOr 30. Rome: Pontificum Institutum Biblicum.

Feigin, Samuel I., and Benno Landsberger. 1955. The Date List of the Babylonian King Samsu-ditana. *JNES* 14: 137–60.

Fiette, Baptiste. 2017. Note sur les toponymes du Sud mésopotamiens, 3: Kar-Šamaš. *NABU* 2017/3: no.70.

Finkel, Irving L. 1980. Bilingual Chronicle Fragments. *JCS* 32: 65–80.

Fitzgerald, Madeleine A. 2002. *The Rulers of Larsa.* Doctoral dissertation submitted at Yale University.

Földi, Zsombor. 2014. Cuneiform Texts in the *Kunsthistorisches Museum Wien*, Part IV: A New Text from Dūr Abī-ēšuḫ" in *WZKM* 104: 31–55.

Földi, Zsombor. 2017. Cuneiform Tablets and the Antiquities Market: The Archives from Dūr-Abī-ešuḫ. *Distant World Journal* 2: 7–27.

Frankena, Rintje. 1957–71. Gula A. Pp. 695–697 in *RlA* 3. Berlin, New York: Walter de Gruyter.

Frayne, Douglas R. 1990. *Old Babylonian Period (2003–1595 BC).* RIME 4. Toronto: University of Toronto Press.

Frazer, Mary. 2016. 'Gilgamesh, King of Ur': The Letter of Gilgamesh in Context. Paper presented at the 62nd RAI, held in Philadelphia, July 11–15, 2016.

Gabbay, Uri. 2014a. A Balaĝ to Enlil from the First Sealand Dynasty. *ZA* 104: 146–70.

Gabbay, Uri. 2014b. *Pacifying the Hearts of the Gods.* Heidelberger Emesal-Studien 1. Wiesbaden: Harrassowitz Verlag.

Gabbay, Uri, and Odette Boivin. forthcoming. A Hymn of Ayadaragalama, King of the First Sealand Dynasty, to the Gods of Nippur. The Fate of Nippur and its Cult during the First Sealand Dynasty. *ZA.*

Gadd, Cyril J., and Reginald Campbell Thompson. 1936. A Middle-Babylonian Chemical Text. *Iraq* 3: 87–96; plate IV.

Galter, Hannes D. 1983. *Der Gott Ea/Enki in der akkadischen Überlieferung. Eine Bestandsaufnahme des vorhandenen Materials.* Dissertationen der Karl-Franzens-Universität Graz 58. Graz: DBV Verlag für die Technische Universität Graz.

Gasche, Hermann. 1989. *La Babylonie au 17e siècle avant notre ère: approche archéologique, problèmes et perspectives.* MHE II/1. Ghent: University of Ghent.

Gasche, Hermann, James A. Armstrong, Steven W. Cole, and Vahagn G. Gurzadyan. 1998. *Dating the Fall of Babylon. A Reappraisal of Second-Millennium Chronology.* MHE II/ IV. Ghent: University of Ghent and the Oriental Institute of the University of Chicago.

Gasche, Hermann, Michel Tanret, Steven W. Cole, and Kris Verhoeven. 2002. Fleuves du temps et de la vie: Permanence et instabilité du réseau fluviatile babylonien entre 2500 et 1500 avant notre ère. *Annales. Histoire, Sciences Sociales* 57/3: 531–44.

Gasche, Hermann, et al. 2007. The Persian Gulf Shorelines and the Karkheh, Karun, and Jarrahi Rivers: A Geo-Archaeological Approach. First Progress Report—Part 3. *Akkadica* 128: 1–72.

Gentili, Paolo. 2002. The 'Strange(r)' Month Names of Tell Muhammad and the Diyāla Calendars. *Egitto e Vicino Oriente* 25: 203–30.

George, Andrew R. 1992. *Babylonian Topographical Texts.* OLA 40. Leuven: Peeters Press and Department Oriëntalistiek.

George, Andrew R. 1993. *House Most High. The Temples of Ancient Mesopotamia.* MC 5. Winona Lake: Eisenbrauns.

George, Andrew R. 2005. AMAR ANNUS: The God Ninurta in the Mythology and Royal Ideology of Ancient Mesopotamia. (State Archives of Assyria Studies Vol. 14.) xvi, 242 pp. Helsinki: University of Helsinki, Neo-Assyrian Text Corpus Project, 2002. *Bulletin of the School of Oriental and African Studies* 68 (2): 307–09.

George, Andrew R. 2007. The civilizing of Ea-Enkidu: an unusual tablet of the Babylonian Gilgameš epic. *RA* 101: 59–80.

George, Andrew R. 2009. *Babylonian Literary Texts in the Schøyen Collection.* CUSAS 10. Bethesda: CDL Press.

George, Andrew R. 2011. Other Second-Millennium Royal and Commemorative Inscriptions & Sumero- Babylonian King Lists and Date Lists. Pp. 89–125; 199–209 in *Cuneiform Royal Inscriptions and Related Texts in the Schøyen Collection,* ed. Andrew R. George. CUSAS 17. Bethesda: CDL Press.

George, Andrew R. 2013. *Babylonian Divinatory Texts Chiefly in the Schøyen Collection.* CUSAS 18. Bethesda: CDL Press.

Gibson, McGuire. 1992. Patterns of Occupation at Nippur. Pp. 33–54 in *Nippur at the Centennial,* ed. Maria deJong Ellis. CRRAI 35=OPSNKF 14. Philadelphia: University of Pennsylvania Museum.

Gibson, McGuire. 2012. Nippur. Pp. 116–22 in *The Oriental Institute 2011–2012 Annual Report,* ed. Gil J. Stein. Chicago: The Oriental Institute.

Gibson, McGuire. 2016. Nippur. Pp. 128–29 in *The Oriental Institute 2015–2016 Annual Report,* ed. Gil J. Stein. Chicago: The Oriental Institute.

Gibson, McGuire, Donald P. Hansen, and Richard L. Zettler. 1998–2001. Nippur. B. Archäologisch. Pp. 546–65 in *RlA* 9. Berlin, New York: Walter de Gruyter.

Glassner, Jean-Jacques. 1986. *La chute d'Akkadé. L'événement et sa mémoire.* BBVO 5. Berlin: Dietrich Reimer Verlag.

Glassner, Jean-Jacques. 1993. Chronologie élamite et chroniques mésopotamiennes. *NABU* 1993/2: no.38.

Glassner, Jean-Jacques. 1997. L'historien mésopotamien et l'événement. *Mètis. Anthropologie des mondes grecs anciens* 12: 97–117.

Glassner, Jean-Jacques. 2004. *Mesopotamian Chronicles.* Writings from the Ancient World 19. Atlanta: Society of Biblical Literature.

Goddeeris, Anne. 2002. *Economy and Society in Northern Babylonia in the Early Old Babylonian Period (ca.2000–1800 BC).* OLA 109. Leuven: Peeters.

Goddeeris, Anne. 2016. *The Old Babylonian Legal and Administrative Texts in the Hilprecht Collection Jena.* TMH 10. Wiesbaden: Harrassowitz.

Goetze, Albrecht. 1945. The Akkadian Dialects of the Old-Babylonian Mathematical Texts. Pp. 146–51 in *Mathematical Cuneiform Texts,* ed. Otto Neugebauer and Abraham Sachs. AOS 29. New Haven: American Oriental Society and the American Schools of Oriental Research.

Goetze, Albrecht. 1947. Historical Allusions in Old Babylonian Omen Texts. *JCS* 1: 253–66.

Goetze, Albrecht. 1957. On the Chronology of the Second Millennium. *JCS* 11: 53–61; 63–73.

Goetze, Albrecht. 1964. The Kassites and Near Eastern Chronology. *JCS* 18: 97–101.

Grayson, Albert K. 1975. *Assyrian and Babylonian Chronicles.* TCS 5. Locust Valley: J.J. Augustin Publisher.

Grayson, Albert K. 1980–83. Königslisten und Chroniken. Pp. 77–135 in *RlA* 6. Berlin, New York: Walter de Gruyter.

Green, Margaret W. 1975. *Eridu in Sumerian Literature.* Dissertation presented at the University of Chicago.

Groneberg, Brigitte. 1980. *Die Orts- und Gewässernamen der altbabylonischen Zeit.* RGTC 3. Beihefte zum TAVO. Wiesbaden: Dr. Ludwig Reichert Verlag.

Guichard, Michaël. 2016. Guerre et diplomatie: Lettres d'Iluni roi d'Ešnunna d'une collection privée. *Semitica* 58: 17–59.

Haas, Volkert. 2003. *Materia Magica et Medica Hethitica.* Berlin, New York: Walter de Gruyter.

Hallo, William W. 1957. *Early Mesopotamian Royal Titles: A Philologic and Historical Analysis.* AOS 43. New Haven: American Oriental Society.

Hallo, William W. 1975. Toward a History of Sumerian Literature. Pp.181–203 in *Sumerological Studies in Honor of Thorkild Jacobsen,* ed. Stephen J. Lieberman. AS 20. Chicago, London: The University of Chicago Press.

Hallo, William W. 1983. Dating the Mesopotamian Past: The Concept of Eras from Sargon to Nabonassar. *Bulletin of the CSMS* 6: 7–18.

Hallo, William W. 1991. The Royal Correspondence of Larsa: III. The Princess and the Plea. Pp. 377–88 in *Marchands, diplomates et empereurs. Etudes sur la civilisation mésopotamienne offertes à Paul Garelli*, ed. Dominique Charpin and Francis Joannès. Paris: Éditions Recherche sur les Civilisations.

Hamidović, David. 2014. Alphabetical Inscriptions from the Sealand. *Studia Mesopotamica* 1: 137–55.

Hamza, Hussein A. 2011. Tall Muḥammad. The Eighth Season of Excavations. Pp. 405–16 in *Between the Cultures. The Central Tigris Region from the 3rd to the 1st Millennium BC.* Proceedings of a conference held at Heidelberg, Jan. 22–24, 2009, ed. Peter A. Miglus and Simone Mühl. HSAO 14. Heidelberg: Heidelberger Orientverlag.

Hartman, Louis F., and A. Leo Oppenheim. 1950. *On Beer and Brewing Techniques in Ancient Mesopotamia. JAOS* Suppl. 10. Baltimore: American Oriental Society.

Haussperger, Martha. 2012. *Die mesopotamische Medizin aus ärztlicher Sicht.* Baden-Baden: Deutscher Wissenschafts-Verlag.

Heimpel, Wolfgang. 1986. The Sun at Night and the Doors of Heaven in Babylonian Texts. *JCS* 38: 127–51.

Heimpel, Wolfgang. 1987. Das Untere Meer. *ZA* 77: 22–91.

Heimpel, Wolfgang. 1998–2001. Nanše. A.Philologisch. Pp. 152–60 in *RlA* 9. Berlin, New York: Walter de Gruyter.

Heinz, Marlies. 1995. Migration und Assimilation im 2. Jt. v. Chr.: Die Kassiten. Pp. 165–74 in *Zwischen Euphrat und Indus, Aktuelle Forschungsprobleme in der Vorderasiatischen Archäologie.* K. Bartl, R. Bernbeck and M. Heinz, ed. Hildesheim: Georg Olms.

Hinz, Walther. 1967. Elams Vertrag mit Narām-Sîn von Akkade. *ZA* 58: 66–96.

Hoffmann, Inge. 1984. *Der Erlaß Telepinus.* THeth. 11. Heidelberg: Carl Winter Universitätsverlag.

Høljund, Flemming. 1989. Dilmun and the Sealand. Pp. 9–14 in *Northern Akkad Project Reports.* Vol. 2. Ghent: University of Ghent.

Hölscher, Monika. 1996. *Die Personennamen der kassitenzeitlichen Texte aus Nippur.* IMGULA 1. Münster: Rhema-Verlag.

Hommel, Fritz. 1904. *Grundriss der Geographie und Geschichte des Alten Orients. Erste Hälfte: Ethnologie des Alten Orients. Babylonien und Chaldäa.* 2nd edition. München: C.H. Beck'sche Verlagsbuchhandlung.

Horowitz, Wayne. 1998. *Mesopotamian Cosmic Geography.* MC 8. Winona Lake: Eisenbrauns.

Horsnell, Malcolm J.A. 1999. *The Year-Names of the First Dynasty of Babylon* Mesopotamia. 2 vols. Hamilton: McMaster University Press.

Hritz, Carrie. 2010. Tracing Settlement Patterns and Channel Systems in Southern Mesopotamia Using Remote Sensing. *Journal of Field Archaeology* 35 (2): 184–203.

Hritz, Carrie, Jennifer Pournelle, and Jennifer Smith. 2012. Revisiting the Sealands: Report of Preliminary Ground Reconnaissance in the Hammar District, Dhi Qar and Basra Governorates, Iraq. *Iraq* 74: 37–49.

Hruška, Blahoslav. 1969. Das spätbabylonische Lehrgedicht 'Inannas Erhöhung'. *ArOr* 37: 473–522.

Hunger, Hermann. 1968. *Babylonische und assyrische Kolophone.* AOAT 2. Kevelaer, Neukirchen-Vluyn: Verlag Butzon & Bercker and Neukirchener Verlag.

Huot, Jean-Louis. 2014. *L'*E.babbar *de Larsa aux IIe et Ier millénaires (Fouilles de 1974 à 1985).* BAH 205. Beyrouth, Damas: Presses de l'IFPO.

Hüsing, Georg. 1906. Karduniaš. *OLZ* 9(12): 663–65.

Jacobsen, Thorkild. 1939. *The Sumerian King List.* AS 11. Chicago: The University of Chicago Press.

Jacobsen, Thorkild. 1940. Historical Data. Pp. 116–200 in *The Gimilsin Temple and the Palace of the Rulers at Tell Asmar,* ed. Henri Frankfort. OIP 43. Chicago: The University of Chicago Press.

Jacobsen, Thorkild. 1975. Religious Drama in Ancient Mesopotamia. Pp. 65–97 in *Unity & Diversity. Essays in the History, Literature, and Religion of the Ancient Near East,* ed. Hans Goedicke and Jimmy J.M. Roberts. Baltimore, London: The John Hopkins University Press.

Johns, Claude Hermann Walter. 1913. *Ancient Babylonia.* Cambridge: Cambridge University Press.

Jursa, Michael. 1995. *Die Landwirtschaft in Sippar in neubabylonischer Zeit.* AfO Beih. 25. Vienna: Institut für Orientalistik der Universität Wien.

Jursa, Michael. 2007. Die Söhne Kudurrus und die Herkunft der neubabylonischen Dynastie. *RA* 101: 125–36.

Keetman, Jan. 2017. Notes on of the god *Ja'u* and *Bīt-Ja'kīn. NABU* 2017/1: no. 18.

Kilmer, Anne D. 1963. The First Tablet of *malku = šarru* together with its Explicit Version. *JAOS* 83: 421–46.

King, Leonard W. 1907. *Chronicles Concerning Early Babylonian Kings.* 2 vols. London: Luzac and Co.

King, Leonard W. 1915 (Reprinted 1969). *A History of Babylon, from the Foundation of the Monarchy to the Persian Conquest.* New York: AMS Press.

Kingsbury, Edwin C. 1963. A Seven Day Ritual in the Old Babylonian Cult at Larsa. *HUCA* 34: 1–34.

Klein, Jacob. 1998–2001. Namtar. Pp. 142–45 in *RlA* 9. Berlin, New York: Walter de Gruyter.

Klengel, Horst. 1983. Bemerkungen zu den altbabylonischen Rechtsurkunden und Wirtschaftstexten aus Babylon (VS 22: 1–82). *AoF* 10(1): 5–48.

Koldewey, Robert. 1911 (Reprinted 1972). *Die Tempel von Babylon und Borsippa.* WVDOG 15. Osnabrück: Otto Zeller Verlag.

Komoróczy, Géza. 1976. Das Pantheon im Kult, in den Götterlisten und in der Mythologie. *Orientalia N.S.* 45: 80–86.

Kraus, Fritz R. 1951. Nippur und Isin nach altbabylonischen Rechtsurkunden. *JCS* 3: 1–228.

Kraus, Fritz R. 1964. Briefschreibübungen im altbabylonischen Schulunterricht. *JEOL* 16: 16–39.

Kraus, Fritz R. 1968. Sesam im Alten Mesopotamien. *JAOS* 88: 112–19.

Kraus, Fritz R. 1980. Der Brief des Gilgameš. *AnSt.* 30: 109–21.

Kraus, Fritz R., and Horst Klengel. 1983. Spät-altbabylonische Briefe aus Babylon (VS 22: 83–92). *AoF* 10(1): 49–63.

Krebernik, Manfred. 1987–90. Lugal-a'abba. P. 109 in *RlA* 7. Berlin, New York: Walter de Gruyter.

Krebernik, Manfred. 1993–97. Mondgott. A.I. In Mesopotamien. Pp. 360–69 in *RlA* 8. Berlin, New York: Walter de Gruyter.

Krebernik, Manfred. 2003–05. ^{d}peš-gal. P. 436 in *RlA* 10. Berlin, New York: Walter de Gruyter.

Krebernik, Manfred. 2009a. Šarrat-EANNA. P. 74 in *RlA* 12(1/2). Berlin, New York: Walter de Gruyter.

Krebernik, Manfred. 2009b. Šarrat-Ninua. P. 76 in *RlA* 12(1/2). Berlin, New York: Walter de Gruyter.

Krebernik, Manfred. 2009c. Šarrat-Nippur, UN-gal-Nibru. Pp. 76–77 in *RlA* 12(1/2). Berlin, New York: Walter de Gruyter.

Krebernik, Manfred. 2011. Sonnengott. A.I. In Mesopotamien. Philologisch. Pp. 599–611 in *RlA* 12(7/8). Berlin, New York: Walter De Gruyter.

Krebernik, Manfred. 2012. S/Šugallītu(m). Pp. 256–57 in *RlA* 13(3/4). Berlin, New York: Walter De Gruyter.

Kutscher, Raphael. 1976. Josef Bauer, *Altsumerische Wirtschaftstexte aus Lagasch.* Rome, Biblical Institute Press, 1972. *BiOr* 33: 195–98.

Labat, René. 1939. *Le caractère religieux de la royauté assyro-babylonienne.* Paris: Librairie d'Amérique et d'Orient Adrien Maisonneuve.

Lafont, Bertrand. 2010. Sur quelques dossiers des archives de Girsu. Pp. 167–79 in *Why Should Someone Who Knows Something Conceal It?, Cuneiform Studies in Honor of David I. Owen on His 70th Birthday,* ed. Alexandra Kleinerman and Jack M. Sasson. Bethesda: CDL Press.

Lambert, Wilfred G. 1957–71. Götterlisten. Pp. 473–79 in *RlA* 3. Berlin, New York: Walter de Gruyter.

Lambert, Wilfred G. 1967. The Gula Hymn of Bulluṭsa-rabi. *Or.* 36: 105–32.

Lambert, Wilfred G. 1974. The Home of the First Sealand Dynasty. *JCS* 26: 208–10.

Lambert, Wilfred G. 1975. The Historical Development of the Mesopotamian Pantheon: A Study in Sophisticated Polytheism. Pp. 191–200 in *Unity & Diversity. Essays in the History, Literature, and Religion of the Ancient Near East,* ed. Hans Goedicke and J.J.M. Roberts. Baltimore, London: The John Hopkins University Press.

Lambert, Wilfred G. 1982. The Hymn to the Queen of Nippur. Pp. 173–218 in *zikir šumim. Assyriological Studies Presented to F.R.Kraus,* ed. Govert van Driel, et al. Nederlands Instituut voor het Nabije Oosten Studia Francisci Scholten Memoriae Dicata 5. Leiden: Brill.

Lambert, Wilfred G. 1987–90a. Lugal-irra and Meslamta-ea. Pp. 143–45 in *RlA* 7. Berlin, New York: Walter de Gruyter.

Lambert, Wilfred G. 1987–90b. Lugal-namtarra. P. 150 in *RlA* 7. Berlin, New York: Walter de Gruyter.

Lambert, Wilfred G. 1987–90c. Manzi'at/Mazzi'at/Mazzât/Mazzêt. Pp. 344–46 in *RlA* 7. Berlin, New York: Walter de Gruyter.

Lambert, Wilfred G. 1990a. The Name of Nergal Again. *ZA* 80: 40–52.

Lambert, Wilfred G. 1990b. Samsu-iluna in Later Tradition. Pp. 27–34 in *De la Babylonie à la Syrie en passant par Mari.* Mélanges J.-R. Kupper, ed. Önhan Tunca. Liège: Université de Liège.

Lambert, Wilfred G. 2007. *Babylonian Oracle Questions.* MC 13. Winona Lake: Eisenbrauns.

Landsberger, Benno. 1954. Assyrische Königsliste und 'Dunkles Zeitalter.' *JCS* 8: 31–73; 106–33.

Laursen, Steffen T. 2016. Symbols of Dilmun's royal house—a primitive system of communication adopted from the late Indus world? *Arabian archaeology and epigraphy* 27: 2–18.

Laursen, Steffen, and Piotr Steinkeller. 2017. *Babylonia, the Gulf Region, and the Indus: Archaeological and Textual Evidence for Contact in the Third and Early Second Millennia B.C.* MC 21. Winona Lake: Eisenbrauns.

Lauth, F.J. 1880–81. Remarks on the name Šišku, *apud* Theophilus G. Pinches. Notes on a New List of Early Babylonian Kings: being a Continuation of the Paper read December 7th, 1880. *PSBA* 3: 37–48.

Leemans, W.F. 1960a. *Foreign Trade in the Old Babylonian Period.* SDIOA 6. Leiden: Brill.

Leemans, W.F. 1960b. The Trade Relations of Babylonia and the Question of Relations with Egypt in the Old Babylonian Period. *JESHO* 3(1): 21–37.

Leemans, W.F. 1960c. *Legal and Administrative Documents of the Time of Ḫammurabi and Samsuiluna (mainly from Lagaba).* SLB I(3). Leiden: E.J. Brill.

Leemans, W.F. 1968. Old Babylonian Letters and Economic History. A Review Article with a Digression on Foreign Trade. *JESHO* 11: 171–226.

Leemans, W.F. 1973. Quelques remarques à propos d'un texte concernant l'administration des terres vieux-babylonienne. Pp. 281–92 in *Symbolae Biblicae et Mesopotamicae Francisco Mario Theodoro de Liagre Böhl Dedicatae,* ed. Martin A. Beek et al. Leiden: E.J. Brill.

Leichty, Erle, and Christopher B.F. Walker. 2004. Three Babylonian Chronicle and Scientific Texts. Pp. 203–12 in *From the Upper Sea to the Lower Sea. Studies on the History of Assyria and Babylonia in Honour of A.K. Grayson,* ed. Grant Frame. PIHANS 101. Leiden: Nederlands Instituut voor het Nabije Oosten.

Linssen, Marc J.H. 2004. *The Cults of Uruk and Babylon. The Temple Ritual Texts as Evidence for Hellenistic Cult Practice.* CM 25. Leiden, Boston: Brill and Styx.

Litke, Richard L. 1998. *A Reconstruction of the Assyro-Babylonian God-Lists, AN: ^{d}A-nu-um and AN: Anu ša amēli.* TBC 3. New Haven: Yale Babylonian Collection.

Maekawa, Kazuya. 1985. Cultivation of Legumes and mun-gazi Plants in Ur III Girsu. Pp. 97–118 in *BSA* 2. Cambridge: University Press.

Matthews, Lucy P. 1970. *The First Dynasty of Babylon: History and Texts.* Doctoral dissertation submitted at the University of Birmingham.

Maul, Stefan M. 1994. *Zukunftsbewältigung.* BagF 18. Mainz: Verlag Philipp von Zabern.

McCown, Donald E., Richard C. Haines, and Donald P. Hansen. 1967. *Nippur. I. Temple of Enlil, Scribal Quarter, and Soundings. Excavations of the Joint Expedition to Nippur of The University Museum of Philadelphia and The Oriental Institute of the University of Chicago.* OIP 78. Chicago: The University of Chicago Press.

Meissner, Bruno. 1891. Babylonische Pflanzennamen. *ZA* 6: 289–98.

Metab, Amal. 1989–90. Excavations at Tell Muhammad. *Sumer* 46: 127–59 [in Arabic].

Metab, Amal., and Hussein A. Hamza. 2003–04. Excavations in Tell Muhammad (Season 8, 1999). *Sumer* 52: 358–84 [in Arabic].

Michalowksi, Piotr. 1989. *The Lamentation over the Destruction of Sumer and Ur.* MC 1. Winona Lake: Eisenbrauns.

Michalowksi, Piotr. 1998–2001. Nisaba. A.Philologisch. Pp. 575–79 in *RlA* 9. Berlin, New York: Walter de Gruyter.

Michalowski, Piotr, and Gary Beckman. 2012. The Promulgation of the Name of the third Year of Rim-Anum of Uruk. Pp. 425–3. in *The Ancient Near East, a Life! Festschrift Karel Van Lerberghe,* ed. Tom Boiy, et al. OLA 220. Leuven, Paris, Walpole: Peeters.

Middeke-Conlin, Robert. 2014. The Scents of Larsa : A Study of the Aromatics Industry in an Old Babylonian Kingdom. *CDLJ* 2014 : 1 http://www.cdli.ucla.edu/pubs/cdlj/2014/cdlj2014_001.html.

Miglus, Peter A. 2003–05. Palast. B Archäologisch. Pp. 233–69 in *RlA* 10. Berlin, New York: Walter de Gruyter.

Milano, Lucio. 1993–97. Mehl. Pp. 22–31 in *RlA* 8. Berlin, New York: Walter de Gruyter.

Mittermayer, Catherine. 2009. *Enmerkara und der Herr von Arata. Ein ungleicher Wettstreit.* OBO 239. Fribourg, Göttingen: Academic Press and Vandenhoeck & Ruprecht.

Moon, Jane, et al. 2014. *Ur Region Archaeology Project: Report 2014.*

Moon, Jane, et al. 2015. *Ur Region Archaeology Project: Report 2015.*

Moon, Jane, et al. 2016. *Ur Region Archaeology Project: Report 2016.*

Moorey, P. Roger S., and Oliver R. Gurney. 1973. Ancient near Eastern Seals at Charterhouse. *Iraq* 35: 71–81.

Nashef, Khaled. 1982. *Die Orts- and Gewässernamen der mittelbabylonischen und mittelassyrischen Zeit.* RGTC V = TAVO 19. Wiesbaden: Dr. Ludwig Reichert Verlag.

Neumann, Jehuda, and R. Marcel Sigrist. 1978. Harvest Dates in Ancient Mesopotamia as Possible Indicators of Climatic Variations. *Climatic Change* 1(3): 239–52.

Nijhowne, Jeanne. 1999. *Politics, Religion, and Cylinder Seals: A Study of Mesopotamian Symbolism in the Second Millennium B.C.* BAR International Series 772. Oxford: John and Erica Hedges.

Nougayrol, Jean. 1971. Nouveaux textes sur le ziḫḫu (II). *RA* 65: 67–84.

Novotny, Jamie. 2016. 'Synchronistic King List (Ass 14616c)', *The Royal Inscriptions of Assyria online (RIAo) Project*, The RIAo Project, 2016. http://oracc.museum.upenn.edu/riao/king lists/synchronistickinglist/ [accessed May 2, 2017].

Oelsner, Joachim. 1974. Neue Daten zur sozialen und wirtschaftlichen Situation Nippurs in altbabylonischer Zeit. *ActAnt.* 22: 259–65.

Oelsner, Joachim. 1976. Zum Pantheon von Nippur in altbabylonischer Zeit nach den Personennamen der Rechtsurkunden. *Or.* 45: 110–15.

Oppenheim, A. Leo. 1937–39. Studien zu den nichtsemitischen Nuzi-Namen. *AfO* 12: 29–39.

Oppenheim, A. Leo. 1970. The Cuneiform Texts. Pp. 1–101; Figures and Plates in *Glass and Glassmaking in Ancient Mesopotamia*, ed. Axel von Saldern, et al. The Corning Museum of Glass Monographs 3. Corning: The Corning Museum of Glass Press; London, Toronto: Associated University Presses.

Oppenheim, A. Leo. 1977. (Revised Edition; 1964) *Ancient Mesopotamia, Portrait of a Dead Civilization.* Chicago: University of Chicago Press.

Paulus, Susanne. 2014a. *Die babylonischen Kudurru-Inschriften von der kassitischen bis zur frühneubabylonischen Zeit.* AOAT 51. Münster: Ugarit-Verlag.

Paulus, Susanne. 2014b. Babylonien in der 2. Hälfte des 2. Jts. v. Chr.—(K)ein Imperium? Ein Überblick über Geschichte und Struktur des mittelbabylonischen Reiches (ca. 1500–1000 B.C.). Pp. 65–100 in *Imperien und Reiche in der Weltgeschichte: Epochenübergreifende und globalhistorische Vergleiche,* ed. Michael Gehler and Robert Rollinger. Teil 1. Wiesbaden: Harrassowitz Verlag.

Peterson, Jeremiah. 2014. A Journey of the Boat of An to Nippur During the Reign of Rīm-Sîn I. *StMes* 1: 319–31.

Peterson, Jeremiah. 2016. UET 61, 74, the Hymnic Introduction of a Sumerian Letter-Prayer to Ninšubur. *ZA* 106: 33–41.

Pientka, Rosel. 1998. *Die spätaltbabylonische Zeit. Abiešuḫ bis Samsuditana. Quellen, Jahresdaten, Geschichte.* 2 vols. IMGULA 2. Münster: Rhema.

Pinches, Theophilus G. 1884. [Untitled contribution]. *Proceedings of the Society of Biblical Archaeology* 6 (May): 193–198; 2 plates.

Pinches, Theophilus G. 1915. *The Babylonian Tablets of the Berens Collection.* Asiatic Society Monographs 16. London: The Royal Asiatic Society.

Pittman, Holly, and Steve Renette. 2016. The Material Culture of Al-Hiba: Glyptic and Ceramic Evidence. Paper presented at the 10th ICAANE as part of the workshop "Ancient Lagash: A Workshop on Current Research and Future Trajectories," held on 27 April, 2016 in Vienna.

Podany, Amanda H. 2002. *The Land of Hana. Kings, Chronology, and Scribal Tradition.* Bethesda: CDL Press.

Podany, Amanda H. 2014. Hana and the Low Chronology. *JNES* 73 (1): 51–73.

Podany, Amanda H. 2016. A Goddess and her Community: Insights into a Late Old Babylonian Neighborhood in Terqa. Presentation held on July 15, 2016 at Philadelphia during the 62nd Rencontre Assyriologique Internationale.

Poebel, Arno. 1947. *Miscellaneous Studies.* AS 14. Chicago: The University of Chicago Press.

Postgate, J. Nicholas. 1984. Processing of Cereals in the Cuneiform Record. Pp. 103–13 in *BSA* 1. Cambridge: University Press.

Postgate, J. Nicholas. 1987a. Notes on Fruit in the Cuneiform Sources. Pp. 115–44 in *BSA* 3. Cambridge: University Press.

Postgate, J. Nicholas. 1987b. Employer, Employee and Employment in the Neo-Assyrian Empire. Pp. 257–70 in *Labor in the Ancient Near East,* ed. Marvin A. Powell. AOS 68. New Haven: American Oriental Society.

Postgate, J. Nicholas. 2003–05. Palast. Einleitung. Pp. 195–200 in *RlA* 10. Berlin, New York: Walter de Gruyter.

Potts, Daniel T. 1997. *Mesopotamian Civilization: The Material Foundations.* London: Athlone Press.

Potts, Daniel T. 2006. Elamites and Kassites in the Persian Gulf. *JNES* 65(2): 111–19.

Potts, Daniel T. 2010. Cylinder Seals and Their Use in the Arabian Peninsula. *Arabian archaeology and epigraphy* 21: 20–40.

Pournelle, Jennifer R. 2003. *Marshland of Cities: Deltaic Landscapes and the Evolution of Early Mesopotamian Civilization.* Doctoral Dissertation submitted at the University of California, San Diego.

Powell, Marvin A. 1984. Sumerian Cereal Crops. Pp. 48–72 in *BSA* 1. Cambridge: University Press.

Powell, Marvin A. 1987–90. Maße und Gewichte. Pp. 457–517 in *RlA* 7. Berlin, New York: Walter de Gruyter.

Powell, Marvin A. 1994. *Metron Ariston:* Measure as a Tool for Studying Beer in Ancient Mesopotamia. Pp. 91–119 in *Drinking in Ancient Societies. History and Culture of Drinks in the Ancient Near East. Papers of a Symposium held in Rome, May 17–19, 1990,* ed. Lucio Milano. Padua: Sargon srl.

Prażak, Roman. 2001. Salt tolerance of *Triticum monococcum* L., *T. dicoccum* (Schrank) Schubl, *T.durum* Desf. and *T. aestivum* L. seedlings. *Journal of Applied Genetics* 42(3): 289–92.

Pruzsinszky, Regine. 2009. *Mesopotamian Chronology of the 2nd Millennium B.C. An Introduction to the Textual Evidence and Related Chronology Issues.* DÖAW 56. Vienna: Verlag der ÖAW.

Purves, Pierre M. 1943. Elements other than Akkadian and Sumerian. Pp. 183–280 in *Nuzi. Personal Names.* OIP 57. Chicago: The University of Chicago Press.

Ravn, Otto E. 1929. The Rise of Marduk. *ActOr.* 7: 81–90.

Reiner, Erica. 1974. *The Series ḪAR-ra = ḫubullu. Tablets XX–XXIV.* MSL XI. Rome: Pontificum Institutum Biblicum.

Renfrew, Jane M. 1984. Cereals Cultivated in Ancient Iraq. Pp. 32–44 in *BSA* 1. Cambridge: University Press.

Renfrew, Jane M. 1985. Finds of Sesame and Linseed in Ancient Iraq. Pp. 63–66 in *BSA* 2. Cambridge: University Press.

Renger, Johannes. 1967. Götternamen in der altbabylonischen Zeit. Pp. 137–72 in *Heidelberger Studien zum Alten Orient.* Festschrift A. Falkenstein zum 17. Sept. 1966, ed. Dietz-Otto Edzard. Wiesbaden: Otto Harrassowitz Verlag.

Renger, Johannes. 1970. Zur Lokalisierung von Karkar. *AfO* 23: 73–78.

Renger, Johannes. 1995. Institutional, Communal, and Individual Ownership or Possession of Arable Land in Mesopotamia from the End of the Fourth to the End of the First Millennium B.C. *Chicago-Kent Law Review* 71: 269–319.

Richardson, Seth. 2002. *The Collapse of a Complex State: A Reappraisal of the End of the First Dynasty of Babylon, 1683–1597 B.C.* 2 vols. Doctoral dissertation submitted at Columbia University.

Richardson, Seth. 2005. Trouble in the Countryside *ana tarṣi* Samsuditana: Militarism, Kassites, and the Fall of Babylon I. Pp. 273–89 in *Ethnicity in Ancient Mesopotamia,* ed. Wilfred H. van Soldt, et al. CRRAI 48=PIHANS 102. Leiden: Nederlands Instituut voor het Nabije Oosten.

Richardson, Seth. 2010. Writing Rebellion Back Into the Record: A Methodologies Toolkit. Pp. 1–27 in *Rebellions and Peripheries in the Cuneiform World,* ed. Seth Richardson. AOS 91. Winona Lake: Eisenbrauns.

Richardson, Seth. 2012. Early Mesopotamia: the Presumptive State. *Past & Present* 215(1): 3–49.

Richardson, Seth. 2015a. Samsuditana and the sixty-armed horde. *NABU* 2015/2: no.37.

Richardson, Seth. 2015b. Re-digging Hammurabi's canal. *NABU* 2015/4: no.94.

Richardson, Seth. 2016. The Many Falls of Babylon and the Shape of Forgetting. Pp. 101–42 in *Envisioning the Past Through Memories. How Memory Shaped Ancient Near Eastern Societies,* ed. Davide Nadali. Cultural Memory and History in Antiquity 3. London: Bloomsbury.

Richardson, Seth. 2017. Sumer and Stereotype: Re-forging 'Sumerian' kingship in the Late Old Babylonian Period. in *Conceptualizing Past, Present and Future.* Sebastian Fink and Robert Rollinger, ed. Melammu Symposia 9. Münster: Ugarit-Verlag.

Richter, Thomas. 2004. *Untersuchungen zu den lokalen Panthea Süd- und Mittelbabyloniens in altbabylonischer Zeit.* AOAT 257. 2. Auflage (1999). Münster: Ugarit Verlag.

Rochberg-Halton, Francesca, and Paul Zimansky. 1979. The University of Iowa Cuneiform Texts. *JCS* 31: 127–48.

Röllig, Wolfgang. 1970. *Das Bier im Alten Mesopotamien.* Berlin: Gesellschaft für die Geschichte und Bibliographie des Brauwesens e.V.

Römer, Willem H.Ph. 1967–68. Studien zu altbabylonischen hymnisch-epischen Texten (3). *WO* 4: 12–28.

Römer, Willem H.Ph. 2001. *Hymnen und Klagelieder in sumerischer Sprache.* AOAT 276. Münster: Ugarit- Verlag.

Römer, Willem H.Ph. 2004. *Die Klage über die Zerstörung von Ur.* AOAT 309. Münster: Ugarit-Verlag.

Rositani, Annunziata. 2003. *Rīm-Anum Texts in the British Museum.* Nisaba 4. Messina: Dipartimento di Scienzie dell'Antichità dell'Università degli Studi di Messina.

Roux, Georges. 1960. Recently Discovered Ancient Sites in the Hammar Lake District (Southern Iraq). *Sumer* 16: 20–31.

Rubio, Gonzalo. 2009. Scribal Secrets and Antiquarian Nostalgia: Writing and Scholarship in Ancient Mesopotamia. Pp. 155–82 in *Reconstructing a Distant Past.* Festschrift J.R. Silva Castillo, ed. Diego A. Barreyra Fracaroli and Gregorio del Olmo Lete. AulaOr. Suppl. 25. Barcelona: Editorial Ausa.

Rubio, Gonzalo. 2011. Gods and Scholars: Mapping the Pantheon in Early Mesopotamia. Pp. 91–116 in *Reconsidering the Concept of Revolutionary Monotheism,* ed. Beate Pongratz-Leisten. Winona Lake: Eisenbrauns. Pp. 91–116.

Rutz, Matthew, and Piotr Michalowski. 2016. The Flooding of Ešnunna, the Fall of Mari: Hammurabi's Deeds in Babylonian Literature and History. *JCS* 68: 15–43.

Sallaberger, Walther. 1993. *Der kultische Kalender der Ur III-Zeit.* UAVA 7. Berlin, New York: Walter de Gruyter.

Sallaberger, Walther. 1996. *Der babylonische Töpfer und seine Gefässe nach Urkunden altsumerischer bis altbabylonischer Zeit sowie lexikalischen und literarischen Zeugnissen.* MHEM 3. Ghent: University of Ghent.

Sallaberger, Walther. 2004. Pantheon. A.I. In Mesopotamien. Pp. 294–308 in *RlA* 10. Berlin, New York: Walter de Gruyter.

Sallaberger, Walther. 2012. Bierbrauen in Versen: Eine neue Edition und Interpretation der Ninkasi-Hymne. Pp. 291–328 in *Altorientalische Studien zu Ehren von Pascal Attinger* mu-ni u_4 ul-li_2-a-aš $\hat{g}a_2$-$\hat{g}a_2$-de_3, ed. Catherine Mittermayer and Sabine Ecklin. OBO 256. Fribourg and Göttingen: Academic Press Fribourg and Vandenhoeck & Ruprecht.

Sallaberger, Walther. 2013. The Management of Royal Treasure. Palace Archives and Palatial Economy in the Ancient Near East. Pp. 219–55 in *Experiencing Power, Generating Authority. Cosmos, Politics, and the Ideology of Kingship in Ancient Egypt and Mesopotamia,* ed. Jane A. Hill, et al. Philadelphia: University of Pennsylvania Museum of Archaeology and Anthropology.

Samet, Nili. 2014. *The Lamentation over the Destruction of Ur.* MC 18. Winona Lake: Eisenbrauns.

Sanati-Müller, Shirin. 1990. Texte aus dem Sînkāšid-Palast. Dritter Teil. Metalltexte. *BagM* 21: 131–213.

Sanati-Müller, Shirin. 2000a. Ein zweites Nabi-ilišu-Jahresdatum. *BagM* 31: 87–91.

Sanati-Müller, Shirin. 2000b. Texte aus dem Sînkāšid-Palast. Zehnter Teil: Holztexte—Elfter Teil: Fragmentarisch erhaltene Texte. *BagM* 31: 93–176.

Sassmannshausen, Leonhard. 2000. The Adaptation of the Kassites to the Babylonian Civilization. Pp. 409–24 in *Languages and Cultures in Contact. At the Crossroads of Civilizations in the Syro-Mesopotamian Realm,* ed. Karel Van Lerberghe and Gabriella Voet. CRRAI 42=OLA 96. Leuven: Peeters.

Sassmannshausen, Leonhard. 2001. *Beiträge zur Verwaltung und Gesellschaft Babyloniens in der Kassitenzeit.* BagF 21. Mainz: Verlag Philipp von Zabern.
Sassmannshausen, Leonhard. 2004a. Kassite Nomads: Fact or Fiction? Pp. 287–305 in *Nomades et sédentaires dans le Proche-Orient ancien*, ed. Christophe Nicolle. CRRAI 46=Amurru 3. Paris: Éditions Recherche sur les Civilisations.
Sassmannshausen, Leonhard. 2004b. Babylonian Chronology of the 2nd Half of the 2nd Millennium B.C. Pp. 61–70 in *Mesopotamian Dark Age Revisited.* Proceedings of a conference held at Vienna 8–9 November 2002, ed. Hermann Hunger and Regine Pruzsinszky. ÖAW 32. Vienna: Verlag der Österreichischen Akademie der Wissenschaften.
Schramm, Wolfgang. 2001. *Bann, bann! Eine sumerisch-akkadische Beschwörungsserie.* GAAL 2. Göttingen: Seminar für Keilschriftforschung Göttingen.
Selz, Gebhard J. 1989. *Altsumerische Verwaltungstexte aus Lagaš. Teil 1. Die altsumerischen Wirtschaftsurkunden der Eremitage zu Leningrad.* FAOS 15,1. Wiesbaden: Franz Steiner Verlag.
Selz, Gebhard J. 1990. Studies in Early Syncretism: The Development of the Pantheon in Lagaš. Examples for Inner-Sumerian Syncretism. *ASJ* 12: 111–42.
Selz, Gebhard J. 2015. Uru-kù(-g). P. 497 in *RlA* 14 (5/6). Berlin, New York: Walter de Gruyter.
Seri, Andrea. 2013. *The House of Prisoners.* SANER 2. Boston, Berlin: Walter de Gruyter.
Seux. Marie-Joseph. 1967. *Épithètes royales akkadiennes et sumériennes.* Paris: Letouzey et Ané.
Sigrist, Marcel. 1976. *Ninurta à Nippur. L'Économie du culte pendant la période d'Isin et Larsa.* Doctoral dissertation presented at Yale University.
Sigrist, Marcel. 1977. Offrandes dans le temple de Nusku à Nippur. *JCS* 29: 169–83.
Sigrist, Marcel. 1980. Offrandes aux dieux à Nippur. *JCS* 32: 104–13.
Sigrist, Marcel. 1984. *Les sattukku dans l'Ešumeša durant la période d'Isin et Larsa.* BiMes 11. Malibu: Undena.
Sigrist, Marcel. 1990. *Larsa Year Names.* IAPAS 3. Berrien Springs: Andrews University Press.
Sigrist, Marcel, Uri Gabbay, and Mark Avila. 2017. Cuneiform Tablets and Other Inscribed Objects from Collections in Jerusalem. Pp. 311–36 in *The First Ninety Years. A Sumerian Celebration in Honor of Miguel Civil*, ed. Lluís Feliu, Fumi Karahashi, and Gonzalo Rubio. SANER 12. Boston, Berlin: Walter de Gruyter.
Skaist, Aaron. 1994. *The Old Babylonian Loan Contract. Its History and Geography.* Jerusalem: Bar-Ilan University Press.
Slotsky, Alice L. 1997. *The Bourse of Babylon. Market Quotations in the Astronomical Diaries of Babylonia.* Bethesda: CDL Press.
Sollberger, Edmond. 1965. A three-column *Silbenvokabular A.* Pp. 21–28 in *Studies in Honor of Benno Landsberger on his Seventy-Fifth Birthday*, ed. Hans G. Güterbock and Thorkild Jacobsen. AS 16. Chicago: University of Chicago.
Sommerfeld, Walter. 1982. *Der Aufstieg Marduks. Die Stellung Marduks in der babylonischen Religion des zweiten Jahrtausends v. Chr.* AOAT 213. Kevelaer, Neukirchen-Vluyn: Verlag Butzon & Bercker and Neukirchener Verlag.
Sommerfeld, Walter. 1985. Der Kurigalzu-Text MAH 15922. *AfO* 32: 1–22.
Stamm, Johann J. 1968. *Die akkadische Namengebung.* Mitteilungen der Vorderasiatisch-Ägyptischen Gesellschaft 44. 2nd edition (1939). Leipzig: J.C. Hinrichs Verlag.
Stein, Peter. 2000. *Die mittel- und neubabylonischen Königsinschriften bis zum Ende der Assyrerherrschaft.* JBVO 3. Wiesbaden: Otto Harrassowitz Verlag.

Steinkeller, Piotr. 1987. The Name of Nergal. *ZA* 77: 161–68.
Steinkeller, Piotr. 2001. New Light on the Hydrology and Topography of Southern Babylonia in the Third Millennium. *ZA* 91: 22–84.
Steinkeller, Piotr. 2013a. Corvée Labor in Ur III Times. Pp. 347–424 in *From the 21st Century B.C. to the 21st Century A.D.* Proceedings of the International Conference on Sumerian Studies Held in Madrid, 22–24 July 2010, ed. Steven Garfinkle and Manuel Molina. Winona Lake, IN: Eisenbrauns.
Steinkeller, Piotr. 2013b. How did Šulgi and Išbi-Erra Ascend to Heaven? Pp. 459–78 in *Literature as Politics, Politics as Literature.* Festschrift Peter Machinist, ed. David S. Vanderhooft and Abraham Winitzer. Winona Lake, IN: Eisenbrauns.
Steinkeller, Piotr. 2013c. More on the Nature and History of the Goddess Nanaya. *NABU* 2013/4: no.65.
Steinkeller, Piotr. 2015. Introduction. Labor in the Early States: An Early Mesopotamian Perspective. Pp. 1–35 in *Labor in the Ancient World.* Proceedings of a Colloquium held at Hirschbach (Saxony) April 2005, ed. Piotr Steinkeller and Michael Hudson. The International Scholars Conference on Ancient Near Eastern Economies, vol.5. Dresden: ISLET-Verlag.
Steinkeller, Piotr. 2017. The Locations of the Canal Hammurabi-nuhuš-niši and of the Fortress Dur-Abi-ešuh: A New Proposal. Paper presented at the 63rd RAI held at Marburg, July 24–28, 2017.
Stol, Marten. 1971. Zur altmesopotamischen Bierbereitung [Review of Röllig, W. *Das Bier im alten Mesopotamien*]. *BiOr* 28: 167–71.
Stol, Marten. 1976. *Studies in Old Babylonian History.* PIHANS 40. Leiden: Nederlands Historisch-archaeologisch Instituut te Istanbul.
Stol, Marten. 1979. *On Trees, Mountains, and Millstones in the Ancient Near East.* Leiden: Ex Oriente Lux.
Stol, Marten. 1983–84. Cress and its Mustard. *JEOL* 28: 24–32.
Stol, Marten. 1985a. Beans, Peas, Lentils and Vetches in Akkadian Texts. Pp. 127–39 *BSA* 2. Cambridge: University Press.
Stol, Marten. 1985b. Remarks on the Cultivation of Sesame and the Extraction of its Oil. Pp. 119–26 in *BSA* 2. Cambridge: University Press.
Stol, Marten. 1987. Garlic, Onion, Leek. Pp. 57–80 in *BSA* 3. Cambridge: University Press.
Stol, Marten. 1987–90. Malz. Pp. 322–29 in *RlA* 7. Berlin, New York: Walter de Gruyter.
Stol, Marten. 1991. Old Babylonian Personal Names. *SEL* 8: 191–212.
Stol, Marten. 2001. A Rescript of an Old Babylonian Letter. Pp. 457–65 in *Veenhof Anniversary Volume, Studies Presented to Klaas R.Veenhof...65th Birthday*, ed. Wilfred H. van Soldt. PIHANS 89. Leiden: Nederlands Instituut voor het Nabije Oosten.
Stol, Marten. 2004. Wirtschaft und Gesellschaft in altbabylonischer Zeit. Pp.641–975 in *Mesopotamien. Die altbabylonische Zeit.* OBO 160/4. Fribourg, Göttingen: Academic Press, Vandenhoeck & Ruprecht Verlag.
Stol, Marten. 2003–05. Öl, Ölbaum. A. In Mesopotamien. Pp. 32–33 in *RlA* 10. Berlin, New York: Walter de Gruyter.
Stol, Marten. 2006–08. Ration. Pp. 264–69 in *RlA* 11. New York: Walter de Gruyter.
Stone, Elizabeth C. 1977. Economic Crisis and Social Upheaval in Old Babylonian Nippur. Pp. 267–89 in *Mountains and Lowlands: Essays in the Archaeology of Greater Mesopotamia*, ed. Louis D. Levine and T. Cuyler Young Jr. Malibu: Undena.

Stone, Elizabeth C. 1987. *Nippur Neighborhoods.* SAOC 44. Chicago: The Oriental Institute of the University of Chicago.

Stone, Elizabeth C. 2003. Remote Sensing and the Location of the Ancient Tigris. Pp. 157–62 in *The Reconstruction of Archaeological Landscapes through Digital Technologies.* Proceedings of the 1st Italy-United States Workshop, Boston, Nov. 2001, ed. Maurizio Forte and Patrick R. Williams. BAR International Series 1151. Oxford: Archaeopress.

Streck, Michael P. 2000. *Das amurritische Onomastikon der altbabylonischen Zeit.* Band I. AOAT 271/1. Münster: Ugarit-Verlag.

Streck, Michael P. 2009–11. Schilf. Pp. 182–89 in *RlA* 12. Berlin, New York: Walter de Gruyter.

Talon, Philippe. 1997. *Old Babylonian Texts from Chagar Bazar.* Akkadica Supplementum X. Brussels: FAGD—ASGD.

Tammuz, Oded. 1996. The Location of Lagaba. *RA* 90: 19–25.

Tanji, Kenneth K., and Neeltje C. Kielen. 2002. *Agricultural Drainage Water Management in Arid and Semi-Arid Areas.* FAO Irrigation and Drainage Paper 61. Rome: Food and Agriculture Organization of the United Nations.

Thureau-Dangin, François. 1927. La chronologie des trois premières dynasties babyloniennes. *RA* 24: 181–98.

Thureau-Dangin, François. 1951. La chronologie de la première dynastie babylonienne. Pp. 229–58 in *Mémoires de l'Institut national de France, Académie des inscriptions et belles-lettres* 43/2. Paris: Imprimerie nationale.

Tiele, Cornelis P. 1886. *Babylonisch-Assyrische Geschichte, Handbücher der alten Geschichte I/IV, 1. Teil: Von den ältesten Zeiten bis zum Tode Sargons II.* Gotha: Friedrich Andreas Perthes.

Van De Mieroop, Marc. 1992a. Reed in the Old Babylonian Texts from Ur. Pp. 147–53 in *BSA* 6. Cambridge: University Press.

Van De Mieroop, Marc. 1992b. Wood in the Old Babylonian Texts from southern Babylonia. Pp. 154–62 in *BSA* 6. Cambridge: University Press.

Van De Mieroop, Marc. 1993. The Reign of Rim-Sin. *RA* 87: 47–69.

Van De Mieroop, Marc. 1994. The Tell Leilan Tablets 1991. A Preliminary Report. *Or.* 63: 305–44.

Vanderhooft, David, and Wayne Horowitz. 2002. The Cuneiform Inscription from Tell en-Naṣbeh: The Demise of an Unknown King. *Tel Aviv* 29: 318–27.

van der Toorn, Karel. 1986. Judges XVI 21 in the Light of the Akkadian Sources. *Vetus Testamentum* 36(2): 248–53.

van Dijk, Jan. 1966–67. L'hymne à Marduk avec intercession pour le roi Abī'ešuḫ. *MIO* 12: 57–74.

van Driel, Govert. 2003–05. Pfründe. Pp. 518–24 in *RlA* 10. Berlin, New York: Walter de Gruyter.

van Ess, Margarete. 1991a. Die Keramik: Die Typen und ihre Verbreitung nach Zeitstufen. Akkad- bis altbabylonische Zeit. Pp. 90–99 in *Uruk. Kampagne 35–37. 1982–1984. Die archäologische Oberflächenuntersuchung (Survey),* ed. Uwe Finkbeiner. AUWE 4 Text. Mainz: Philipp von Zabern.

van Ess, Margarete. 1991b. Die historische Topographie von Uruk-Warka. Altbabylonische Zeit. Pp. 204–06 in *Uruk. Kampagne 35–37. 1982–1984. Die archäologische*

Oberflächenuntersuchung (Survey), ed. Uwe Finkbeiner. AUWE 4 Text. Mainz: Philipp von Zabern.

van Koppen, Frans. 2004. The Geography of the Slave Trade and Northern Mesopotamia in the Late Old Babylonian Period. Pp. 9–33 in *Mesopotamian Dark Age Revisited. Proceedings of an international conference of SCIEM 2000 (Vienna 8th–9th November 2002)*, ed. Hermann Hunger and Regine Pruzsinszky. Denkschriften der Gesamtakademie 32. Contributions to the Chronology of the Eastern Mediterranean 6. Vienna: Verlag der Österreichischen Akademie der Wissenschaften.

van Koppen, Frans. 2010. The Old to Middle Babylonian Transition: History and Chronology of the Mesopotamian Dark Age. *Ägypten und Levante/Egypt and the Levant* 20: 453–63.

van Koppen, Frans. 2013. Abiešuh, Elam and Ashurbanipal: New Evidence from Old Babylonian Sippar. Pp. 377–97 in *Susa and Elam. Archaeological, Philological, Historical and Geographical Perspectives.* Proceedings of the International Congress held at Ghent University, Dec. 14–17, 2009, ed. Katrien De Graef and Jan Tavernier. MDP 58. Leiden, Boston: Brill.

van Koppen, Frans. 2017. The Early Kassite Period. Pp. 45–92 in *Karduniaš: Babylonia under the Kassites. Babylonien zur Kassitenzeit.* Proceedings of the Symposium held in Munich from 30 June to 2 July, 2011, ed. Alexa S. Bartelmus and Katja Sternitzke. Berlin, Boston: Walther de Gruyter.

Van Lerberghe, Karel. 1986. Un 'Elamite' à Sippar-Amnānum. Pp. 151–55 in *Fragmenta Historiae Aelamicae.* Mélanges offerts à M-J. Steve, ed. Léon de Meyer, et al. Paris: Éditions Recherche sur les Civilisations.

Van Lerberghe, Karel. 1995. Kassites and Old Babylonian Society. A Reappraisal. Pp. 379–93 in *Immigration and Emigration within the Ancient Near East.* Festschrift E. Lipiński, ed. Karel Van Lerberghe and Antoon Schoors. OLA 65. Leuven: Peeters.

Van Lerberghe, Karel, and Gabriella Voet. 2009. *A Late Old Babylonian Temple Archive From Dūr-Abiešuḫ.* CUSAS 8. Bethesda: CDL Press.

Van Lerberghe, Karel, and Gabriella Voet. 2010. Kassite Mercenaries at Abiešuḫ's Fortress. Pp. 181–87 in *Why Should Someone Who Knows Something Conceal It?, Cuneiform Studies in Honor of David I. Owen on His 70th Birthday.* A. Kleinerman and J.M. Sasson, ed. Bethesda: CDL Press.

Van Lerberghe, Karel, and Gabriella Voet. 2016. Dūr-Abiešuḫ and Venice. Settlements In-between Great Rivers. Pp. 557–63 in *Libiamo ne' lieti calici. Ancient Near Eastern Studies Presented to Lucio Milano on the Occasion of his 65th Birthday by Pupils, Colleagues and Friends*, ed. Paola Corò, et al. AOAT 436. Münster: Ugarit-Verlag.

Van Lerberghe, Karel, Marten Stol, and Gabriella Voet. 1986. *Old Babylonian Legal and Administrative Texts from Philadelphia.* OLA 21. Leuven: Peeters.

Van Lerberghe, Karel, David Kaniewski, Kathleen Abraham, Joël Guiot, and Elise Van Campo. 2017. Water Deprivation as Military Strategy in the Middle East, 3.700 years ago. *Méditerranée* [Online. : http://mediterranee.revues.org/8000]

van Seters, John. 1983. *In Search of History. Historiography in the Ancient World and the Origins of Biblical History.* New Haven: Yale University Press.

van Soldt, Wilfred. 2015. *Middle Babylonian Texts in the Cornell University Collections. I. The Later Kings.* CUSAS 30. Bethesda: CDL Press.

van Zeist, Willem, and Sytze Bottema. 1999. Plant Cultivation in Ancient Mesopotamia: The Palynological and Archaeological Approach. Pp. 25–41 in *Landwirtschaft im Alten Orient*, ed. Horst Klengel and Johannes Renger. BBVO 18. Berlin: Dietrich Reimer Verlag.

Veenhof, Klaas R. 1991. Assyrian Commercial Activities in Old Babylonian Sippar—Some New Evidence. Pp. 287–303 in *Marchands, diplomates et empereurs*. Festschrift Garelli, ed. Dominique Charpin and Francis Joannès. Paris: Éditions Recherche sur les Civilisations.

Veldhuis, Niek. 2008. Old Babylonian Documents in the Hearst Museum of Anthropology, Berkeley. *RA* 102: 49–70.

Veldhuis, Niek. 2017. Words and Grammar: Two Old Babylonian Lists. Pp. 356–88 in *The First Ninety Years: A Sumerian Celebration in Honor of Miguel Civil*, ed. Lluís Feliu, et al. SANER 12. Berlin, Boston: Walter de Gruyter,

Vincente, Claudine-Adrienne. 1992. *The 1987 Tell Leilan Tablets dated by the Limmu of Habil-kinu*. Doctoral dissertation submitted at Yale University (1991).

von Soden, Wolfram. 1976. Einige Fragen zur Geschiche von Isin. *Or.* 45: 105–09.

von Soden, Wolfram. 1995. *Grundriss der akkadischen Grammatik*. 3., ergänzte Auflage. AnOr 33. Rome: Editrice Pontificio Istituto Biblico.

Waerzeggers, Caroline. 2012. The Babylonian Chronicles: Classification and Provenance. *JNES* 71: 285–98.

Waerzeggers, Caroline. 2015. The Neo-Babylonian chronicle about Sabium and Apil-Sîn: a copy of the text (BM 29440). *NABU* 2015/2: no. 54.

Waetzoldt, Hartmut. 1981. Zu den Strandverschiebungen am Persischen Golf und den Bezeichnungnen des Hōrs. Pp. 159–83, maps in *Strandverschiebungen in ihrer Bedeutung für Geowissenschaften und Archäologie*. ed. Jörg Schäfer and Wilhelm Simon. Ruperto Carola Sonderheft. Heidelberg: Universität Heidelberg.

Waetzoldt, Hartmut. 1985. Ölpflanzen und Pflanzenöle im 3. Jahrtausend. Pp. 77–96 in *BSA* 2. Cambridge: University Press.

Waetzoldt, Hartmut. 1987. Compensation of Craft Workers and Officials in the Ur III Period. Pp. 117–41 in *Labor in the Ancient Near East*, ed. Marvin A. Powell. AOS 68. New Haven: American Oriental Society.

Wang, Xianhua. 2011. *The Metamorphosis of Enlil in Early Mesopotamia*. AOAT 385. Münster: Ugarit Verlag.

Wasserman, Nathan. 1995. Sîn goes to Fishing. *NABU* 1995/3: No. 71.

Weadock, Penelope N. 1975. The *Giparu* at Ur. *Iraq* 37 (2): 101–28.

Weidner, Ernst F. 1926. Die grosse Königsliste aus Assur. *AfO* 3: 66–77.

Westenholz, Joan G. 1997. *Legends of the Kings of Akkade*. MC 7. Winona Lake: Eisenbrauns.

Westenholz, Joan G. 2007. Inanna and Ishtar—The Dimorphic Venus Goddesses. Pp. 332–47 in *The Babylonian World*, ed. Gwendolyn Leick. New York, London: Routledge.

Wetzel, Friedrich, Erich Schmidt, and Alfred Mallwitz. 1957. *Das Babylon der Spätzeit*. WVDOG 62. Berlin: Verlag Gebr. Mann.

Wiggermann, Frans A.M. 1998–2001a. Nergal. A.Philologisch. Pp. 215–23 in *RlA* 9. Berlin, New York: Walter de Gruyter.

Wiggermann, Frans A.M. 1998–2001b. Nin-Šubur. Pp. 490–500 in *RlA* 9. Berlin, New York: Walter de Gruyter.

Wiggermann, Frans A.M. 2008. A Babylonian Scholar in Assur. Pp. 203–34 in *Studies in Ancient Near Eastern World View and Society*. Festschrift Marten Stol, ed. Robartus J. Van der Spek. Bethesda: CDL Press.

Wiggermann, Frans A.M. 2010. Siebengötter (Sebettu, Sebittu, Sibittu). A.Mesopotamien. Pp. 459–66 in *RlA* 12. Berlin, New York: Walter de Gruyter.
Wilcke, Claus. 1976–80. Inanna/Ištar (Mesopotamien) A.Philologisch. Pp. 74–87 in *RlA* 5. Berlin, New York: Walter de Gruyter.
Winckler, Hugo. 1893–97. Bruchstücke von Keilschrifttexten. Pp. 516–47 in *Altorientalische Forschungen.* Reihe I(6). Leipzig: Verlag von Eduard Pfeiffer.
Wiseman, Donald J., and Jeremy A. Black. 1996. *Literary Texts from the Temple of Nabû.* CTN IV. London: British School of Archaeology in Iraq.
Wu, Yujin. 1994. *A Political History of Eshnunna, Mari and Assyria During the Early Old Babylonian Period (From the End of Ur III to the Death of Šamši-Adad)*, Suppl. to *Journal of Ancient Civilizations* No 1. Changchun: Institute of History of Ancient Civilizations.
Woolley, Leonard. 1954. *Excavations at Ur: A Record of Twelve Years' Work.* London: E. Benn.
Woolley, Leonard. 1965. *The Kassite Period and the Period of the Assyrian Kings.* UE 8. London: The British Museum and the University Museum, Pennsylvania.
Wright, Henry T. 1981. The Southern Margins of Sumer: Archaeological Survey of the Area of Eridu and Ur. Pp. 295–345 in Robert McC. Adams, *Heartland of Cities.* Chicago: University of Chicago Press.
Yoffee, Norman. 1998. The Economics of Ritual at Late Old Babylonian Kish. *JESHO* 41(3): 312–43.
Zadok, Ran. 2014. On Population Groups in the Documents from the Time of the First Sealand Dynasty. *Tel Aviv* 41: 222–37.
Zimansky, Paul, and Elizabeth Stone. 2016. Tell Sakhariya and Gaeš. Pp. 57–66 in *Proceedings of the 9th International Congress on the Archaeology of the Ancient Near East, 9–13 June 2014, Basel.* Vol.3, ed. Oskar Kaelin and Hans-Peter Mathys. Wiesbaden: Harrassowitz Verlag.
Zimmern, Heinrich. 1911. Zur Herstellung der großen babylonischen Götterlisten An = (ilu) Anum. *Berichte über die Verhandlungen der Königlich-Sächsischen Gesellschaft der Wissenschaften* (BSGW) 63/iv: 83–125.
Zomer, Elyze. 2016. 'Game of Thrones': koningen in strijd in de Laat Oud-Babylonische periode. *Phoenix* 62.2: 52–63.
Zomer, Elyze. forthcoming. *Various Middle Babylonian Literary Texts from the Frau Professor Hilprecht-Collection.* TMH 11. Wiesbaden: Harrassowitz
http://www.urarchaeology.org/babylonian-public-building-at-tell-khaiber; accessed on 22 October 2015.

Indexes

Index of Geographical Names

Index of Deities

Index of People

Index of Professions

Index of Akkadian and Sumerian terms discussed

General Index

Index of cuneiform sources

CPSIA information can be obtained
at www.ICGtesting.com
Printed in the USA
JSHW020822110423
40171JS00004B/261

9 781501 519437